A

TENNESSEAN ABROAD

OR

LETTERS

FROM

EUROPE, AFRICA, AND ASIA

BY

RANDAL W. MacGAVOCK, A.M., LL.B.

A MEMBER OF THE NASHVILLE BAR

REDFIELD

110 AND 112 NASSAU STREET, NEW-YORK

1854

TYPOGRAPHY OF
TUBBS, NESMITH & TEALL,
29 Beekman st.

TO

MY FATHER

THESE LETTERS

Are Affectionately Dedicated.

THE AUTHOR.

PREFACE.

The increased facilities for locomotion and the recognised brotherhood of nations have brought the advantages of travel within the reach of many to whom they were formerly denied. Thousands are every year availing themselves of this pleasantest method of gaining correct ideas of the men and manners of the time, and visiting for themselves the classic spots which have for so many ages inspired the soul of the poet, and guided the pencil of the painter. In this pilgrimage to the shrines of the Beautiful and the haunts of the Romantic, America has not been without her representatives. There is scarcely a spot in the Old World that gems the page of history or lives in the poet's song, where the foot of our countryman has not pressed. Some travel from curiosity, others to gain knowledge, while not a few, like the birdling of Jenny Lind, go, "not knowing why."

In the Spring of 1851, the author found himself in one of these categories—precisely which, he leaves it with the reader to determine. Of one sin, however, he holds himself innocent—the *malice prepense* of writing a book. During an absence of nearly two years, he had ample time and opportunity to visit all the more interesting portions of the three grand divisions of the Eastern hemisphere. The following Letters are his impressions of those scenes, and of the various people that inhabit them. They were written originally for the perusal of personal friends, and not for the critical eye of the great public. The partiality of those friends and their flattering reception of them are the responsible party for their present appearance before this august censorship. They were published some time since in one of the leading journals in Tennessee, and subsequently copied into the prints of other States. For much of the historical matter they contain, the author acknowledges his indebtedness to several European travellers who have preceded him in his tour of observation; and if aught of genial feeling or poetic fervor breathe through the following pages, he owes much of it to the companionship that shed continual sunshine over the weariness of travel, and to the gentle hands that were gathering flowers by his side for this bouquet of A Tennessean Abroad.

The Author.

CONTENTS.

A TENNESSEAN ABROAD.

LETTER ONE.

SHIP WATERLOO, CAPT. HARVEY,
Banks of Newfoundland.

Introduction—Prospects of visiting Europe—Reasons for going—Preparation for the Voyage—Parting with Friends—The Waterloo—Passengers—The Steam-tug—New-York Bay—Fight among the Sailors—The midnight cry of Murder—Man overboard—Sermon at Sea—Storm near the Banks—Icebergs, etc.

"I'm on the sea; I'm on the sea,
I am where I have longed to be,
With the blue above and the blue below,
And joy wherever I go."

FOR some years past I have cherished the hope that it would be in my power to realize the fondest dreams of a life passed in literary pursuits and professional duties, and make a tour in foreign lands, whose history, language, people, institutions and customs, I have heard and read so much about, but which no one has written of or represented so as to enable me to appreciate what I now anticipate. Some persons are content if they have a well-written history or book of travels, over which they can go into ecstasies without the trouble of locomotion, and at the same time enjoy the cosy fireside, and perfume of the well-filled meerschaum; but with me it only creates a desire to see with my own eyes, and learn for myself, things I have failed to realize in books. Through some freak of fortune, or misfortune, as time may determine, I found my inclination to leave home become so strong, I was willing to yield to the solicitations of those who desired my company, leave my business, part with my family and friends, and all who are near and dear to me, and be a rover for eighteen months or more in foreign climes. As the day fixed for our departure drew near, my anxiety became intense. I was ready even before the time to bid adieu to my native land, with a heart full of anticipated pleasure.

On Saturday, at noon, I found myself on board the splendid ship Waterloo, belonging to the Star Line, bound for Liverpool, and commanded by Captain Harvey. Here I found assembled those who were to constitute my fellow-passengers across old ocean's wave, numbering some thirty-five persons, great aud small, for the cabin, and forty-five for the steerage. Here, also, I found assembled a few chosen friends whom I had known in college-life, and who had come to the dock to take leave, and express their good wishes for my safe return and happiness. After a short time allowed by our accommodating captain for leave-taking, we were dragged by the tug Achilles out into the middle of East River, amid the shouts and waving of those on shore. We stood in the stream for about half an hour, waiting for two of our party, who had gone out to purchase books for perusal during the voyage, thinking they had ample time. They soon returned, and found, much to their surprise, that we had left the dock. Their only chance was to get some one to row them out in a yawl, which they soon found without difficulty. As they were pulling out to us, we laughed at them most heartily, which dispelled for a time the gloom which seemed to pervade all on deck. All being aboard, the tug comes up and hitches on, and off we move for our destination. While wending our way slowly out to Sandy Hook, we had a fine opportunity of indulging our romantic ideas and enjoying the beautiful scenery on New-York Bay, which is said by some to surpass any in the world, not excepting even the Bay of Naples, rendered immortal by the pen of the gifted Byron. The great city of New-York, the emporium of the new world, with her lofty spires and immense structures, surrounded by a forest of masts, indicating her commercial importance; Brooklyn, her sister city just opposite, with her beautiful residences and public edifices; together with Hoboken, Jersey City, Governor's Island, and other places, all possessing their attractions, combine to render the panorama exceedingly beautiful. About dusk the steamer left us outside the Hook, and returned to the city, leaving us to make our way across old ocean's wave as fast as the wind might carry us. In a few moments the hoarse voice of the mate was heard crying "All hands ahoy!" but instead of the command being obeyed, it was followed by the cry of "Fight—fight—fight!" when all on deck simultaneously made their way to the forecastle, from whence the cry proceeded. As I expected, the crew were all pretty much fuddled, and as usual on starting out they deemed it necessary to take a round or so, in order to prove each other's pugilistic attainments. The officers immediately interfered, and finding that John Barleycorn was the *causa belli*, ordered him to be placed under lock and key, which being done, order was restored, and Jack went kindly to the mast-head singing the jolly seaman's song.

All sails being set, and night having begun, I took one last lingering look at the highlands of New-Jersey, and repaired to my state-room, where I found my trunks snugly stored away, and all the little conveniences requisite for a sea voyage. The cabin I found to be larger than usual and much better furnished, while the appointments of this noble vessel of over one thousand tons were admirable, and the attendance without a fault. In crossing the Atlantic, I would advise all travellers who prefer real comfort and quietude, and have the time, by all means to take a packet-ship in preference to a steamer. In the American line will be found every luxury and convenience one can desire. The commanders generally are the very best of seamen, and conduct themselves at table, and wherever duty calls them, as gentlemen and men of intelligence; the crews excellent, being selected from the first class seamen, who always know their duty, and are faithful in its execution. Aside from these considerations, I would prefer going eastward in a packet ship on the score of safety and dryness of the deck: you are more liable to accident in a steamer from various causes; while their decks are always damp, being forced through the waves against a head wind, throwing the spray from stem to stern, making it exceedingly unpleasant; as it is always desirable to be as much on deck as possible, there being only two remedies for sea-sickness, according to the advice of our captain, viz., breathing the pure air, and the free use of brandy. The latter remedy I have found very acceptable to some, judging from their repeating propensities. Not being affected by sea-sickness, I of course could feel but little sympathy for my friends who seemed to be suffering agonies, yet I could fully appreciate their unpleasant situation, and did all in my power to alleviate their sufferings and cheer up their drooping spirits. I was somewhat surprised they should have been affected so early in the action, particularly as we had little or no wind and consequently a calm sea. It is really distressing to witness the prostration of all your fellow-passengers for the first four or five days, after which they become habituated to the motion of the vessel, and are ready to laugh at the many little sayings and doings while sick. To give you some idea of the feeling of a sea-sick person, I will merely relate one or two incidents that occurred among our party during their agonizing moments. Nearly all said they wished they were on *terra firma*, and one of the married members of the party remarked to me with great earnestness, that he was a pretty old fool for leaving his wife and children, to cross the ocean, knowing he would be deathly sick; and if the Lord spared him, he was certain he never would leave home again. Another gentleman of the party came out one morning on deck to breathe the fresh air after being immured for several days in his berth, and in his peculiar way said he would just like to shout one long God d—n for relief sake. He had hardly uttered the words when his eyes rested on two Reverend gentlemen, one of whom told him he had as well take that back; whereupon onr friend commenced making all sorts of apologies, saying really he did not know he was near, or he would have been more guarded; but in truth he really felt just that way.

On the third day after our departure we found it disagreeably cold, and as the stoves were left in New-York for a summer voyage, we were compelled either to take exercise on deck, or keep ourselves warm by rolling up into our bunk, which I found anything but agreeable. Fortunately for our comfort, we reached the Gulf stream on the fourth day, where a very pleasant temperature greeted our trembling limbs, being some eight or ten degrees warmer than any other part of the ocean. There is something very curious about this stream, of which so much has been said and written. Many theories have been advanced, and with some degree of plausibility, relative to the causes of this remarkable phenomenon of nature. Some say it is occasioned by an under-current flowing from the Pacific (which is considerably higher than the Gulf of Mexico) through the Isthmus of Darien; while others have contended it is produced by the trade winds from the coast of Africa, meeting the waters of the mighty Mississippi, and forcing it northward by way of the Island of Cuba along our coasts to the banks of Newfoundland, where its force is broken, and its waters disseminated and lost in immensity. The stream is forty or fifty miles wide, running at the rate of four miles per hour, with a temperature ten degrees warmer than other parts of the ocean.

We were driven by adverse winds considerably out of our way, having gone to the southward about six points, which will make our voyage longer than was anticipated. Nothing occurred from the time we set out until the sixth day, except the spouting of whales, floating of sea-weed, and pieces of some wreck, which the captain said might have been floating for six months, but which appeared to me to be of recent happening.

On the afternoon of the sixth day, while we were all on deck, passing our time variously as suited our inclinations, some playing at backgammon, some reading, others conversing, we were alarmed by a sudden squall which came upon us while we were under full sail, without a moment's warning. Before the captain could give orders for reefing the sails, our mainsail was rent in twain, the flying-jib and jib-boom carried off, and the ship thrown on her beam-ends, much to the alarm and consternation of the passengers. I was not at all disconcerted, because I had seen vessels in much greater straits, and knew there was no real danger, but was considerably amused at some of the passengers, who were probably never at sea before. One of the clergy said he trusted in the saving power of the Almighty; another gentleman said he was prepared for the event, so let her rip and be d——d; while a certain old gentleman bid good-bye to his wife and daughter—the ladies almost gave up the ghost—and the servants rolled into their bunks, and covered up their heads negro-like, until the wind subsided.

On the night of the seventh day, being Saturday, we assembled around the table in the gentlemen's cabin to drink the usual toast of "wives and sweethearts," which all seemed to enter into with a hearty zest. At a late hour we retired, expecting to pass the night in undisturbed repose. We were not exactly right in this matter. While we were all sleeping away the still watches of the night, with nought to disturb us save the occasional tread of the officer on deck, we were aroused by the awful cry of "Murder—murder—murder!" accompanied by a terrible scuffling on deck, as if some one was being stabbed. The cry of murder is at all times alarming, but when one is awakened from a sweet sleep by such a cry, it becomes still more terrible. Thinking it might be a mutiny, (although mutinies are out of vogue now,) I hurried on deck, and found, much to my relief, it was nothing more than the cry of a steerage passenger, who was laboring under a fit of *mania a potu.* He had crawled without observation during the night under one of the benches; the noise I mistook for wrestling, was his endeavor to disengage himself from the legs of the bench—imagining them to be sailors attempting to cast him overboard. The officers, with their usual dispatch, had him immediately conducted to his quarters, and all was quiet again.

The next morning the passengers all assembled in the cabin, to hear service by the Right Rev. Bishop Otey, of Tennessee, assisted by Parson McDougal of England. The morning service being over, the sermon having begun, we were alarmed by the cry of "Man overboard!" All rose instantly from their seats, and hurried on deck, to learn the truth of the matter. Sure enough, a man was overboard; and who should it be, but the *mania a potu* man, who alarmed us so much during the previous night. Fortunately for him, the vessel was standing almost still, there being little or no wind. When he rose, he swam like a duck, and caught the rope thrown out by the sailors, by which they drew him up into the ship. All the steerage passengers assembled around the poor fellow, who looked perfectly frantic, and began questioning him as to the whys and wherefores. He said he knew the captain wished him to jump overboard, for the sailors had been after him for several days. He then commenced relating several fish-stories, all of which evinced that he was not sane, yet sufficiently rational to jump into the sea when the ship was standing still with empty sails. In a few moments the excitement subsided, and the Bishop proceeded with his sermon; which was listened to with great attention and interest. After the conclusion of the sermon, I accepted the invitation of the physician belonging to the ship, and accompanied him to the steerage, wishing to see every thing, and let nothing escape. Here I found men, women and children, from almost every nation and clime, all having different tales to tell; some were going back to their native land after a wife, children, sister, or brother, while others were dissatisfied with America, and were returning to old England, where all those who are dissatisfied with our institutions usually come from. All seemed to be getting along remarkably well; I heard no complaint, except from one old woman, who told the doctor she hoped he would give the crazy man a potion to make him sleep; he annoyed her very much during the night by pulling her nose—all of which he solemnly denied.

For the last few days the winds have been adverse, and we have made little or no progress, being out of our course, towards the banks of Newfoundland, which we wished to avoid on account of the ice, etc. The eighth day was decidedly the most eventful we have had since our departure. At noon the skies began to lower, and the winds to rage, indicating a severe storm. Then appeared about a thousand porpoises and one or two whales, indicating, as the sailors say, a high wind. About three o'clock it seemed as if the spirits of the mighty sea were awakened from their dreams—

> "He that has sailed upon the dark blue sea
> Has viewed at times, I ween, a full fair sight."

The wind blew a perfect hurricane, and the short high sea was perfectly furious, lashing about in all directions with the madness of a maelstrom, and with a violence that apparently nothing could resist. Heavy squalls and thick weather added to the fearful tempest that was raging. The officers and crew of our noble vessel, which rode the waves like a thing of life, were all on the alert to a man, wrapped in their oil-skin dresses and water-proof overcoats, ready to meet the worst. All sails were immediately reefed, we stood full three hours with our head to the wind, buffeting the waves which rolled mountain high, as something superior to human work; our ship stood it well, and came out with flying colors. It was truly a magnificent scene; one that I would not have missed for any consideration. Could we have divested ourselves of its reality, it might be likened to a fancy picture in which some strange and curious dance was being represented between the sea and the ship. But our danger was too great for such thoughts. The fact of our being near the banks of Newfoundland, and the region of floating icebergs, was too strongly impressed upon our minds, to allow any visionary thoughts to possess us at the time. The captain, after the winds had subsided, and the waves had assuaged, remarked it was the severest storm he had witnessed for three years past. I feared I would not have the opportunity of seeing a storm at sea, but my wishes were realized, and

I can truly say I never beheld a scene so fearful, and at the same time so sublime.

Next morning we found ourselves on the banks of Newfoundland, and in the region of floating icebergs, which we have been trying to avoid for three days past. During the day we saw three icebergs, the nearest being about three miles off. It is truly a grand sight to see these immense fields of ice drifting on the bosom of the mighty deep, while the rays of the burning sun reflect a dazzling light on the waters round about. From these crystal plains rise, sometimes lated, sometimes in groups, elevations of thirty feet or more in height. In the spring, these fields begin to drift along in solemn procession to the southward, in which direction they hold their steady course, whether in calm or in spite of adverse winds. In my next you shall have a description of our voyage to our journey's end.

LETTER TWO.

IRISH CHANNEL, below Liverpool.

Journalizing—Better Prospects ahead—Speaking a ship—Interesting Jury Trial at Sea—Amusements—Irish News—Uproar on board—Sea Fowls—White Rat—Cabin Passenger lashed to the shrouds by the Sailors—Sunset at Sea—Cape Clear by moonlight—Bursting of Champagne Corks—Incidents in the Irish Channel.

THERE is no established mode of journalizing at sea, as every person has his own peculiar way of seeing and noting incidents *en route*. In looking over my little journal, I find many things worthy of comment, but must omit them in this sheet, in order that I may give prominence to the more interesting features of the voyage, and relieve you from the tedium of perusal.

In my last, written some fifteen days since, from the Banks of Newfoundland, I mentioned our ill luck in meeting unfavorable winds, which seemed to impede our progress in spite of our anxiety to proceed and our experience in nautical matters; but fortunately, while we were feeling something as Jonah did when the whale swallowed him, (rather down in the mouth,) a spanking breeze sprung up and carried us at a fine rate for several days. But this good luck was not of long duration; we had scarcely got through congratulating the captain, when adverse winds began to blow, and continued for several days, driving us a great way out of our course, towards the north of Ireland.

The day after we left the Banks we spoke the Belona, a ship bound for New-York from Liverpool. No day has elapsed since our departure without being in sight of a sail; this was the first vessel that came near enough to pass the usual compliments—such as the hoisting of flags and interchange of longitude. This ship came near enough to hear the shouts of the emigrants which crowded her decks. As an American citizen, my heart exulted with pride and admiration as I heard the shouts that filled the air when we hoisted from the spanker jib the stars and stripes of our free and happy country, to whose shores they were going like the Israelites of old to the promised land.

During a long voyage passengers are compelled to resort to all sorts of ways to kill time and make the monotony tolerable. Amusements of every description are brought into repute, and each one's ingenuity is taxed to diversify and render them interesting. After we had exhausted our patience in playing the various games, such as whist, chess, backgammon, shuffleboard, etc., etc., we resorted to trials by jury and publication of newspapers, both of which furnished an infinite deal of amusement. Cases of assault and battery, libel, and breach of promise were tried regularly. One of our legal friends officiated as judge, Mr. L. as clerk, an Englishman as sheriff, and your humble servant, together with a gentleman from Philadelphia, were the counsellors. The cases were all decided by the court against the defendants; and the verdicts were champagne for the crowd at Cape Clear. Our judge was exceedingly punctilious about maintaining the dignity of the court, and having the causes conducted in order. He fined several gentlemen two or three bottles of champagne for contempt of court. Among the sufferers was your old friend, who was fined two bottles for taking a seat beside his honor on the bench.

Nothing has created so much amusement during our passage as the newspapers, which are read out every day at table. We are indebted to one of our party who is known at home as the knight of the gray goose quill, for the publication of the first paper, called the

Waterloo Budget, which created great merriment. Some of the gentlemen, thinking rivalry the road to success, started another paper called the Stormy Petrel, which also created considerable merriment, and caused a deal of laughter and comment. These papers were kept up until good taste suggested their discontinuance. To give you an inkling of the contents of these papers, I will make a few extracts, selecting those that were received with most applause:

EXTRACTS

From the Waterloo Budget and the Stormy Petrel, published on board the Waterloo, at Sea.

WATERLOO BUDGET.—*Alarming Incident.*—As the Waterloo was on her late passage from New-York to Liverpool, the officer on watch and all in the vicinity were greatly startled and alarmed towards what Burns termed the "sma' hours," by a grating or jarring sound which appeared as if it proceeded from the ship's bottom. Some thought it might be caused by that natural phenomenon, a sub-marine earthquake. Others thought the ship's keel had dragged over some rocks. But "great effects proceed from little causes;" it finally turned out to be no more nor less than the voices of sundry gentlemen, in full chorus over that classical ditty "Uncle Ned." The participants at last accounts were doing as well as could be expected.

Lusus Naturæ.—Cases are given by travellers of districts of country in Arkansas and Texas, where the ague is so violent as to cause chickens to shake all their feathers off. We have recently had brought under our notice something quite as strange, viz., a *rat* which on a voyage to Europe became perfectly *white*, the result, doubtless, of paleness and disgust caused by sea-sickness. The poor fellow was on his way to the World's Fair.

Squalls.—The next debate by that enlightened body, the *Latitudinarians,* will be on the question, "What are the causes of squalls, as well when the mercury is up in the barometer, as when it is down?" Bachelors are expected to participate in the discussion.

Ladies' Fashions.—Joseys and sacks for promenading, with a very pretty style of cottage bonnets, something on the coal scuttle order. Hair, *à la Grecque,* when a reef occasionally gets shaken out of it.

Prices Current.—Whiskey Punch—The stiffest article, quick sale and the demand steady. Porter—Pretty good demand for the best. Lemonade—Flat. Whiskers and Moustaches—Black in good demand, much sought after and but little in market; red and foxy, a perfect drug, the market being largely overstocked; gray scarce, and no call for them.

Would be exchanged.—A pair of "sea-legs" for any thing that could toddle about on the solid earth—shape or length immaterial, as the advertiser is desperate.

METEOROLOGICAL TABLE.

First Week.	*Second Week.*	*Third Week.*
Wind. { Squall, Squallier, Squalliest.	Wind. { Calm, Calmer, Calmest.	Wind. { Contrary, Contrarier, Contrariest.

Wanted, by an individual, (not a doctor,) any amount of patience; application to be made at the weather side of the quarter deck, the first rainy day, when the wind is from the north-east.

Stormy Petrel.—*Singular Incident.*—Our peaceful community was very much startled from its propriety on Sunday last by a great outcry, and the rumor that something as yet unclassified in natural history had been discovered in the rigging of the vessel. All hands rushed upon deck, and beheld an object at some elevation in the rigging. Some supposed it to be a bird, while others thought it was a novel species of turtle that had crept out of the ocean. The bird theory was principally advocated by a gentleman from Brummagem, who unhesitatingly declared his conviction that it was only a lark; some of the more timid passengers were considerably alarmed, but were re-assured by the chivalrous Johnson, who informed them "*it was all right.*" On further investigation, it appeared that the object in question was a gentleman from Tennessee, who having ventured up the rigging, in violation of well established maritime law, was seized by the sailors and lashed fast, as an example to all land lubbers. He was not allowed to come down from his bad elevation, until he had engaged to come down with a modicum of grog for his captors.

The sea—the sea—I'm on the sea,
I'm where I don't want to be;
With the sky above and the sea below,
And nought but salt water wherever we go.
Oh! the ship doth pitch and the ship doth toss,
And bumps you about till you're sore and cross;
It upsets your soup and it spills your tap,
And it pours out your grub in your neighbor's lap:
I wouldn't be here, if I could once more see land,
I wouldn't—I wouldn't—if I would may I be d—d!

Many other pieces were read which would bear insertion, but as postage is heavy, and patience rare, I will not insert them.

During our passage we were followed by sea fowls of various descriptions far away from land. It is really surprising to watch their movements. The gull, which is the largest and most common, will follow a vessel for days without even resting on the waters, except occasionally when they dart down to catch a fish, or a crumb from the ship.

A few evenings since, one of our passengers was disturbed in his berth by a strange visitor in the shape of a rat, but being of a different hue from rats generally, it was doubted for a time whether the gentleman was correct in his supposition about its being a white rat. The following day the mysterious visitor again appeared, and was seen by several—all of which the mate confirmed, stating that he saw it come on board in New-York, from a China ship.

I have often heard persons expatiate on the beauties of a sun-set at sea, and expected to find it far more beautiful than any thing we landsmen are blessed with; but I was sadly disappointed, as we were not favored with a clear evening sky during the passage, and in the absence of the many hues created on land by reflection, it failed to present to my mind the beauties I anticipated.

On the evening of the twenty-second day, while we were all out on the quarter-deck, hoping to be soon in sight of land, we were aroused by the voice of a female in the steerage crying, "A duck, a duck, a fish-duck!" which immediately put us on the look-out. After gazing and straining our eyes in fruitless attempts for some time, one of the sailors descried Mizen Head from the mast-head, which verified the woman's duck story.

In a short time after this joyous news, the captain pointed out to us the highlands of Cape Clear, which appeared to me in the distance like a small cloud on the horizon; but as we drew nearer and nearer, the land became more distinct, and was visible to the naked eye. After we were fully satisfied that Cape Clear was really in view, it was suggested by one of the party that we might as well call out that champagne imposed by the Honorable Court. All acquiesced, and the wine circulated freely, making us feel happy and disposed to witticism and merriment.

The following day we were blessed with another calm, and stood out in the Channel without moving the least for eight hours; about dark a breeze sprung up, and we made a fine run as far up as Great Owen's Head, where we will lie until morning. The scenery along the shores of Wales looks very beautiful in the distance, although very rugged. I was strongly reminded, while looking at the many little farms inclosed by hedges and ditches, of some of the closely cultivated portions of New-England. Every spot of ground seems to be in a high state of cultivation.

You will be surprised to learn that the hills along these shores are clad with snow, which appears a little singular so late in the season.

The steam tug is now waiting to carry us into Liverpool, which I am anxious to reach, having been out twenty-six days.

LETTER THREE.

WATERLOO HOTEL, Liverpool, Eng.

Arrival at Liverpool—Appearance of the City from the River Mersey—The Docks—Public Buildings—Monuments—Railroad Stations—Markets—Hotels—Draught Horses—Visit to Birkenhead—Marriage in Church, &c.

ON the morning of the 8th, the good ship Waterloo cast anchor in the Mersey, three miles below the city, near the Lock Fort, after a voyage of twenty-six days. Here, the captain informed us, we had to remain until he could go after a custom-house officer to examine our trunks, all of which appeared absurd to those over-anxious to reach the land. Several of us, determined not to be cheated out of a good breakfast, accepted the invitation of the captain and went ashore, leaving our luggage on the ship. After procuring lodgings for the party, and partaking of an excellent breakfast, we returned in the steam-tug to the Waterloo, where we found all on deck, anxiously awaiting our return. In a few minutes the baggage and passengers were transferred from the ship to the tug, and off we started, giving three hearty cheers for the Waterloo and her crew, which was responded to by the officers and sailors with heartfelt enthusiasm.

We are now in the hands of the custom-house officer, whose duty requires a thorough examination of all baggage entering the port in order to detect smuggling and to receive duties on articles of prohibition. English reprints and cigars are immediately taken, if discovered, and also daguerreotypes and line engravings. Several of our party paid duty on these articles. As a general thing their examinations are nominal, particularly if the person presents a genteel appearance, for they merely ran their hands hurriedly through the contents of the trunks, frequently leaving things undiscovered which would otherwise bring revenue to the government. Many avail themselves of their good looks, and pass through the custom-house without detection.

The approach to Liverpool does not come up to my expectations, although the docks give it an appearance altogether different from what we are accustomed to, rendering it very attractive to the lovers of architectural skill. These docks of world-wide reputation, standing for miles along the river, are the pride of the city and Great Britain, and justly so, for they show to mankind what mighty works of commercial convenience labor and skill can produce. The cost of these docks was immense; more, probably, than any other nation is able to bestow upon one city.

Liverpool is comparatively a new place, but its immense tonnage, which now almost equals that of London, and its growing importance in a commercial point of view, render it, next to the metropolis, the greatest city in the kingdom. Those who now look at the Tyre of Great Britain, view its spacious docks where flags of all nations float gaily in the breeze, traverse its wide streets and observe its noble public buildings, handsome shops and commodious dwelling-houses, must find some difficulty in believing it has sprung from an insignificant fishing village within the period of little more than a century, whose inhabitants in the days of "good Queen Bess" found themselves compelled to pray for the remission of a tax, which they were unable to pay, styling themselves of "Her Majesty's poor and decayed town of Liverpool." The greatest and most remarkable changes, however, have taken place within the last eighty years. There are still living many persons, with memories nervous in age, who with feeble voices speak of their native town abounding in fields, orchards, and gardens, pleasant places which have gradually faded from sight before the magic touch of improvement; broad streets, squares and palaces only now appearing, where wild flowers hung pendulous in the sunbeam, and the loudest noise was that of merry children at play, or the carolling of the cuckoo in mid-air. Year by year the town has been extending and spreading, until its former features have departed, leaving no traces of early recollection and no spot to quiet reflection in the mind of the antiquary.

Liverpool has done much towards beautifying her public buildings, which are real ornaments—and at the same time substantial. It would be impossible to give in the space of a letter an accurate description of the various public buildings, and I will merely touch upon the general features of the most attractive.

The corner-stone of the custom-house, which is a very large and substantial building, was laid in 1828, with much ceremony. The style of this edifice is Ionic, and designed somewhat in the shape of a double cross with four points of great extent. The main front is 430 feet in length, and surmounted by a cupola and dome 127 feet from the ground, the crown of which is supported by a tasteful circle of Corinthian columns, between which are placed sixteen perpendicular windows, admitting a strong flood of light in the spacious room below. The windows in the upper story are semicircularly arched; the lower portion of the building is rusticated. The custom-house and post-office is a stately building, well adapted for all commercial and postal purposes. In front of this building there is a bronze statue erected by the corporation to the memory of Huskisson, through whose powerful mediation the building was commenced.

The exchange building next claims our attention. Its foundation was laid in 1803, and the total cost was £110,888. It is one of the largest buildings in the city, occupying three sides of a quadrangle, measuring 194 feet by 180, the area being 3,492 feet, and twice the size of the Exchange, London. It is built of reddish-colored stone in the Doric fashion.

In the centre of the area of the Exchange is the Nelson Monument, in which I was greatly disappointed, having heard and read very exaggerated accounts of its beauty. It is altogether different in structure from any monument in the States, being made of bronze placed on a plain stone pedestal. The design is very good, and reflects credit upon Mr. C. Wyatt, also upon Westmacott, who modelled it. It is a circular pedestal surmounted with a statue of Nelson holding in his left hand four crowns, emblematical of his four victories, and in his right the flags taken in battle. In the rear is a figure of Britannia lamenting his loss, while the hand of a skeleton, emblematical of death, reaches from behind the folds of one of the flags and rests upon his heart. Around this are four allegorical statues representing in different attitudes the appearance of great grief. It has upon it this inscription: "*England expects every man to do his duty.*" The monument weighs twenty-two tons, and cost £9,000.

St. George's Hall is just being completed. It is the largest and most beautiful edifice in the city. It has a concert room capable of accommodating more persons than any other in this kingdom. This building is to be used as an assembly room. While we were visiting this hall we called into a church very near, and were ushered by the sexton into the clerk's room, who invited us very kindly to be seated. In a minute or so he turned to me and asked if I had my license? License for what, said I? To be married, he replied. We all commenced laughing, and he soon discovered his mistake, and made the matter plain by telling us that he was expecting a bridal party, and concluded we were the persons wishing to be united in the holy bonds of wedlock. In a short time the *genuine* bridal party entered the church, and we witnessed for the first time a marriage in old England.

The Sailors' Home is decidedly the most tasty building in the city, and acquires additional importance from the fact that the corner-stone was laid by Prince Albert, (*I mean in the eyes of Englishmen.*)

The railroad stations of Liverpool are very costly, being built of solid stone and covered with glass.

The market places of this city are very superior. St. John's market is a building 180 feet long, 100 broad, containing five avenues. There I had an opportunity of seeing some of the fine beef and mutton that I had heard so much about, and I assure you it surpasses any thing that I have ever seen in our country. The fish market is also very superior; but the vegetables and fruits were very inferior.

There is no place more refreshing in the city limits than St. James' Cemetery. It presents a remarkable appearance, being formed in a deep dell or quarry, which for many years contributed its stone in the erection of various public works. The area contains 44,000 square yards of ground used for interments, while the length is 1500 feet, breadth 270, and depth 60 feet. The western side and north end are covered by a thick shrubbery, sloping gradually from the top of the cemetery to the bottom; the eastern wall is occupied by 105 catacombs, the entrances to which are four feet six inches wide, seven feet high, and finished with rustic masonry; they are approached by inclined planes. There are one or two chaste tombs in the cemetery, but most of them are very inferior. I was told while there by the sexton that twenty thousand persons had been interred within this small place, which seems almost incredible.

The hotels here are called excellent, but really they are far inferior to our American hotels in every particular. They are nothing more than large coffee-houses with lodging rooms attached. The idea of one taking his meals all alone is rather anti-democratic for Americans, and more particularly a Westerner. You go into the coffee-room and call for what you wish, which is served up in a few minutes by females, in large old-fashioned white caps, which makes one feel like laughing more than eating. Nothing has attracted my attention more than the draft-horses that I see in the streets. Their size and capabilities are really wonderful; as a general thing they are about sixteen hands high, and in proportion. They are in excellent order, and look as sleek as a new hat. Yesterday I counted as many as thirty steam-pressed bales of cotton on one wagon, and drawn by only two horses, which would be considered a tremendous load on our turnpikes for a team of six horses. Being rather curious, I stopped the driver and inquired what he fed his horses with; and he told me that steamed beans and corn were mostly used, but that every thing was steamed. Yesterday afternoon we accepted the invitation of a friend living in Birkenhead, just opposite the city, and visited the Park, containing over one thousand acres, and made at the expense of the corporation of Birkenhead, which contains about thirty thousand inhabitants. It is the largest park in this part of England, and certainly possesses many attractions. It is inclosed by an iron fence, with massive stone gate-ways, and laid out most beautifully in walks and flower beds. In the centre is an artificial stream, filled with swans, over which are thrown aërial bridges. Statuary of various kinds are placed in the most prominent parts of the Park, all together making it exceedingly beautiful.

After viewing the Park satisfactorily, we accompanied our friend to his residence, where we passed the evening most delightfully.

LETTER FOUR.

HUCKNALL, near Newstead Abbey, Eng.

Departure from Liverpool—Manchester—Posting to Rousley—Visit to Haddon Hall and Chatsworth—Visit to Sherwood Forest—Newstead Abbey, etc.

HAVING remained in Liverpool sufficiently long to see every thing that a stranger finds to engage his attention, and to recruit after a long voyage, we took the *rail* to Manchester, passing through a tunnel one mile and a half in length, and over a champaign country beautifully hedged, and under a fine state of cultivation. Being in what is called the express train, which carried us at the rate of sixty miles per hour, you can readily imagine our chance of forming any correct idea of the qualities of the land, products, etc.

Long before we reached the City of Mills, our attention was attracted by the thousand and one chimneys reaching almost to the clouds, and enveloping the whole country round about with coal-smoke, giving the city an old and dingy appearance, and rendering it next to an impossibility for the ladies to keep their faces clean. Here we met several Americans from the Eastern States, who like ourselves were anxious to go through and examine the principal mills, and compare them with our own. Upon inquiry we were told that we would find no difficulty in gaining admission; but our experience, I am sorry to say, was quite the contrary, for we were refused admission at two or three places—which was quite enough for our patience. They stated that they had been so much visited during the month, and that there were so many mechanics and manufacturers in the country, that they preferred keeping closed doors. There are certainly a great number of mills here, and their manufactured articles are justly prized by the kingdom; but really, without boasting, I think that our mills can fully compete with them in all respects, and in a few years, I hope to see in operation manufactures on a much grander scale in our own Tennessee.

From Manchester, we proceeded by post to a little village called Rousley, in the county of Derby, through an exceedingly broken and somewhat romantic country. From the Peaks of Derby, we had a fine view of nearly the whole county and portions of those adjacent. To an American accustomed to the White, Alleghany, and Cumberland mountain scenery, it would not be much thought of; but here in England they call it a *lovely panorama*. I was exceedingly amused at an old gentleman who asked me if I did not consider that a very wild region, which is more thickly populated than any portion of Tennessee. You can imagine how one accustomed to the dark swamps and thick cane-brakes of Arkansas must have given vent to his risibles.

Travelling by post-coaches still remains in use where the locomotive has not been introduced, and it reminds me very much of our stage travelling—with the exception of the *style*, which we utilitarians would abandon as useless trumpery. The driver is quite as consequential, and the freedom of speech is equally as unrestrained as you find with us, which is much more agreeable than being confined in a close car where you can neither see nor hear any thing with satisfaction.

Arrived at the little village of Rousley, we put up at an inn called the Peacock, which is about two hundred years old, and has great reputation as a place where fishermen and sportsmen congregate to carry on their amusements, and indulge in their favorite sports. Near this village is the old castle of Haddon Hall, now owned by the Duke of Rutland. It is unoccupied, but is kept in good order by the Duke as a monument of antiquity. Soon after the conquest this property was owned by the Avenells, from whom it came to the Vernons. The last male heir of this family, Sir John Vernon, was commonly called the King of the Peake, on account of his hospitality and magnificent mode of living. He died during the seventh year of Elizabeth, and Haddon passed by marriage with one of his daughters into the possession of the family of the Manners, and was their principal seat till the beginning of the last century. In the time of the first Duke of Rutland, in the reign of Queen Anne, seven score servants were maintained in this ancient seat of English hospitality. The situation of Haddon is very beautiful. It stands on a shelving and rather elevated mass of the first limestone, overlooking the entire dale and its meandering Wye, backed by an extensive wood and surrounded by beautiful trees. At first sight it has more the appearance of an old fortress, than what it really is, a hall, chiefly in the Elizabethan style, and without any effectual defences. The building in its present form is not in the least calculated for defence or protection against a besieging force, according to the military tactics of any period, though there can be but little doubt that this mansion, which was the work of different ages, occupies the site of a Norman castle, portions of the lower part of which may be traced in the walls of the towers which overlook both the upper and lower portals. It is said to be decidedly one of the finest specimens of a hall of the olden time in existence. The old tower with narrow loop-holes, and gloomy, uncomfortable rooms, is the only part which retains that *stern* character, the peculiar feature of the iron age when "every man's hand was against his fellow;" that age of darkness and military despotism which succeeded the destruction of the Roman power by the savages of the North. The old part of Haddon is said to have been built before the conquest; and as a quiet country seat of the English gentry in the eighteenth century, kept still in good repair, with all its ancient honors about it, just as deserted by the family one hundred and seventy years ago, and really retaining all that character, as if they had quitted it yesterday, is a beautiful specimen of that age.

There can hardly be conceived a more striking contrast to the sombre grandeur of Haddon Hall, than is exhibited by the splendid magnificence of the neighboring pile of Chatsworth, the country seat of the Duke of Devonshire. The former of these buildings, as remarked by an English writer, is "one of the most perfect and most curious of the class of castellated houses now remaining, but when viewed as a whole, is almost devoid of all real elegance, or comfortable convenience, and fitted only to entertain a horde of licentious retainers." In the latter edifice we perceive a unity of design and adaptation of parts, not only beautiful when separately considered, but also deriving new beauties from their connection with the other portions of the structure to which they belong. The various divisions of the edifice harmonize with each other, and combine with the adjacent scenery to constitute a picture of surpassing elegance and splendor. We were ushered through the entire building, out-grounds and conservatories, and I feel safe in saying that it is the most beautiful, comfortable, and elegant structure in all England, not excepting even Windsor Castle. To describe the park with its three thousand deer, the gardens with their extensive conservatories, water-falls, fountains and statuary, the castle with its extensive libraries, ancient paintings and statuary, would require more space than I can allow in this letter. But notwithstanding the great magnificence of Chatsworth, I must say that the antiquity and associations connected with Haddon Hall made it more interesting to me. It remains as a model of domestic arrangements of the noble families of former times, and as a picturesque object suited to the bold and romantic landscape of which it forms a prominent part; and it is also deserving great attention from artists and amateurs as affording examples of elaborate and beautiful workmanship in the carved panelling of its wainscotted apartments, and in the elegant tracery of some of the ceiling.

The next places of interest were Sherwood Forest and Newstead Abbey, both of which possess attractions and associations dear to every Englishman—the former as the place where "bold Robin Hood and his merrie men" used to practise their daring exploits, and the latter as the home of the gifted Byron. As we passed through this legendary neighborhood, surrounded by the haunts of Robin Hood and his band of outlaws, so famous in ancient ballad and nursery tale, it recalled vividly the romantic faith and impressions of our boyhood, and caused a thrill of delight to animate a heart which is not always glad. My remembrances of "merrie Sherwood" are of the pleasantest kind; for often during my earlier life have I dwelt with wonderment over the pages of some little book giving a description of the great deeds once done in this classic region. This locality, which was once a mighty forest, now teems with mouldering ruins and noble remnants of the grandeur of bygone ages. Among the many interesting spots that give character to the neighborhood, Newstead Abbey is the most prominent, and particularly interesting to Americans, as they are generally great admirers of the poet. As we drew near to the Abbey, a most glorious scene burst upon the view. On the right hand lay a splendid sheet of water, fringed with young woods that bow their whispering homage o'er the margin, reflecting all the depth and brightness of the tranquil heavens; aquatic wild birds studded the silvery surface, as though they had a "vested interest" in the place, and possessed a "protective order" against all molestation. A romantic water-fall, and the ruins of a rustic mill, together with the gentle murmuring of the foaming falls, added to the richly wooded country around, served to complete a picture upon which memory, so long as "she holds her zeal," will love to dwell. Turning to the left, the venerable Abbey rises in solemn grandeur, the long and lovely ivy clinging fondly to the rich tracery of a former age. As we first gazed upon these old walls, and remembered that it was here, even among the comparative ruins of a building once dedicated to the sacred cause of religion by the monks of old, that the great genius of Byron was first developed—here that he paced with youthful melancholy the halls of his illustrious ancestors, and trod the lonely walks of the banished monks—we involuntarily commenced repeating those beautiful lines from his own pen, in which he speaks of the decay of his much loved home:

"Newstead! fast falling, once resplendent dome;
Religions shrine; repentant Henry's pride;
Of warriors, monks and Danes, the cloistered tomb,
Whose pensive shades around thy ruins glide;
Hail to thy pile! more honor'd in the fall
Than modern mansions in their pillar'd state:
Proudly majestic frowns thy vaulted hall,
Scowling defiance on the blasts of Fate."

Newstead was founded by Henry the Second, in the year 1170, as a priory of Black Canons, an order having for their tutelary patron St. Augustine, and practising great austerity of life. It was dedicated to the Virgin Mary, and there is still to be seen in one of the niches of the chapel, in a state of preservation, a sculptured Virgin and child. It continued a priory until the time of Henry VIII., who, in his zeal for the temporal welfare of himself, and to the consternation of the then religious world, set about the wholesale destruction of all the monastic institutions of the country. It was afterwards granted by the same royal favor to Sir John Byron, who converted it into a residence of more than ordinary splendor. During the troubles which marked the history of the great rebellion, which ended in the martyrdom of the unfortunate King Charles the

First, the Byrons distinguished themselves as warm adherents of royalty, and Newstead sustained the siege from the parliamentarians; thus as Lord Byron says:

> "The Abbey once, a regal fortress now,
> Encircled by insulting rebel powers;
> War's dread machines thy threatening brow,
> And dart destruction in sulphurous showers."

On the death of Charles, the Byron estate was placed under sequestration. During the civil war, in 1643, Charles the First marked his high sense of Sir John Byron's loyalty and devotion by raising him to the peerage, and immediately after the restoration Charles the Second restored Newstead to its late owner, from whom it descended to Lord Byron. In the year 1818, Colonel Wildman, the present esteemed owner, purchased it from the poet, who was compelled to dispose of it on account of pecuniary difficulties, for the sum of £100,000; and has since, by judicious alterations and im provements, proved himself a most worthy owner of a place at once the pride of the forest and the admiration of thousands who have by his courtesy been permitted to traverse its spacious galleries and venerable halls. We had the pleasure of seeing Col. Wildman, who was very kind in conducting us through the various apartments of the Abbey and explaining every thing to us. He was a class-mate and early friend of the poet, and in speaking of Lord Byron he would almost go into ecstasies.

From the Abbey we came to this place, which has the honor of being the last resting-place of the departed great, his remains having been removed by his sister, Augusta Maria Leigh, from Missolonghi in Western Greece. His remains are deposited in the Byron vault, in a small church and still smaller village. He should have been buried where he requested, at Newstead, between his favorite dog and faithful servant. But he needs no monument or epitaph to perpetuate his memory; it will live when all monuments shall have crumbled away.

LETTER FIVE.

STRATFORD-ON-AVON, Eng.

Visit to Birmingham—Its Manufactures, etc.—Visit to Kenilworth and Warwick Castles—The Home of Shakspeare.

WE are now nearly in the centre of England, and in the great workshop of the kingdom, where almost every thing that the human mind can conceive of is manufactured. From a very early period Birmingham has been renowned for its manufactures in steel and iron. This trade is now carried on to an extent elsewhere unequalled. The principal branches of it are plate and plated wares, ornamented steel goods, jewelry, japanning, papier maché, cut-glass ornaments, steel pens, buckles and buttons, cast-iron articles, guns, steam-engines, etc. We found no difficulty in gaining admission, as at Manchester, into the principal establishments. They were particularly polite in carrying us through and showing the entire process by which they manufacture their various articles. We were particularly struck with the manner of making papier maché articles, which are so beautiful, and which appear to us so difficult and intricate. The process is very simple when we look at it, and causes us to wonder why it has not been more generally used. The first thing is to cut out of common brown paper the articles to be made, which is pasted together and placed in an oven of a certain temperature to be dried. It is then taken out and varnished with a very thick black coating, the mother-of-pearl being imbedded in the varnish. The article is now complete with the exception of the finishing polish, which is nothing more than rubbing and varnishing.

Birmingham is connected with London and various places by means of canals, and forms a centre of railway communication with every part of the kingdom. There is nothing in Birmingham to attract the stranger, aside from the mills. Her public edifices and monuments are of a mean description, and deserve no particular notice.

Not far from Birmingham is the famed Castle of Kenilworth, around which linger so many historical associations and pleasing reminiscences.

"Shrine of the mighty, can it be
That this is all that remains of thee?"

Among the venerable remains of the once magnificent dwellings of princes—alternately the prisons and the "plaisance" of royalty—there cannot be one more deserving the notice of the admirers of picturesque beauty than this old castle, which, notwithstanding the corroding hand of Time, still retains such vestiges of its former extent and grandeur as are powerfully calculated to impress the mind of the beholder with a vivid idea of the magnificence of the feudal ages, and the instability of all things human. As I stood upon the bridge erected by the Earl of Leicester for Queen Elizabeth to enter the castle, and viewed its ivy-clad battlements and majestic towers, which are now fast mouldering to decay, yet still "elegant in their ruins and dignified in their disgrace," I was inspired with thrilling emotions of the deepest awe and veneration. Imagination involuntarily takes wing, and forcibly brings to remembrance the departed glory of all those mighty cities, whose renown in arts and arms filled the world with wonder and astonishment, and whose builders decreed that they should be the imperishable monuments of the genius of science and of conquest. Who, for instance, can behold the ruins now unfolded to our view, without exclaiming, in the sublime and energetic language of the inspired writer, "How is the mighty fallen!" All who have read Sir Walter Scott are perfectly familiar with the strange and romantic history of Kenilworth. The only part of the original fortress of this once lordly structure now remaining is the keep, generally known as Cæsar's Tower, the walls of which are in some places ten feet thick. The remains of the additions made by John of Gaunt, Duke of Lancaster, are termed Lancaster buildings. In a part of the ruins termed Leicester buildings are to be seen the relics of the great hall, a fine baronial room eighty-eight feet in length and forty-five in width. Although the erections of Leicester are of the most recent date, they have the most ancient and ruined appearance, being built of a brown, crumbling stone, not well adapted for durability. "We cannot but add," says Sir Walter Scott, "that this lordly palace, where princes feasted and where heroes fought, now in the bloody current of storm and siege, and now in the games of chivalry, where beauty dealt the prize which valor won, all is now desolate. The bed of the lake is now a rushy swamp, and the massy ruins of the castle only serve to show what their splendor once was, and to impress upon the mind of the visitor the transitory value of the humble happiness of those who enjoy an humble home in virtuous contentment."

From the castle of Kenilworth we went to Warwick, only a few miles distant, which is also one of the noblest specimens of ancient grandeur this country now possesses. Owing to the recent death of the Countess of Warwick the doors of the Castle were closed to all visitors, and we were denied the privilege of going through those ancient halls and comparing them with others. The porter, however, who was a good-natured and well-fed Englishman, was kind enough to conduct us over the grounds, and show to us some old relics that belonged to the giant Guy, Earl of Warwick. Among the many curious things I noticed was his armor, his sword weighing twenty-two pounds and about seven feet in length, and his shield, helmet, breast-plate, walking staff and tilting pole are all of enormous size and undoubtedly very ancient; the horse armor, on which is an inscription nearly obliterated, is of a later date. A large pot, called "Guy's pot," and his flesh fork, are really curious; the pot holds one hundred and seventy gallons, and the weight with the fork eight hundred and seven pounds. Five of our party got into this pot, and there was room, like a *buss*, for one more. This enormous vessel is now used by the Warwick family for a *punch-bowl*, and is filled three times in succession on the day when each heir of the Castle attains his majority.

This is a place of much importance and great interest, from its being the chief seat of men whose names are intimately connected with the most prominent events of English history. The present Earl takes pride in keeping it in good repair, and it is now said to be among the most desirable country abodes in England.

We are now in the town of Stratford, the birth-place and home of the "sweet swan of Avon," the immortal Shakspeare. One always attaches to the cradle of greatness the idea of romance and beauty, for it is almost impossible to conceive that the genius of poetry could emanate from a little unpretending village such as I found this place to be. It is a clean, quiet town, pleasantly situated on the Avon, and surrounded by meadows, but its pretensions to celebrity would be small but for the *magic of a name* which has penetrated into every region where civilized man has trodden. While here we visited the theatre, being rather curious to know how they would represent the characters of the great master of the drama in his native place. After groping our way through narrow streets and lanes for some time, we at last found the Adelphi of Stratford in an obscure part of the village. The door was kept by a *woman*, and the house was very small and plain, while the performance was miserable, reflecting no credit on the dramatic corps; it was such as would be hissed even in the theatre of *Bowery*.

The house in which the poet was born still stands on the north side of Henley street, as a relic of the departed. As we entered the low but honored roof from whence came forth the man whose writings are for all time, I could but smile at the extreme simplicity and primitiveness of every thing about it. The floor is paved with stones that, characteristically enough, are cut up into a host of splinters and fragments, as if really hacked by a butcher's cleaver. On one side is an old-fashioned log-cabin fireplace, with cozy sitting places on either side; for in those smoky days, with penetrating draughts coming in on all sides, happy was he who was privileged to take a chimney-corner. In the room where Shakspeare was born, are inscribed on the walls, floor, window glass, and every other part of the room, the autographs of visitors desirous of doing honor to the memory of the departed, or themselves, according to circumstances. Among the many, I saw Sir Walter Scott's name cut with a diamond on the window glass.

After seeing the birth-place, we proceeded to the village church, where Shakspeare's honored relics are entombed. The slab that covers the grave is the plainest in the church, being outside the chancel between his wife and eldest daughter, with the inscription written by himself:

"Good friend, for Jesvs sake forbear
To digg the dvst enclosed heare;
Blest be ye man yt spares these stones,
And cvrst be he YT moves my bones."

LETTER SIX.

OXFORD, England.

The University—Students—Public Buildings—Libraries—Arundelian Marbles—Monument to Cranmer, Ridley, and Latimer—Boat-racing—Blenheim, etc.

WE are now in Oxford, the seat of one of the most celebrated universities of Europe—distinguished alike for its antiquity and influence upon the institutions and government of England. For here it is that the nobility for generations have resorted to acquire that early training and mental discipline necessary to render them capable to discharge the duties of office and manage the affairs of state. Here also have been educated many of those master spirits renowned in the arts and sciences, whose writings have shed light upon the world, and given to England a character for belles-lettres scholarship more enduring than the rock of ages. It is a place of very remote antiquity, as the period of its origin is involved in obscurity. The first fact connected with it that is known with certainty is, that in the reign of Alfred, who once resided here with his three sons, the place was noted for a monastery which was founded in the year 727. The origin of the university, like that of the town, is involved in obscurity. The first places of education here appear to have been schools for the instruction of youth. The earliest charter of privileges to the university as a corporate body is of the 28th Henry III., and it was in 1603 that the university obtained from James the First the privilege of sending two members to Parliament.

The university now contains twenty colleges and five halls, and numbers upon the books of the different colleges and halls 5,400 members. We may therefore say that Oxford is the city of colleges, for without them it would have nothing to recommend it to particular notice.

The buildings of the different institutions present a very antiquated appearance. Many of the walls are fast crumbling to decay, being built of a soft friable sandstone, which is easily affected by the influence of the atmosphere, and gives to the buildings a sombre and gloomy aspect. The students, however, as they walk through these dark halls with their loose, flowing robes, gaze upon the old structures with pride and admiration, saying to themselves, "We come here to gather knowledge from the experience of those who have gone before us—and what place more fitting to burn the midnight taper than those venerable halls erected by the munificence of our ancestors?" The students of Oxford conduct themselves with gentlemanly propriety and decorum, and every thing seems to move on like clock-work. A rebellion is out of the question, as no one dares presume to do aught against the rules of the institution, knowing that he would be instantly detected and brought to condign punishment. No one until recently could enter this university unless he had been received or baptized in the established Church of England, and consequently a religious influence pervades the entire establishment, and gives it a tone which in all probability it would not otherwise possess.

In Oxford there are many very superior libraries, among which the Bodleian Library is particularly worthy of notice. It was founded by Sir Thomas Bodley, at the close of the sixteenth century, on the remains of one established by Humphrey, Duke of Gloucester. This library is said to contain, perhaps, the most valuable collection of books and manuscripts in Europe. A description of its wonders and treasures would require far more time and space to do them the least measure of justice than I can here bestow. We passed around the quadrangle with its galleries one above another, and their alcoves on each side, with their thousands upon thousands of volumes of all languages and tongues neatly arranged on shelves, with convenient steps to them, and desks furnished with pen and ink for the use of those who seek this vast repository of the learning of the world. Some of the manuscripts which the polite official showed us were represented to be twelve, fourteen, and fifteen centuries old. A copy of the first authorized edition of the Bible, and the first ever printed, was also exhibited, besides many other things equally rare and curious. The collection of writings in Sanscrit is large enough alone to form a respectable library. Then there is a room appropriated for the reception of all the best periodicals from every country on earth—an assemblage of works which in ages to come must be exceedingly valuable. After visiting the library, we went to a room containing Arundelian Marbles, so called from Thomas Howard, Earl of Arundel, by whom they were procured in Greece, and brought to England. They are curious specimens of antiquity. I did not examine the various objects with their inscriptions with any degree of minuteness, as they were all hieroglyphical to me, and besides there has been published a full and accurate account of every article in the collection, with drawings of the same.

In the middle of the street, fronting Baliol College, is a stone cross, marking the spot where Latimer, Ridley, and Cranmer were burned at the stake as martyrs during Mary's reign. And near this memorable place is a beautiful monument erected by public subscription to the memory of those pious men, who laid down their lives for refusing to subscribe to the Romish doctrine of transubstantiation. The Church of England regard this spot with peculiar interest and veneration.

After seeing every thing in the city worthy of the stranger's attention, we walked through one of the beautiful meadows near by, to the banks of the *great river* Thames, to witness the annual boat-race, in which the students take great pride. This race comes off every May, between the students of the different colleges. Each college has a beautiful boat constructed of light materials, and built with an eye to speed. Each boat has eight oars, manned by those selected by their comrades for skill and strength. The oarsmen are beautifully equipped in all the colors of the rainbow, and evince great pride in keeping all things in ship-shape. Several thousand persons assembled on the banks of the river to witness the sight, which was really exciting. To see twenty boats of different colors, all running after another with great speed, is a scene well worthy of the emulation of the young aspirants, and the attention of those who come many miles to witness it.

Near the city of Oxford is Blenheim, the magnificent seat erected in the reign of Queen Anne, for the celebrated Duke of Marlborough. This elegant structure was designed by Sir J. Vanburgh, and one million pounds was granted by Parliament for its erection. The interior is splendidly adorned, and contains a valuable collection of pictures, and a library of more than 17,000 volumes, and an elegant chapel. The gardens are extensive, and the park, consisting of 2,700 acres, is richly wooded, and the grounds are laid out with great taste. It is now the residence of one of the descendants of the original Duke, none of whom have done any thing to reflect honor upon their distinguished ancestor.

LETTER SEVEN.

LONDON, England.

The Great Industrial Exhibition—The National Representation—Our own Country—Americans in London—Her Majesty and the Royal Family.

WELL, here we are at last in the very midst of modern Babylon—the city of *busses, cabs, clamor, crowds, industry, poverty, and imperial splendor*—the great metroplis of England, and of the civilized world. After procuring comfortable apartments in a convenient part of the city, and making due preparations for several weeks' sojourn, we commenced our labors of sight-seeing. The first object of attraction was of course the Crystal Palace, which has been the topic of conversation and newspaper speculation in all parts of the world ever since it was projected. I regretted exceedingly that we were not here to witness the opening of the exhibition, in the presence of Her Majesty, Prince Albert, and the royal family, which is said to have been the grandest display of regal splendor ever witnessed in London. The opening was successful beyond the most sanguine expectations of those particularly interested. Every thing was conducted with perfect order and system, and the day passed off in peace and quietude, much to the gratification of the Queen and all her subjects. When I first beheld this truly magnificent structure, with all its contents, I was utterly bewildered, and experienced pretty much the same feeling that a *greenhorn* would upon his first entance into a fancy store. I saw so many beauties, that I was completely at a loss which to look at first, or to tell which I liked most. To give you any thing like a correct idea of the Exhibition would require volumes, and then I would fail, for no pen is adequate to delineate perfectly all that is here to be seen. I have read many accounts, and listened to the descriptions of many, but they all fail to come up to my ideas of the magnificence of the undertaking. As you have long since read descriptions of the building in the prints, and are perfectly familiar with its structure and dimensions, it is unnecessary for me to notice it, further than to say that it is a wonderful work, furnishing a remarkable example of the triumph of human genius and skill. Mr. Paxton, the superintendent of the gardens at Chatsworth, who designed the Crystal Palace after the Duke of Devonshire's conservatory, so arranged it as to furnish ample room for the display of all the various specimens of human industry, whether directed to the productions of art or the creations of nature, in the smallest allowable space, and in a light to afford opportunities for a fair examination. In a word, order and system were to be secured in an assemblage, where, from the multitude of objects and visitors, confusion and disorder were naturally to be feared. The entire palace is so arranged and divided into compartments as to furnish every convenience for the reception of the various offerings of industry; and each division is marked with the names of the different countries represented, so as to prevent any confusion or mistake. This arrangement also furnishes a great facility to visitors in enabling them to compare the articles of the different countries with the aid of the catalogue, without the perplexity of asking and being asked questions.

The first object that attracted my attention upon entering was a glass fountain, occupying the central place in the building. It is a very curious piece of work, showing the extent to which glass can be employed for decorative purposes, and exhibits the beauty of the material in large works. Near four tons of crystal or flint glass are employed in the construction of this fountain, which may be, without much difficulty, converted into a superb candelabrum. It is kept constantly in play—scattering the pure clear water in a hundred fantastic shapes, which falls into a marble basin in which are to be seen fish of every hue and shape. Around this cooling fount were assembled the representatives of nearly every nation and clime in the world, who furnish subjects of study quite as interesting to me as their industrial products. The lively Frenchman, neatly dressed and restless, as if he wished to see all at one sight, as he passed quickly from object to object, could not fail to be distinguished from the heavy Dutchman, who, with hands crossed behind his back *à la* Napoleon, surveyed each specimen in the great collection with the keen scrutiny of a Jew, intent upon receiving his due, even to the pound of flesh. The grave-looking Turk was there, with his flowing robes and turban of ample folds encircling his head, and the Persian, whose pants drawn tight around his ankles and the seat depending below the calves of his legs, and a loose jacket thrown over his shoulders, with a species of turban set carelessly upon his head, betrayed his eastern origin too plainly to be mistaken. The Spaniard was known by his proud look, and our own countrymen by their free and independent bearing; the Tunisian by his olive complexion, moustaches, and queer-looking blue cap and abundance of beard; and the Chinese by his eyes with the outward corners thrown upwards, the head shorn except on the top and back, his long queue hanging almost to his heels, and his dress not unlike the under garment of a woman. The Italian was present, known by his brown complexion and dark hazel eye; and lastly, the burly Englishman, by his half-open mouth as he waddled along among the products of industrial skill, panting for breath, and thinking of brown ale and roast beef, and ready to swear that the English excelled all people of the earth. So much then for the variety of races at the World's Fair, though the subject, so far from being exhausted, has only been glanced at.

As I said in the beginning, it would be useless to attempt a description of the contents of the Fair in the short space assigned to a letter. All that I can hope to do is to speak of the general effect and the comparative representations of the different nations. The articles exhibited are all of the very best quality, showing that great pains was taken to produce the perfection of art and taste. One is here surrounded by the results of the efforts of thought in almost every direction in which the human mind has tried its powers. The mineral, the vegetable, and the animal kingdoms, have contributed the material upon which man has worked; and the various arts by which these have been made to assume every variety of form, for use or ornament, have here the most ample illustration. Here an opportunity is offered, unequalled in the world's history, for us to learn what, through times past, man has aimed at—what he has reached in the present, and what may be the powers of advancement which still remain for him.

The United Kingdom of Great Britain, as anticipated, was represented in all her glory. Every thing that could be done was done to make her industrial products compare with that of the great family of nations. Machinery, and manufactured articles of every description, both for utility and ornament, were displayed to the greatest possible advantage. Being more interested in the success of the Exhibition than any other nation, and being the immediate recipient of all the benefits accruing, it is natural to suppose that she would excel those countries that had nothing to gain further than a desire to be well represented, and whose products had to be conveyed from great distances, at a very heavy expense. Next to England and her Provinces, France seems to be most fully represented. Her apartments are arranged in the real French style, and her contributions are of the most elegant and costly character. Austria is among the first—her products are of the most remarkable character. The porcelain, glass, and sculptured articles are very striking examples of those classes of manufacture. The contributions from Prussia, Spain, Italy, Turkey, and nearly all the European nations are highly important, each one of which would furnish subject matter for a volume. The Eastern countries, although far removed, are well represented in their articles of curious workmanship.

In speaking of the various countries that have sent their contributions to the Exhibition, I find that I have omitted our own United States, from which so much was expected, and I am sorry to say so little realized. Nearly the first object that attracted my attention upon entering the Palace was the *American Eagle* perched aloft in one of the most conspicuous places, holding the stars and stripes in her talons, and bearing the motto, *E Pluribus Unum*, in letters large enough to read a half mile off. Seeing the old bird holding a lofty bearing and wide-spread pinions, as if she were guarding the treasures of all the States, my national pride was aroused, and I immediately repaired to her quarters, thinking that I would there find something far more interesting than the contributions of any other nation. But my expectations were not realized; I mistook the old bird's meaning, for instead of guarding her industrial products she was spreading her wings over an immense desert, with an oasis only here and there, to relieve the dull monotony. As my eye ranged round this comparatively unoccupied portion of the building, my ardor was a little cooled, for after making such a large demand for space, we had failed to occupy one third appointed to us. When the Commissioners were assigning to the several nations of the earth their places in the Palace, our Minister secured a space larger than any of the rest, according to the extent and capabilities of the country, which, if occupied as he anticipated, would have reflected honor upon the whole nation. In no one branch of industry is the United States fairly or adequately represented; in this all Americans here agree. The North, or New-England States, are not represented either as to the extent, the progress, or the variety of their manufactures. The Middle States, which are second to none in the invention and construction of machinery, have here but three or four machines, which are very good of their kind, but fail to give to the mechanics of England the faintest idea of our progress in this particular. The Western and Southern States, so rich in their agricultural resources and variety of products, are, I may say, not represented at all, for out of the many kinds of cotton cultivated, we find here but samples of seven, while the different varieties of sugar in the State of Louisiana are represented by one specimen from a single plantation. The question naturally arises to the inquiring mind as to the causes of this *magnificent* failure. The main cause lies at the door of the committee at Washington, who rather threw cold water upon the undertaking, and failed to infuse into our people the spirit of rivalry, by acquainting them officially with the extent of the Exhibition. Secondly, Congress has unfortunately made no appropriation, as in other countries, to assist exhibitors; and this has tended to strengthen the third cause, the remoteness of the scene of action, which rendered the transmission of our contributions expensive and inconvenient. What we have is very good, but the great difficulty is, we have so little that it makes comparatively no show at all. Powers' Greek Slave attracts more attention than any thing else, and deservedly, for it is decidedly the most beautiful piece of statuary in the Exhibition, and reflects honor upon the distinguished sculptor and his country. Daguerreotypes, piano-fortes, and India-rubber manufactures are largely illustrated; also agricultural machines, lard oil, and fancy soaps. The most wonderful thing, however, in the American collection, is an iron safe, with one of Hobbs' locks. It is so constructed that no person but the inventor can open it. Mr. Hobbs placed two hundred pounds in this safe, which he offers to any man in England who can pick the lock, and at the same time wagers one hundred pounds that he can pick, in fifteen minutes, any lock in England, not excepting even Chub's celebrated lock, which is now used in the vaults of the Bank of England, and upon which there have been delivered many lectures. Such a proposition appeared ludicrous to the advocates of Chub's lock, who endeavored to laugh Hobbs out of countenance by saying that he was either deranged or half-witted even to suppose that his lock could not be picked by an *Englishman*, who are generally more expert in such things than any other people. Hobbs, however, like a true Yankee, was not to be hoodwinked in this manner. He demanded a fair trial, which was readily granted, and in the presence of several Bank officers he succeeded with the simplest kind of an instrument in picking their favorite lock, which was considered the very best ever invented. The officers present stood by and looked at Hobbs with perfect amazement, wondering how he managed to pick Chub's lock in fifteen minutes' time with so little difficulty. On the evening that this feat was performed a lecture was to be delivered on Chub's lock, and the officers who witnessed the picking, desirous of saving the character of the lecturer, dispatched a messenger to inform him that Chub's lock was no more; but it was too late, the lecturer had commenced, and there was no remedy. If Hobbs' invention proves to be what he represents, it will be a triumph worth talking about. I also noticed a caloric engine, which the inventor states has many novelties, and will eventually supersede the use of steam; but I rather think it will not turn out as represented, as it appears to be but a modified arrangement for heating and cooling air, produced by some gases not named, under a piston, as in Ericsson's ordinary engine.

After all said and done, the United States will derive more benefit from this grand exhibition than any other nation. She has not contributed much, but she has sent some of her ablest mechanics here to note the contributions of other countries, which they will carry home for adoption and improvement.

The Queen and the royal family visit the Exhibition nearly every morning at half-past nine. The doors are opened for the people about ten o'clock, and those who go early have a fine opportunity of seeing her Majesty. She walks about the Palace with her suite, and examines the different articles with much interest. The stranger would fail to recognise her in the multitude were it not for the great deference paid to her by her subjects, who seem to idolize her. As she passes through the crowd on her way to the carriage, which stands at a private door, the people standing on either side of the avenue take off their hats and return her salutations with great deference. In appearance the Queen is not remarkable; her figure is short and rather embonpoint, her hair and eyes light, and her countenance indicative of nothing more than benevolence. Prince Albert is certainly fine-looking, but falls far short of the description given of him in the English prints. He is devoted to his Queen and family, and holds a high place in the affections of the English people.

LETTER EIGHT.

LONDON, England.

Visit to Westminster Abbey—The Houses of Parliament—The Members—The Thames, Bridges, and Tunnel.

> "From hence we may that antique pile behold,
> Where regal heads receive the sacred gold;
> It gives them crowns, and does their ashes keep;
> There made like gods, like mortals there they sleep;
> Making the circle of their reign complete,
> The suns of empire, where they rise they set."

WESTMINSTER ABBEY has been called, with much propriety, the Pantheon of the glory of Britain; for it is its monuments and ancient remains which render the Abbey so precious to Englishmen, and all those who admire the works of by-gone ages. Here lie nearly all of the kings, queens, princes, statesmen, philosophers, and poets of England, from the time of Edward the Confessor to George the Second. It is essentially the home of the mighty dead—for here sleep the illustrious men who have adorned life by their virtues, or enlightened the world by their labors in the various departments of human knowledge, who have reigned as the fathers of the people, ruling in the fear of God, or have governed with an iron rod, and in the indulgence of their passions have violated every law human and divine. Their ashes repose here in peace · their souls are with Him who gave them being, and will hereafter call them to stand at the bar of eternal judgment.

As we walked through the avenues of this venerable structure, and gazed on the monumental inscriptions of the departed, a crowd of thoughts rushed upon my mind, reminding me forcibly of the many historical associations connected with it; for aside from being remarkable as the depository of the great and good, it has been the place where the Roman Catholic magnate once celebrated mass with more than eastern splendor—where the Puritan once poured forth his fervent but holy exhortation. Here the terrible sentence of excommunication has been launched forth in all its terrors, and here the first English Bible issued from the press. Here, also, the magnificence and pomp of the regal coronation have followed the solemn and beautiful burial service for the dead.

This truly noble specimen of Gothic architecture was originally founded in the seventh century, by Sebert, King of the East Saxons, in the year 610; but being afterwards destroyed by the Danes, it was rebuilt by King Edgar in 958. Edward the Confessor again rebuilt the abbey and cathedral on a larger scale, in 1066, when Pope Nicholas II. constituted it the place of inauguration of the Kings of England, and gave it the form of a cross, which thenceforward became the usual form for cathedral building in England. Henry III. made large additions to the abbey in 1245. Henry VII. also made an addition, which is regarded as a remarkable specimen of architecture, yet adds nothing to the beauty of the building, as it is not in keeping with the original design. In the general plunder of monasteries and church property, which distinguished the reign of Henry VIII., this abbey, among others, suffered severely; but it was more injured by the Puritans in the great civil war, who left it in a state of dilapidation. Sir Christopher Wren was afterwards intrusted with the task of repairing the great national edifice, which is now greatly improved, and stands a monument that every true Englishman is proud of.

The monuments in the Abbey are, generally speaking, of a very plain and unostentatious character, particularly those that mark the resting-places of the truly great. Thus, Milton, Dryden, and rare Ben Jonson. But the sepulchres of the kings are somewhat different. Here we find great efforts made at the grand, the ornate, and the beautiful. Mary, styled the "bloody Mary," and her sister Elizabeth, both repose in the same tomb, and one monument covers them both. I looked with melancholy interest on the monument erected by James I. in honor of his mother, Mary, Queen of Scots. There are very many interesting objects to be seen here, and among them we were shown the chair used at the coronation of the Kings and Queens of England. It was made in the reign of Edward I., and presents nothing remarkable for beauty of form or costliness of material. Immediately under the seat is fixed the stone of Scone, from Scotland, which was formerly used at the crowning of the Scottish kings. The chair itself is perfectly plain, and appears to have been hacked and carved with penknives not a little, by persons desirous of cutting their names upon the coronation chair of English monarchs. I noticed among the monuments one erected to the memory of the unfortunate Major André, Adjutant-General to the British army in America. It sets forth his melancholy end, the esteem in which he was held both by his friends and his foes, and concludes by stating that his remains had been deposited in November, 1821, in a grave near the monument.

I left the old abbey with a feeling of reluctance; for in the short space of time allotted, I could take barely a glance at objects that were well worth a day's reflection.

Just opposite Westminster Abbey, on the banks of the Thames, or *Tems*, as the English term it, is the Palace of Westminster, or new Houses of Parliament, which is, without doubt, the most important architectural work which has been undertaken in this country since the re-edification of St. Paul's Cathedral. The old Houses having been destroyed by fire, Oct. 15, 1839, the present magnificent structure was commenced, from the designs of C. Barry, Esq., in 1840, and is now rapidly approaching completion. The plan of this truly national edifice is extremely simple. It is constructed entirely of hard magnesian limestone and cast-iron, in the Gothic style of architecture, and will endure, in all probability, as long as England continues its present form of government. The towers of this enormous building are crowned by majestic symbols of the British monarchy; its walls are girt with the heraldic insignia of a long race of kings; its chambers glow with all the associations of chivalry, religion, and of justice; and when completed, it will stand a monument of enduring splendor to the reign of the present dynasty.

To convey to you some idea of the magnitude of Westminster Palace, I will give the dimensions of the whole building. The eastward presents a frontage of nearly one thousand feet. When complete, it will cover an area of nine statute acres. The great tower at the southwestern extremity, which has already been raised to the height of one hundred and eighty feet, will ultimately reach the gigantic elevation of three hundred and forty-six feet. Its cubic contents exceed 15,000,000 feet, being one-half greater than St. Paul's, and it contains not less than between five and six hundred distinct apartments, amongst which will be a chapel for Divine worship formed out of the crypt of old St. Stephen's. As far as I am able to judge, I regard the structure as perfect in arrangement, detail, warming, ventilation, and all other conveniences.

After examining the architectural beauty and utility of the building, we went into the halls of legislation, which I have always had a desire to see, and compare with our own national bodies. We were fortunate in procuring seats where we could see and hear every thing distinctly in the House of Commons, and I must say that I was really disappointed in the appearance of the body, their demeanor, and manner of conducting business. A very important resolution was under consideration while we were there, viz., a resolution condemnatory of the punishments inflicted during the disturbances in Ceylon; of the conduct of Lord Torrington, the late governor of that island; and of that of Earl Grey, in signifying her Majesty's approbation of Lord Torrington's conduct during and subsequent to the disturbances. The debate was heated, and we had a fine opportunity of hearing the best speakers of the House under favorable auspices; and I feel safe in saying that not one of them would have been regarded with us as either effective or eloquent. It did not strike me as a dignified body, but on the contrary, was, if any thing, a little worse than our House of Representatives. The members were very generally engaged in conversation, or moving about during the debate, and all sat covered except him who for the time occupied the floor in speaking. During a man's speech, he is frequently annoyed and the House thrown in confusion by the cry of *Hear*, *hear*, *hear*, which is generally followed by the deep, hoarse voice of the Speaker calling out *Order*, *order*, *order*. Very tart and occasionally acrimonious language was used in debate; most generally, however, it was hypothetical, and qualified in the end, so as to be harmless or retracted. The members are arranged, as with us, on opposite sides of the chamber. Those who support the government or administration sit on the right of the Speaker, and those opposed on his left.

We next went into the House of Lords, which presents a more dignified appearance than the Commons, but failed to impress me with that veneration and respect that I always experienced when I entered the Senate Chamber at Washington. We had the pleasure of hearing the Duke of Argyle, Lord Brougham, and several other distinguished Lords, upon a bill to suppress the sale of spirituous liquors. The subject certainly was not one calculated to bring out the powers of the speaker, yet it gave us an opportunity of forming an estimate of the body. I was struck with this fact in all the speaking that I heard in the House of Lords and Commons, a degree of hesitation or stammering, which is very unpleasant to the ear, and spoils the beauty of language. The oratory of Americans in the legislature, on the stump, at the bar, and in the pulpit, is far superior to any thing that I have yet heard in this country.

From Westminster Bridge we had a fine view of the *great Thames* and the seven bridges that span its channel, which are like so many bee-hives, with the tide of humanity going each way. It is really astonishing to think of the vast amount of commerce carried on in this river, which we in the States, accustomed to the great inland sea, would call nothing but a large creek. Yet small and filthy as it is, we see the vessels of all nations floating upon its surface, indicating an amount of trade no where else to be seen.

The bridges across the Thames are generally built of stone at an immense cost. They are too low to make much show, but are substantial structures, every way suited to accommodate the public.

From Westminster Bridge we drove down the Surrey side of London to the great Tunnel, through which we passed. This extraordinary undertaking was originally projected and carried out by Sir T. K. Brunel, and is an enduring monument of his skill and enterprise, notwithstanding it has failed in its results as a passway, most persons preferring to cross on the bridges. It consists of a square mass of brick work, thirty-seven feet wide by twenty-two high, containing in it two archways, each of the width of sixteen feet four inches; each road is thirteen feet six inches wide, and fifteen feet six inches high, and footpaths three feet wide. There is a central line of arches separating the two passages, some of them wide enough for a carriage to go from one side of the Tunnel to the other. Between these archways are gas lamps and stalls for refreshments, trinkets, &c., kept by females, who are exceedingly annoying to visitors. The entire length of the Tunnel is thirteen hundred feet, and the thickness between the vault of the Tunnel and the Thames above, fifteen feet. It cost £611,000. Toll, one penny. To civil engineers, or persons interested in scientific pursuits, this structure possesses great attractions, for it is regarded as the most extraordinary triumph of science and perseverance in all England.

LETTER NINE.

London, England.

Excursion to Windsor Castle—The Palaces of London—The Royal Mews—Amateur performances at the Devonshire House—The Royal Italian Opera, etc.

Taking advantage of a clear sun and cloudless skies, which Londoners are rarely permitted to enjoy, we formed an agreeable party, and made an excursion to Windsor Castle, one of the country seats of Her Majesty the Queen.

It is beautifully situated on a lofty eminence about twenty miles from London, and possesses many attractions to render it an agreeable retreat from the noise and bustle of a city life. It does not equal Chatsworth, which I have previously described, either in the extent of the grounds, the magnificence of the castle, or the elegant manner in which the various apartments are furnished. Visitors are permitted to go over every part of the castle except the Queen's private apartments, which are inaccessible, except by an order from the Lord Chamberlain during her absence. The state-rooms are fitted up in very good style, and the walls are adorned by a great number of paintings by the most eminent masters, which the visitor is permitted merely to glance at, being ushered by the guide in rapid succession from one room to another. Windsor Castle has been the principal seat of British royalty for upwards of seven centuries. The Saxon kings had a palace here long before the conquest. The present castle was founded by William the Conqueror, but was almost rebuilt by Edward III., with the assistance of the celebrated William Wykeham, who superintended the works. Great alterations were subsequently made by Sir Jeffrey Wyatville, during the reign of George IV. St. George's Chapel is an elegant specimen of florid Gothic architecture. It is the most interesting portion of the castle, as it contains the stalls of the Knights of the Garter, and the remains of some of the most distinguished characters of England. George III. and his Queen, George IV., the Princess Charlotte, the Duke of Kent, the Duke of York, William IV., and Queen Adelaide are deposited in the vaults of this chapel; also Edward IV. and his Queen. Henry VI., Henry VIII., Jane Seymour, and Charles I. are here interred. The keep, or round tower, in the centre of the castle, is perhaps the most remarkable part of the building. It is of great height, and furnishes a beautiful view of the parks and surrounding country. Here James I. of Scotland was confined, and here the Queen frequently resorts to enjoy the pure air and the luxury of quiet meditation.

From Windsor, we repaired to Buckingham Palace, the city residence of the Queen, which is regarded as the most elaborate and magnificent building of the kind in London. It was commenced during the reign of George IV., who after the most lavish and extravagant expenditure, exceeding £600,000, abandoned it as altogether unfit for the pageantries of royalty, and but little suited as a place of residence for his *Majesty.* William IV. not liking the building or the situation, it was not occupied until the accession of Victoria, when various alterations, additions, and improvements were made in accordance with her wishes, and the requirements of an *increasing family.* As it now stands it is an ornament to the city, and a building in every way suited for the residence of the royal family.

After examining the palace, we walked around to see the royal mews, which are very near. The state carriage is a superb piece of workmanship, being elaborately carved, finished with gilt work, and adorned with all the devices of royalty. The carriages used on ordinary occasions, numbering some forty-five or fifty, are substantial, but not very elegant or expensive. The state horses are the most beautiful animals I ever saw, being almost perfect in form, size, and color. The Queen has in all about three hundred horses, many of which are very superior. What sense can there be in having so many carriages and horses for the use of one little woman and her children, when one third of the number would answer every purpose? But in monarchies the whims and caprices of the sovereign must be indulged—it matters not how foolish and extravagant—and at the expense of the *democracy*, the fruits of whose labors are applied to uphold the false dignity of the nation.

Several of the London palaces have rooms beautifully fitted out in theatrical style for the exhibition of amateur performances. Those who assist in the plays are from private circles, who volunteer their services merely to gratify the lord of the house, or benefit some laudable institution in need of pecuniary assistance. The guests are always ticketed by the lord, notwithstanding they are required to pay enormously for the honor of being invited. These performances are always select, and generally wind up with a ball and supper, which adds much to the enjoyment of the evening.

The Duke of Devonshire gave one of these entertainments recently at his city residence, in Picadilly, for the benefit of the "Literary Guild." Sir E. B. Lytton's comedy was represented most beautifully, and a new farce of the old extravagant school, which seems to have been written for the purpose of showing the talents of Mr. C. Dickens, in what is called a "personation" part. Mr. Dickens sustained himself in his usual manner, displaying great versatility of genius, and some drollery in the system of disguising and counter-disguising. The evening wound up with a ball and a supper, and every thing was conducted in superior style.

London is now full of attractions of every description. All the various places of amusement are in full blast, affording to foreigners visiting the Exhibition an opportunity of passing their evenings pleasantly. The opera houses are peculiarly attractive at this time, being fortunate in procuring for the season the best talent in Europe. Mesdames Sontag, Castellan, and Grisi are all here, and you can well imagine what a sensation they create among the uppertendom of London.

The Queen honors one of the opera houses nearly every evening with her presence, accompanied by distinguished foreigners. Her presence is always a sure guarantee for a brilliant house, as many persons go there to show their loyalty, and others merely to gaze on her Majesty's little round face.

LETTER TEN.

LONDON, England.

Excursion to Epsom—Tower of London—Docks and Vaults, etc.

A FEW days since, the great city of London was in a perfect state of commotion—cabs, busses, and postillions were hurrying to and fro in every direction. Lords and ladies, gentlemen and cockneys, together with the stranger from every clime, were in a perfect state of excitement, indicating to the calm observer that something of more than ordinary interest was on the tapis. Having previous intimation through a friend that the celebrated Derby stake would come off on that day, we agreed to make an excursion to Epsom, and mingle for a time among the sportsmen of England. Failing to procure a private conveyance, we hurried across London bridge to the railroad station, where we found some two or three thousand persons endeavoring to obtain tickets and seats. Seeing this eager crowd pushing and scuffling in their efforts to get ahead of each other, my friend remarked that our chance of witnessing the races was rather slim. I replied to him not to fear, that I would play a *Yankee* trick upon them and get tickets before our time. Assuming an *air consequential*, (for I believe it was not nature,) I passed along through the crowd, saying, "Gentlemen, allow me to pass *if you please*." Thinking that I was either a railroad official, or person wishing to attend to something very urgent, they politely gave way, and I procured tickets without any difficulty. But this was the smallest part of the trouble; after getting our tickets we found it still more difficult to get seats, as none were secured. As the train, numbering some fifty or sixty cars, came alongside the platform, the rush to get seats was intense, in which several persons were seriously injured.

By purely physical force, we succeeded in getting seated in a first class car, while many were compelled to wait for the next train. In a few minutes we found ourselves at the Epsom station, which is very near the race-course. Here we came in contact with footmen, and persons in every sort of conveyance, making their way to the great place of excitement. Upon reaching the hill-top where the principal stand is situated, our eyes rested on a perfect sea of humanity, all eager to get good positions, in order to see the race advantageously. I was disappointed in the appearance of the course. It is very uneven, and entirely without improvement, with the exception of the central stand, which is very large and fine. The track is about fifty yards in width, and one mile round, inclosed with a simple wooden railing. You are of course aware, that in England they race exclusively on the turf, which they say is far preferable to our mode of ploughing and harrowing. I do not know how this is exactly, not being well versed in such things; but it strikes me, that in moist weather the suction on the turf would very much impede the progress of the horses. During the day we witnessed several races, and all sorts of games and tricks for money, by the lower classes, very like those that are to be seen in the obscure parts of our sporting grounds. At three o'clock the grand Derby stake came off, and I do assure you it was a magnificent sight—surpassing any thing of the kind that I ever saw. Thirty-three horses were entered, and every one run out, something unprecedented in the Derby stake. The horses all appeared to be of the best blood and training, and are doubtless excellent racers, but I feel confident in saying that Tennessee can produce a better horse than any one in this stake. Englishmen would say that this was an Americanism—but if proved, it would turn out a truism. However, I should not complain, as it surpassed any thing, take it altogether, to be seen in the States. Thirty-three horses running together, beautifully housed, with riders dressed in all the colors of the rainbow, and with eight or ten thousand people on the ground to witness them, is a sight not often to be seen in any country. Epsom is more resorted to by the masses than any other place in England, but the Queen and the nobility frequent and patronize Ascot Heath, near Windsor Castle. It is farther removed from London than Epsom, and consequently is not so much crowded on race days.

After seeing the race we returned to London and visited the Tower, which possesses more interesting reminiscences than any other building in the city. Its glory is all in the past. Take from it its early history, and you divest it of every thing, since so far from being an imposing object to the eye, it shows itself only as a huddled up mass of buildings, some of them very much modernized, and none of them, with the exception of the new barracks, particularly dignified in appearance. The only part of the old building worthy of attention, is a lofty upright sructure distinguished by the name of the "White Tower," which, with the turrets and its angles, forms a bold and conspicuous architectural object in the views from various points. This part of the building is supposed to have been erected by the Conqueror, about 1078, who employed Gundulph, Bishop of Rochester, for his architect. It is a quadrangular, and nearly square edifice, measuring about 116 feet on one side, and 96 on the other, and is about 90 feet high, exclusive of the turrets at the four angles.

This tower was originally used as a royal palace, but during the reign of Elizabeth it was converted into a dungeon, and continued to be used for that purpose until the year 1820. Thistlewood and his associates in the Cato street conspiracy were the last prisoners confined within its walls, five of whom were executed on the 1st of May, in the same year. The vault where Sir Walter Raleigh was confined, and in which he wrote his History of the World; the spot where Mary Queen of Scots was executed; the execution block and axe, are pointed out to the visitor as objects particularly worthy of notice. The Tower has been the depository of the crown jewels from the reign of Henry IV.; here are preserved the coronation regalia, including the new imperial crown, and other emblems of royalty used by the sovereigns of England at their coronation, the value of which is estimated at more than three millions of money. The crown worn by Victoria is valued at *one million sterling.* The celebrated diamond of Runjeet Singh, Koh i Noor, the tale of which is so momentous, and the value of which is so great, being computed to be worth £2,000,000 sterling, is usually deposited here, but is at present placed in the Exhibition for *show*, being secured by an iron case and box, which is in itself a very ingenious piece of mechanical contrivance.

In this Tower there are very many curious things worthy of attention, and among them I must mention the Horse Armory, erected in 1826, in a low and not very wide room, built in the Gothic style. Here are ranged a long line of British monarchs and warriors, on their war steeds, and cased in complete armor, the whole forming a very interesting record of the various changes which have taken place in the use of armor, from the time of Edward the First to that of James the Second. The ceiling of this room is characteristically ornamented with devices and decorations, composed of spears, pistols, and other military weapons. On the right of this armory is another room of similar dimensions, containing specimens of the different kinds of firearms in use at various times since the first invention of gunnery; also, swords, helmets, girdles, and Chinese military dress, taken in the conflicts between the British and Chinese. The Tower is altogether an exceedingly interesting place, about which much can be said and written, but I must forbear.

Near the Tower are the celebrated docks of London, which contain more shipping than any other place in the world. The accommodation, however, enormous as it is, is proportionally very inferior to that of Liverpool, which I have described in a previous letter. One cannot fully appreciate the power, the wealth, and the world-wide commerce of London until he visits her shipping, where are to be found concentrated the evidences of a commerce, and of a concourse of nations no where else to be seen. The warehouses and vaults are truly extraordinary, and the volume of value of their contents cannot but overwhelm the beholder. For instance, the tobacco warehouses will alone contain twenty-four thousand hogsheads, and are rented by government at £14,000 a year. The tea warehouses erected in the last few years are capacious enough to hold one hundred and twenty thousand chests of tea; while the vault of the same establishment, covering an area of eighteen acres, will contain the incredible quantity of sixty thousand six hundred pipes of wine. While we were making our way through these catacombs, I was forcibly reminded of the dark recesses of the Mammoth Cave. The deep shadows, the impenetrable gloom, imperfectly illumined by the torches carried by the attendant coopers, which cast their red glare a brief space, and serving only to make "darkness visible," the long fringe hanging from the walls, the long rows of huge barrels, and the deep silence that prevailed, all conspired to invest a commonplace matter of fact with an air almost of romance and mystery. The atmosphere in these vaults is precisely the same that we find in large caves, and the visitor must be careful not to indulge too freely in the different wines that are offered to him by the attendant if he wishes to come out as he went in. You do not feel the effects of the delicious draught while you are in the vault, but as soon as you reach your native climate its influence begins to operate, and you find yourself almost imperceptibly in a delightful state of intoxication.

LETTER ELEVEN.

LONDON, England.

St. Paul's Cathedral—Meeting of the Charity Schools—The Ragged Schools—Pauperism—Hospitals—Markets, etc., etc.

In a previous letter I gave you a description of Westminster Abbey, which is without doubt the most imposing and interesting structure to be seen in England; but of all the religious edifices of London—amounting to upwards of seven hundred, and composing the most prominent share of its architectural splendor—there is none more worthy of attention, or more calculated to awaken the curiosity of the visitor, than St. Paul's Cathedral. It does not lay claim to great antiquity, neither does it possess those early associations which render the Abbey so interesting; yet from its vast dimensions, great height, and commanding position, it may be regarded as the most conspicuous edifice of the metropolis, while its architectural merits make it one of the most magnificent. The ancient Gothic cathedral, which originally stood on the same spot, was destroyed in the great fire of London, 1666, when the erection of the present building was intrusted to that master architect, Sir Christopher Wren, under whose direction it was completed in 1715. The first stone of the new cathedral was laid on the 21st of June, 1675, by the architect and his lodge of freemasons. The trowel and mallet used on this occasion are still preserved in the Lodge of Antiquity, of which Sir Christopher was Master. The general form, or ground plan, is that of a Greek cross, having a very large dome arising from the intersection of the nave and transept. There seems to be a combination of the several styles of architecture—adopted, doubtless, to give the building a modern appearance—but upon the whole, the Corinthian and Composite orders seem to prevail. The principal entrance or front is extremely noble. It is adorned with a rich and beautiful portico consisting of twelve lofty columns, above which are eight more, ranged in pairs, supporting a triangular pediment, the entablature of which represents the conversion of St. Paul, executed by Bird, in low relief. On the apex of this pediment is a colossal figure of St. Paul, with two of equal size at each end, representing St. Peter and St. James; and along the summit of the front are the statues of the four Evangelists. The whole rests on an elevated base, the ascent to which is formed by twenty-two steps of black marble. The angles are surmounted by two elegant turrets of a chaste and uniform character, each terminating in a dome, ornamented with a gilt pine-apple; the north turret contains the belfry, the south turret the clock. In front of this magnificent portico is a marble statue representing Queen Anne, in the robes of state, holding in her hands the emblems of royalty, together with figures representing Great Britain, Ireland, France, and America. There are two other entrances to each end of the principal transept which correspond to the main portico, with the exception of the figures of the Apostles—the royal arms and regalia supported by angels, and the representation of a phœnix rising from the flames. The east end of the bnilding is semi-circular, and is ornamented with two rows of pilasters and a variety of fine sculpture. The dome, which is upwards of four hundred feet from the pavement below to its summit, rises in beautiful and majestic proportion, attracting the attention and admiration of every one that beholds it. This dome is terminated by a lantern and globe weighing about seven tons, and on the top of the whole is placed the emblem of Christian faith.

Although the external appearance of St. Paul's is very attractive, one is utterly unprepared from an outward view to form any adequate conception of the effect of the interior. The unexpected loftiness of the vaultings, and of the long range of columns and piers which meet the vision, produces an effect of wonder and surprise. The view upwards into the interior of the dome is extremely striking. It is so constructed as to show a spacious concave in every direction, and light from the lantern above pours down its illumination with beautiful effect upen the whole, as well as the great colonnade that encircles its basement. In this rotunda is the Whispering Gallery, which you have heard so much about. It derives its name from the well-known reverberation of sounds, so that the softest whisper is accurately and distinctly conveyed to the ear at the distance of a hundred feet, which is the diameter of the dome. The echo is so great that the stroke of a carpenter's hammer below produced a sound equal to the report of a cannon, or the bursting of a thunder cloud. As you ascend the staircase to the whispering gallery, you pass near the library, which contains, I suppose, a valuable collection of ecclesiastical and evangelical works, but the flooring, consisting of upwards of two hundred pieces of oak, is pointed out as the object most worthy the attention of a casual visitor. The clock-works are well deserving the notice of the curious, as they are extraordinary in size and quality. From the library you can go to the stone gallery which surrounds the exterior dome above the colonnade, and from this elevation, *when the atmosphere is clear*, the view around is very fine. As the staircase above this becomes very steep, narrow, and dark, not many visitors can be prevailed on to go higher; and yet there is much to repay both the trouble and apprehension attending the ascent. Just before I ascended to the ball a lady from France came down in perfect ecstasies, saying in her own tongue, "Oh, what a pretty view of your great city—how charming—what a nice place to take the fatal leap!" From the summit of this cathedral the stranger can acquire a more correct idea of the geography of London and its environs than he could by looking at maps and traversing its various streets in cabs and busses for the space of six months. Some years ago there appeared an extraordinary Panorama of London from St. Paul's, designed by Horne, and executed by Parris, which is now being exhibited at the Coliseum in Regent's Park. It is a work of superior merit, and well deserving the attention of those desirous of obtaining an insight into the intricacies and mysteries of modern Babylon.

Having given you but an imperfect idea of this magnificent cathedral, I now proceed to describe the anniversary meeting of the charity children, which I had the extreme pleasure of attending recently.

In 1782, the assemblage of the children clothed and educated in the parochial schools, took place for the first time in St. Paul's, where they have since annually been collected, and the effect of such a scene as that presented on this occasion could not be surpassed in any part of the world. In its way, the exhibition was quite as bewildering to my senses as that of the great Crystal Palace in Hyde Park, at present the wonder of the world. The grand spectacle of between six and seven thousand children, dispersed on raised platforms round the gigantic nave of the cathedral, the tiers of benches gradually elevated nearly to the top of the columns upon which the dome rests, decked out in party colors, with banners to represent the various schools from whence they are sent as representatives—the boys separated from the girls, and the whole mass arranged with an eye to symmetry and pleasing contrast—is easier to look at and admire than describe. Add to this a dense and animated assemblage of spectators of more than twelve thousand, who filled the vast interior to its very extremities, while in the background, the great organ, with its pendent choir of eighty or a hundred singers, arrayed in white surplices, together with drums and trumpets, served to render the picture complete, making a *coup d'œil* truly magnificent. The prayers on this occasion were intoned by the Rev. R. Shutte, and the lessons read by the Rev. W. J. Hall. The sermon appropriate to the ceremony and its praiseworthy object was preached by the Archbishop of Canterbury; the text, from Proverbs xix. 2: "That the soul be without knowledge it is not good," was made the theme of an eloquent, judicious and impressive discourse on the advantages of a liberal education. The singing of the children was of course the object of general interest, and the important feature of the day. The 100th Psalm, before the prayers, sung by so many thousand fresh voices with perfect intonation and unison, produced a thrilling effect, and on the whole surpassed every thing of the kind that I have ever heard.

After the services had concluded, I met a medical friend from Philadelphia, whom I invited to accompany me to Field Lane Ragged School, which is of more recent origin than those institutions that assembled in St. Paul's. Here we had an opportunity of seeing the offspring of the last of creation, the real miseries of London. The school-room is situated in that part of the city set apart as the abode of poverty, vice, and crime—a fit place for such an institution. When we entered the room, the teachers, who are females, were very polite in offering us seats, showing the improvement of their little ragged pupils, and explaining the objects and manner of conducting the institution. I do wish that you had been seated with us in the midst of this congregation of poverty-stricken children, varying in their age from one to twenty years. I am confident that you would agree with us in saying that there is nothing in our glorious land half so low, half so pitiable. Englishmen may write, talk, and preach what they please about the horrors of our peculiar institution; they may send their abolition emissaries across the water, with pockets well filled, to preach a crusade against our liberty and our laws; but they had better consider the deplorable condition of their own population, one tenth of which is now supported by charity, and whose condition both in a physical and moral point of view is far inferior to that of the slave owned by the most cruel of masters. Our colored population are provided with every thing calculated to render them comfortable, and life happy. They are worked moderately, clothed comfortably, fed abundantly, and provided for when they get old and decrepit—while the poor of this great metropolis are devoid of all these blessings.

My friend being connected with one of the Medical Universities of Pennsylvania, and desirous of gaining as much information as possible relative to the manner of conducting such establishments in London, proposed that we should visit St. Bartholomew's Hospital, at which there are a number of students and any quantity of subjects both living and dead for them to operate upon at their leisure. This hospital is the oldest and best in the city; having been founded by Rahere, the minstrel and poet of Henry I., in 1102. It owes much to the munificence of Henry VIII., who endowed it at the Reformation with an annual revenue, and profits largely at times by the liberality of private benefactors. The annual income of this hospital averages about £32,000. This establishment is conveniently arranged, and cleanliness, returning health, and comfort pervade all its apartments. The professors were very polite in conducting us through the different rooms, and explaining the symptoms of several patients who were singularly affected. I am not a medical man, yet I took a great deal of interest in examining the different institutions of this description which add so much to the character of London One thing I noticed, and with some pride too, as it is an American invention, that chloroform is invariably used in amputations which are attended with much pain—a fact not generally known with us, who always apprehend danger from its use.

From St. Bartholomew's Hospital we visited Smithfield Market, which is very near. This is considered the greatest market for live cattle in the world; it is situated in the centre of the city, and covers an area of six acres and a quarter. Markets have been held here from time immemorial, it being mentioned by writers as far back as the tenth century, as a place where horses and cattle are sold. It is nothing more than a square of unsightly pens, which are filled on market days with cattle, sheep, and pigs, besides any quantity of trading and swindling speculators, who infest the whole neighborhood. The citizens have been endeavoring for many years to get Parliament to remove this market-place, which is undoubtedly a great nuisance, to some point in the suburbs; but as bills before Parliament are somewhat like their bills in Chancery, they have as yet received no encouragement, and the market must continue an eyesore and grievous nuisance to all in its vicinity. At Smithfield we concluded that while we were visiting such places we might as well go to the well-known market of Billingsgate, about which we read so much in *Punch*, etc. Fish of all kinds in season are on sale here daily; the market opens at five o'clock in the morning and continues during the day. I was altogether disappointed in the place; it is a little narrow, filthy, and cramped up affair, where a gentleman would dislike exceedingly to venture. But being out sight-seeing, I made my way through, much to the amusement of my friend, who stood on the outside. As I walked along, the fish-women accosted me at every step, pressing me to buy the fish or periwinkles, which they sell by the bushel. After I completed the task of wading through fish, women, and periwinkles, we went to a place adjoining the market called the Three Tuns Tavern, which is a celebrated fish ordinary. Here we were furnished with a fish dinner in perfection, which, added to the busy scene on the ever moving *Tems*, induced me to forget the market from whence they came and the *delicate* hands that prepared them. But enough of the fish stories.

LETTER TWELVE.

LONDON, England.

Westminster Hall—Public Buildings—Monuments—Parks, Streets, and Gardens—Dinner and Soirée at the American Minister's—The Duke of Wellington, Lord John Russell, etc.

IT is always natural for one to frequent those places of public attraction in which they are most interested, and which pertain to their own sphere of life; consequently, I have found myself day after day within the walls of Westminster, attending the proceedings of the various courts, and witnessing the administration of justice according to the tenets of that jurisprudence which our ancestors early adopted, and which we have subsequently aided in improving. Before noticing the conduct of the different courts as compared with our own, a brief account of this Hall, around which linger so many remarkable associations, will not be out of place. It is said to be one of the largest rooms in Europe unsupported by pillars, being 238 feet long, 68 feet broad, and 90 feet high; and has a carved roof of chestnut wood, most curiously constructed in the Gothic style of architecture. The interior, as well as the stone moulding that runs round the Hall, is adorned with angels supporting the arms of Edward the Confessor, or those of Richard II. with the hart couchant under a tree, and other devices of the latter monarch, under whose reign it was used as a banqueting room to the ancient palace of Westminster. To give you some idea of the dimensions of this Hall, I will quote from history a fact which seems almost incredible, which is, that Richard II. held his Christmas festival here, accompanied with all that splendor and magnificence for which his court was conspicuous; and that on these occasions, twenty-eight oxen, three hundred sheep, and fowls without number were consumed—requiring two thousand cooks to prepare the feast, which was attended by ten thousand guests.

Since Richard's time the Hall has been used for a variety of purposes. Parliament often sat here—Cromwell was inaugurated here—the coronation feasts of all the sovereigns were held here; and here likewise have been held various important State trials, one of which finds no parallel in the annals of English jurisprudence. I allude to the trial commenced in 1684, in which was presented the extraordinary spectacle of a sovereign defending himself before a jury composed of his own subjects—a trial which occupied one hundred and thirty days at intervals from the period of its commencement. In this Hall the voices of some of the greatest men in history have been heard—men whose virtues and whose eloquence are now pointed to by teachers as models for the rising generation. Here the fierce and withering invective of Burke, and the impassioned eloquence of Sheridan and Warren Hastings, have been heard and felt, which of itself is sufficient to make the place almost sacred.

The High Court of Chancery is now held in the new House of Lords, which I have previously described. The Vice Chancery, Exchequer, Queen's Bench, and Common Pleas Courts are held in a series of small, close, and disagreeable apartments entering into Westminster Hall, which are wholly unsuited for court rooms, being too small to accommodate even the members of the bar. In these rooms I had an opportunity of listening to the opinions and arguments of some of the first men in England, on cases of great interest and importance to the government as well as individuals. When I first entered, my attention was directed to the peculiar manner in which the members of the court were dressed, which is so entirely at variance with our democratic way of doing things, and at the same time so useless, that I was forced to give utterance to my thoughts, and smile at what seemed to me the mere trappings of monarchy, put on to attract the eyes of the ignorant, who are always influenced more by sight than common sense. The judges are required, while on the bench, to be clothed in long purple robes, made of silk, with capes of the same material covering the shoulders, with white cravats and white wigs made of horse hair, or fine wire, curled all over the head with the exception of a small place just on the top, where there is a patch representing baldness. The members of the bar are required to wear black robes, white cravats, and wigs of the same material, but differently shaped and curled, and with no patch on the top. This mode of dressing certainly gives to the members of the legal profession a very venerable and dignified appearance, and is well calculated to create a feeling of reverence among the people—particularly those who believe that wisdom always lies under gray hairs; but in this age of progressive democracy in America, all such trappings would be cast aside as utterly useless and anti-utilitarian. In the speeches of those members of the bar that I had the pleasure of listening to, I discovered that hesitancy and stammering which I noticed in the House of Parliament and in the pulpit—which is not only disagreeable to the ear, but contrary to all rules laid down by the old masters. Demosthenes had the fault, and corrected it by placing pebbles in his mouth and practising elocution on the sea-shore—a task that I would recommend to all those that I have heard to undertake immediately, if they desire to become fluent speakers.

The proceedings of the different courts are conducted with great accuracy and precision; the decorum is perfect, and the arguments of counsel evince a degree of research and study that we do not often see in our own country. You will be pleased to know that the opinions of some of our jurists are received, and frequently quoted in the higher courts as excellent law, and precedence often given over the best English authorities. Indeed, I have heard Marshall, Story, and Greenleaf quoted by the best lawyers of the London bar quite as often as any of the English writers. In law reform we are far ahead of the mother country, and before the lapse of many years we will be able to show an improved system of jurisprudence that they may well receive and adopt.

I had intended giving you a description of the Bank of England, Custom House, Post Office, Treasury Department, and other public buildings, but I have devoted so much space in previous letters to descriptions of places of more importance, that I must pass them over by merely stating that they are all very large and superior buildings, every way suited to their different purposes, and great ornaments to the city.

Next to the public buildings, the monuments and national statues of distinguished public characters, which are open to the view of every passing traveller, are worthy of notice. Some possess great interest from historical associations, others from the excellent workmanship which they exhibit, while many are utterly worthless and uninteresting.

The most remarkable monument in the city is called "The Monument," to distinguish it from the rest. It was built by Sir Christopher Wren, at a cost of £13,700, in commemoration of the great fire of 1666, which destroyed nearly the whole of the city. Next to St. Paul's Cathedral it is the most prominent object to the view, being a large shaft 202 feet in height, surmounted with a blazing urn of gilt brass, which serves as a kind of beacon to guide the steps of the stranger while wending his way through the east end. It is of the fluted Doric order, with appropriate devices on the pedestal, emblematical of that fearful event, which marked an era in the history of the great metropolis. On one side is a bas-relief by Cibber, representing King Charles, surrounded by Liberty, Genius, and Science, giving directions for the restoration of the city; on the other side there are Latin inscriptions, descriptive of the destruction of the city, and the restoration. Within the column is a spiral staircase, of black marble, having three hundred and forty-five steps, by which the visitor can gain access to the iron balcony, from which a noble prospect is presented to the eye no where else to be seen. The wonders of nature are certainly objects of grandeur and sublimity well calculated to arouse the highest inspirations of the poet; but from this monumental pile is presented a scene far more interesting than any thing in nature. Here one looks down upon the dwellings of more than two millions of human beings, innumerable churches of every Christian denomination, with their spires and turrets pointing to the skies, seven bridges spanning the ever-flowing tide of the Thames, where float the masts of all nations. All these objects, and the contemplation of the various pursuits, occupations, and conditions of life in this little world, form an *ensemble* worthy of the greatest admiration.

Next to "The Monument," the Nelson Column in Trafalgar Square is most conspicuous as well as imposing. It is of the Corinthian order, and consists of a tall shaft placed on a square pedestal, and surmounted by a colossal statue of Nelson, having on its four sides bronze bas-reliefs of the hero's four principal engagements, viz., St. Vincent, Copenhagen, Nile, and Trafalgar. The design of the various figures is good, and the monument is every way worthy to commemorate the death of a man who rendered great service to his country, both at sea and on land.

The York Column, in St. James' Park, is also worthy of notice. It is a plain Doric structure, surmounted with a bronze statue of the Duke of York, representing him in a flowing robe, with a sword in his right hand, and in his left the insignia of the Order of the Garter.

Besides these monuments there are many equestrian statues erected at different periods, to commemorate the deeds of public men, and among those of a recent date, that erected in honor of the Duke of Wellington attracts most attention. Just in front of Apsley House, the mansion of the Duke, in Green Park, there is a triumphal arch of the Corinthian order, forming an entrance from Piccadilly, and also one of the grand approaches to St. James' Park and Buckingham Palace. It is one of the most conspicuous and elegant structures in the city. On the principal front are four columns, supporting a portico, the arch itself being adorned with ivy Corinthian pilasters; the opposite front is nearly similar; in the centre there is a vaulting part, which is divided into richly carved compartments, and the gates, which are of beautifully bronzed iron work, are adorned with the royal arms. On the summit of this arch is placed a colossal bronze statue of the old Duke, which is so striking in its resemblance to the original that no man need inquire what it is.

This statue is situated near three of the most celebrated parks in the city, viz., St. James', Green and Hyde Parks; and from its summit you may see in the afternoon all the elegant establishments, fine horses, servants in livery, and fashionables, who drive in these favorite places, to breathe the pure air and enjoy the pleasure of gazing and being gazed upon with quizzing glasses, which are regarded here as utterly indispensable both with gentlemen and ladies. To a stranger who has nothing to occupy his time but sight-seeing, I would recommend a visit on a clear afternoon to Rotton Row in Hyde Park; and here he will see horsemen of every grade, vehicles of every description, and costumes as various as the climes which produce them, all together forming a scene of great attraction and amusement. The ladies of London are excellent horsewomen, and quite equal to our Western girls, although taught in different schools. They sit the horse beautifully, and manage the reins with perfect ease and grace, without the least exhibition of fear, being entirely independent of their beaux, who are, generally speaking, very *sorry* riders. The city of London is celebrated the world over for the number, extent, and beauty of its parks, which have very properly been termed the "lungs of the city;" for here the laboring classes, who have no opportunity of seeking recreation in the country, can resort after the fatigue of the day, and inhale the pure air, which is so essential to health and comfort, and here also the children of the poorer classes are permitted to enjoy their sports without interruption.

In Hyde Park there are very many attractions calculated to interest the stranger. First and foremost is the Crystal Palace, now the great wonder of the world, about which you have been reading for the last year, and which continues to be resorted to by increased numbers daily. Indeed, it becomes more interesting to me every time I visit it, for it is very much like going into a large city with innumerable attractions—the longer you stay and the better you become acquainted with the geography of the place and the position of things, the more you appreciate it. New contributions from different countries are coming in every day, and in the course of a few more weeks, the Exhibition will be far more attractive than it was at the opening.

It is now Whitsuntide, and the laboring classes from every part of the kingdom are taking advantage of the holidays and the reduction of fare on the railroads, to visit the great Exhibition. Every train that arrives is filled even to the tops of the carriages with hundreds of persons who were never before out of sight of the smoke of their own chimneys, all eager to see the exhibition of their own labor compared with that of other countries.

From the Crystal Palace flows the Serpentine river, which is much resorted to during the summer months for the purpose of bathing. Vast numbers of persons assemble here on a Sunday, between the hours of two and six, chiefly on the north side from Piccadilly to Kensington Garden, where there is a beautiful promenade in view of the rich and luxuriant foliage of the trees and shrubbery, forming a lovely contrast to the immense pile of brick in the city. On the western extremity of the river there is a very elegant stone bridge, and also an artificial waterfall, which add much to the beauty of the stream. Near the river are two powder magazines; the great government store of gunpowder, in which are deposited upwards of one million rounds of ball and blank cartridges, ready for immediate use. I think a more suitable place might be selected for the dangerous storehouse than in the midst of a populous city. Not far from Hyde Park are the beautiful grounds called Regent's Park, which is one of the most atractive and agreeable places about London. It contains a variety of objects worthy of attention, such as the villas of the nobility and private gentlemen, the Zoological and pleasure gardens, winter gardens, and Royal Botanical Gardens; all of which places are pointed out by the citizens as well worth the stranger's examination.

From this park leads Regent street, one of the great thoroughfares of the city. It is much wider than the generality of streets, and is well built up, but falls far short of Broadway in point of activity or elegance. Indeed, I do not believe that any city in the world can produce on one street such a large number of elegant establishments, and such a scene of activity as are to be witnessed from the "buck tower" of the great American metropolis. The streets in the east end of London are narrow and tortuous, but well lighted and kept perfectly clean. Those in the west end, which are more modern, are laid out upon a more liberal scale, and present a more inviting appearance than the antique-looking portion of the old city. The police regulation is far superior to that of any city in the world; they are selected from the best men in the country, and are compelled to go through the same training as soldiers, in order to qualify them to discharge the arduous duties of their office with promptness and energy. The average strength of the London police is about five thousand, who are distributed into eighteen divisions, distinguished by different alphabetical letters, each being attached to a certain locality or district, in each of which is a station or rendezvous, from which point the duty is carried out. This admirable system was put into operation in 1830 by the late Sir Robert Peel, and has proved equal to his expectations in every particular—in a word, is perfect.

I cannot conclude this letter without alluding to a dinner party and soirée recently given by the Hon. Abbott Lawrence, at his residence in Piccadilly, which is said to have been one of the grandest banquets of the season. The guests at the dinner party were but few, consisting of some select friends among the nobility and several Americans. After the banquet in the evening, Mrs. Lawrence threw open her superb saloons for the reception of visitors, and in a few minutes they were occupied by guests from all nations. Nearly all the nobility were present, the *corps diplomatique*, and many Americans, which constituted an assemblage of rare brilliancy. Mr. L. lives in excellent style and entertains well, being blessed with the *wherewith*, and that peculiar gift of nature, the *suaviter in modo*, which makes every one feel comfortable and at home. He is very particular in his attention to Americans, (who are very numerous at present,) and has acquired a degree of popularity among the nobility that rarely falls to the lot of a foreign minister. Among the distinguished guests of the evening was the Duke of Wellington, now the greatest man in Europe. He is very old and feeble, but yet retains some of that fire that burned so brilliantly in early life. He honored the company with his presence the greater part of the evening, and seemed to enjoy the society of Americans more than that of any other nation. He says that he admires the American people, and would visit our country if he were only a few years younger. Lord John Russell was also present, but so very small that he was not visible in the crowd more than once or twice during the evening. To look at him, you would never suppose that he was the Lord Premier of Great Britain, as there is nothing attractive either in his conversation or personal appearance. He still clings on to the Ministry, but there is no telling how long he will be retained. He is indebted to the great Exhibition for his retention in office, and it is supposed by the *quid nuncs* that as things fall back in the quiet channel, and the Exhibition fever subsides, a new ministry will be formed, and little John required to resign his office and its honors.

LETTER THIRTEEN.

CHESTER, England.

Departure from London—Railways and Stations—Agriculture in the Southern Counties—Scenery on the banks of the Wye—Visit to the Hills of Great Malvern—The Cureall Establishment—The appearance of Chester, its Antiquity, etc.

AFTER a sojourn of some four or five weeks in the great metropolis of England, each day of which was occupied with some new scene of interest, we made our departure on the Great Western Railway, on a tour of pleasure to the counties bordering upon Wales. In previous letters I have spoken of the magnitude, the population, the wealth, and the great importance of London; but all these descriptions fail to convey so correct an idea of the real character of the place as is furnished by its railway termini—those gates of the world, through which enter the produce and representatives of all nations. Like those in Liverpool and all other large towns throughout England, they are constructed on a scale of magnificence and costliness that would utterly astound the advocates of railways in our country. To give you some idea of these magnificent structures, I will describe the above-named station, which was the first erected in London, having been completed in the year 1838, at a cost of £125,000. You approach an extensive range of buildings for the reception of passengers through a noble propylon, or architectural gateway, having four lodges connected with it, intermediate to which, and in connection with the whole, are large, lofty, and ornamental gates of cast iron. The propylon is a most successful adaptation of the Grecian Doric. The extreme length of the entrance is upwards of three hundred feet, and the columns are higher than those of any other building in London, measuring from the pavement to the top of the columns, forty-four feet two inches; the diameter at the base being eight feet six inches. The public hall, general meeting room, lost baggage and various other offices, are all very commodious and convenient. The walls of this station are in imitation of granite; the ceiling is panelled, deeply recessed, fully enriched, and connected with the walls by boldly designed ornamented consoles. Over the door of the general meeting room is a sculptured group, representing most beautifully Britannia, with Mercury and Science on either side. This company, which is interested, either directly or indirectly, in more than twelve hundred miles of railway, has very fine stations at every place of importance, at each of which a certain number of officers are constantly stationed to prevent accidents, and see that every thing is conducted with order and precision. On all the routes they have three classes of carriages, which are constructed differently from ours, being divided into three apartments instead of having all in one. The seats run entirely across the carriage, and face each other. Each apartment is capable of holding eight persons on the broad gauge, and six on the narrow. The first class carriages, which are used only by the nobility and foreigners, are exceedingly comfortable, being well cushioned with spring-bottom seats. The second class carriages, which are most generally used, are precisely like the first with the exception of the cushioned seats. Persons going short distances always take this class, as there is a very great difference in the fare. The third class are very neat, but not very comfortably arranged, and are used only by the lower classes. The expense of travel in this country is enormous, far exceeding any part of the United States. You can travel from Maine to Texas with the same amount of money that it would require to convey you through the kingdom of Great Britain. The reason of this difference in travel is to be attributed to the great expense of building roads in England. With us the right of way is a small matter, while here it amounts to millions, and aside from this consideration, the actual cost of railroads in America is about one third of that in this country.

The Great Western Railway passes through the richest and most beautiful agricultural region in England. The farms along the line are hedged in with the well-trimmed hawthorn, and are cultivated upon principles far better than is to be seen in any other part of the country. The crops all look clean and promising, and the stock, which are of superior breed to any that I have seen, are well-conditioned, giving evidence that things are in a prosperous situation. The houses of the peasantry in this part of England are neater, better built, and altogether more comfortable than those of the north. Having travelled on the above named road as far as Gloucester, we took a post coach for Chepstow, by way of Monmouth, in order to view the scenery on the river Wye, which is described by writers as very like the Rhine in point of beauty and romance. It is certainly the most beautiful scenery in England, but like all of Nature's works in this country, it is on a miniature scale. The most interesting object on the Wye is the ruins of Tintern Abbey, which belongs to the Duke of Beaufort. It is situated on the edge of a lofty precipice overhanging the stream, from the summit of which the visitor can view all of South Wales and several counties in England. The ruins are covered with ivy, and present a very picturesque appearance. The monastery was founded in the year 1131 by Walter de Chase. At the dissolution, the site was granted to Henry, second Earl of Worcester, ancestor to its present possessor. This county once constituted part of Wales, but now belongs to England, being one of that number lopped off at different periods to gratify the whim or caprice of the sovereign. An old Welshman travelling in the coach informed me that Wales lost a county every century, a process of diminution which must, if it continues, soon efface the distinctive features of the Welsh race. From the beautiful banks of the Wye, we continued our journey to the Hills of Great Malvern, in Worcestershire, a place recently rendered celebrated throughout England on account of the marvellous cures said to have been effected by Dr. Wilson, the great leader among the advocates of the Hydropathic system. The object of our visit was to see an American friend who is in delicate health, and is now undergoing the various processes of wrapping in wet sheets, steaming, dieting, exercising, and bathing. He told me that he thought he had improved very much since he had commenced the treatment, and in fact looks much better; but I think it is to be attributed more to the regular exercise and diet, breathing pure air, and drinking pure water, than the system of ablutions that they are required to go through. There are a great number of invalids at this place from different countries, and among them several of our own countrymen who have been persuaded that hydropathy will cure any and all diseases. Bathing is undoubtedly greatly conducive to health, and should be practised by every one, but there is a medium in all things. The idea of wrapping people up in wet sheets and blankets like mummies, steaming them almost to suffocation, and then plunging them into cold water, seems to me to be an absurdity, and contrary to all reason. Like Mesmerism, it is necessary for the patient to have faith in order to effect a cure. Faith works wonders; it makes a man sometimes believe that black is white—converts the vilest sinner into a Christian, and will ultimately revolutionize the world.

From Great Malvern we came to this place, which is the oldest and most curious city in England. It is situated on a rocky eminence, and surrounded by the ancient walls, built while a Roman station, forming a delightful promenade, and commanding fine views of the river Dee, and the neighboring scenery. The houses are constructed in a very singular manner, being excavated from the rock to the depth of one story beneath the level of the ground on each side, and having porticoes running along the front, affording a covered walk to pedestrians, and beneath them are shops and warehouses on a level with the streets. The castle, which is now used for barracks, and the old cathedral, are the most interesting buildings in the city. The former was erected during the reign of William the Conqueror, and the latter was the church of the dissolved abbey of St. Warburgh. Chester is the place where Edward of Caernarvon received the submission of the Welsh in 1300. It was besieged and taken by the parliamentary forces in 1645.

About three miles from Chester, on the banks of the river Dee, is Eaton Hall, the seat of the Marquis of Westminster. It is a superb mansion, rebuilt in the Gothic style, and is fitted up in great splendor. Among the paintings in the gallery I observed two by West, which are regarded by judges as very superior. One represents Cromwell dissolving the Parliament, and the other the landing of Charles II. Next to Chatsworth, the seat of the Duke of Devonshire, Eaton Hall may be regarded as the most magnificent and desirable country residence in England.

LETTER FOURTEEN.

MENAI STRAIT, near Britannia Bridge, Wales.

Tour through North Wales—Vale of Llangollen—Capel Cerrey—Vale of Llanberis—Snowdon—Slate Mines—Character of the Country and People—Tubular and Suspension Bridges—Isle of Anglesey—Marquis of Anglesey's Column, &c.

AFTER passing through the densely populated cities and highly cultivated farms which greet the eye on every side in Old England, one experinces pleasures altogether different as he approaches the mountainous region of North Wales. Here he is, comparatively, in a wild country, surrounded by lofty cliffs, deep ravines, and uninterrupted silence, save only the occasional bleating of the mountain lamb, and the echo of the miner's hammer in the far-off hills. The transition being so sudden, and so great, it is almost impossible to realize that you are in a country governed by the same laws, and acknowledging the same sovereign authority. The face of nature, the character of the people, their habitations and their language, are as different as you can well imagine, and you would never dream of being in Britain's realm were it not for the gaudy livery of her Majesty's mail-carriers, and the occasional mention of the name of the young Prince of Wales.

Leaving the railroad near the little town of Llangollen, we passed through a beautiful vale of the same name, in which are to be seen many romantic views, and places of picturesque beauty. Among the places of interest on the roadside are yet to be seen the remains of Valle Cruces Abbey, founded in 1200. They are covered with ivy, and shaded by lofty ash trees, and near the ruins is Ellisey's Pillar, erected by Conceres to perpetuate the memory of his ancestor Ellisey, who was killed fighting against the Saxons, in 607.

The only mode of public travel through this portion of Wales is by post coach, which compels tourists who desire to examine particular places, either to lie over a stage, or procure a private conveyance, in which he can travel at his leisure. Preferring this mode, we left the little town of Cowen, and proceeded to Cape Cerrey, a romantic place near several lakes much resorted to by anglers, as they abound with trout, grayling, and salmon. Here we found an excellent inn, which was not only "licensed to sell ale, porter, and spirituous liquors to be *drunk* on the premises," but allowed the guests of the house the extraordinary privilege of trying their luck with the hook and line in the waters of the placid lakes. Being no fisherman, either by nature or acquirement, I abandoned the idea of watching the floating cork, and allowed myself to be conveyed by the dulcet tones of a harp, touched by the hands of a blind Welshman, into the land of dreams and sweet repose.

On the following morning we made an early start for the Vale of Llanberis, which presents by far the most beautiful scenery to be seen in North Wales. On one side, the lofty and majestic peaks of Snowdon rear themselves nearly four thousand feet above the level of the sea, furnishing a panorama of natural beauty which fully compensates the tourist for the fatigue and annoyance which he must necessarily undergo in his ascent upon a miserable donkey, about the size of a large goat, which is urged along the rugged pathway by the constant pelting and hideous shouts of the guide, who is always close at hand, holding on to the tail of the poor animal. At the foot of the mountain are the remains of Dolbardern Castle, covered over with ivy and roses, and presenting a view of the lake and snow-clad hills around that is really enchanting. Just opposite this old castle there is the most extensive slate mine in the whole country, which furnishes London and the greater part of the kingdom with materials for building and covering houses. The proprietors have recently constructed a railroad from the mines to Menai Straits which is kept in constant employment in the conveyance of slate which is transported in vessels to every port almost in the nation.

Wales is not an agricultural country, but depends chiefly upon raising sheep, and its mineral resources, both of which are exceedingly profitable, being in constant demand, and giving employment to nearly the entire population. The people of Wales are naturally industrious and frugal, and although few of them can be called rich, they are generally independent, relying exclusively upon their own labor for support. The houses of the peasantry in this country are more substantial and comfortable than you find in England, being built entirely with slate-stone, and covered either with the same material or wheat straw. They have no floors but the hard clay, and no chimney save a small aperture in the roof, through which the smoke from the peat fires gradually finds its way out after smoking the inmates almost to suffocation. But around a Welshman's house everything is kept pretty clean and healthful; here no poverty or beggary meets the stranger's eyes, but on the contrary every one seems to be blessed with plenty and contentment.

After enjoying the beautiful scenery in the Vale of Llanberis, we hastened to Menai Straits being impatient to gaze on the Britannia Bridge, the pride of England, the wonder of the age, and the greatest achievement in engineering that the world ever saw. The pen and pencil of gifted writers who are familiar with the science of engineering have frequently been employed to delineate this stupendous undertaking—this masterpiece of human skill; and whatever difference of taste or opinion may have prevailed in determining the character of the various sketches, all have been unanimous in their admiration of the intellect which could plan, and the skill which could erect such magnificent and astonishing structures, contrasted with which, in a scientific point of view, all other works of the kind, both in ancient and modern times, sink into comparative insignificance. No description of ours can give to the man of science, or general reader, an adequate idea of the magnitude and grandeur of the work, for it is a subject which none but a mechanical genius, familiar with the principles upon which the mighty fabric is based, is capable of describing; and all that we can hope is, to give you some general idea of the Tubular Bridge, as it appeared to us. You are aware that it had its origin from the peculiar difficulties to be encountered and overcome in carrying the Chester and Holyhead Railroad over that great arm of the sea, known as the Menai Strait. Originally it was intended to appropriate one side of Telford's celebrated suspension bridge, which, with its light and beautiful tracery, spans the strait about a mile below the site of its massive successor; but it soon became evident that so light a fabric would not answer for heavy trains; that the line could never be considered complete, or commensurate with the requirements of the public, unless carried by a rigid instead of a flexible structure over the stream. Various plans were suggested by Mr. Stephenson, the engineer-in-chief, but they met strenuous opposition in Parliament, and were dismissed on the ground that they would interfere injuriously with the navigation, which was more to be regarded than all railroad communications. Some new experiment of engineering was therefore required, and an engineer bold and skilful enough to conceive such an expedient, and to apply it. That engineer was found in Mr. Stephenson, who, having matured the plan in his own mind, made all calculations, and being fully satisfied as to the perfect feasibility of the work, presented it to the Committee of the House of Commons, for their consideration. When this description of bridge was explained to the members of the committee, the plan was received with general incredulity. The engineer, however, was satisfied that the thing was practicable, and determined not to give it up. A bill was ultimately obtained, and the gigantic undertaking was commenced and completed in the year 1849.

An immense tube, upwards of sixteen hundred tons in weight, suspended in the air, and through which railway trains should pass, was a magnificent conception, and now that it has been successfully tried and found to answer every purpose in furnishing adequate means of communication for the great mercantile transport between London and Dublin, it gives a character to its projectors as enduring as the work itself. The bridge consists of hollow rectangular tubes, sustained in their position by no other power than that which they derive from the strength of their materials and the manner in which they are constructed. They are made of plates of wrought iron from one half to three fourths of an inch in thickness, firmly riveted together so as to form a single and continuous structure, one tube (or connected series of tubes) serving for the passage of the up, and the other of the down train. The total length of each line of tube is said to be 1513 feet, which is formed by the union of four separate lengths of tubes, two of longer and two of shorter dimensions. The two main lengths of tube, each measuring 472 feet, pass from the tower constructed of solid masonry at high tide, on the Caernarvon and Anglesey shores, to the central tower raised in the middle of the strait, to the height of 210 feet, and based on a rock formerly covered by high water. The shorter portions of tubes connect the land towers on either side with the abutments which terminate the embankment, upon which the line of railway is carried, and by which the shores of the strait are approached. These tubes, formed entirely of wrought iron, were constructed on the Caernarvon shore, and afterwards floated by means of pontoons and raised to the required elevation by the use of powerful hydraulic presses. There are three towers attached to this bridge, which were run up and built around the tubes after they had been elevated to the height of one hundred feet above the water. The sides of these stupendous masses of masonry are tapered with a straight batter, by which the size of the upper part is reduced, and greater firmness given to the mass, with a corresponding boldness in the character of the design. These vast monuments rising up from the depths of the sea are equally as curious and wonderful as the tubes themselves. To give you some idea of the magnitude of these structures, I will describe the dimensions of the Britannia tower, which stands in the centre of the strait. It weighs about 20,000 tons; it is 62 feet by 52 feet 5 inches at the base, and 55 feet by 45 feet 5 inches at tube level. Its height from high water is 199 feet, and its total height is 221 feet 8 inches, which is far above the topsail of the largest vessel. The amount of stone contained in this stupendous work is said to be no less than 1,500,000 cubic feet. At the termination of the abutments on the land ends there are four colossal statues of lions, executed in the Egyptian style. The appearance of these enormous statues, lifting their limestone foreheads in the face of every train, defying the tempest and the storm, and guarding as it were the entrance to these caverns of wonder, show conclusively to the stranger that the Britannia bridge is the pride of the whole nation.

Policemen are always stationed at the bridge to regulate the trains, and conduct visitors through the tubes, a duty which they perform very faithfully, considering they are not allowed to receive any compensation from the thousands of people that flock there daily to see it. After being conducted through one of the tubes, the visitor can, if he chooses, return on the top of the bridge, which is reached by means of lofty stone steps in the interior of the tower on either side. The roof is nearly flat and covered with prepared canvas—making it perfectly safe as a place of promenade. The prospect from the towers is truly magnificent. Standing on their summit, you find yourself surrounded with a scenery of great diversity and picturesque beauty, forming at once a panorama of gorgeous sublimity. On one side the Isle of Anglesey, with its highly cultivated fields and green meadows, extends in rolling beauty before the eye; while on the other, the horizon appears bounded or rather fortified by that large range of mountains, about forty miles in length, which bears the name of Snowdonian mountains, and among which extends the lofty patriarch of the group, described in the beginning of this letter. On the east and west are to be seen glittering in large masses the Irish Sea and St. George's Channel, connected together by the narrow strait, whose silvery course, meandering in the chasm beneath, is dotted here and there with the spreading sail and little islands, ornamented with the humble yet beautiful cottage of the fisherman. About a mile below the great tubular bridge there gracefully hangs across the stream in a festoon, which in the annals of science will ever encircle the name of Telford, his celebrated suspension bridge. And not far off the eye of the visitor will wander instinctively to a lofty monument standing on the summit of a rocky eminence on the Isle of Anglesey, erected by the people to commemorate the military services of their countryman William Henry, Marquis of Anglesey. In fine, the scene from this bridge is grand and romantic, presenting to the eye at one glance the wonders of science and the beauties of nature.

LETTER FIFTEEN.

VICTORIA HOTEL, Lakes of Killarney, Ireland.

Tour through the South of Ireland—Cork Harbor—Cork—Blarney Castle—Nature of the Country and Condition of the People—Lakes of Killarney, etc.

THE introduction of steam has done more to unite the interests and harmonize the intercourse of nations than all the legislative acts or governmental policies that were ever created by human ingenuity. The time was, within the memory of men now living, when a trip across the Irish channel was considered about as great an undertaking as a voyage at the present day to our Eldorado on the Pacific—when a people living under the same laws, and acknowledging the same sovereign authority, knew less of each other than they do now of their brethren who people the shores of America. But in this age of enlightenment and improvement in steam navigation, a trip from Holyhead to Dublin, or the city of Cork, is regarded as a mere pleasure excursion; and the facilities for traversing the Island from one extremity to the other by railroad are so admirable, that the toil of travel is just sufficient to enhance the pleasure and brace the frame—acting on the blood like *Pat's potheen*, and sharpening the appetite for a good mess of his *baked potatoes*. There is no country on this side of the water so interesting to an American tourist as old Erin's Isle. Between the two people there exists an identity of sentiment, consanguinity, affinity, sympathy, and mutual love, no where else to be seen. Many of our best citizens emigrated hence—some of whom have rendered signal service to the country both in the field and in our council chambers, and whose names are now intimately blended with the history of the mighty West. In return we have done much for Ireland. On our hospitable shores her people have found a refuge and asylum from oppression and misrule. And during the prevalence of the famine which threatened destruction to her peasantry, we opened our coffers with a liberal hand, and emptied our granaries without money and without price into her seaboard towns, saving thousands upon thousands from the most horrid of all deaths—starvation.

Wishing to see the country in all its parts, and form my own estimate of the real character of the lands and condition of the people, I concluded to visit the south first, by way of Cork, and then make my tour by land to the northern counties. The steamers that run between Holyhead and Cork are of the most substantial character, but not very comfortably arranged for the accommodation of cabin passengers—particularly those accustomed to travel on the floating palaces of the great Mississippi. Very few persons visit this part of Ireland except on business, and consequently owners of boats have paid but little attention to style or convenience. But one can afford to put up with these things occasionally, when he has in contemplation a treat in the way of beautiful scenery, which has given so much celebrity to the harbor at Cork. When our boat entered the land-locked bay, a panorama of surpassing beauty was presented to our view. The neat little town of Cove (now called Queenstown, in commemoration of a visit from the Queen) first meets the eye, with its environs rising terrace above terrace abruptly from the clear waters below, embracing the picturesque beauty of the lofty hills which overhang the spacious basin of the inner harbor. As we glided along the placid waters, our attention was drawn to the beautiful outline of the coast, the bright headlands, and sweet islands around which were numerous vessels of various sizes, some reposing at anchor, and some with their white sails spread to the sun, skimming along like things of life. Several of these islands are filled with public works. Haulboline has its dock-yard and naval stores, and Spike Island its battery and barracks, beyond which we could trace with the eye the shore sweeping in a magnificent curve, and dotted with smiling villas, till narrowing at either side, the basin is guarded by Carlisle fort on the left, and that of Camden on the opposite headland. We now entered the windings of the river Lee, whose scenery is still more beautiful. Its banks are filled with summer residences, bathing eastablishments, and monuments of past ages. The ruins of the old castle on the left bank still remain, and is pointed out by Pat as the place where William Penn, the broad-brimmed founder of the Keystone State, embarked for the new world—a tradition of doubtful character, as several places lay claim to the same honor. Just opposite the castle, on a lofty eminence, is a monument recently erected by a wealthy tailor of Cork, in honor of Father Mathew and the Temperance cause. It is a plain and unobtrusive structure, but serves to show the high repute in which the great Apostle of Temperance is held in his native town. Beyond this we had a fine view of the city, the quays, and the beautiful hills around, which present *in the distance* a prospect of rare beauty, soon, however, to be dispelled by an utter disgust for the place and every thing about it. The city is built on low marshy ground, as its ancient name, Coreagh, imports. The streets are irregular in character, and the houses are mostly in a dilapidated condition, showing conclusively that it is fast going to decay. The poor-houses are filled to overflowing, and the streets from morning until night are literally blocked up with a variegated mass of squalid humanity that sways and surges around the stranger on every side, pulling his garments, thrusting their hands into his face, and filling his ears with all the discordant sounds of blatant mendicancy, ranging through the whole diapason of beggars' oratory, from the shrill squeak of the pinched infant in the arms of the snivelling beldame, to the unmanly whine of some stalwart vagabond who puts the soft pedal upon his strong lungs and gives utterance to the oft repeated song, "Your honor, for God's sake give us a penny to buy something to eat." This destitution and misery is not confined to the city of Cork alone; it extends in a greater or less degree over the whole country, but more particularly in the south and west, where the Celtic race predominates. Wherever we went evidences of decay, poverty, and distress were visible, not only in the habitations, but in the appearance of the people, many of whom are utterly destitute of the necessaries of life. In the bog lands the condition of the peasantry is really deplorable, and no one who has not witnessed it can possibly conceive their manner of living, or realize that they are beings like ourselves, subject to the same diseases and possessing the same wants. To convey to you some idea of the real state of things in this portion of Ireland, I will describe a hovel on the roadside that was pointed out by the coach guard as the habitation of a very large family. Being curious to see life in all its various phases, I descended from the coach and entered a narrow aperture serving as a doorway into a miserable place about the size of a Tennessee pig sty, and quite as cleanly. Here a scene was presented that I hope never to see again—a widow with ten small children, hovering around a peat fire, without garments to protect them from the weather, or food to sustain their physical wants. Their little home had no floor or bed, save a small heap of straw in one corner, and their only dependence for bread was upon the liberality of those who chanced to pass by the doorway. This is not an isolated case, but only the picture of many others of the same sort.

Various causes are assigned for the poverty of the country: some say, it is owing to the failure in the potato crop; others, to bad legislation, and monopoly of the lands by absentees; and not a few contend that it is to be attributed to the influence of Catholicism. But the real cause in my opinion, as far as I had an opportunity of judging, is the bad system of agriculture, which has a tendency to exhaust the lands and render them unfit for tillage. Thousands of acres have been abandoned in the last few years, as utterly worthless, and the population have emigrated to foreign parts, leaving whole counties almost in a state of nature. The lands in this portion of Ireland were originally superior to any in the kingdom, but are now valueless; while the farms of England and Scotland yield abundantly. Let them change their present system, and enrich their farms with manure or compost, and a delightful result will follow. But there is no hope of such a change soon; the people are disheartened and tired of the country; emigration to America is the subject of their thoughts by day and dreams by night. Every one that can raise a few pounds, immediately sets sail for the new world, which is regarded here as the promised land for the oppressed of all nations. According to the census just taken by authority of the government, it is estimated that the diminution of the population of Ireland in the last three years exceeds two millions, and is rapidly on the increase. Most of these emigrants go to the United States, many of whom make industrious and respectable citizens, while others remain in their original condition.

Having given you some idea of the ancient city of Cork, I will now describe two places Irishmen always go into ecstasies about, viz., Blarney and Killarney. The former is renowned in history for its beautiful groves and the fine stronghold of the McCarthys in olden times. Much of the ancient buildings have disappeared, but the donjon keep and lofty tower still stand a princely monument of departed glory. Our guide was a joyous old dame, weighing something less than two hundred pounds; and had evidently kissed the famous stone so often that she believed fully in all its magic properties; at least she was willing to impress us with the belief, in order to make her fee as large as possible. After some persuasion we agreed with the old lady, that we should not think of leaving the castle without seeing at least the stone that imparts to those who kiss it such rare power, and we accordingly mounted the flight of steps that lead to the summit of the northeast angle, when she pointed out a stone bearing the date of 1703, and worn by the lips of thousands who have visited it as sleek as a new silk hat. Happy is he whose lips touch it, if there be any truth in legends, or the old woman's story, and what traveller will gainsay them? Had Demosthenes kissed the Blarney stone, instead of filling his mouth with pebbles, his eloquence would have been all the sweeter, though not a whit less passionate. Scott, Lockhart, and Maria Edgeworth, have all tried its virtues; and who will not confess the source from whence Father Prout drew all his inspiration? From the summit of this old ruin we had a beautiful survey of the little river called Comane, and the lake surrounded by a graceful fringe of trees, with paths and grottoes for the accommodation of those who desire to visit the famous castle.

A few hours' ride by rail and post coach brought us from the castle to the lakes of Killarney, which are much resorted to in summer by travellers who are fond of enjoying the beauties of nature. The lakes are three in number, and all connected with each other, forming a bed or basin between the lofty hills, deep, sinuous, and gorgy, preesenting every variety of feature of land and water scenery. Writers have compared them to the lakes in Scotland and Switzerland, which surpass them in sublimity, though not in the beauties of softer scenery. To an American, accustomed to the broad expanse of our northern lakes, Killarney seems in miniature, and he feels as if he were looking at the soft beauties of nature on a very small scale. The hotels on the shore are very comfortable, and the traveller has every inducement to come here, in the way of good living and exquisite scenery. But there is one great objection to this place; you cannot enjoy any thing in quietude for the beggars, who harass the stranger wherever he goes, rendering his visit to Killarney a source of vexation and disagreeability instead of enjoyment.

LETTER SIXTEEN.

DUBLIN, Ireland.

Appearance of the City—Poor-Houses—Police—Parks and Monuments—O'Connell's Vault—Railway to Galway and Line of Steamers to the United States.

NEXT to London, this city may be regarded as the largest and most important in the kingdom, being beautifully situated near a bay of the same name, which always affords a safe and commodious harbor for vessels of the largest capacity. The Anna Liffy flows through its centre, furnishing water sufficient to accommodate boats of light draught, and acting as a kind of drain, carrying off the filth of the city. Over this stream are seven substantial bridges connecting the main streets, which were built at different periods, and consequently present various styles of architecture according to the improvements of the age.

The time has been when this city was regarded by strangers as a place of great beauty and attraction, but through some cause or other it has gone down in the last few years, and now presents the appearance of neglect and dilapidation. The public buildings, some of which are very large and elegant, are kept in good repair, and several of the principal thoroughfares still retain their ancient importance; but the great majority of the streets and private houses show conclusively that the blight visible in every part of the south and west has had its desolating influence upon the metropolis of Ireland. You will be surprised to learn that the poor-houses in this city are pointed out to the stranger as among the most interesting and worthy objects of his notice. What we would keep in the background is here placed in the foreground, and the officers take almost as much pride in explaining the operations of the institution, and hearing the comments of visitors, as an American would in relating the battles of his country. They are certainly very laudable undertakings, that reflect credit upon the government. They are conducted upon principles of a superior nature—dispense much good, and relieve many who are in misery; yet they fail to meet the demands of the public. Thousands and thousands of poor creatures who are compelled to live from hand to mouth—not knowing today where the morrow's meal is to come from—would be glad to receive shelter from the pitiless storm in these asylums of charity; but they are turned from the doors daily, for want of room, and are compelled to seek their living by begging in the streets. The city authorities have made every endeavor to prevent this mode of obtaining subsistence, by adopting a strict police regulation, which has thus far proved utterly useless, from the fact that the people cannot procure labor whereby to gain the necessaries of life, and they cannot compel a man to starve.

The police of Ireland is better, probably, than that of England, being composed of the first young men in the country, and required to undergo a thorough drilling before they are received or allowed to enter upon the regular duties of their office. The government owes much to this body of men, who are stationed in every neighborhood, for the preservation of peace and quietude. Were it not for their efficiency and promptness in quelling riots and keeping the masses in subjection, Ireland would soon be the scene of another revolution. During my stay here I have witnessed several reviews of the constabulary and military in the Phœnix Park, a place of great natural beauty, and much adorned with gravel walks and a large granite monument in the centre, called the Wellington Testimonial. On these occasions the visitor has an opportunity of witnessing the largest, best drilled, and most efficient corps of men in the kingdom. It is certainly a beautiful sight to stand on some eminence and watch this large body of men go through the various evolutions of military tactics with so much precision and grace; but when one reflects upon its utility, and considers the enormity of taxation laid upon the people to keep up an idle soldiery, he loses all interest in the dazzling display, and becomes utterly disgusted with monarchies and every thing connected with them.

The public monuments in this city are well deserving our notice, as they all commemorate some historical event, or great man's character. Next to the Wellington Testimonal in Phœnix Park, there is a tall shaft rising from the centre of Sackville street, to the height of about two hundred feet, which is called the Nelson Monument. It is a very substantial structure, and contains some ingenious carving representing the four great battles in which Nelson figured, and about which Englishmen can talk for ever. The most interesting testimonial of this character, to me, was a vault in the Catholic Cemetery near the city, which contains the remains of the celebrated Daniel O'Connell, a man who occupied a high position in the affairs of state, and whose memory is now embalmed in the heart of every true Catholic. The vault is built of plain stone above the ground, with a heavy iron door, upon which is inscribed simply the name of O'Connell, which contains more than any epitaph that could be written. In fair weather this door is kept open, and the splendid coffin, covered with crimson velvet and gold plates, can be seen by all who are curious to gaze upon it. While we were standing at the door, several females came up with baskets filled with flowers, which they scattered over the vault with great care, uttering at the same time something inaudible, which we took to be prayers for the salvation of the departed.

Duing the last few weeks an unusual degree of excitement has been created by the commercial men of this city relative to the prospect of establishing a line of steamers between New-York and the town of Galway on the western shore of Ireland. Every preparation was made to receive the passengers that were expected to come over in the North America, which had engaged to make the trial trip. The citizens of Galway enlarged their public houses—made arrangements for a grand entertainment and tournament. The railroad company fitted up their cars expressly to convey the passengers directly through to this city, and the success of the undertaking was regarded as absolutely certain—when the news came that the owners of the steamer had abandoned the idea. I think that if they succeed in establishing this line, the voyage between the two countries may be shortened at least two days, and the dangers of the Irish Channel avoided; but there is no such prospect at present. Liverpool has monopolized the trade too long, and the influence of her commercial men is so great that it will be utterly impossible to change or establish a new line.

LETTER SEVENTEEN.

LONDONDERRY, Ireland.

Difference between the Northern and Southern parts of Ireland—Belfast—Scenery on the Coast—Giant's Causeway—Death of a young Scotchman—Wreck of an American Vessel —Irish Hospitality—Londonderry—The River Foyle, etc.

AFTER a tour through the southern counties of Ireland, where desolation and want meet the view on every side, one feels, as he passes along the highly cultivated fields of the north, as if he were transported into another land, among a different race of people. Here there is comparatively no beggary or misery; the lands are better cultivated, the houses of the peasantry more comfortable, and the towns present a more thrifty and business-like appearance. The question naturally suggests itself to the mind as to the causes of so great a change in the same country, and the only answer that can be given, is the difference in the character of the people. Those that inhabit this section of Ireland are descended principally from the Scotch, and have inherited to a considerable degree their habits of industry and frugality; while on the other hand the descendants of the Celtic race are by nature less provident, and consequently not so prosperous.

The city of Belfast is the largest and most beautiful place in North Ireland, and is connected by rail with Dublin and the interior counties, making it a place of considerable importance in a commercial point of view, aside from its extensive interest in linen manufactures. It is rather a singular sight as you approach the city, to see large fields covered over with immense quantities of linen put out to bleach, giving them in the distance the appearance of a winter scene after a heavy fall of snow. The linens of Belfast are regarded as the best in the world, and constitute the principal article of their merchandise. The streets are wide, built up with great regularity, and kept perfectly clean and decent, which is a little more than can be said of most cities. The docks are extensive, and always present a scene of activity which is far more interesting to a man who lives in a progressive country than the dull monotony of inertness every where visible in the south and west.

Near the docks there is a large archway about one hundred feet in height, which was erected two years ago to receive Victoria, when she honored Pat with a visit. It is constructed of wood, and constitutes one of the most prominent objects in the city. On one side is inscribed in letters of living light, "God save the Queen," and on the other, in the Irish language, "One hundred thousand welcomes to you." The Queen's reception is said to have been warmer here than at any other place she visited during the tour—a demonstration of loyalty that gratified her beyond measure, as it was wholly unexpected. She returned to Buckingham Palace highly pleased with her Irish subjects, and expressed the opinion that they were a better people than the world gave them credit for.

Leaving Belfast, we passed along the sea-shore in an Irish jaunting car, to the Giant's Causeway, which is a pleasant day's drive over a beautiful road, and through scenery of great singularity and wildness. The Causeway is regarded here as one of the wonders of the world, and is resorted to by thousands every week during the summer months, who are curious to behold and admire the works of nature. After enjoying a good dinner at the Causeway House, and getting rid of the swarm of specimen venders that infest the whole neighborhood, we proceeded quietly with our guide down a narrow pathway to the sea-shore, where we were shown for the first time this great phenomenon. Like almost every one that goes there, we were at first sadly disappointed—having actually stood upon the rocks without being aware of it—inquiring of our guide all the while, "Where is the Causeway?" But this disappointment was not of long duration, for when we came to examine into its formation and singularity, we felt fully compensated for our trouble. It consists of a series of stone columns extending several hundred yards into the sea, with a gradual descent forming an inclined plane. Each block is about one foot in diameter, and varies in length from three to six feet, fitting into each other with as much nicety and precision as if it were done with the hand of art. No two of these columns are alike in shape; some are hexagons, some heptagons, and others octagons, and every other conceivable formation. The beauty of the Causeway has been very much impaired of late years by the removal of the most curious blocks to different parts of the world as specimens for exhibition. You will find them in London, Paris, and even in Philadelphia—and, as a matter of course, in Barnum's Museum.

After viewing the Causeway to our satisfaction, we consented to be rowed in a small boat by four sturdy Irishmen into the caves, more in conformity with custom than any pleasure we expected to derive, for we were pretty well convinced before starting that they were humbugs, exaggerated in order to squeeze a few more shillings out of the visitor's pocket. They repaid us, however, by rowing the boat out into the sea, from which we had a beautiful view of the lofty heights formed of a succession of columns, and extending for miles beyond as far as the eye can reach. Our guide was particularly loquacious, and grew quite eloquent in his description of the attack made by the Spanish Armada upon one of the heights, which they battered down in the night with cannon balls, thinking it was the Castle of Dunlose, about four miles off. He also pointed out a place formed of a succession of small fluted columns resembling pipes, and called the Spanish organ, from its similarity to that instrument. These heights are always covered with sea fowl of every description, that congregate there to receive shelter and build their nests in the fissures of the rock. Quite a melancholy accident took place there a few weeks since. A young man from Edinburgh, in the morning of life and of great promise, descended from the summit to the distance of about fifty feet in an attempt to reach one of these nests, when he became dizzy, lost his support, and fell about two hundred feet into the sea. His body was found some four days after by his brother, much mutilated and disfigured.

The northern shore of Ireland is considered by navigators as exceedingly dangerous, on account of the high seas and great number of rocks forming ledges below the surface of the water, and extending for miles in some places from the main land. Several wrecks have taken place during the present month, and among them an American vessel from St. John, loaded with lumber. The crew were all saved by fishermen, who picked them up here and there on planks upon which they floated all night in the storm.

The city of Londonderry, so celebrated in history on account of its long and memorable siege, is the most beautifully situated and interesting place in Ireland. The old wall that surrounded it originally is still kept in good repair, and stands as a monument of its former strength. The public buildings all present an antique appearance without any evidence of dilapidation, and the population is composed of decidedly a better class of people than it has been our fortune to meet with elsewhere on this side of the channel. Here we saw something of Irish hospitality and the fine old Irish gentleman in his true element.

Londonderry is a place of considerable commerce; vessels of the largest capacity come up the Foyle, and steamers of the first class ply daily to Glasgow and Liverpool. At this season of the year the docks are always crowded with laborers going to Scotland to aid them in gathering in their harvest, after which they return to their families and occupy the intervening time in tending their flocks and growing potatoes.

LETTER EIGHTEEN.

GLASGOW, Scotland.

The River Clyde—Dumbarton Castle—Glasgow—Trip to Ayr—Birthplace of Burns—Alloway Kirk—Brig of Doon, etc.

IN my last letter I gave you a description of the scenery on the river Foyle—the pride of Londonderry—out of which we sailed in a magnificent steamer, called the Thistle, for the shores of Caledonia, passing *en route*, by moonlight, the lofty heights of the Causeway, the chalk bluffs, and several beautiful islands dotted here and there with the thatch-covered cottages of the Irish peasantry. Wishing to enjoy a sea-view of the Highlands and the Firth of Clyde, so celebrated in Scottish song, we gave orders to the steward, before retiring, to have us up by the dawn of day—an injunction obeyed most implicitly, for Aurora had scarcely emerged from the waters when all on board were aroused by a loud voice crying out, "The rock! the rock! the rock!" Many of the passengers, supposing the vessel was in danger of being stranded on some fearful breaker, rushed forth from their berths in their morning gowns, with glaring eyes and distended mouths, expecting every moment to hear the crash and feel the shock, but were agreeably disappointed when the captain informed them that there was no danger, as the rock was two miles off—pointing out at the same time a lofty object in the shape of a cone, rising some forty or fifty feet above the surface of the water. This singular rock stands, solitary and alone, several miles from the main land, serving as a beacon for vessels nearing the Scottish shore. The captain of our ship told us, *and we have no reason to doubt its truth*, that a bold fresh water spring rises from the summit and flows perpetually down the sides of the rock into the sea, furnishing sailors with the pure element to mix with their vile liquor without the trouble of making a landing. Beyond this rock, in the dim distance, the lofty peaks of Ben Lomond, and the whole range of southern highlands, were presented to our view, forming a scene of panoramic beauty far surpassing my expectations, and equalling in every respect the descriptions given by different writers. In a short time we found ourselves ascending the Clyde, which is in a commercial point of view the most important river in Scotland, being navigable at high water for the largest class of merchant vessels as far as Glasgow. The river as far up as Dumbarton Castle is very wide and beautiful, with many villas and several flourishing towns on the banks, but beyond this it is very narrow and uninteresting except to practical minds, fond of looking at ship yards and dredging machines. Large sums of money have been expended of late by the city of Glasgow in deepening the channel and making the stream wider, an undertaking of great magnitude, evincing a degree of enterprise that we rarely see in any city. Several thousand Irish laborers are now employed night and day, with their shovels and spades, in excavating the banks and conveying the dirt in boats to the low lands below, which are subject to inundation at high tide. In a few years this river, which was originally very small and unimportant, will become, by human ingenuity and labor, the largest in the kingdom.

Dumbarton Castle is one of the four fortresses stipulated to be kept up at the time of the union between Scotland and England, and, accordingly, it is still in repair, and occupied by a garrison. It is situated on a rock rising from the point of junction of the Leven and Clyde, to the height of two hundred and sixty feet, measuring a mile in circumference, terminating in two sharp points, one higher than the other, and covered over with houses and batteries. Previous to his being sent to England, Wallace was confined in this castle, the governor of which was the notorious Sir John Menteith, who betrayed him. One of the peaks of the rock is now called Wallace's Seat, and a part of the castle Wallace's Tower, in which can be seen a huge two-handed sword said to have belonged to that hero. During the wars which desolated Scotland in the reign of Queen Mary, this formidable fortress was taken by Captain Crawford, a distinguished adherent of the King's party, by means of scaling ladders, in the night time, choosing for his dangerous experiment the place where the rock was highest, and where, of course, less pains were taken to keep a regular guard. The exploit at the time was considered very extraordinary, but in this day and generation of ours, when men do every thing and stop at nothing, it would be regarded as mere child's play.

The city of Glasgow is the great commercial metropolis of Scotland, and in wealth, population, and manufacturing importance, the third city in the United Kingdom. It cannot be called a beautiful place, although it possesses many attractions. The streets are wide, well paved, and kept perfectly clean, and the houses all present a similarity of architecture, and are constructed without an exception of white stone found in the neighborhood. Like most of the cities in this country, it is rich in religious, charitable, and philanthropic institutions, which are supported by annual donations to the amount of fifty thousand pounds. Among the most important establishments of this kind which we visited are, the Asylum for the Houseless Poor, Asylum for Indigent Old Men and Orphan Boys, Institution for Destitute Young Females, and work-houses, all of which are conducted upon superior principles, and do much towards improving the condition of the masses, and elevating the tone of society. Among the many beautiful houses dedicated to the worship of God, the venerable Cathedral erected by Bishop Achaius, in 1136, is the most conspicuous. It occupies the highest point in the city, and stands, like the awful Genius of the place, in perfect preservation, surrounded by the remains and memorials of twenty-five generations. In the centre of the Necropolis, near this ancient structure, stands a beautiful monument erected to the memory of John Knox, the great ecclesiastical reformer. It is a plain and substantial structure, designed more to represent the true character of the man, than as an ornament to perpetuate the name of the architect, or gratify the vanity of those who projected it.

The first object that strikes the eye of the stranger in Glasgow, is the monument recently erected in George's Square to Sir Walter Scott. It is in the form of a fluted Doric column, about eighty feet in height, with a colossal statue of the great Minstrel on the summit. The figure is half enveloped in a shepherd's plaid, which hangs in graceful folds on the *wrong arm*, and the expression of the countenance is characterized by that air of *bonhomie* and shrewdness which distinguished the great writer. Directly in front of Sir Walter's pillar, in the same square, there is a fine pedestrian statue, in bronze, by Flaxman, of the lamented Sir John Moore, who was a native and resident of this city. To the right of the statue, in an angle of the square, there is also a noble figure of James Watt, in bronze, and of colossal magnitude. It is intended, as opportunity offers, to place the statues and monuments of other eminent men around the inclosed area of this small but handsome square, which is now ornamented with shrubberies and walks, so that in course of time it will become a sort of open Pantheon, dedicated to the illustrious dead.

Standing on the balcony of my hotel, which fronts on George's Square, I have before me one of the finest architectural vistas in the city. On one side the lofty spire of St. George's Church, one hundred and sixty-two feet in height, catches the eye, surmounting a building obviously too small for such a vast superstructure. Somewhat nearer, on the same side, is the Dissenting Chapel, in which the celebrated Dr. Wardlaw officiates, an elegant building, in the Grecian style of architecture. On the other side George street is presented to the view, extending for about two miles in a straight line, and forming an uninterrupted succession of blocks of the same description. Immediately in front of me the lofty colonnade of the Royal Exchange rises above every other object. This splendid fabric is built in the florid Corinthian style of architecture, and is surmounted by a lantern, which forms at night one of the most conspicuous objects in the city. As a whole, this building is regarded as one of the most striking of the kind in the kingdom. Its general effect is grand and impressive, though some of the details may be liable to the objections of a refined criticism.

The streets of Glasgow present an uninterrupted scene of activity, and the smoke, which almost obscures the light of the sun, shows conclusively that her manufacturing establishments are carrying on an extensive business, which must in the course of a few years render it a wealthy, populous, and influential city.

Wishing to see the birth-place of Burns, the great Scottish Bard, and the scene of Tam o' Shanter's route, so much talked of and admired, we formed an agreeable party and ran down by railroad to a little town called Ayr in the space of two hours. Here we procured at one of the inns a drosky, and drove out about two miles to the little cottage where Burns was born. The original erection was a *clay bigging*, consisting of two apartments, the kitchen and the *spence*, or sitting-room. The cottage was built by Burns's father, on a small piece of leased land, which he designed for a nursery, but gave up that idea when he was employed by Mr. Ferguson as his gardener and overseer. On removing to Locklee he disposed of his leasehold to the corporation of shoemakers in Ayr, to whom the house and ground still belong. It is occupied at present by an old lady as an ale-house, and every one that goes there is expected to drink to the memory of the departed in a mug which has been used for the purpose ever since the poet's death. In the interior of the kitchen we were shown a recess, where stood the bed in which Burns was born, also several articles of furniture said to have belonged to the family. Proceeding a little further, we saw "Alloway's auld haunted kirk." This interesting building has long been roofless, but the walls, which are very thick and built of stone only one story in height, are pretty well preserved, and it still retains the old bell on the east end, as a memento of its ancient importance. Every piece of wood-work about the house has long since been removed to make snuff-boxes and other memorials of this celebrated spot. The churchyard of Alloway has now become a fashionable burying place. Its little area is almost filled with modern monuments to the memory of persons, many of whom have been brought from considerable distances to take their rest in this doubly consecrated ground. The poet is not interred here, as might have been expected, but at Dumfries in the extreme south of Scotland. A few yards from the kirk a well trickles down into the Doon, where formerly stood the thorn on which "Mungo's mither hang'd hersel," and just beyond is the "Auld Brig" of Doon, which figures so conspicuously in the tale of Tam o' Shanter. The age of the structure is unknown, but it is evidently of great antiquity. Between the kirk and the brig, on an elevation, stands the monument erected in 1820 by voluntary contribution, at a cost of upwards of £4,000. It is a beautiful structure, and contains, in a circular apartment on the ground floor, several articles appropriate to the place, various editions of the poet's works, a snuff-box made from the wood-work of Alloway Kirk, a copy of the original portrait of Burns by Nasmyth, and the Bible given by Burns to his Highland Mary. The monument stands in the centre of a square acre, which is beautifully inclosed and adorned with shrubbery of every description. In a small grotto at the south side of the inclosed ground we were shown the two far-famed statues of Tam o' Shanter and Souter Johnnie, by Mr. Thom, of Ayr. They are well executed, and represent the characters in the drinking scene to perfection.

From the base of the monument we obtained a splendid view of the picturesque scenery of Dover and the surrounding country, which has acquired so much celebrity through the writings of the inimitable bard. It is certainly beautiful, and every way suited to inspire the imagination and elevate the thoughts of a poetical genius.

LETTER NINETEEN.

STIRLING, Scotland.

Farming in the South of Scotland—Hotels—Expense of Travel—Highland Scenery—Lochs Lomond and Katrine—The Trosachs—Stirling Castle, etc.

IN previous letters I have given descriptions of the system of farming in England and Ireland, which varies materially from that in this country, owing to the great difference in the qualities of the land and manner of culture. Scotland is naturally divided into highlands and lowlands, and the surface of the country is consequently exceedingly diversified. The general average is inferior to that of England, although many of the valleys are highly productive. It is supposed, that estimating the whole extent of the country, exclusive of lakes, at 19,000,000 acres, scarcely so many as 6,000,000 are arable—that is, less than one third; whereas in England the proportion of arable land to the entire extent of the country exceeds three fourths. The inferiority of the climate also renders this country less desirable in an agricultural point of view than either England or Ireland, as exhibited by contrasting the phenomena of vegetation in the several divisions. Notwithstanding the very advanced state of agriculture in the southern counties of Scotland, the crops are not reaped with the same certainty as in England; nor do the ordinary kinds of grain arrive at the same perfection. Various fruits, also, which ripen in the one country, seldom arrive at maturity in the other, and never reach the same perfection; while different berries acquire in Scotland somewhat of that delicious flavor which distinguishes them in still higher parallels. The highlands of this country are barren and unproductive, and fit only for grazing purposes—a source of wealth entered into very largely by the tenantry. In the lowlands, which lie principally in the south, the farms are not divided up into small parcels or patches as in other portions of Great Britain, but on the contrary, they are very extensive, and remind me very much of the broad acres in our western fields.

The internal communication throughout Scotland is so extensive, and the facilities of locomotion so great, that one may accomplish the usual tour through the Highlands in a few days, without much annoyance or fatigue. Carriage roads extend over the whole country; and in consequence of the excellent materials which abound in all parts of Scotland, and of the greater skill and science of Scottish trustees and surveyors, their turnpike roads are better built and superior in every respect to those in England. Notwithstanding the irregularity of surface is so unfavorable to artificial inland navigation, we find a number of large canals, of considerable length, upon which are carried on an extensive traffic. Many railroads are also in progress, and some completed, connecting the most important points of communication, and rendering the facilities of travel and transportation exceedingly convenient for those who are able to stand up under exorbitant charges. Every thing that one requires while travelling through Scotland has to be paid for about three times over. The fares on canals, railroads, and post-coaches are much dearer even than in England, and the hotel bills are really alarming to a backwoodsman unaccustomed to "roast beef and two dollars a day." One can afford, however, to be gouged in this manner for a short time, if he has any romance in his composition, and loves to gaze upon the beauties of nature, which are scattered profusely in every direction over the whole country. To describe the Highland scenery would be a work of supererogation and presumption on my part, as every one who has perused the writings of Sir Walter Scott and the letters of the numerous tourists through this country, are almost as familiar with every lake, hill, and dale in Scotland, as the Highlanders themselves. But in order to furnish you with a connecting link of our journey, I will describe briefly the scenes that we passed through *en route* from Glasgow to this place—a tour usually made by persons who do not desire to penetrate the extreme north, and which embraces the finest lake scenery and most beautiful highlands in Scotland. Leaving the city of Glasgow early in the morning, we proceeded down the river Clyde on a small steamer, with a full complement of passengers, as far as Dumbarton, where we took the rail for the foot of Loch Lomond, ("the lake full of islands,") which is unquestionably the pride of Scottish lakes. Here we found a small steamboat waiting to convey us to the northern extremity of the lake to an excellent inn called Tarbet, which is snugly ensconced in a little vale at the foot of Ben Lomond. The lake is twenty-three miles in length, and its breadth, where greatest, at the southern extremity, is five miles, from which it gradually grows narrower, till it terminates in a narrow prolonged sheet of water. Numerous islands of every varying form and outline which fancy can frame, stud the unrippled surface of the water, and the old ruins of the strongholds of the Macfarlanes still stand as monuments of the past; while the lofty peak of Ben Lomond, rising more than three thousand feet above the level of the sea, serves to complete the view, and form a picture of natural beauty that is really sublime. Reaching Tarbet early in the day, we concluded to make use of our time and visit Loch Long, about three miles distant, which is considered by many as very beautiful, but far inferior to Loch Lomond in every particular. It is formed by an arm of the sea, and navigable in high tide as far up as a little place called Arroquhar, formerly the seat of the chief of the clan Macfarlane. Our guide—whom we found to be like all other guides, exceedingly communicative, and willing to tell all he knew and more too—

informed me that this was the loch up which the Norwegians sailed when they invaded Scotland with a fleet of sixty vessels, ravaging the country on all sides, and on reaching the head of the loch they drew their boats across the isthmus into Loch Lomond, and committed the same depredations on its shores. Near the head of the loch is a fantastic peak called Ben Arthur or the Cobbler, from its resemblance to a shoemaker at work—a place where all strangers are decoyed by the guide in order that they may run their hands a little deeper into your pocket, and excuse themselves when you express your disappointment, by saying that *every body goes there*, which is very consoling to a man feeling conscious that he has been *gouged*. However, we shall not complain, as we were fully compensated on our return to the inn, by an invitation from one of the lairds to attend a Scottish *fête* in the neighborhood, which we accepted, as you might suppose, being unwilling to allow such a favorable opportunity to pass for seeing the Highland character on its native heath. Here we were interested beyond measure in the costumes of the different clans, and their manner of dancing, each one having different ways of adjusting their plaids, and peculiarities of step easily distinguished by the looker on. The Macgregors, Macfarlanes, and all the neighboring Macs, were there with their *bonnie lasses*, "tripping the light fantastic toe," to the squeak of the *bagpipe*, until the shades of evening admonished them that it was time for them to repair to their homes. On the following morning we crossed the placid waters of Loch Lomond in a pleasure boat to the cataract of Inversnade, the scene of Wordsworth's beautiful poem to the "Highland Girl." Here we procured a drosky and crossed over a narrow and rugged pathway to Loch Katrine, so elegantly described by Sir Walter Scott, in the Lady of the Lake. Just as we came in sight of the water we saw the little boat that was to convey us to the Trosachs, puffing away about two miles from the starting point—leaving us, as we supposed, to pass the day in a miserable little hovel, *licensed to sell ale and cider, to be drunk on the premises*. Fortunately, however, we had in our party a tall six-footer from the *far west*, who proposed to hail the boat, a suggestion received with a smile, as they all doubted the power of his lungs to make himself heard at so great a distance. But suiting the action to the word, he raised his stentorian voice to its highest key, and actually succeeded in rendering himself audible and bringing the boat back to the shore—an achievement worthy of Rob Roy, or any of the McGregors who once roved the region about Loch Katrine to the terror of all the neighboring clans. To give you a description of this beautiful sheet of water is impossible, as no one can convey to the distant reader an adequate idea of the works of nature. It must be seen, and the many associations connected with it felt, in order to appreciate its varied beauties. The loch is of a serpentine form, encircled by lofty mountains, and is ten miles in length, attaining, in some places, a breadth of two miles. The scenery which fringes its shores is wild and romantic, reminding me very much, from its similarity, of Lake George in New-York. In sailing along towards the Trosachs, I discovered many arms of the lake—here a bold headland, where black rocks dip in unfathomable water—there the white sands in the bottom of a bay, bleached for ages by the waves. On the north side there is a solid ledge of rock, which rises two hundred feet above the lake, down which a hundred little streams rush with incredible noise and velocity into the basin below. On the opposite shore the wild goats climb where they have scarce room for the soles of their feet, and the water eagle sits in undisturbed majesty on his well-known rock, where he gazes with composed indifference on the sight-seekers below. The scene is closed by a view of the Trosachs, (Troschen, bristled territory,) which is

> "So wondrous wild, the whole might seem
> The scenery of a fairy dream."

Here we found an excellent inn, much resorted to during the summer months by tourists, and persons wishing to avoid the heat and dust of the cities, where we procured refreshments, and proceeded by post coach to Stirling, passing *en route* the Bridge of Turk, the "Coilantogle Ford," where Fitzjames and Roderic Dhu met face to face, and steel to steel—and the romantic village of Callender, surrounded by wooded crags and pastoral inclosures.

The town of Stirling is delightfully situated on an eminence near the river Forth, and bears in the distance a beautiful and imposing appearance, but possesses nothing to interest the stranger, except the old castle, which was built and for a long time used as the residence of royalty. It was frequently taken and retaken after protracted sieges, during the wars which were carried on for the independence of Scotland, and is now occupied by soldiers—being one of the four fortresses which, by the articles of the Union, are always to be kept in repair. Among the many interesting things pointed out to the stranger in the old castle is one of the apartments called Douglas's Room, in consequence of the assassination of William, Earl of Douglas, by the hand of James II., after he had granted him a safe conduct;—a deed of great historic interest, which is beautifully expressed in those lines from the Lady of the Lake,

> "Tetarver, within whose circuit dread,
> A Douglas by his sovereign bled."

The view from the towers of the castle is extremely magnificent. "To the north and east are the Ochil hills, and the windings of the Forth through the carse of Stirling, with its fertile fields, luxuriant woods, and stately mansions. On the west lies the vale of Menteith, bounded by the highland mountains. The Campsie hills close the horizon on the south, and in the foreground, on the east, are the tower, the Abbey Craig, and the ruins of Cambuskenneth Abbey."

About one mile from Stirling is the celebrated battle-field of Bannockburn, which has been aptly termed the Marathon of the North. It was on this memorable spot that Edward II., with one hundred thousand men, was so signally defeated by Robert Bruce, with only thirty thousand, sustaining a loss of thirty-six thousand men, and seven hundred barons and knights—one of the most brilliant victories in the annals of military glory. The view from the eminence on which the battle was fought, is very extensive, varied, and beautiful. According to tradition the royal standard was pitched in a stone, having a round hole for its reception, and thence called the Bare Stone. The remaining fragments of this stone, protected from the depredations of persons visiting the spot by a frame-work of wire, are still shown as a precious remembrance of Scottish valor.

LETTER TWENTY.

EDINBURGH, Scotland.

General Appearance of Edinburgh—Old Town and New Town—Population—Hospitals—Holyrood Palace—The Castle—Public Buildings—Monuments—Excursion to Melrose Abbey—Abbotsford—Dryburgh, etc.

AMONG the numerous cities we have visited in the kingdom of Great Britain, the metropolis of Scotland is unquestionably the most beautiful and attractive. Instead of approaching the "Heart of Midlothian" through mean and squalid suburbs, as in most places, the stranger is gradually introduced into streets of a highly respectable character; the abodes of poverty being for the most part confined to gigantic piles of buildings, in the older parts of the city, where they serve as ornaments rather than otherwise, and contribute essentially to the picturesque grandeur of the place. Of late years Edinburgh has acquired the epithet of modern Athens, a title conferred by writers on account of its literary character, and striking resemblance in situation to that ancient and renowned city. In panoramic beauty, its site is certainly unequalled by any city that I have yet seen on this side of the waters, which, taken in connection with the curious disorder of the buildings in the Old Town, and the symmetrical proportions of the streets in the New, presents to the eye a picture of rare and singular grandeur. From Calton Hill, which rises higher than the tallest spire near the centre of the city, and is ascended by a flight of stone steps, the visitor is furnished with a view of the environs that will fully repay for the trouble and fatigue of climbing.

> "Traced like a map the landscape lies,
> In cultured beauty stretching wide;
> There Pentland's green acclivities;
> There Ocean with its azure tide;
> There Arthur's Seat; and gleaming through
> The Southern wing, Dunedin blue;
> While in the orient Lammer's daughters,
> A distant giant range, are seen,
> North Berwick-Law with cone of green,
> And bass amid the waters."

It is not natural or artificial beauties alone that render Edinburgh so attractive, for many of its localities teem with recollections of "the majestic past," and are associated with events of deep historical importance. Many of its localities have been invested with interest no less engrossing by the transcendent genius of Sir Walter Scott, who has done more for Scotland than Scotland ever did for herself. His writings have not only refreshed and embellished the incidents of history, but have conferred on many a spot previously unknown to fame, a reputation as enduring as the rock of ages. In literary eminence, also, Edinburgh claims a distinguished place, and its prosperity depends essentially upon its college and schools, and still more essentially upon the courts of judicature. The former attract many youths from great distances who are desirous of obtaining a liberal education at a moderate expense; the latter afford employment for the gentlemen of the legal profession, who constitute at least one third of the population in the higher and middle ranks of society, a proportion greater than you will find in any other city. Do not understand me that all subsist solely by their professional gains; a considerable number of them are gentlemen wholly independent of their profession, who have joined the body on account of the *status* which they acquire from the learning and accomplishment of its members.

Edinburgh has no extensive manufactures like its sister city Glasgow, and is consequently exempt from those sudden mercantile convulsions productive of so much misery in large manufacturing towns. Printing and publishing are carried on more extensively than any other branch of industry. In this department, Edinburgh far surpasses all the towns of the kingdom, London only excepted; many of the most valuable and popular works of the age emanating from her press. According to the recent census there appears to be a greater numerical disproportion in the sexes than there ever was before; the tables show an excess of the females amounting to upwards of sixteen thousand. Upon inquiry, I was informed by an intelligent gentleman residing here, that this strange fact is mainly to be attributed to the stationary or retrograde state of industrial occupation in the city, the young men being obliged to seek for employment in other fields of enterprise, while the weaker sex, less adventurous, and less able to indulge the spirit of adventure where it exists, are compelled to remain in the place of their nativity and maintain themselves as domestics, or in any other way that opportunity offers.

Of the public edifices it may be observed, that while the greater number are distinguished by chaste design and excellent masonry, there are none of those sumptuous and elegant structures which, like St. Paul's or Westminster Abbey, Parliament House, and many other places throughout the kingdom, strike the beholder with wonder, and astonish alike by their magnitude and their architectural splendor. In no city, however, is the general standard of excellence so well maintained; although you find no edifice here to overwhelm the imagination by its magnificence, there are comparatively few to offend taste by their deformity or meanness of design.

The hospitals of this city for the education and maintenance of poor and fatherless children, or children whose parents are in indigent circumstances, are decidedly the most imposing structures and proudest ornaments to be seen any where in Scotland. Out of ten or twelve buildings termed hospitals, Heriot's and Donaldson's are the largest and conducted on the most extensive and improved plans. The former owes its foundation to George Heriot, jeweller to James VI., more familiarly known to us as the "jingling Geordie" of "The Fortunes of Nigel." The latter was founded by a printer of Edinburgh, who died in 1830, and bequeathed the greater part of his estate, amounting to nearly £200,000, for the purpose of building and keeping in operation a hospital for poor boys and girls. The course of instruction in these institutions is very thorough, embracing the classics, the modern languages, and all the various branches of a complete English education. Pupils are admitted between the ages of seven and ten, and generally leave at fourteen, unless superior scholarship appears to fit them for prosecuting some of the learned professions, in which case the period of their term is prolonged, with the view of preparing them for the studies of the University. Upon leaving the hospitals, each boy is furnished with a Bible, and other useful books, with two suits of clothes of their own choice.

Those who leave the institutions for the purpose of learning a trade are allowed ten pounds annually for five years, and have five pounds at the termination of their apprenticeship; and those who desire to enter some of the learned professions are sent to college for four years, during which time they receive thirty pounds a year.

Aside from these advantages given to the poor, other benefits have resulted from the application of the surplus funds belonging to these institutions to the establishment of free schools and bursaries, or exhibitions, which are always open to those who do not belong to the hospitals, bringing thereby the advantages of a substantial education within the reach of every citizen, however humble.

Among the ancient buildings of Edinburgh the Palace of Holyrood is the most interesting. By those acquainted with the early history of Scotland, it is considered as almost sacred, and visited with the same feeling of reverence that possesses an American when he visits the tomb at Mount Vernon. The building has undergone so many changes from time to time in the way of alterations and additions, that it would be difficult to determine the prevailing style of architecture, or to affix a precise date to any part of it. It is in the form of a quadrangle, with a central court, and is flanked on the front with double castellated towers, imparting to it that military character which the events of Scottish history have so frequently proved to have been requisite in her royal residences. The only objects of interest now to be seen in the Palace are the *bed of Queen Mary*, which remains in the same state as when last occupied by that unfortunate princess, and the *closet* where the murderers of Rizzio surprised their victim. Stains are still shown by the cicerone at the door of the apartments, which she in an air theatrical told us were produced by the blood of the murdered man. The largest room in the Palace is the Picture Gallery, which is filled with pieces of colored canvas, in gilt frames, called portraits, and said to be likenesses of all the Scottish kings; but they are executed in such a barbarous style that you would find it difficult (without a guide) to determine whether the artist intended them for likenesses of Scottish kings or Africans. The Duke of Hamilton (hereditary keeper) occupies the Palace while in Edinburgh, and on public occasions it is still used for levees and entertainments. During his absence it is thrown open for the inspection of strangers, who, as at all such places throughout Great Britain, are expected to drain their pockets of small change for the benefit of stupid cicerones, whose presence tends more to annoy and mar the pleasure of a visit, than will compensate for the little information they retail in their oft repeated story.

After going through the halls of old Holyrood, we proceeded up High street, familiarly known as the place where John Knox, the great reformer, lived and preached. The building having fallen into a very dilapidated state, was ordered several years since to be taken down, but a subscription for its preservation was immediately raised by some of the more public-spirited of the citizens, and this interesting old relic permitted to remain as a memorial of its former occupant. It has recently been restored by the purchasers, who have taken great care to preserve every feature of the building, and placed a family within to exhibit it to strangers and protect it from spoliation. As we entered the old house, my attention was attracted by the following admonitory inscription over the door:

"*Lufe. God. above. al. and. your. neebour. as. yourself.*"

And close beneath the window from which Knox is said to have preached to the populace, I observed a rude effigy of the reformer stuck up on the corner in the attitude of addressing the passers by. The old arm-chair and several other interesting pieces of furniture used by John Knox are shown to visitors, and a beautiful steel engraving of the building is furnished at a very moderate price. Pursuing our way up High street, we came to the Castle, which occupies the most prominent site in Edinburgh, and may be said to form the nucleus around which the city has arisen. The period of its foundadation is involved in mystery. The earliest name by which it is known in history is *Castrum Puellarum*, or "The Camp of the Maidens," from the daughters of the Pictish kings being reared and tutored within its walls. Like most of the fortresses in Scotland, it has experienced vicissitudes peculiar to her early history, and was frequently taken and retaken by various conflicting parties. It is one of the four fortresses which, by the articles of Union, are to be kept constantly fortified, and contains at present accommodation for two thousand soldiers, and space sufficient in the armory to hold thirty thousand stand of arms. There is nothing very curious or interesting in the structure of the Castle. It consists of a series of irregular fortifications, which were at one time considered impregnable; but at the present age it is regarded as utterly useless. Many things connected with great historical events are exhibited in the Castle by an order from the Lord Provost, which is never refused when properly applied for. The Scottish regalia are to be seen in an apartment called the crown room every day from twelve to three o'clock. These insignia of royalty consist of a crown, a sceptre, and a sword of state; along with them is also shown the Lord Treasurer's rod of office, found deposited in the same old oak chest in which the regalia was discovered by Sir Walter Scott. Compared with the crown jewels of England, they are of small value; but taken in connection with the many associations connected with them, they are inestimable. The room where Queen Mary gave birth to James VI., in whom the crowns of England and Scotland were united, the huge piece of artillery called Mons Meg and his wife Meg, are also exhibited to strangers, besides a number of other interesting things too numerous to mention.

Besides these old buildings which are interesting mainly on account of the associations connected with them, the city of Edinburgh can boast of many modern structures that are fit to adorn any place. Among them may be mentioned the High School, Parliament House, St. Giles' Cathedral, and the Royal Institution for the Encouragement of the Fine Arts in Scotland. The latter named building contains the paintings of the Scottish artists—comprehending specimens of Wilkie, Etty, Turner, Maclise, Stanfield, Roberts, and other artists of distinction.

The monuments of this city attract more attention probably than any other objects. They are very numerous, and some of them exceedingly beautiful and costly. On Calton Hill, which I have alluded to in the beginning of this letter, there are several monuments worthy of notice; but as I am pressed for space, and wish to notice others of more importance, will merely mention their names. The first that attracts the notice of the visitor is the graceful monument to Dugald Stewart; and close by one of equal beauty to Professor Playfair. Upon the summit of the hill stands Nelson's Monument, a structure more ponderous than elegant, but which, though wholly destitute of grandeur of design, becomes impressive from its great size and elevated position. Near it is the Old Observatory, and twelve columns of the National Monument, an unfinished structure intended to commemorate the *heroes* who fell at Waterloo. The splendor of the projected building (which was to be a literal reproduction of the Parthenon) was worthy of a better cause, where

Scottish valor achieved some glory, unaided by allied powers. In the centre of St. Andrew's Square, which is in the most beautiful part of the city, there is a monument erected to the memory of Lord Melville; it rises one hundred and thirty feet in height, besides the statue, which measures fourteen feet more. The design is that of a Trojan column, the shaft being fluted, instead of ornamented with sculpture as in the ancient model. Throughout the principal streets are to be seen a number of bronze statues representing the different sovereigns, and other distinguished characters in Scottish history; but the most important testimonial in the city is the monument to Sir Walter Scott, which was designed by George M. Kemp, and completed in the year 1844. It is situated in the most public part of Prince street, the great thoroughfare of Edinburgh, is constructed of a beautiful quality of sandstone, and is two hundred feet in height; a stair of two hundred and eighty-seven steps conducts to the gallery at the top. "In each part of the monument, above the principal arch, are six small niches, making a total of twenty-four in the main structure, besides thirty-two others in the piers and abutment towers. These niches are to be occupied by sculptural impersonations of the characters, historical and fanciful, portrayed in the writings of Sir Walter. The following statues now occupy the four principal niches which crown the four lowest arches, viz.: the statue of Prince Charles, (from Waverley,) drawing his sword; Meg Merrilies, (from Guy Mannering,) breaking the sapling over the head of Lady Bertram; Lady of the Lake, stepping from a boat to shore; and the Last Minstrel, playing on his harp. Under the arches in the monument is a beautiful marble statue of Scott, by Steel; a fine work of art, and said to be a most faithful likeness. The inscription is appropriate, and the monument well worthy to commemorate the genius of the departed great.

After viewing the monuments in the city, we made an excursion to "fair Melrose," which is situated in the vale of the Tweed, near the foot of Eildon Hill. The village at present is utterly devoid of interest; but the country round about is every where fertile and picturesque; while the famous Abbey yet stands in beauteous ruins, presenting to the eye the finest specimen of Gothic sculpture and Gothic architecture ever reared in this country. A few miles beyond Melrose is Abbotsford, the home of Sir Walter, situated on a bank overhanging the south side of the Tweed, which here makes a beautiful sweep around the declivity on which the mansion stands. Though irregular in its proportions, the building as a whole produces a very striking effect. The visitor is ushered in by a porchway, adorned with petrified stag-horns, into a hall which is richly panelled with carved oak, from the palace of Dunfernshire; behind the cornice there is a line of coats-armorial richly blazoned, belonging to the families who kept the borders. The floor is of black and white marble from the Hebrides, and the walls are hung with ancient armor, and various specimens of military implements. We were then conducted into the armory, a narrow, low arched room, which runs quite across the house, having a blazoned window at either extremity, and filled with smaller pieces of armor and weapons. This apartment communicates with the drawing-room on one side, and the dining-room on the other. The former is a lofty saloon, with wood of cedar, and furnished with antique ebony furniture, carved cabinets, all of beautiful workmanship. The latter is a very handsome apartment, richly carved with black oak, and contains a fine collection of pictures, the most interesting of which are the family portraits, and the head of Queen Mary in a charger the day after she was beheaded. The library, which is the largest of all the apartments, is a magnificent room, fifty feet by sixty. The collection of books in this room amounts to about twenty thousand volumes, many of them extremely rare and valuable. Adjoining the library is the study in which Sir Walter wrote all of his works. His writing table, old arm-chair, and clothes worn at the time of his decease, are here shown to visitors by a cicerone employed by Mr. Lockhart, Sir Walter Scott's son-in-law, who now occupies the mansion, and allows it to be visited at all times by strangers, who are conducted through all the apartments and out-grounds.

Not far from Abbotsford and near Melrose is the Abbey of Dryburgh, which is the most melancholy-looking spot that could have been selected for the last resting place of Sir Walter. The building is almost entirely demolished by the work of time, and the only portions that are now standing are the gable of the nave of the church, the ends of the transept, part of the choir, and St. Mary's aisle. In the latter, which is by far the most beautiful part of the Abbey, are to be seen, side by side, the plain granite tombs of Sir Walter, his wife and only son, the late Col. Scott. There is no inscription on the tomb but his name, which speaks more than any epitaph that could be written. His name will live when the stone slab that now covers his mortal remains will have crumbled away; and his writings, which embrace all the beauties of the English language, will be as familiar for centuries to come as household words.

LETTER TWENTY-ONE.

PARIS.

The French Fêtes—Dinner—Theatricals and Concerts at the Hôtel de Ville—Visit to Versailles—The President's Festival at St. Cloud—Reception at the English Embassy—Ball at the Hôtel de Ville—Grand Review and Sham Fight in the Champ de Mars—Dramatic Representation at the Opera, etc

BEFORE this letter reaches you, the telegraph will have conveyed the news of the recent festivities in Paris—a succession of brilliant scenes that will long be remembered throughout the world. The Prefect of the Seine, in the name of the great city of Paris, and I may say, in that of the French nation, invited the Chief Magistrate and civic dignitaries of London, the Mayors of the different towns in England that were represented at the Exhibition, the Royal Commissioners, the Executive Committee, and all those who were in any way associated with that great work, together with a host of other distinguished foreigners, to accept the hospitalities of la belle France, upon her own soil. The generous invitation was cordially accepted; and for five days this gay metropolis and her magistrature, with a profuse expense, with the most excellent judgment, with the most perfect taste, with the most kindly feeling, and with most untiring zeal, have endeavored to show their guests that they did not underrate the importance of the occasion, or the effect it was calculated to produce, not only at home, but over public opinion throughout the civilized world. The year 1851 will hereafter constitute an important era in the history of Europe. The Exhibition of the Industry of all Nations at London first gave it an impulse, and all the events that from time to time have sprung out of it, together with those likely to ensue, are calculated to confirm and strengthen the belief that some great result is yet to be accomplished. Indeed, much has already been accomplished towards inculcating the relation of friendship, peace and good-will, between two of the most powerful and hitherto most hostile nations in Europe. Ever since the inglorious defeat of Napoleon by the allied powers on the field of Waterloo, the French people have entertained a bitter hatred towards England, have burned for an opportunity to wipe out what they consider a stain upon their escutcheon. But what do we now see? France extending the hand of fellowship to the Lord Mayor of London and his numerous retinue, in a manner unknown to Englishmen, and wholly unexpected. The city of Paris not only gave her English guests a free passage by land and sea, but for the first time abolished the passport system, and what was perhaps still more agreeable, the inspection of John Bull's portmanteau at Boulogne and the barriers—a courtesy unheard of in the English works on etiquette, and which, it is to be hoped, may teach them a lesson in politeness and cordiality of feeling.

The *Fêtes* were opened on Saturday the 2d inst. with a sumptuous dinner, given by M. Berger, the Prefect of the Seine, in behalf of the city of Paris, at the Hôtel de Ville. No place could have been selected more appropriate for the opening of the festivities—a palace distinguished alike for its magnificence and architectural beauty—the residence of the Prefect, and the head-quarters of the *Corps de Ville*, or municipality of Paris. About six o'clock the whole of the vast range of rooms, fitted up for festive receptions, were thrown open, and the invited guests began to assemble. At a lale hour the Lord Mayor of London and his suite arrived, dressed in courtly style, and full of consequence. M. Berger welcomed them to the hospitalities of Paris in a manner peculiarly happy, in which he alluded to the position of his own country and that of Great Britain among the nations of the earth, and the importance of cultivating relations of amity and friendship between the two people. The Lord from London, after being informed by an *interpreter* at his elbow as to the purport of the *Frenchman's* remarks, replied in the same complimentary strain, and pledged in a bumper of good old *Rhenish* wine the future and growing friendship of France and Great Britain. The dinner party was composed of some of the most distinguished men of the two countries, besides many from other nations, who happened to be in the city, and whose presence added much to the enjoyment and brilliance of the occasion.

At nine o'clock the cloth was removed, and the guests were ushered into a room appropriated for theatricals. The best performers in the city were selected, and a comedy arranged for the evening was presented in real *French* style, much to the amusement of the party. The closing scene of the evening was decidedly the most interesting. The comedy being concluded, the guests were attracted to the Grand Saloon by the sound of many voices and music of surpassing beauty. All of the first-rate musicians that could be procured, assisted by one hundred operatic voices, and conducted by the celebrated Strauss, were placed on an elevated stage in one end of the brilliantly illuminated room, where they discoursed music of the most select character in a manner highly creditable, and much to the gratification of all who had the pleasure of being present.

The following day being Sunday, (which is *the* day in France,) the same circle of guests, and thousands more, were invited by the Prefect of Paris to visit the galleries and sylvan shades of Versailles, rendered especially attractive by the announcement that the *grandes eaux* would be seen in full play. From an early hour in the morning until late in the afternoon the powers of accommodation of *rive droite* and *rive gauche* railways were put to a severe test by the incessant crowds besieging their termini, and asking to be conveyed at any price to the palace of all the glories of France. They proved equal to the emergency; and train after train, with two locomotives and one mile in length, crammed within and without, were dispatched with a degree of order and punctuality which is rarely seen in other countries on such occasions.

Versailles is situated about four leagues from the capital, and contains a population of 30,000 inhabitants. The château and two small palaces called the Grand Trianon and Petit Trianon constitute the only attractions of the place. The palace was built by Louis XIV., at the enormous cost of forty millions sterling, including the gardens and fountains. It is considered the finest palace in the world, and certainly possesses attractions far superior to any thing to be seen in England. It belongs to the government, and is kept up at an enormous expense, as a place of resort for strangers. The company were first ushered though the state apartments, which are six miles in length, beautifully furnished, and filled with paintings of the old masters and modern artists of merit, forming a complete history of France, and furnishing the visitor with a collection of the fine arts no where else to be seen. After viewing and admiring the beauties of the château, the company were invited into the gardens, where the waters of innumerable fountains sparkled in the glowing sunshine of as lovely a day as ever dawned. The aspect of the grounds, filled with beautiful avenues, broad sheets of water, exotics from every clime, statuary, promenaders attired in every conceivable hue, and the feathery jets spouting in a thousand forms, was brilliant in the extreme. As the hour approached for the principal fountain in the *Piece de Neptune* to launch its maze of glittering sprays into the air, the sloping bank of turf which forms a vast amphitheatre around it became more and more densely crowded with spectators. At about five o'clock the Lord Mayor of London and the invited guests made their appearance in a space immediately in front of the fountain allotted to those who were provided with cards of invitation. Over one hundred thousand persons were present on this occasion, and when the Prefect gave the signal for the outbreak of the waters, a stream of jets crossing each other in the most graceful curves, spread itself out high and wide over the seething surface of the great basin, accompanied by the martial strains of music and the shouting of the populace, and forming upon the whole a scene of incredible splendor. After remaining some time contemplating the spectacle before them, the vast crowd gradually began to move, and poured its streams through the various gates of the park once more to invade the railway stations.

The gorgeous festival given by the President of the Republic in the galleries and gardens of St. Cloud, on Monday evening, constituted the third of the series of *fêtes*, and will long be remembered by all who had the pleasure of witnessing the happy reception given by Louis Napoleon to the Lord Mayor of London, in the favorite château of his uncle, the Emperor. The palace, which is now the summer residence of the President, is beautifully situated on the Seine, two leagues west of Paris, and is one of the most elegant and interesting country seats in all France. The buildings and outgrounds are on a small scale compared with Versailles, but it is far more desirable as a place of residence, and certainly much better suited for Napoleon, who, unlike his predecessor the King, has no *responsibilities* to look after, and consequently requires but little room in his state of *single blessedness.* The Corinthian order prevails in the construction of the outer walls, and the interior is fitted up in a style that smacks more of royalty than republicanism. Valuable furniture and costly ornaments adorn the state apartments, and the walls are hung with Gobelin tapestry, containing exquisite copies from the series of paintings executed by Rubens for Marie de Medicis. The park, which is about four leagues in circumference, is beautifully diversified, presenting varieties of wood and water, patches of level sward, and picturesque acclivities of the most agreeable character. At three o'clock, the hour appointed for the reception, the road to St. Cloud was lined with the elegant equipages of the invited guests, the dazzling display of the military, and thousands of people assembled on the sidewalks to witness the gorgeous retinue. Arrived at the palace, the President and the Lord Mayor of London promenaded through the state apartments and gardens, accompanied by their suites, and receiving the civilities of their guests amid the playing of fountains and sweet strains of martial music, until the banqueting hour was announced. Here a scene was presented that reminded me very much of an American barbecue. The table was set in the *Salle de l'Orangerie*, where the events of the 18th Brumaire took place, a long and plain room measuring about one hundred and forty by seventy feet. As soon as the doors were opened, the crowd rushed in, ladies and all, making a general scramble for the edibles and wines, equal to the famous mob at the recent entertainment at Guildhall in London. The French officers, who constituted a considerable part of the company, acted on this occasion in a manner totally different from the real character of French gentlemen, and very disrespectfully to their invited guests. They contrived in the general struggle to occupy the best places at table; eating and drinking half the spoils of war, spilling the remainder in the struggle, and swallowing more ice than might have served to cool the ardor of the whole French army, doubtless to mark their delicate appreciation of similar proceedings on the part of John Bull at Guildhall. But, bating these trifles, which were, perhaps, only concessions to English habits and tastes, we have ample reason to be thankful for the bounteous hospitalities and festivities at St. Cloud.

The following afternoon the Marquis and Marchioness of Normanby gave a grand reception, which may be considered as part of the exhibition fêtes, the intention being to do honor to those who participated in the previous entertainments. The cards of invitation intimated that their "Excellencies would be at home" from three to six, and soon after three nearly all of the guests had arrived at the embassy. Each one's name was called out, and they were received by the ambassador, who stood at the entrance of the second saloon, and introduced them to the ambassadress. At four o'clock the President of the Republic arrived, dressed in plain clothes, as at the fête of St. Cloud, wearing the grand cordon of the Legion of Honor. Soon after he was announced the Prince gave his arm to the Marchioness of Normanby, and proceeded to a beautiful lawn at the back of the *Hôtel*, where seats had been placed for the accommodation of the company, and where they were entertained with military and other airs by an excellent brass band at the extremity of the lawn, relieved occasionally by an orchestra in the gallery of the hotel, and an *American rope-dancer*, who performed all sorts of antics in a manner highly creditable to his profession, and amusing those whose tastes run in that way. Soon after these exhibitions, the doors of the *buffet* were thrown open, and the choicest refreshments in great abundance were at the disposition of the company. The party was one of the largest and most elegant of the season. The company retired gradually at an early hour in order to make the necessary preparations for the grand ball given by M. Berger, the Prefect of the Seine, at the *Hôtel de Ville*, which presented a spectacle of magnificence not often witnessed in the sober working world in which we live, and which might be called the crowning festival of the series, did we not remember that the spectacle of the great review in the Champ de Mars, and the dramatic representation at the opera the following day, were each, in their own peculiar manner, as splendid and as gratifying as those which preceded them.

It is impossible to speak or write of scenes like these, if we express the admiration and approval which they demand, without using language that, to those who were not privileged to be present, may appear exaggerated and fanciful; but even the cooler judgment of those far away, who will merely read of those scenes, will approve the spirit which dictated them, and look hopefully towards the good results that must undoubtedly flow from them. In this ball of unrivalled splendor, the ancient supremacy of this beautiful city in its own unapproachable line has been vindicated to the full. Each element of life, and beauty, and grace, which Paris knows so well how to use, was invoked and answered to the appeal. And if the appeal was somewhat overcharged—if invention, taxed beyond its powers, has here and there approached the verge of extravagance, we must not complain, but attribute all to a worthy and hospitable intention. On this occasion the entire palace was thrown open, and illuminated in a manner far more pleasing to look at than easy to describe. The company, after wending their way through a line of cavalry one mile in length, amid the shouts of the populace on the sidewalks, were ushered into the state apartments by way of the lofty marble staircase upon which were placed corbeils of the rarest flowers, intermingled with tall girandoles of gilt bronze, a blaze of light being poured down on the whole from chandeliers suspended from the roof. The landing above presented even a richer display of shrubs and flowers, and all so arranged as to be in keeping with the hangings of the adjoining rooms. Two ball rooms were fitted out for dancing, the magnificent *Galerie des Fêtes* on the one side, and the *Salle du Trône* on the other. In the former, the celebrated Strauss, who came up from the baths of Vichy to preside at this great festival with a superb orchestra, were stationed on an elevated stage in one end of the room, thus presenting an unbroken view of the entire apartment, with a long range of pillars on each side, and the rays of a thousand wax lights beaming on the curtains of white and yellow silk, on the delicate ornamental paintings of the walls, the many-colored flags of all nations which waved above, and the beauty and grace of every clime below, formed a *coup d'œil* of surpassing brilliancy. The *Salle du Trône* was also fitted up in an elegant manner, and the apartments between the ball rooms were arranged with equal magnificence and taste. Nothing could surpass the beauty of the brocade furniture, tapestry, statuary, and gilt bronzes that every where met the eye. The open Court of Louis XIV. was filled with flowers, and brilliantly lit up, serving as a place of promenade during the night. The play of water in the fountain which occupied the centre of the square, and the odor of the flowers and orange trees placed around, were delightfully refreshing after the heat of the crowded ball rooms. At half-past eleven the ball was at its height, when the President of the Republic and the Lord Mayor of London made their appearance. They were received throughout their progress with every mark of respect, and acknowledged their reception by saluting on each side. It is estimated that six thousand persons were present during the evening, and the arrangements were so complete that not the least confusion arose. Out of this vast assembly our own country was well represented—citizens from nearly every State in the Union were present, and none more largely represented than Tennessee.

On the following day Paris "abandoned itself," to use its own phrase, to a fête that all were permitted to see. The previous fêtes were exclusive and narrowed within particular limits; but when the day arrived for the grand review and sham fight, the whole city as it were turned out, and for the first time exhibited symptoms of a popular holiday. The French leap to the sound of a trumpet, and work themselves up into ecstasies in the midst of the roar of cannon. Republican simplicity and economy is utterly lost sight of and dazzled by the sparkle of epaulets, and only a few minds of the first order ever soar above the *régime* of percussion muskets and revolving pistols. At an early hour of the day hawkers cried the programme of the operations along all the principal streets, which were crowded with working men and women hurrying westward to the all-attractive Champ de Mars. The sea of humanity continued to flow in uninterrupted streams until three o'clock, (the hour appointed for the mock battle,) when the field of action was skirted by deep ranks of an eager, but orderly crowd. Every available point was occupied—housetops furnished perches for thousands. Every elevated garden was converted into a pile of scaffolding, tenanted by enthusiastic spectators armed with telescopes, etc.

Without giving you the details of military operations, which would prove dry and uninteresting, I will merely sketch the general notion of the plan, and the character of the ground. The Champ de Mars is a large open space, bounded by trees on two sides, and stretching in the shape of an oblong square from one of the façades of the Invalides to the river Seine. The field is as turfless as the public square in Nashville, and about as dry and dusty. Opposite the centre of it a substantial stone bridge (the Pont de Vienne) crosses the Seine, not far from the celebrated Champs Elysées, and above the bridge on the opposite bank the ground rises in steep heights and ridges covered with houses. The ridge is termed the Trocadero, and this was the place of battle. One army was supposed to be in the Champ de Mars, the other on the heights of the Trocadero. Those in the field were the attacking body. The bridge of Vienne was supposed to be well defended by the troops occupying the heights beyond it, so that it became necessary for the assailing army not only to attack the Pont de Vienne, but to throw a bridge of pontoons over the river, so as to attack the Trocadero troops in front and flank. This manœuvre accomplished, and the Pont de Vienne forced at the same time, the battle was to be waged among the slopes of the Trocadero, until the invading party, repulsed, recrossed the bridge pursued by their opponents, and the engagement was to end in a pitched battle in the Champ de Mars. This is a faint description of the preconcerted plan of the manœuvre. At three o'clock, the troops, having arrived from their respective barracks, began to take up their stations as above described. I was informed by an officer, that, including the artillery, infantry, and cavalry, there were on the ground nearly fifty thousand men, which I suppose to be correct, as there are more than one hundred thousand troops within the barriers of Paris. Soon after the two conflicting armies were arranged in battle array, Louis Napoleon entered the field, on a noble animal, followed by a gaily uniformed staff, all mounted on handsome chargers, and composed of representatives of every French cavalry regiment, and many belonging to foreign services, among which I noticed English, Prussian, and Tuscan officers. The President as he rode along was warmly greeted by the tribunals and populace, which he received in a manner of becoming grace and dignity. He had been but a few minutes in the field when operations commenced, and the first rush of light infantry was made across the bridge, supported by the fire of field artillery from both the lower and upper sides. Into the minutiæ of the campaign, which lasted one hour and a half, I do not intend to enter, not being sufficiently acquainted with military tactics to give an intelligible description. Indeed, the dust in the field created by the cavalry was so dense that I lost sight of part of the operations conducted in the vicinity of the Pont de Vienne.

The preconcerted engagement went on according to stipulation· the artillery on both sides of the river kept up an incessant fire; the attacking columns, supported by field pieces and cavalry, rushed cheeringly across the bridge, and the roll of musketry swelled upon the breeze like the continuous rattle of drums in the distance. The heights of the Trocadero were thus obstinately contested for nearly an hour, the firing being incessant, and the movement of the troops exceedingly rapid, when the attacking party began to give way. Their drums and bugles sounded the retreat, and they recrossed the bridge, covered by the fire of the artillery, while regiments as yet unengaged advanced to receive the enemy on either flank. Some good artillery movement followed, the retreating party sweeping the bridge with their field pieces, and then retiring, covering the movement by rapid charges of cavalry as the head-quarters of the enemy's columns marched from the bridge. The same manœuvres were four times repeated—first by the tirailleurs—then those of the attacking but repulsed party retreated, and the two lines of artillery opened their fire. Supported in this manner, the cavalry dashed out; their opponents formed into squares, and repulsed them, still, however, retiring and allowing the sharp shooters and artillery to come again into play. In this engagement of the contending parties was contained the whole of the strategy. I was particularly interested during the engagement in observing the powers, docility, and fine qualities of the horses of the cavalry, lancers, hussars, and cuirassiers. They are far superior to those in the English service, and are much better trained to stand the smoke of powder. In the charge these troops uttered a wild shrieking cry, not like the yell of an American Indian, but to the highest notes of a Frenchman's voice. The lancers in charging kept in ranks like cuirassiers, and made no show of using their weapons, holding the points steadily in the air. The cuirassiers and hussars flourished their swords, but neither made any use of firearms, carbines, or pistols. The sham fight being over, the contending armies united their strength, and defiled in long and magnificent procession before the President of the Republic, and distinguished guests in the tribunes—arms presented and bands playing—marching to their respective barracks, highly delighted with the performances of the day. The generals in command of the troops were General Condit, who occupied the Trocadero, and

General Guillabert, whose forces were stationed in the Champ de Mars.

On the same evening, the long and splendid fêtes of the week were concluded with a magnificent opera, confined exclusively to those who were so fortunate as to procure tickets of invitation. The major portion of the entertainments produced for the occasion were evidently chosen with a view of enabling the foreign visitors to form some idea of the immense musical, scenic, and terpsichorean resources of this celebrated place of amusement. They consisted of the first act of Halevy's opera *La Juive*, the fourth act of Meyerbeer's *Huguenots*, and the second act of Auber's *Enfant Prodigue*. Nothing could exceed the magnificence of decoration, and the scenic effects with which those fragments of the glories of the opera were produced. But the greatest event of the evening was an operatic divertissement composed expressly for the occasion, and entitled *Les Nations*. In the words of the programme, the piece is in honor of "the Titans, who by their new conquests have brought steel and iron to obedience." The whole affair was gotten up to represent the Exhibition—the Crystal Palace, and the marvels of art, science, and manufacturing skill collected within it, in which ample homage should be rendered to the various nations which have contributed to that magnificent and wonderful collection. The house was crowded to excess, and the *coup d'œil* was brilliant in the extreme—nearly the entire auditory being in full dress. Most of the distinguished men of France, with the Lord Mayor of London and his suite, were present.

It is impossible to reflect on the brilliant scenes which I have so feebly described without congratulating both the hospitable entertainers and their honored guests, on what each have achieved for their respective countries. From first to last, Paris has worthily maintained her ancient character, as the city of chivalry, and the home of arts. The refined taste and dignified splendor which presided over and illustrated all the proceedings, were in every way worthy to be remembered by all who had the privilege of participation. The *Fêtes* of 1851 mark an epoch in the intercourse between France and England, from which we sincerely hope there will be dated the establishment of relations of peace and amity, based upon the surest of all foundations, a familiar acquaintance on the part of each with the real character and purposes of the other.

LETTER TWENTY-TWO.

ANTWERP, Belgium.

Preparations for a Continental Tour—Arrival in Brussels—Excursion to the Field of Waterloo—The City of Antwerp—Catholic Antiquities—Fête of the Virgin Mary—Character of the Country and condition of the Government.

SEVERAL days previous to our departure from the gay scenes of Paris, the note of preparation might have been heard throughout the Hôtel Meurice in the Rue Rivoli, somewhat louder than usual, much to the annoyance of the English, who generally infest the establishment; and more particularly of our excellent hostess, who disliked the idea of parting with old friends, who had graced her *table d'hôte* so long that she began almost to regard them as members of her family. Couriers and valets de place (who are generally indispensable nuisances) were running to and fro and changing heavy American trunks for light *malle poste bages*, and collecting for their employers all the little essentials requisite for a European tour; and at the time appointed three parties of Americans, forming a goodly number, set off together by way of the railroad for Brussels, the capital of Belgium, passing *en route* through a country wholly devoid of interest, being nothing more than a dreary plain with here and there an interminable avenue, small patches of vines of a short low kind, not trained in festoons, but about straight sticks, and a few queer old towns, drawbridged and walled, with odd old towers at the angles like grotesque faces. Ruinous old buildings of all sorts, sometimes an hôtel de ville, sometimes a guard house, sometimes a low dwelling-house covered with lightning rods, and sometimes an old château with a rank garden prolific in dandelion, are the standard objects that meet the eye, repeated over and over again. The monotony, however, of the country was somewhat alleviated by the excellence and comfort of the cars, together with the politeness and strict attention bestowed on the passengers by the conductor and officers of the road. We reached Brussels in about eight hours, including the detention at the custom house, and procured excellent apartments at the Hôtel Bellevue, situated near the King's Palace, and fronting on the Park, the most convenient and central part of the city. Brussels is a miniature Paris, and to one who has visited the French metropolis and is acquainted with Parisian manners and costumes the similarity will be readily observed. Besides the language, which is the same, (with the exception of the lower orders, who speak only Flemish,) and a certain affectation of French style perceptible in society here, the town of Brussels has its little opera, its cafés like those in the Palais Royal, a palace garden, called the Tuileries, and its Boulevards resembling those of the city of Paris. It has a population of about one hundred and fifty thousand, including the suburbs, and contains many handsome public buildings, distinguished alike for beauty and architectural superiority. The King's Palace, Palace of the Prince of Orange, (the late King of Holland,) Palais de la Nation, built by Maria Theresa for the meetings of the Council of Brabant, Cathedral and Hôtel de Ville, are all beautiful buildings and much admired. In the public squares I noticed several monuments, statues and jets, of some merit. The *Place des Martyrs* contains a large monument, erected over the grave of more than three hundred Belgians, who were killed in the revolution of 1830. It consists of a marble statue of Liberty on a pedestal with a kneeling genius in each of the four corners. Below and around it runs a sort of subterranean gallery or catacomb, which contains the remains of the slain. And in the Place Royal there stands a bronze equestrian statue of Godfrey of Bouillon that attracts much attention. The most remarkable object, however, is one of the jets, situated near the centre of the city, visited by all strangers, and regarded by the citizens with peculiar reverence. It is called the Manikin, and represents an ebon-looking figure in a stooping posture, spouting a small jet of water high in the air, to the admiration of the crowd that always stands around. Once every year this little figure is taken down, dressed up in court style, and carried round the city in state, followed by a large procession, and then replaced on the pedestal assigned for it.

For the last few years Brussels has increased her business operations far beyond any other period. Every branch of industry appears to be thriving, and more particularly her manufactures, the most remarkable of which is that of *lace*, celebrated all over the world. Strangers are allowed to visit these establishments and examine the process of lace making, which is exceedingly curious and interesting. "The peculiarity, in addition to the fineness, which distinguishes it, is, that the patterns are worked separately with most microscopic minuteness, and are afterwards sewed on." Some of these establishments have as many as two thousand females constantly employed, many of whom are required to work in confined dark rooms, into which light is admitted only partially by a small aperture, in order to discipline the eye to spinning the flax to that web-like fineness which constitutes the chief excellence of the fabric.

From Brussels the stranger always visits the field of Waterloo, a beautiful drive of about twelve miles through the *Forest of Soigne*, described by Byron as the Forest of Ardennes. This region of country has been appropriately termed the "cockpit" of Europe, as it has been for ages the ground upon which the powers of Europe have decided their difficulties. Besides the fields of Waterloo and Quatre Bras, through which the road passes, Wavre, Fleurus, Ligny, and the little village of Ramillies, where Marlborough gained one of his victories over the French and Bavarians, lie within the province of Brabant not far from the roadside. Long before reaching Waterloo we were assailed by guides and relic-venders, who make their living like their fathers before them by repeating over to every new comer the same stereotyped story, and selling buttons and bullets manufactured for the purpose, and buried in the ground a short time in order to give them an old rusty appearance. Each guide has at his tongue's end two stories—one for the English and the allied powers, and the other for the French and Americans—which they relate in the most enthusiastic manner.

By a natural instinct they are able to locate the visitor immediately, and if he be an English subject, look out for the high eulogium upon Wellington and his *Spartan band;* but if, on the contrary, he be an American citizen, (who are supposed here to favor the French side of the question,) they will speak of the disadvantageous position occupied by Napoleon, and the failure of Grouchy in executing his orders, which resulted in the overthrow of the French army.

The best view of the field is from the top of the *Mound of the Belgic Lion,* erected to commemorate the spot where the Prince of Orange was wounded. It is a vast heap of earth collected from the field of battle, and thrown up to the height of two hundred feet, beneath which the bones of friends and foes lie indiscriminately together; a flight of steps leads up to the top, which is surmounted by a huge cast lion facing France, with its right paw placed on a globe, conveying the idea of exultation and defiance, which has been denied, and said to be intended only as a memorial, a trophy and a tomb. The field from this eminence presents the appearance of a perfectly open and undulating plain of great fertility and beauty, and the places so renowned in history are now covered with products of peace and industry. The following morning our agreeable party that set out together from Paris found it necessary to separate, as our plans were different; one party started for the cold region of St. Petersburg, another for the banks of the beautiful Rhine, and the third for this curious old city. Antwerp is a strongly fortified place, and contains a population of about eighty thousand. In the height of its splendor and prosperity, during the sixteenth century, it is said to have numbered two hundred thousand, and was the richest and most commercial city in Europe. Its merchants were princes in wealth, and their houses splendid palaces. "During this period as many as twenty-five hundred vessels were sometimes seen at one time, lying in the Schelde, laden with the productions of all quarters of the globe; five hundred loaded wagons on an average entered its gates daily from the country. The amount of money put into circulation annually was enormous; and five thousand merchants met twice every day on the exchange." The decay and fall of its prosperity is attributed to the establishment of the Inquisition, and tyranny of Alva, under the directions of his haughty master, Philip II. of Spain, which drove thousands of industrious citizens to seek refuge elsewhere; and to the memorable siege of fourteen months in 1585, which ended in its capture by the Duke of Parma. Like Brussels, it has of late years improved very much, and although inferior to many places in a commercial point of view, it possesses many attractions for the stranger fond of looking at the curiosities of antiquity, and the works of ancient artists. It would be sufficient to mention the great names of Rubens (who lived here) and of Vandyck, Teniers, Jordaens, Quentin Matsys, etc., who were natives of Antwerp, or its neighborhood, to show the high reputation it deserves for its encouragement of the arts. Although trade and commerce have deserted Antwerp, their consequences, in a variety of instances, particularly in the great works of art produced here, still remain behind; the power and genius of Rubens and Vandyck, whose masterpieces are still to be seen here in the museum and churches, are no where else to be equally understood and appreciated.

In this city the Catholic religion has full sway; nearly all the churches belong to them, and most of the citizens are attached to the Catholic faith. In these old buildings, several of which are very fine, there is much to interest one unaccustomed to such things. In the Dominican church there is a representation of Calvary, an artificial eminence raised against the walls of the church covered with slate or rock-work, and planted with statues of saints, angels, patriarchs, and prophets. On the summit is a representation of the crucifixion, and at the base there is a grotto taken in imitation of the Holy Sepulchre in Jerusalem. As we entered it the body of Christ was presented to our view, encircled with the habiliments of silk and muslin; while to the face of the rock near the entrance are attached boards covered and painted to represent the glowing flames of purgatory, in the midst of which appear a number of faces, bearing the expression of agony, and intended to remind the people of the sufferings of the souls of the wicked in that place of torment. The Cathedral of Notre Dame is one of the largest churches and most beautiful specimens of Gothic architecture in the Netherlands; the great attraction in it, is the celebrated masterpiece of Rubens—the Descent from the Cross; but, to me, the fête of the ascension of the Virgin Mary, taken in connection with the magnificence of the dress, the costliness of the jewels, and the singularity of the Catholic forms, constituted one of the most curious spectacles I have ever witnessed. On the day of this celebration, which is in the month of August, the whole city was crowded with people from the country, who flocked in with their baskets of provisions and gala apparel to witness the fête, affording me an opportunity which I should not otherwise have had of seeing the manners and costumes of the people.

Take it all together, Antwerp is rather a queer old place; particularly to an American, who is so little accustomed to the old way of doing things. Every thing here is done according to law, which applies to every occupation and person, from King Leopold himself down to the lowest fish-monger. While walking through the streets, my attention was attracted to a crowd of persons standing around an iron railing, in which there were fifty or a hundred baskets filled with live craw-fish, which they were selling off at auction to the highest bidder; upon inquiry, I was informed that they were not allowed to sell them privately, but required to carry them to certain places established by law, and sell to the person who gives the highest bid.

Belgium is one of the most beautiful and interesting countries in Europe; the soil is of the best quality, and cultivated upon scientific principles, reminding me forcibly of the manner of culture in England. Since the separation of the Netherlands and the elevation of King Leopold to the throne, Belgium has prospered in a manner that surprises even her own people.

LETTER TWENTY-THREE.

AMSTERDAM, Holland.

Trip from Antwerp to Rotterdam—The Hague—Paintings—Canals and Railroads—Appearance of Amsterdam—Excursions to Haerlem and Brock—Government of Holland, and Condition of the Country.

AFTER spending several days most delightfully in examining the antiquities of Antwerp, we took passage on a Dutch steamer for the city of Rotterdam, a trip occupying eight hours, and wholly devoid of interest. The scenery on the Schelde and Maas, like that of the Mississippi below New-Orleans, is entirely monotonous, having low banks, little or no cultivation, and inferior habitations. The banks of the Maas are covered with wind-mills, all of which were in full operation when we neared the city, presenting a scene entirely new to me, and so singular in appearance, that I could but reflect upon the ingenuity of man and the great variety of ways resorted to in this part of the word to reclaim lands from the water; while we in America had thousands and thousands of acres high and dry, occupied only by a few straggling settlers and the wild beasts of the forest. These mills are nearly all occupied by families who make their living solely by their operations in manufactures, grinding purposes, and in pumping water off the lands, which is absolutely necessary to protect them from the invasion of the sea. They are not confined alone to this region, but are scattered all over the land, as numerous as the sand on the sea-shore, and the stars in heaven. Holland is emphatically a country of wind-mills, canals, dykes, and ditches; without them the visitor would fail to realize his idea of the Dutchman's home, and the Dutchman himself would feel very much like a duck out of water.

The city of Rotterdam, since the separation of Holland and Belgium, has increased rapidly in population and commercial importance. It is built in the form of a triangle, and consists of as many canals as streets; the three principal ones open in the river, and communicate with numerous smaller canals which intersect the town; thus not only keeping the canals constantly supplied with water, but, by the ebbing and flowing of the lake, a circulation is kept up which prevents stagnation and sickness. This city, like most commercial places, possesses few attractions in the way of fine public buildings and monuments of art; but to a stranger who has never seen a Dutch town before, it is particularly interesting. After procuring lodgings at the new Bath Hotel, on the Quay, sufficiently comfortable for one night, we commenced the work of sight-seeing, which is considered by experienced travellers as a matter of no small moment, as it involves in most instances not only expense but fatigue and annoyances without number. Having no special object to see but a bronze statue of Erasmus, erected near the centre of the city on a wide bridge over a canal, we occupied the afternoon in merely walking through the streets and observing the novel and picturesque combination of water, bridges, and shipping in the heart of a populous city. The buildings are mostly constructed with the gables facing the street, and often overhanging the foundation more than a foot, a peculiarity more striking in the narrow thoroughfares, as it frequently occurs that the houses are so close together at the top that the sun never reaches the inhabitants below. This is to be attributed to the insecurity of the foundations, the whole city being built on piles which must settle and give way more or less by the action of time. While examining the structure of the houses as we passed along, our attention was drawn to another Dutch custom which is exceedingly annoying to curious young men who delight in receiving the furtive glances of the fair ones. By means of little mirrors (spions) projecting in front of the windows, and consisting of two pieces of glass placed at an angle of 45° to each other, the one reflecting up, and the other down the street, the Dutch lady may see all that passes outside, without the trouble of going to the window, or the necessity of exposing herself to the vulgar gaze. Here she sits ensconced behind the gauze blind, knitting, sewing or reading, according to her fancy, while we poor fellows go stumbling along blind to all their charms and indifferent to their gaze.

Being excluded by this vile custom from a sight of the Dutch aristocracy, we determined not to be outdone, and proceeded to the *Kirmess*, a sort of fair or carnival that exhibits many peculiarities of character. The streets in the portion of the city where we witnessed this exhibition were lined on either side with booths, in which all kinds of comic representations of a low nature were presented, and every namable trinket offered for sale. In Antwerp, I witnessed the sale of craw-fish and frogs at auction, which is required by a municipal law; and at this fair, gingerbread and pancakes, baked on the spot and cried off to the highest bidder by rosy-cheeked girls, seemed to be in great demand, and created more interest than all else besides. To a stranger who is fond of a good merry laugh, a visit to one of these fairs is worth, of itself, a trip to Holland; for, aside from the various exhibitions and sales at auction, he is furnished with the opportunity of hearing national melodies and witnessing the peculiarities of dress and manners among the lower classes. The servant girls, when being hired, always stipulate with their masters for a certain number of holidays or kirmess-days; and they swarm at these festivals in company with their "sweethearts," (whom they frequently hire for the occasion,) attend in their best gala gowns, the waistband of which usually strikes them just below the armpit, which, together with the gold headband, curious hats, and wooden shoes, forms a complete picture, and subject of mirth for the stranger.

The following morning we started to the Hague, per railroad, as far as the ancient town of Delft, where we changed our conveyance for variety sake, and tried the canal, which we found to be far more comfortable, although less expeditious. This railway, which connects Rotterdam and Amsterdam, the two principal cities in Holland, was the first constructed, and is due to the enterprise of a public company whose affairs are managed by a council of administrators consisting of five commissioners and the engineer. The gauge of this road is two metres—six and a half feet English—from centre to centre of the rails, and the carriages disproportionately wide, which causes an unsteady and disagreeable motion. The officers of the road are exceedingly remiss in their attentions to passengers, and the Dutch customs of singing discordantly and smoking intolerably, render the trip absolutely disagreeable. Upon the canal, however, we fared much better; the boats are large, perfectly clean, well managed, and make between four and five miles an hour. In this country many families live altogether on the water, some of whom were never known to sleep under the roof of a house. They take to a canal boat as naturally as a Westerner to a log-cabin, and have on board what is necessary for their wants in life. You would be surprised to see the largest boats drawn by women, assisted occasionally by a dog harnessed up in the manner of a horse.

The women of Holland are universally larger and more athletic than the men, and with the aid of a strap fastened round the body, they draw for many miles boats to which we in America would attach two or more horses. Indeed, they may be said to do all the work of the country. In the field, shop, dairy, and all other places, she will be seen toiling away, while her husband is seeking his fortune on the ocean, or dragging out a miserable existence in the army or the tap-room.

Arrived at the Hague, which is the most beautiful city in Holland, containing upwards of seventy thousand inhabitants, the seat of government and the residence of the King, we proceeded first to the gallery of paintings, which contains some of the finest works of the Dutch masters. My attention was particularly drawn to two remarkable pictures by Paul Potter and Rembrandt, both of which have been much admired, and justly, by the artists of Europe. The picture of the first named artist represents a young bull, painted as large as life, and which approaches the nearest to deception of any really fine work of art that I have ever seen. This picture was carried to Paris by the French, and was classed by them FOURTH in value of all the paintings then in the Louvre. It is valued at £5,000, which sum was frequently offered by the Dutch government to Napoleon if he would allow it to remain at the Hague.

The other picture represents a surgeon, Professor Tulp, attended by his pupils, proceeding to dissect a dead body. Though an unpleasing subject, it is a most wonderful production. The dead body is perfectly drawn, and resembles in color and appearance all the peculiarities of a subject. The expression of countenance given to the Professor and his pupils standing around the dead body is a true and faithful representation of a dissecting room.

Connected with this gallery is the Royal Cabinet of curiosities, which contains a highly interesting collection of curious workmanship from China. The costumes of that country, illustrated by figures of persons of various ranks, in porcelain, and objects elaborately carved in ivory, mother-of-pearl, soap-stone, or steatite, give most satisfactory insight into the manners and habits of that remote and highly civilized country. The Dutch are the only people who have been permitted heretofore to bring any thing from Japan, and consequently the extensive collection of Japan ware here exhibited is invaluable. Among other objects, a plan of Jeddo, the metropolis of Japan, attracted my attention. It was modelled by the Japanese with the most minute attention to details. Several hundred figures are introduced into it, giving a precise idea of the occupations of the people, the furniture of their houses, their dress, etc.

The private galleries at the Hague are much larger and contain a greater variety of paintings than the public. The most extensive collection is that of the late King, (who died in 1849,) when Prince of Orange. He was a liberal patron of the arts, and left in his palace a large number of splendid paintings, which are now offered for sale.

After rambling during the day through the galleries and streets of the Hague, we took the railroad, and in three or four hours found ourselves safely landed in this city, which may be called the Venice of the North. It is situated at the confluence of the river Amstel with the arm of the Zuyder Zee, contains upwards of two hundred thousand inhabitants, and is constructed in the same manner as I have described the city of Rotterdam. Four large canals running in curves parallel with a semicircular fosse on the outside of the walls, together with the various small canals which intersect the town in all directions, dividing it, as represented, into ninety-five islands, and traversed by three hundred bridges, render it emphatically a city of islands, lacking only the gondola to make it a Venice.

Amsterdam, like Rotterdam, has but few attractions for a stranger aside from the peculiarities mentioned. The streets all present an active appearance, and the spirit of enterprise seems to pervade all classes. During our stay here we have made one or two interesting excursions, which all travellers desirous to learn something of country life and village customs in Holland should see. Our first was to the village of Haerlem, on Sabbath morning, with the view of seeing a lake by the same name, which is now being drained by three large engines, and to attend divine service in the great church of St. Baron, which contains the celebrated organ of Christian Miller, which has become one of the lions of the continent, although surpassed of late years in size and power. The lake of Haerlem, formed by the union of four small lakes, was eleven leagues in circumference, and contained thirteen feet of water, covering an area of 45,230 acres. The States General of Holland sanctioned a plan for converting the bed of the lake into arable and pasture land. Operations were accordingly commenced in 1840, by constructing a water-tight double rampart or dyke and ring canal round the lake, into which the water is pumped up, to be discharged through sluices into the sea. Three enormous pumping engines were erected, each of which is capable of discharging fifty-three tons per stroke, which by constant operation have almost succeeded in converting an inland sea into meadows and fruitful fields.

Having viewed the workings of these mighty engines, and seen the dry land yielding fruit abundantly where the waters of the sea were once gathered together, we repaired to the great church of St. Baron, and enjoyed the excellent music of its organ, which claims supremacy over all other instruments of the kind for its general beauty and sweetness of tone. While standing in the nave of the church listening in silent admiration to its dulcet strains, expecting to retire as soon as it was over, the doors were closed by an officer, and all ingress and egress strictly prohibited until the sermon had concluded. Finding ourselves in a dilemma, we determined to make the best of it, and quietly took a seat and listened for two mortal hours to a sermon that *was all Dutch to us.* The speaker was very vehement in his gestures, and his voice was like the sound of many waters, producing a wonderful influence upon his hearers, who sat like mummies with their heads covered with queer-looking hats, (which they removed only during prayer,) and arms folded with all the resignation of a saint.

The following day we made an excursion to the far-famed village of Brock, celebrated for its beauty and cleanliness. It has about one thousand inhabitants, composed principally of men who have amassed fortunes and retired from business. There is neither horse nor carriage road through the place; so we were obliged to leave our conveyance at a small inn on its outskirts, and to walk through it. "A notice on a sign-board gives warning to strangers that they are not to smoke without a stopper on their pipe, nor to ride through the village, but must dismount and lead their horse at a foot pace." The narrow lanes or foot paths which intersect it are paved with little stones and shells set in patterns, in imitation of mosaic. The houses are mostly of wood, very curiously constructed, and scrupulously painted two or three times during the year with white and green. Many of them have gardens attached, which present the most perfect pictures of prettiness, with their meandering walks and fantastically cut parterres, filled with flowers of gaudiest hue. Each garden is provided with a fish pond, around which are arranged beautiful summer houses, where the family and their guests usually resort in the afternoons to smoke their pipes and sip their beer, coffee or tea. Notwithstanding Brock has been much admired and praised by visitors, it is an exceedingly dull-looking village to one fresh from the busy streets of Amsterdam, which is attributed to the custom of always keeping the front door and windows closed, save for the entrance of the bridal pair after marriage, and for the exit of a corpse for burial. On our return to the city we stopped at a dairy farm by the roadside, where we witnessed the various processes of making the little round cheeses, known all over the world as Dutch cheeses, an article of great traffic, and source of considerable wealth to the province of North Holland. On entering the house we were provided by a young lady with wooden shoes or sabots, in order that we might not carry into their cleanly habitation any mud from our boots. At first we objected to putting them on, but being informed by our guide that it was a custom of the country, we readily complied with her request, and were introduced to the manager of the establishment, who was particularly polite in explaining every thing. The house was in the form of a square—three sides being appropriated for a cow stable in winter, and the other side, including the centre, was set apart for the family. The cows were all grazing on the meadows; but from what I could see I will venture to say that they are much better lodged and cared for than nine tenths of the poor people of Great Britain. The pavement of this house was of Dutch tiles, the walls of deal boards, which were as smooth and as clean as a dining table in a Tennessee log cabin. From one end of the stable to the other runs a gutter, which keeps the stalls perfectly dry and comfortable, while every convenience that could be thought of for such an establishment was here made use of.

The industry, perseverance, cleanliness and hospitality of the Dutch people is universally known and appreciated. Evidences of these good qualities are to be seen in every part of Holland. Here no poverty or beggary meets the stranger's eye, but on the contrary all classes seem to prosper, while the wheels of government move quietly along, giving satisfaction to all, and insuring peace and harmony to a people naturally fond of repose.

LETTER TWENTY-FOUR.

HEIDELBERG, Germany.

Scenery on the Rhine from its Delta to Mayence—Steamboats, Rafts, and Bridges on the Rhine—Cologne—The Seven Mountains—Fortifications at Coblentz—Frankfort on the Main—The Castle of Heidelberg, etc.

" On the banks of the majestic Rhine,
There Harold gazes on a work divine,
A blending of all beauties; streams and dells,
Fruit, foliage, crag, wood, cornfield, mountain, vine,
And chiefless castles breathing stern farewells,
From gray but leafy walls, where ruin greenly dwells.'

THE beauties of "Old Father Rhine" have been for ages past a subject upon which the pens of the poet, the novelist, and the historian have alike exhausted their highest meed of praise. Intimately associated with the historical recollections of Roman conquests, and the feats of chivalric exploit in the feudal periods of the wars and negotiations of modern times of the coronation of kings and the welfare of the neighboring nations, it merits a reputation and possesses an interest that no other stream that flows on earth can lay claim to. The course of "the great inland sea" of our own country is much longer, and its volume much greater; the banks of the beautiful Ohio present a greater variety of scenery, and the natural beauties of the Hudson are infinitely superior, wanting only a few antiquated castles and vine-clad terraces to complete the picture, and render them perfect in panorama.

From Arnheim, where we took the steamer, as high up as a little village called Bonn, twenty miles above Cologne, there is nothing to admire in the scenery of the river. The banks are low and uninteresting, as in Holland, and the villages which lie on them do not require any notice. At Bonn, however, the glories of the Rhine commence with a beautiful cluster of mountains, called the Seibengelirge, and continues to present scenes of equal beauty and variety as far up as the strongly fortified town of Mayence; here the scenery changes again, and offers nothing pleasing to the eye until you reach its source as it flows down from the snow-capped peaks of the distant Alps.

The steamboats on the Rhine, like all that I have yet seen in Europe, have few conveniences, and little or no comfort, except in fair weather, when the passengers abandon the close and heated cabins, and sit out on the deck, which is protected from the rays of the sun by a light awning arranged on pulleys. They are divided into three cabins: 1. The pavilion, usually occupied by English and Americans; 2. The cabin for the continental people; 3. The after cabin for servants and inferior persons. Meals are prepared on board at prices fixed by a printed tariff regulated by the government, and Rhenish wines furnished in abundance at a mere song. Three different companies own these steamers, and convey annually up and down one million of passengers, who go as far as they choose on one boat, make little excursions at the various points of interest, and pursue their journey on the next steamer. In ascending the Rhine I was reminded frequently of life on the Mississippi, in seeing the vast floating islands of timber which the traveller constantly meets with on that river. The rafts on the Rhine are very large, and have the appearance of a floating village, composed of eight or ten little wooden huts on a platform of oak or deal timber. The rowers and workmen sometimes amount to four or five hundred, superintended by pilots and a proprietor, whose habitation is superior in size and comfort to the rest. The boatmen are often accompanied by their wives and families, who carry on spinning, knitting, tailoring, dress-making, and all other domestic pursuits. The consumption of provisions on the voyage is almost incredible, and the expenses are so great that a large capital is necessary to construct and float a raft. The bridges on the Rhine are constructed of boats lashed together and made fast by means of anchors, over which is placed a substantial floor twenty or thirty feet in width, and elevated about four feet from the surface of the water. Rafts and boats are let through by means of a kind of lock in the bridge; which is nothing more than the detachment of four or five boats by the action of the current, forming a space sufficiently wide for the largest craft, and brought back to their proper position by machinery. The original cost of such bridges is much less than they would have to pay for a suspension; but in the end the expense of repairing the boats would counterbalance the difference, and make the new invention far preferable.

Americans usually expect to find beautiful and agreeable cities on the Rhine—a conclusion formed from reading the exaggerated descriptions of letter writers, and listening to the accounts of tourists whose enthusiasm leads them into extremes. There is in truth no city or village from its mouth to its source that is any ways attractive as a place of residence, or even agreeable for a stranger to pass a fortnight. Cologne, renowned all over the world for the manufacture of Eau de Cologne, is the largest and most interesting place on the river; interesting not on account of its beauty or cleanliness, for it can boast of neither, but for its historical associations and curious churches. Traces of the possession of this city by the Romans remain not only in various fragments of walls, originally part of the outer defences, though not far within the city, and in the numerous altars, inscriptions, coins, etc., which come to light nearly every day; but even in the features of character of its inhabitants, who are said to betray their hereditary blood, and to differ in many respects from their German neighbors on the opposite side of the Rhine. The existing outer walls of Cologne are considered very superior, and present one of the most perfect examples of fortifications of the middle ages, with picturesque flanking towers and gate-houses.

They were built between the twelfth and fifteenth centuries, and each nearly five miles in circumference. The Cathedral of Cologne, begun in 1248 by Archbishop Conrad, is still incomplete, but is even in its present state one of the finest and purest Gothic monuments in Europe. A fresh impulse was given to the works on the accession of the present King, who contributed largely to its funds, and the efforts of an association established in Cologne, with branches in all parts of Europe, to collect subscriptions for completing the edifice according to the original design. The architect estimates the cost of finishing it at £750,000, and requiring the constant labor of the workmen for twenty years. The choir is the only part finished, and judging from its superior beauty and elegance, the Cathedral if ever completed will be one of the most uniform and most stupendous Gothic structures existing.

"In a small chapel immediately behind the high altar is the celebrated Shrine of the three Kings of Cologne, or Magi, who came from the East with presents for the infant Saviour. The skulls of the three kings, inscribed with their names, Gasper, Mulchioz and Balthuzea, written in rubies, are deposited in a case of plated silver curiously wrought, surrounded by small arcades, supported on pillars, inclosing figures of the Apostles and Prophets." Many of the jewels belonging to this chapel were taken away and sold at the time of the French revolution, but the precious stones, the gems, cameos, and rich enamels, which still remain, are said to be worth more than two hundred thousand pounds, which will give you a fair idea of its riches and magnificence in its original state. Near this chapel, under a plain slab in the pavement, is buried *the heart of Mary de Medicis*, and in the sacristy are many relics of saints, including a bone of St. Matthew. Many other things of an interesting nature are to be seen in the Cathedral; but to one fond of the curious, a visit to the church of St. Ursula should be made without fail. It is one of the most remarkable structures in Europe, not for any architectural beauty, but as the depository of the bones of St. Ursula's companions. According to tradition, that pious woman with her eleven thousand virgins set sail from Brittany for Rome, and were slaughtered on their return at Cologne by the barbarian Hans, because they refused to break their vows of chastity. "On entering the church these hideous relics meet the eye, beneath, above, around; they are built into the walls, buried under the pavement, and displayed in gaunt array in glass cases about the choir. The saint herself reposes in a coffin behind the altar, while the skulls of a select few of her associates are admitted to the *Golden Chamber* encased in silver, along with a number of other relics, such as one of the stone vessels which held the water that was turned into wine at the marriage in Cana, etc."

Soon after leaving Cologne we came in sight of the Seven Mountains which form the commencement to the beautiful scenery of the Rhine. They are the highest and wildest on its banks, and almost all crowned with a chapel, or the ruin of some ancient tower or hermit's cell, which adds much to their picturesque features. The most interesting of the whole group, from its shape and position, but more than all from the verses of Byron, is the famed Drachenfels, whose precipices rise abruptly from the river side crowned with ruin:

> "The castled crag of Drachenfels
> Frowns o'er the wide and winding Rhine,
> Whose breast of waters broadly swells
> Between the banks which bear the vine,
> And hills all rich with blossomed trees,
> And fields which promise corn and wine;
> And scattered cities crowning these,
> Whose far white walls along them shine,
> Have strew'd a scene which I should see
> With double joy wert *thou* with me."

Many travellers ascend to the summit of Drachenfels to enjoy the beautiful view of the river, and to examine the ruined fragments which were once the seat of a noble race long since extinct, named after the mountain on which they dwelt. Having in anticipation a sufficient amount of climbing in Switzerland, we were satisfied with a view from the river, and proceeded on to the town of Coblentz, situated at the mouth of the Moselle, and regarded as one of the most strongly fortified places in the Prussian dominions. The extensive fortifications, which occupied nearly twenty years to complete, connect the works on the first bank of the Rhine with the lofty citadel of Ehrenbreitstein on the opposite bank, forming a complete bulwark or fortified camp, capable of containing one hundred thousand soldiers, and combining in this structure not only beauty, but a degree of solidity and strength superior to any fortification that we have yet seen. The next place of interest above Coblentz, is the city of Mayence, situated on the left bank of the Rhine, nearly opposite the junction of the Main. It belongs to the Grand Duke of Hesse Darmstadt, and is the most considerable and important town in his dominions; but, as the chief and strongest fortress of the German confederation, it is garrisoned by Prussian and Austrian troops, in nearly equal numbers, and is commanded by a governor elected alternately from either nation for a period of five years. Leaving the Rhine at this point, we proceeded by railroad to Frankfort on the Main, now the seat of the German Diet, and one of the most lively as well as handsome cities in Germany; it is situated on a perfect plain, and is divided into two distinct parts, called the new and old town. The streets in the new town are wide, and many of the houses inhabited by rich merchants, bankers or diplomatists, are literally palaces. "The *old town*, on the other hand, with its narrow streets and quaint wooden buildings, with gables overhanging their basement stories, forms a complete contrast to the new." Many of the houses are of great antiquity, especially in the quarter around the birthplace of Goethe, the poet, and the *Rothschild family*, still inhabited by the Jews of the city. Over the door of Goethe's house we were shown his father's coat of arms, which, by a singular coincidence, bears the poetical device of three lyres, and is pointed out to strangers who visit the place by an old lady, and described in language too pathetic to dwell upon. The citizens of Frankfort have erected a monumental statue of him in the *Allee* or public place; it is of bronze, pedestal and figure, and is a superior work; the subjects of the bas-reliefs are said to be taken from Goethe's works. The most interesting object of this nature, and the pride of the city, is Dannecker's statue of Ariadne, in the garden of a private gentleman. It is placed in a pavilion built for his reception, and is allowed by artists to be one of the most distinguished productions of modern art. I do not profess to be much of a critic in the fine arts, but as far as I am capable of judging, it is, next to the *Greek Slave*, the most perfect and beautiful of all modern statues.

Frankfort is encircled with handsome gardens and agreeable promenades, which, together with its public galleries and places of intellectual resort, make it one of the most agreeable cities in Germany. One or two hours on the railroad brought us from Frankfort to this old town, situated on the Neckar, and renowned for its Castle and University. Being surrounded on either side by lofty hills, Heidelberg is necessarily confined to a single street, nearly three miles in length, and containing about 14,000 inhabitants. The beauty of many places is much exaggerated, but that of Heidelberg cannot be too much extolled. From the ruins of the old Castle which overlooks the entire town and valley below, as far as the Rhine, a panorama is presented calculated to inspire genius, and make it a fit place for the student's home. As an edifice, the University, which was once the pride of Germany, is not remarkable. It is a plain and not very large house, situated in a small square near the centre of the town. The famous Palatine Library, carried off by the Bavarians during the thirty years' war, and restored by Pope Pius VII., now comprises only about 900 volumes, and the entire Library only 120,000 volumes. In the days of its prosperity this institution was overrun with students from all parts of Europe; but the desolating influences of war, time after time, have reduced it almost to ruin, and it at present numbers only three or four hundred students.

"To those fond of the antique, the Castle of Heidelberg presents many attractions. The building displays the work of various hands, the taste of different founders, and the styles of successive centuries; it is highly interesting for its varied fortunes, its picturesque situation, its vastness, and the relics of architectural magnificence which it displays after having been three times burnt, and having ten times experienced the horrors of war." Aside from the Castle itself, many interesting relics of antiquity are shown to visitors, among which are several old wine casks of enormous dimensions.

In a cellar under the Castle is the famous Heidelberg Butt, constructed one hundred years ago; it is the largest wine cask in the world, thirty-six feet long and twenty-four feet high; being capable of holding 800 hogsheads or 283,200 bottles. In former days, when the tierce was filled with the produce of the vintage, it was usual to dance on the platform erected on the top of the tierce. It has, however, remained empty more than half a century, and is now preserved as one of the lions of Heidelberg, and as an evidence of the sumptuous modes of living in ancient times.

LETTER TWENTY-FIVE.

FALLS OF THE RHINE.

Fashionable Watering Places in Germany—Detour to Strasburg—Cathedral at Freiburg—First Adventure on a Diligence—Customs—Cultivation of Tobacco and Indian Corn in Germany—Falls of the Rhine, etc.

HAVING heard a great deal of the fashionable summer resorts in Germany, and feeling a little curiosity to learn something about their way of doing things, and compare them with our own places of the same character, we made visits during the gay season, both to Wiesbaden and Baden Baden, two of the most celebrated watering places now in Europe. Wiesbaden is the capital of the Duchy of Nassau, and residence of the Duke. It is composed almost entirely of lodging houses, and contains a population exceeding twelve thousand. The celebrity of its baths and mineral waters is so great, that visitors in search of health and pleasure flock there from all quarters of the globe, to the amount of fifteen thousand annually. Situated in a kind of basin, formed by the contiguity of several hills, and being a regularly built town, it is necessarily devoid of many of the chief attractions that combine to render such a place pleasant; pure air, shady groves, and fragrant breezes, are out of the question; and all that one may expect to find, is strange tasting water, and extensive gaming at a saloon called the Kursaal, which forms the centre of attraction and gayety. The stranger's attention is soon attracted, as he walks along the streets, by the clouds of vapor arising on all sides out of the ground, produced as is supposed by the numerous boiling springs that abound there. Walking through a long avenue of little short trees, serving as a kind of promenade for the water drinkers, we found the principal spring called the Kochbrunnen (boiling spring) sending forth its heated vapor in volumes, greater than the escape from a steam engine—giving it more the appearance of a caldron in violent ebullition, than a spring of water fresh from the bowels of the earth. From five to eight in the morning, and from six to seven in the evening, are the hours for drinking the water; at which time, ladies and gentlemen from the various hotels and boarding houses repair to the spring, and receiving their portion boiling hot, walk about, glass in hand, discussing its properties, until it is cool enough to be drunk. In taste, it is very much like chicken-broth—and if one did not know the fact, I believe they would not perceive the difference. In a bath, the water is covered with a greasy film or scum, which collects on the surface while cooling; and which, however uninviting it may appear, is the test of its being quite fresh, and not having been used before. The temperature of this water is said to be 156° Fahrenheit, and the volume is so great that after being used both for drinking and supplying the principal baths in the city, it runs over and escapes through the gutters and drains into the Rhine.

The Kursaal, alluded to above, is the most remarkable edifice in Wiesbaden—occupying the east side of a square, the north and south sides of which are lined with colonnades, filled with gay shops, serving as a promenade in wet weather, and a sort of bazaar during the whole of the season. It answers the fourfold purpose of banquet, ball, and gaming room; and forms, as a matter of course, the chief place of rendezvous for the lovers of pleasure. The establishment, however, of the same character at Baden Baden, called the Conversations Haus, is more extensive, and frequented usually by *fashionable gamblers*, who bet on a magnificent scale, and consider it a condescension to put down any thing smaller than a gold piece. "It is let out by the government of Baden to a company of speculators, who pay for the exclusive privilege of opening gambling tables £3,000 annually, and agree to spend in addition 250,000 florins on the walks and buildings." So you may form some idea from this, of the vast sum of money which must be lost every summer by the *dupes* who frequent this *licensed* gaming house. The building is very large, superbly furnished, and conducted on principles different from any thing of the kind either in Europe or our own country. In the afternoon, when dinner is over, the walking colonnades that adorn the front of the Conversations Haus become the fashionable resort, and are crowded with people, sipping coffee and ices, or smoking; the whole space is then covered with chairs and tables, and an excellent band of music is stationed close at hand to enliven the crowd and give zest to the occasion. After this they disperse; some go to their hotels, and others, who are fond of gaming, repair to the brilliant illuminated hall, containing the *rouge-et-noir* and *roulette* tables, which are open, and occupied day and night—but more particularly in the evening, when the stakes become higher and the excitement more intense. Betting at these tables is not confined, as you might suppose, to the gentlemen; but females are often seen at them, and sometimes gamble higher than the men. As a matter of curiosity, we stood five hours one evening at the roulette table watching an old lady from Russia, who played with as much coolness and boldness as the most inveterate gamester. With snuff-box on one side, and rolls of gold on the other, she stood in a crowded room, risking five hundred francs on nearly every turn of the wheel, until she lost thirty thousand francs, a sum of money that would be considered a small fortune by many men even in Germany. One would suppose that after such heavy losses, she would be inclined to leave off for a time; but such was not the case. On the following evening, she was again at the table with her well-filled purse, and met with no better success—but on the contrary, not only lost largely at hazard, but had two thousand francs taken from her pocket by one of the light-fingered gentry who always frequent such places.

The situation of Baden Baden is far more beautiful and better suited for a summer residence than Wiesbaden. Embosomed among hills, forming an offset to the Black Forest range, and seated on the banks of the Oos—a stream which, though not magnificent in size, once formed the boundary line between the Franks and Allemanni—it affords a retreat for the denizens of European cities, that is truly grateful and invigorating. As places of fashion and elegance, neither of the German watering establishments can compare with Newport, Saratoga, or Cape May. The assembly rooms are poorly attended. The hotels are conducted on a small scale, and the visitors usually assort themselves into exclusive parties, which forbids any thing like sociability or gayety of any kind. The Conversations Haus, for those addicted to gaming, and the mineral waters for the invalids, seem to constitute the sole attraction.

Leaving Baden Baden, we made a detour across the Rhine, for the purpose of seeing the celebrated Cathedral at Strasburg—depositing our baggage at a little town called Kehl, on the German shore, to avoid examination and the annoyance of custom-house officers, who are usually more persevering in France than any other country. Soon after crossing on the bridge of boats, we came in sight of the lofty spire of the Minster, which is several miles distant from the river, and situated in the centre of the city. At first we were disappointed in the height of the edifice, but as we drew nearer to it, and ascended the great flight of steps that lead to its summit, we were fully convinced there was no exaggeration, either as to its altitude or beauty. Like many cathedrals in Europe, it stands in an unfinished state; but to the lover of architectural symmetry, its perfect proportions and delicacy of workmanship cannot fail to create admiration. According to measurement, the spire rises four hundred and seventy-four feet above the pavement, twenty-four feet higher than the highest Pyramid of Egypt, and one hundred and forty feet higher than St. Paul's, in London. The view from its summit, although extensive, is wholly uninteresting; presenting nothing to the eye but barren plains and a multitude of rusty-colored tiled roofs, with three and sometimes four stories above the eaves. In the interior, we were shown a beautiful marigold window, the glass of which was painted in the fifteenth century; and the famous clock in one of the transepts, made by an artist of Strasburg, to replace the old one which had fallen to decay. The full mechanism is set in motion at twelve o'clock; at which time a number of ludicrous figures, made of wood, are exhibited, and required to perform by some invisible means various antics, better suited for a puppet-show than the church of God.

Returning to Kehl, where we left our baggage, we proceeded to Freiburg, per railway, which is also remarkable for its Minster. It is the only Gothic church in Germany which is finished, and which has escaped destruction from fire and the violence of war. In appearance, it resembles very strikingly the Cathedral at Strasburg, and is equally admired for the delicate symmetry of its proportions, and the good taste of its decorations. At Freiburg we passed the night, and were lulled to sleep by the exquisite strains of martial music in honor of the Prince of Russia, who had just arrived *en route* for Switzerland. The following morning we procured seats on the diligence for the Falls of the Rhine. Being our first adventure, we followed the advice of *old stagers*, and occupied what they call the Imperial, corresponding with the outside seat on our coaches. Three in number, we started off in high spirits, expecting a nice day's drive. The sky was cloudless, and every thing promised well; but our hopes were destined soon to be changed, for we had scarcely emerged from the lovely valley of the Black Forest, when a storm dark and direful came upon us. The *coupe*, *intérieur*, and *rotonde* were all crowded with phlegmatic Germans, who thought more of their well-filled pipes than the comfort of us poor outsiders. Overcoats were of no avail, and umbrellas perfectly useless, as the wind turned them wrong side out as fast as we raised them. For four long hours, we bore the peltings of the pitiless storm like so many martyrs; but at last our patience was exhausted, and in a fit of desperation, we ordered our trunks to be taken off at a wayside inn, where we passed the night. This was our first and last adventure on a lumbering diligence. After the excitement was all over, and we snugly ensconced around a cheerful fire discussing the impoliteness of European travellers, and the discomforts we had to encounter, a pleasant breeze was created by the daughter of our host, who entered the room with a bright, merry face, bearing an old-fashioned clothes horse, upon which we recognised sundry familiar articles thoroughly drenched, which she proposed roguishly to dry, while we were discussing the dinner prepared for us. At the table, our merriment was increased by seeing two moustached gentlemen salute each other with a kiss, first on one side of the mouth and then the other, a custom that prevails in Germany; which appears quite as ludicrous to an American as seeing two ladies meet and kiss each other in our own streets and public places. Nearly overpowered with laughter, we repaired to our chambers, where we found another German custom that completely did us up for the night. Being considerably longer than the people of this country, we found our beds two or three feet too short, and instead of having a pillow at the head of the bed, it was placed at the foot, and was so large that we could not determine at first whether it was intended for the pillow or the bed. In this dilemma, we summoned our Yankee ingenuity, and managed to arrange things to suit us sufficiently to insure a good night's rest, and pleasant dreams of our first adventure on a diligence. The following morning we procured a carriage, and proceeded to the Falls of the Rhine, passing *en route* several patches of tobacco and Indian corn, far inferior in size and quality to the crops of our Tennessee negroes, cultivated during the holidays. Notwithstanding the Germans smoke more than any people in the world, they know nothing about the cultivation of the plant; and as to the cultivation and uses of Indian corn, they are utterly ignorant.

Entering Switzerland, we soon reached the "hell of waters," as the Falls of the Rhine have been termed by an English poet. The river above the falls is about three hundred feet broad; and the height of the fall is said to be seventy feet, although it does not look so high. Two isolated pillars of stone standing in the middle of the stream, divide the volume of water into three shutes. "The river, after its leap, forms a large semi-circular bay, as it were to rest itself, the sides of which are perpetually chafed by the heaving billows." English travellers and English writers always go into ecstasies about these falls; but an American who has heard the roar, and seen the mighty rush of waters at Niagara, would pronounce it a swindle, and inferior even to many cataracts in the United States, that have no reputation beyond the sound of their waters.

LETTER TWENTY-SIX.

GENEVA, Switzerland.

Government of Switzerland—Character of the People—General aspect of the Country—Towns—Lake Lucerne—Mt. Righi—Pedestrian Tour through the Pass of the Furka and the Bernese Oberland—Rhone Glacier—Falls and Avalanches—Lake Leman and the Castle of Chillon—Geneva, etc.

WE are accustomed to look upon the little republic of Switzerland as "the land of liberty," isolated from the friends of free institutions and oppressed by the neighboring nations. No traveller from the United States ever enters her borders without experiencing at first that homelike feeling of independence and individuality that pervades every part of our happy country. The air seems purer—he breathes more freely, and feels that he is in a country and amidst a people of similar institutions and sympathies. Indeed, nature and nature's God must have designed this mountainous region for a republic—as an oasis in the great desert of political despotism.

"The palaces of nature, whose vast walls
Have pinnacled in clouds their snowy scalps,

And throned eternity in icy balls
Of cold sublimity, where forms and falls
The avalanche—the thunderbolt of snow;
All that expands the spirit, yet appals,
Gather around the summits, as to show
How earth may soar to heaven, yet leave vain man below."

No part of the continent is so well suited for the germination of the seed of liberty as Switzerland; and all that is wanting to make the country prosperous and the people happy, is a proper understanding and appreciation of the system of representation as demonstrated in our own country, a regeneration of her social relations, and a fair trial allowed her by the monarchies of Europe. It is not my intention to trouble you as to what might be done, but to give you some idea of the present condition of the government and character of the people, as far as I am capable of judging, during a sojourn of several weeks. The favorable anticipations awakened by historical associations in our mind, as we approached the land of Tell and Winkelried, were wofully falsified, for the most part, on arriving upon the spot. Although democratic principles have made rapid strides in almost all the countries since 1830, we ascertain, upon inquiring into the political state of this country, that the government is nearly powerless—a confederacy without unity—split into parties by religious dissensions and opposing political interests—and nearly every canton either torn by contending factions, or actually split in two, and as much dissevered as though it consisted of two separate states. In times past the united and valiant forces of the little republic not only withstood the shocks of foreign invasion, secure in the mountain fastnesses, but shattered and annihilated the apparently overwhelming armaments of Austria and Burgundy, not in one battle, but in nearly every action in which they were engaged; and now she must submit to every thing, and, as a necessary consequence, must endure the diplomatic insults heaped upon her on all sides. The demoralizing effect produced upon the Swiss by that system of foreign military service, which they thought had become necessary to the existence of the community, the overpowering deluge of the French Revolution, and the great influx of travellers for the last half century have contributed largely to bring about this result. Instead of finding those simple and guileless manners, which in times past were associated with the name of the inhabitants of these mountains, we encountered a people who are actuated by a spirit of time-serving and a love of money that is really surprising. Every where that we nave stopped, and more particularly on the main routes of travellers, we had to contend with extortionate inn-keepers, obsequious valets, and beggars without number, who infest every village, waterfall, and post station in the country. Patriots are scarce in the land of Tell; and the people who have enjoyed freedom longer than any other in Europe, are principally distinguished for fighting the battles of any master, however tyrannical, who will give the highest price for their services.

The poverty of the land, its slight capabilities of improvement, its deficiency of resources in proportion to the extent of its population, have compelled the Swiss to resort to manufactures for a livelihood. Notwithstanding the natural disadvantages of an inland country, into which the raw material must be conveyed almost exclusively on the axle, over snowy passes, and by long journeys, they have been overcome; and in the excellence of her manufactured articles Switzerland now competes, as shown in the Exhibition, with any country in Europe, not excepting even England.

With regard to the natural beauties of Switzerland, there can be but one sentiment of admiration. The sublimity and diversified grandeur of its scenery is unequalled, perhaps, by any country in the world. The presence of the Alps covered with perpetual snow and reflected in the crystal waters of an hundred lakes—the singular appearance of the glaciers—the music of the waterfalls, and the fearful sound of the distant avalanche, the thunderbolt of snow, constitute its chief features of attraction, and combine to create in the mind of the visitor those thoughts and feelings so eloquently described in the lines of Rogers, in his description of the Alps:

"Who first beholds those everlasting clouds—
Those mighty hills, so shadowy, so sublime,
As rather to belong to heaven than earth—
But instantly receives into his soul
A sense, a feeling, that he loses not—
A something that informs him 'tis an hour
Whence he may date henceforward and for ever?"

Aside from the natural peculiarities of Switzerland, we were much interested in the appearance of her towns, some of which exhibit many curious marks of antiquity; their buildings are frequently found unchanged since a very early period; and in Lucerne, Freiburg, Basle, Berne, and in several other instances, the feudal fortifications, with battlements and watch-towers, remain perfectly preserved. In nearly all of them are to be seen in the public places fountains consisting of a Gothic ornamented pillar, surmounted by a figure of a man, usually some hero of Swiss history, or the figure of some animal or bird peculiar to each canton, and regarded as almost sacred by the people. In Berne they have great reverence for the bear, and not only have his effigy on the coins, sign-posts, fountains, and public buildings of the canton, but keep living specimens of their favorite, maintained at the public expense. "The connection between the town and the animal is accounted for by the ancient tradition, that on the day on which Berchtold laid the foundation of Berne, an enormous bear was slain by him on its destined site. In 1798 the French army took possession of Berne, and led the bears away as captives to the city of Paris, where they were deposited for safe keeping in the Jardin des Plantes. After a series of years, the ancient order of things was restored at Berne, and Martin, their ancient pensioner, was returned to his home, where he is still provided for by the city authorities, and exhibited to strangers as one of the curiosities of the place.

No country in Europe has so many peculiarities of manner, customs and costumes, as are to be seen in Switzerland. Each canton possesses some distinguishing characteristics, and it is really surprising to see people living so near to each other and differing so widely in their habits and manners of dress. This difference is confined in a great measure to the females, who remain at home and do all the work, retaining their ancient simplicity, while the men are travelling about as volunteers, mountain guides, or soldiers for some other government.

At the Falls of the Rhine, where we entered Switzerland, we procured a *char-à-banc* and proceeded to Lucerne, by way of Zurich, one of the handsomest and most flourishing towns in the republic—crossing the high chain of the Albis, and passing through the most desirable portions of the country. This was our first, and I hope the last adventure in a *char-à-banc*, which my travelling companion from

South Carolina and myself concurred in pronouncing inferior in point of looks and comfort to an Irish jaunting car—so much dreaded by the English. If you wish to see this vehicle, take the body of an old-fashioned gig, and place it sideways on one of our rock wagons, to which you must attach two bone-yard horses in tandem, by means of rope traces, collars running in a conical shape about two feet higher than the horse's neck, and bridles very like those used by the ploughmen of the West—and you will have the whole turn-out in perfection.

Lucerne is the residence of the Papal Nuncio, and is beautifully situated on the borders of Lake Lucerne, which is considered by many as the finest and most interesting of the Swiss lakes, between the giant Pilatus and Righi, and in sight of the snowy Alps of Schuytz and Engelberg. It is not a place of any considerable trade, but the absence of this is more than compensated by the picturesque beauty of the mountain crowned with old feudal watch-towers, and the placid waters of the lake rippled only by the paddles of pleasure boats, and the struggles of the weary stag fleeing from the hunter's coil.

It was here that we left the great highway and made the necessary preparations for ascending Mt. Righi—a description of which may be of interest, as it will convey to you some idea of Alpine pedestrian journeys. Our first care was to procure a knapsack similar to those used by our volunteers in the Mexican war, in which we placed a change of garments and sundry little requisites, such as Murray's hand-book and Kelley's road map of Switzerland; in addition to which we were provided with waterproof coats, double-soled shoes filled with hob-nails, a flask to hold brandy or krischwasser, and an alpenstock, all of which are indispensable upon mountain journeys. The alpenstock is a pole about six feet long, with an iron spike at one end for use, and a chamois' horn for show at the other. Those who have tried it, can fully appreciate its uses as a staff and leaping-pole, but chiefly as a support in descending the mountains: it then becomes, as it were, a third leg. It enables one to transfer a part of the weight of the body from the legs to the arms, which is a great relief in descending long and steep hills. By the aid of it, the chamois-hunters glide down snow-covered slopes almost perpendicular, checking the velocity of their course when it becomes too great, by bearing back, and driving the point deeper in the snow. In crossing glaciers, it is also very useful, to feel the strength of the ice, and ascertain whether it be free from crevices and able to bear the weight. From Lucerne we went to Weggis on the lake boat, where we commenced the toilsome ascent of Mount Righi, which is situated between the lakes of Zug and Lucerne, and is celebrated on account of its isolated position; separated from other mountains, in the midst of some of the most beautiful scenery in Switzerland, affording an uninterrupted view on all sides, and serving as a natural observatory, commanding in clear weather a panorama hardly to be equalled in extent and grandeur among the Alps. It has also the advantage of being accessible; no less than three mule paths lead up to the summit, so that it is daily resorted to in the summer by hundreds of travellers from all parts of the world.

From Weggis the path is less steep and a little shorter than the other two, winding along the outside of the mountain in constant view of the lake, furnishing something to please and interest at every step. At the end of each mile there is a resting place and a fresco painting, representing our Lord's Passion, where the weary traveller halts to draw his breath and inquire how much farther it is to the Culm or mountain house. After walking pretty steadily for about three hours, we encountered great quantities of snow, which had fallen the previous night, rendering our farther progress extremely difficult and disagreeable; but as we had a fearless guide who was well acquainted with the landmarks and accustomed to wading through such obstructions, we hurried on, and at last reached the summit, after climbing five long hours. The *Culm*, or culminating part of the mountain, is an irregular space of ground of some extent, destitute of trees, and covered nearly always with snow. Here we found a large inn, constructed of wood, and capable of affording tolerable accommodation, considering the height, for about one hundred persons, although double this number sometimes manage to pass the night under its roof. He that happens to be on the summit of Mount Righi in clear weather, may consider him self exceedingly fortunate, as but few are allowed that privilege, the atmosphere being almost always filled with a cloudy vapor that ascends perpendicularly from the valley, enveloping the mountain, and rendering a view utterly out of the question. At times, however the mist disappears, and the glories of the morning sun are revealed to the wonder-stricken pilgrim in all its grandeur. A glare of light in the east, which gradually dims the flickering of the stars, is the first token of its appearance; it soon becomes a streak of gold along the horizon, and is reflected in a pale pink tint upon the snows of the Bernese Alps. Summit after summit gradually assumes the same glittering hue; the darkness between the horizon and the Culm is next lighted up; forests, lakes, hills, rivers, towns, and villages become more and more distinct, and the whole panorama is spread out before you in all its wonder and diversified beauty. On one side the lofty chain of the Albis, running parallel with the Zurich, and the distant range of the Black Forest hills in Germany, are visible to the eye; on another, the Jura chain, the town of Lucerne, with its coronet of towers, and Tell's Chapel, on the spot where he shot the tyrant Gessler; on another, the beautiful lake of Lucerne and the magnificent white chain of the high Alps of Berne, Unterwalden, and Uri, in one unbroken ridge of peaks and glaciers; and lastly, the Alpine chain, which extends uninterruptedly along the horizon, including the pre-eminent peaks of Doedi, Glaerwisch, and Sentis, while the middle distance embraces the region famous in history as the cradle of Swiss freedom, and the bloody conflict between Suwarrow and Massena.

After taking a satisfactory survey of this wide-spread panorama, extending over a circumference of three hundred miles, we descended by way of the same path to Weggis, where we met the little steamer and proceeded through the lake of the Four Cantons to Fluellen, situated in the midst of what they here call Tell's country. The scenery on this lake is unsurpassed in Europe, and is celebrated not only for its beauty, but the many historical associations connected with it. Its shores are a classic region, the sanctuary of liberty, and memorable events are here recorded which will ever be dear to the lovers of freedom. A short distance beyond Fluellen is the little village of Altorf, the capital of the canton of Uri, the poorest and least populous in the confederation. Its only claim to in terest the traveller is in connection with William Tell. Our guide pointed out to us a stone fountain, on the public square, surmounted with statues of the dauntless crossbowman and his child, which is said to mark the spot where he stood when he shot the apple off his son's head. Near this fountain there is another to perpetuate the spot where the lime tree stood, upon which Gessler's cap was stuck, for all men to do obeisance to it as they passed, and to which the child was bound, to serve as a mark for his father's bolt.

Leaving this region, we passed the Devil's Bridge, crossed the snow-covered Furca, and reached in safety, after two days' travel, the Hospice of the Grimsel, an inn of the rudest kind, originally occupied by monks, who entertained those who travelled from necessity, and afforded gratuitous aid to the poor, but now daily occupied, during the summer months, by travellers for pleasure. It is a massive building, of rough masonry, designed to resist a weight of snow, and with few windows to admit the cold, which is disagreeable in the warmest season. Its situation is dreary in the extreme, in a rocky hollow, upwards of a thousand feet below the summit of the pass, surrounded by soaring peaks and steep precipices. During the winter one servant remains in the house, with a sufficient provision to serve during the period of his banishment, and several dogs to find out the approach of wanderers; for even in the depth of winter, this snow-bound habitation is resorted to by traders from Hasti and the Vallais, who exchange the cheese of one valley for the wine and spirits of the other. In the neighborhood of the Hospice are two of the most remarkable glaciers of Switzerland, the Aar and the Rhone. The former is eighteen miles long and from two to four broad, but is covered to a great extent with rubbish, which mars its beauty; while the Rhone presents a face as clear and dazzling as a sunbeam. It fills the head of the valley from side to side, and appears piled up against the shoulder of the Gallenstock, whose tall peak overhangs it. It is impossible to give you a correct idea of this "magnificent sea of ice;" its extent, thickness, yawning crevices, variety of formation, and extreme purity, are truly wonderful. The river Rhone is supplied from a cavern of ice beneath this glacier, which is estimated at 5,400 feet above the sea. Remaining all night at the Hospice of the Grimsel, we started early the next morning for Grindelwald, stopping *en route* at Handek, near which are the falls of Aar, considered the finest in Switzerland. They are more than two hundred feet high, which, taken in connection with the quantity and rush of water, the gloom of the gorge into which it precipitates itself, and the wild character of the rocky solitude around, renders it far more interesting to the traveller than either the Reichenbach, Giesbach or Staubbach, all within a circuit of fifty miles, and each possessing more celebrity on account of their being accessible and situated nearer Interlachen and Thun, the favorite summer resorts of the English. Grindelwald is decidedly one of the most romantic places in Switzerland, being situated in a valley formed on one side by the Eigher, or Giant, the Mittenberg, (middle mountain,) and the Wetterhorn, (Peak of the Tempests,) between which issue out two magnificent glaciers, bordered with forests of fir, which form, as it were, a graceful fringe to the white ice, while the verdant meadows, with which they are almost in contact near their bases, contrast agreeably with the frozen peaks above. Long before we reached the mountain village, our ears were saluted with the shrill sound of the *alpine horn*, blown by an old soldier, living in a small chapel, who makes his bread by the charity of strangers, who always stop and listen to his wild music. The horn is simply a rude tube of wood six or eight feet long, without ornament or beauty; but the sounds that emanate from it are truly wonderful, particularly when returned to the ear by the echoes repeated from the tall cliffs of the Wetterhorn, refined and softened like an aerial concert among the crags. We were also entertained on the road-side, as we descended into the valley, by young females, who pick up a few *batzen* by singing *Ranz des Vaches*—certainly the wildest chorus that ever was heard by human ears, not excepting even the songs of our Indian hunters. The Swiss song is not composed of articulate sounds, but one in which the voice is used as a mere instrument of music, more flexible than any which art can produce—sweet, powerful, and thrilling beyond description.

Pursuing our journey, we passed through Interlachen, Thun and Berne, to Vevay on Lake Leman, near which is the famous castle of Chillon, familiar to all who have perused Byron's Prisoner of Chillon. Before reaching Vevay, we met some of our dearest friends, with whom we crossed the mighty deep, and separated in Belgium, with the understanding that we should soon meet again and continue our journey together; but they had changed their route, and we parted once more, and finally, I fear; for when travellers divide in Europe, there is no certainty of their coming together again. While we were interchanging salutations, and plans of travel, the diligence left me far behind, and it was in vain that I exerted my pedestrian powers to overtake it; the delivery of the mail was of more importance to the conductor than the comfort or convenience of a passenger. I did not regret this, however, as I was repaid for a walk of ten miles by beholding a beautiful sunset on the snow-covered hills that bound the horizon of Lake Leman. I was all alone, descending the long slope of the mountain by a serpentine road, and gazing in wonder and admiration upon the spots that inspired the genius of a Rousseau, a Byron, and other gifted authors. It was an evening for reflection; thoughts of the past, the glories of the present, and the bright hopes of the future, all conspired to create emotions that will not soon be forgotten.

The following morning we drove along the shore of the lake to the renowned castle of Chillon, romantically situated on an isolated rock, surrounded by deep water, but within a stone's throw of the road, with which it communicates by a wooden bridge. The castle is now converted into a magazine for military stores, but is always shown to strangers by a young woman of some beauty, who dilates considerably upon the "good old times," etc. We were ushered through the dungeon where Bonnivard was confined, saw the ring in the pillar to which he was chained, and the stone floor at its base, worn by his constant pacing to and fro. This pillar is a record of the past, being covered all over with the handwriting of tourists desirous of associating their names with those who have acquired greatness and renown. Among many hundred I observed those of Byron, Shelley, Rousseau, Sue, Dana, and Peel, who have visited the castle and communicated their impressions to the world in terms too familiar to dwell upon. Leaving Chillon, we proceeded upon the deep blue waters of the lake to Geneva, the metropolis of Switzerland, stopping a short time at Lausanne, the place where Gibbon wrote his celebrated work on the rise and downfall of the Roman Empire.

Geneva is one of the most beautiful and active inland cities in Europe. It is the great focus of attraction for travellers of all nations, fifty thousand being the number calculated to pass through the city annually. The river Rhone divides the city into two parts, the water of which is so very blue that it resembles the discharge of indigo from a dyer's vat. "As a town, Geneva possesses but few attractions; it has no fine public buildings, and scarcely any *sights*." It is owing to its beautiful environs, to the commanding view of Mont Blanc, to the charming scenery of its lake, and to its position on the great high road from Paris to Italy, that it has become a place of so much resort and importance.

LETTER TWENTY-SEVEN.

Simplon Pass, Switzerland.

Valley of Chamouni—Ascent to the Mer de Glace—Adventure—View of Mont Blanc from the Flegere—Hospice of St. Bernard—Dogs—Monks—Morgue—The Simplon Road, etc.

Leaving the shores of Lake Geneva, we proceeded in a diligence through a very uninteresting country into Savoy, one of the dependencies of the Sardinian government. Although this route is much travelled during the season by visitors to the valley of Chamouni, it possesses but few facilities and conveniences to enhance one's comfort. The hotels of Switzerland, as a general thing, are excellent; but in this particular region a person may undertake to keep the seventh day without any danger of breaking it: man and horse are entertained in the same house, and their food about on a par, with the exception of the cooking—beds of straw and one waiter for all. The monotony of the country and the inferiority of the hotels were almost forgotten when we thought of the many beauties in reserve for us at Chamouni, and observed the peculiarities of manner and custom presented for our contemplation, as we jogged along in the slow-going diligence. It happened to be one of the days set apart by the people for a public fair or exhibition of the stock of the neighborhood. The women seemed to be the chief managers of the show, as every one we met was driving a black pig with a cord fastened around the neck and body, or leading a cow by the horns to the village near by. For curiosity, we sallied out into the public square to see how such fairs were conducted, and to examine the nature of the animals offered for sale. Taking us to be persons wishing to buy, a buxom young girl, about sixteen, approached us and commenced dilating upon the fine qualities of a large milch cow that we happened to be noticing. She talked so glibly, knowingly and earnestly, that we were disposed to humor the joke, and ask questions about the age of the cow, etc.; whereupon she immediately lifted the head of the animal, opened its mouth, and showed us the marks on the teeth and the ring on its horns, with as much self-possession and accuracy as the most experienced cow dealer. When she had finished we thanked her for the information she gave us, and told her that we were not purchasers, but merely travellers from a distant land who wished to see every thing in her country. Wishing us a happy and prosperous journey, she turned to a real customer and disposed of her cow.

When we reached the village of Chamouni it was after night-fall, and the little square in front of our hotel was illuminated with torch-lights by the friends of an Englishman who had been seen through a telescope during the day on the summit of Mont Blanc. At twelve o'clock the *hero* returned with a long retinue of guides, and expatiated largely to an eager crowd on the many trials, troubles, difficulties and dangers that he had to encounter, wondered how any human being ever summoned courage to perform such a feat, and thanked God that he was spared to return once more to a habitable region and receive the congratulations of his English friends.

Taking his word for it, we concluded not to ascend Mont Blanc so high, but compromised by going to the Mer de Glace, which is neither difficult nor dangerous. Just before reaching Montanvert, a place where refreshments are kept for the accommodation of visitors during the season, we had quite an adventure. One of our party, a gentleman from Boston, concluded he would try the velocity of a stone down the mountain, and accordingly set one in motion, which unfortunately came in contact with a cow before it rolled very far, and to our astonishment the poor animal was hurled with incredible speed to the foot of the mountain. Knowing that we could be of no service to the creature after such a roll, we continued our journey to the Mer de Glace, which is one of the most beautiful sights in Alpine scenery, and wonderful beyond description. The view of this enormous sea of ice is one of the most striking of these scenes of wonder; its great extent, the beauty of its purity, the color and depth of its crevices, surrounded by a thousand nameless pinnacles, render it enchanting and romantic in the extreme.

Many persons cross the Mer de Glace, and go as far as the Jardin or island in the ice; but we dispensed with that privilege—descended the mountain by way of the Glacier, and ascended a mountain called the Flegere on the opposite side of the valley of Chamouni, which affords one of the best views of Mont Blanc. Near the summit of the Flegere is a small *châlet*, where we procured a very good dinner, served in a homely way, but very palatable to a hungry man. After discussing our dinner, we went out and watched the last rays of the setting sun, sinking behind the snow-covered peak of Mont Blanc. The valley beneath was invisible, and we were separated entirely from the inhabitants of the village by a cloud that was as dark and impenetrable as night itself. The panorama presented a picture of singular grandeur and beauty—the time was auspicious, the associations grand, and its recollections imperishable. Returning to Chamouni, we found the owner of the cow we had killed and the syndic of the village awaiting our arrival. The case was properly presented on the part of my friend, who contended that it was an accident. After a great deal of talking and ten thousand gesticulations, my friend was permitted to go, provided he remunerated the owner of the cow.

Leaving Chamouni the following morning, we passed through the Tête Noire to Martigny, and thence to the snow-covered pass of St. Bernard, where we were entertained one night at the Hospice by the monks, who devote their lives to the service of their fellow-men whose pursuits oblige them to traverse these dreary fields in seasons of danger, and the weary traveller who visits their lonely habitations through curiosity. The Hospice is a massive stone building, well adapted to its perilous situation, which is on a very high point of the pass, and exposed to the heavy storms of winter. The building is capable of accommodating more than one hundred persons comfortably; the monks are unremitting in their attentions, and charge nothing for their services—leaving it to the option of the guests to place what they choose in a small bag in the chapel. The room appropriated to visitors is large and convenient; it is hung with many drawings and prints, and is furnished with an excellent library and piano. About the house I saw several St. Bernard dogs, which are altogether different in their appearance from what I had supposed; instead of having long hair, it is short and thick, and their general appearance is very like the large-sized cur of our country—they are very heavy and strong, and capable of enduring more than any other animal. Near the Hospice is what they term the Morgue, or place where they expose the dead bodies found in the snow, which are placed in the frozen position in which they were found; it is a place of melancholy interest, containing the remains of the unfortunate victims for ages past. No one can visit the Hospice of St. Bernard without the satisfaction of being amply compensated for his pains.

Taking leave of the good old monks, we returned to the village of Martigny, and are now wending our way through deep snows over the celebrated Pass of Simplon into Italy.

This remarkable road was built by Napoleon soon after the battle of Marengo, with the view of facilitating the communication between France and Italy, and the ultimate subjection of the latter. It was the first carriage road constructed across the Alps, and now stands as one of the monuments of Napoleon's greatness. To give you some idea of the colossal nature of the undertaking, it may be mentioned that the number of bridges, great and small, constructed for the passage of the road, exceeds six hundred, in addition to the more vast and costly constructions, such as terraces of massive masonry, miles in length, of ten galleries, either cut out of the stone, or built of solid limestone, and of twenty houses of refuge to shelter travellers, and lodge the laborers constantly employed to take care of the road. The cost of this road is said to have averaged four hundred thousand francs per league. The travel over the Simplon road has gradually increased, and it is at present one of the greatest thoroughfares in all Europe.

LETTER TWENTY-EIGHT.

MILAN, Italy.

First Town in Italy—Lago Maggiore—Passports—Examination of Luggage—Milan—Reception of the Emperor—Excursion to Lake Como, etc.

"O Italy! how beautiful thou art!
Yet I could weep; for thou art lying, alas!
Low in the dust: and we admire thee now
As we admire the beautiful in death!"

CROSSING the Alps over the great Simplon road, we passed the first night in a neat little village near the border, called Domo d'Ossola. It was our intention to go on as far as Baveno, situated on Lago Maggiore; but owing to the depth of snow on the Pass, our progress was impeded, and we were compelled to lie over until the following morning. Domo d'Ossola is a small and unimportant town, with few points of interest, save that it is Italian, which was quite enough for us in the *beginning*. The peculiar construction of the houses, with their many-shaped chimneys, colonnades, streets with awnings, shops filled with sausages, maccaroni, and garlic—lazy-looking monks, apparelled in brown-colored gowns, with bare mahogany-looking legs, intermixed with donkeys, well-fed priests, and females veiled with the mantilla, combined to complete a picture at once novel and curious to our eyes.

At Baveno we left the diligence and made an excursion in a small sailing boat to the Borromean Islands, situated in the upper and most beautiful portion of the lake. These islands are two in number, originally barren rocks, now rendered beautiful by the hand of art. Isola Bella consists of ten terraces, the lowest built on piers placed in the lake, rising in a pyramidal form, one above another, and covered with statues, obelisks, vases, and other ornaments. There is a very good hotel on the island, and a garden filled with all kinds of exotics; the orange, citron, myrtle, and pomegranate flourish in abundance, and I have also observed the aloe, cactus, sugar cane, coffee plant, and a camphor tree upwards of twenty feet in height. The Isola Madre is somewhat larger than the former, and situated near the centre of the lake, from which there is a lovely view of the snow-clad Alps, the Simplon Pass, and innumerable little villages on the borders of the water. This island has more natural beauty than the Isola Bella, and also contains a garden worthy of the highest praise.

Leaving our little boat at this point, we boarded the steamer and proceeded to the other extremity of the lake, where we rejoined the diligence at a small town called Sesto Calende, on the Austrian frontier. Here we had a deal of trouble with our passports, luggage, etc. Not satisfied with booking minutely every item in our passports, they tumbled the contents of trunks about with as much *nonchalance* as an old sailor would a wallet of worn-out clothes. Forgetting that we had to undergo an examination, our weapons were left in the trunks, and unfortunately discovered by the Austrian police. The first thing discovered was a six-barrelled revolver, then a stiletto, balls, powder, caps, etc., all of which were drawn out one by one, to the consternation of the bystanders, and to the discomfiture of the owner, who rather feared the consequences, knowing that they were contraband, and that two Americans had recently been imprisoned for much slighter causes. One of the officers intimated that it looked rather suspicious, talked of imprisonment, etc.; but fortunately the captain of the boat came to our assistance, and volunteered to carry them back to the Sardinian government and forward them to Genoa, where they have been received. This difficulty was hardly disposed of when another one arose between a chestnut woman and a Boston Yankee, who happened to be in the diligence. He purchased her chestnuts, and she, Italian-like, wanted to cheat him out of a penny; while he, true to his breeding, resisted "at all hazards and to the last extremity." The dispute grew higher and higher—the crowd gathered around and sided with the woman—and at last the police interfered, and the Yankee got his penny. Laughing heartily at the scene just narrated, we rolled on over the Simplon road through antique villages to the city of Milan. It was night when we entered the massive portal of the Arco de la Pace. The spire of the great cathedral was illuminated, and the figure of the Madonna on the summit shone so brightly that its rays were visible at the distance of many miles. Driving through the Corso, which is a well paved and handsome street, we arrived at a magnificent house, called the Hotel de la Ville, guarded by Austrian soldiers, and the great place of attraction for strangers, who were curious to witness and participate in the pomp and parade exhibited at the reception of the youthful Emperor, Francis Joseph. The following day was Sunday, and the whole city seemed to be alive with the *military;* white coats and epaulets were to be seen in all directions, busy about the arrangements of the day, as the entire reception devolved upon them, the citizens refusing to have any thing to do with the young tyrant—not even the bestowal of ordinary civilities. At the hour of ten the different regiments, mustering upwards of sixty thousand, were assembled on the parade ground near the Arco de la Pace, and called the Piazza d'Armi. It was a magnificent sight; every thing was conducted with perfect order, and the various evolutions of a military review were displayed to the Emperor, in all the pomp and circumstance usual on such occasions.

This being over, he was conducted by this strong guard through the principal streets of the city to the great cathedral, where he knelt and repeated to himself his prayers, while the people stood gazing with vulgar curiosity, anxious to see how the youth bore his honors, and wishing in their hearts any thing but good for his welfare. In appearance, Francis Joseph is tall and slight, rather awkward in address, and wanting in the usual marks that distinguish nature's great men. His reception here must have been any thing but gratifying; there was no enthusiasm, and the people seemed utterly indifferent whether he approved or disapproved of their conduct. During his stay here he feared to remain in the city at night, but went out every afternoon to a fortified town in the neighborhood, and returned the following morning guarded by a regiment of cavalry. How different is it with our President, elevated *voce populi*, and moving among them without fear in the streets of our capital, unguarded and unattended. The more I see of the governments of Europe, the more I admire and appreciate our own; and there is nothing in my opinion so well calculated to make a man patriotic and attached to the union of the States and the perpetuity of our institutions, as a tour of observation among the nations of Europe.

But let us leave this topic for the present, and return to the Duomo or Cathedral, which is considered externally the finest building on the continent. It is the third, and some say the fourth reedification of the original structure, the first being destroyed by Attila, the second by fire, the third by Frederic the First. The first stone of the present Duomo was laid in 1636, and is yet unfinished. Napoleon did much towards bringing it to its present form, and gave an impulse to the works that must always be appreciated by the admirers of architectural beauty. The interior of the building is handsome, but not equal to some other cathedrals in Italy, or in keeping with the exterior, which is beautiful beyond description. View it from any point, and it strikes the beholder with wonder and admiration; but in order fully to understand the merits of the structure, the stranger should ascend the summit, which is reached by two staircases winding in a turret of open tracery. Here the eye rests upon a perfect flower garden, in which nearly every plant is exquisitely represented in white marble, baskets of fruit, cherubs' heads, sunflowers, lilies, and statuary of the rarest workmanship.

A noble view of the plains of Lombardy studded with cities and villages is also presented to the eye, embracing some of the finest lands in Italy. From the cathedral we visited the dilapidated convent of Santa Maria della Grazie, which contains a work of art better known perhaps than any other in the world: the Last Supper, by Leonardo da Vinci. It is one of the wonders of Milan, and may at one time have deserved all the praise bestowed upon it, but at present I defy any man to detect any part of the original expression of any single face or feature on the canvas; not even the coloring is now visible. Aside from the damage it has sustained from damp, decay and neglect, it has been so retouched upon and repainted, and that so badly, that many of the heads are now positive deformities, with patches of paint sticking all over them, and utterly distorting the expression. After looking at this vestige of art, we went into the theatre of La Scala, which is one of the largest and finest in Italy. The form of the house is a semi-circle, with the ends produced and made to approach each other, and it is capable of accommodating 3600 persons comfortably. We did not have the pleasure of hearing an opera within its walls, it being closed on account of the late troubles in Lombardy.

From Milan we made an excursion to the Lake of Como by railroad, a very pleasant little trip, performed in one day. The lake is about forty miles long, and fed principally by the Addo. Taken all together it is the most beautiful sheet of water in Italy, and surpasses in the richness of its tropical vegetation any lake I ever saw.

Many villages adorn its banks, besides the palaces and gardens of Villa d'Este, Villa of Count Taverna, Madame Pasta and Taglioni. No one should visit Milan without availing themselves of the beauties of nature reflected in the bright waters of Como.

LETTER TWENTY-NINE.

VENICE, Italy.

Trip to Venice by way of Verona—Entrance in a Gondola—Piazza of St. Mark—Canals—Churches—Palaces—Excursion to the Lido—Reception of the Emperor.

"There is a glorious city in the sea:
The sea is in the broad, the narrow streets,
Ebbing and flowing; and the salt sea weed
Clings to the marble of her palaces."

OUR journey between the two great cities of Lombardy was not only interesting on account of the number of objects presented for our contemplation, but furnished a variety of travel, which relieved us from the usual tedium of a long distance. At Milan the diligence was placed on the railroad, with the passengers in it, and conveyed to the town of Treviglio, where horses were in waiting to carry us to Bergamo, and thence to the ancient city of Verona, by way of Brescia and the foot of Lago di Garda.

In pleasant Verona we passed an entire day in visiting fair Juliet's tomb, the house of the Capulets, and the great Roman Amphitheatre. The tomb, which is now shown to strangers in the garden of the *Orfanotrofio*, is of reddish marble, originally used as a washing-trough, but so much broken by sentimentalists that but a small portion now remains to designate this imaginary spot. The house of the Capulets has now degenerated into a most miserable little inn, occupied by noisy vetturini and low Italians—a fact well calculated to destroy all associations connected with the mansion. The Roman Amphitheatre, however, is a rich monument of the early periods, standing in the centre of the Piazza di Bra—a spirit of old time, among the familiar realities of the passing hour. The interior is nearly perfect, and so well preserved and carefully maintained, that every row of seats is there unbroken. The old Roman numerals are yet visible over some of the arches, and there are corridors and staircases, and subterranean passages for beasts, and winding-ways, above ground and below, as when the fierce thousands rushed in and out, eager to witness the bloody shows of the arena. Nestling in some of the arches and hollow places of the walls, now, are smiths, with their forges, and small dealers of various kinds, and there are green weeds, and flowers, and grass upon the parapet. But little else is changed. After walking all around and through the mammoth structure, examining every part with the greatest interest, we climbed up to the topmost round of seats, which is one hundred feet from the pavement, furnishing not only a fine view of the magnitude and beauty of the interior, but a lovely panorama of the city and its vicinity, closed in by the distant Alps.

Leaving Verona in the afternoon, on an excellent railroad, we passed through Padua, situated between two ranges of mountains in a narrow valley, filled with grape vines trained on trees, and laden with the most delicious fruit, to the renowned city of Venice. It was late in the night when we reached the station. The officers kindly passed our luggage without the trouble of examination. In the twinkling of an eye the gondoliers had us in keeping, and before we knew by what, or how, we found that we were gliding up a street—a phantom street—the houses rising on both sides of the water, and the long black boat gliding on beneath their windows. It appeared like a heaven, and all was so silent and strange that it was difficult to realize that we were passing through a populous city inhabited by human beings like ourselves. We proceeded up the Canal Grande as far as the Porte di Rialto, where we branched off and continued to hold our course through narrow streets and alleys, all filled and flowing with water. Some of the corners where our way led us were so narrow and acute that it seemed impossible for the long slender boat to turn them; but the skilful gondoliers, with a low, melodious cry of warning, sent it skimming on without a pause. Sometimes the rowers of another dark-looking boat, like our own, echoed the cry, and slackening their speed, as we did ours, would come dashing past us like a dark shadow. At last we reached our hotel, which was once an ancient palace, now converted into a house of entertainment. Feeling no disposition to sleep after passing through such fairy-like scenes, we quietly seated ourselves around a cheerful fire, talked of home and friends, wishing in our hearts that you were with us to share the beauties of this curious old city.

Dreaming of gondolas, palaces, and the Merchant's Daughter, I rose on the following morning and saw the sun rise in splendor (after being obscured for many days) on objects that no words of mine can describe. I looked out on boats and barks—on masts, cordage, flags—on groups of busy sailors, working at the cargoes of their vessels—on wide quays, strewn with bales, casks, merchandise of all kinds—on huge men-of-war, lying at anchor in stately indolence—on islands, crowned with gorgeous domes and turrets, and where golden crosses shone in the light, atop of wondrous churches springing from the sea. "Going down upon the margin of the green sea, rolling on before the door, and filling all the streets, we came upon a place of such surpassing beauty and such grandeur, that all the rest was poor and faded in comparison with its absorbing loveliness." It was the great Piazza of St. Mark, so renowned in story and rich in elegant structures. On the east side stands the old palace Ducale, once the residence of the Doges of Venice, a building much injured and blackened by time, yet more magnificent than all the palaces of Italy. Adjoining it is the Cathedral of San Marco, gorgeous in the wild luxuriant fancies of the East; not far from its porch, a lofty tower called the Campanile, standing by itself, and rearing its proud head high towards heaven, commands a view of the Lido and the Adriatic sea. Near it is a second tower not so lofty as the first, but far richer in its decorations, bearing on its summit a great orb, gleaming with gold and deepest blue; the twelve signs painted on it, and a mimic sun revolving in its course around them; while above, two Herculean statues made of bronze hammer out the hours upon a sounding bell. Two ill-omened columns of red granite—one having on its top a figure with its sword and shield, the other a winged lion—and an oblong square of elegant houses of the whitest stone, surrounded by a light and beautiful arcade filled with jug-shops and busy people, all combined to complete the enchanted scene. After standing for some time admiring first one object and then another, we entered the door-way of San Marco, surmounted by huge gilt horses brought from the Hippodrome at Constantinople when that city was taken by the Crusaders, and ornamented with mosaic of the largest and most costly workmanship. The vestibule extends along the whole front, in the centre of which there is a lozenge of reddish marble, marking the place where Pope Alexander III. and the Emperor Frederic Barbarossa were reconciled, through the intervention of the Venetian Republic. The vaulting is covered with mosaics, and around the walls stand numerous columns of precious marble, brought from the East. The interior is extremely rich; the walls and columns are of precious marbles, the vaulting covered with old mosaics, with gold ground, and the floor is of tesselated marble. In the sacristy we were shown many precious stones and metals, glittering through iron bars, and exhibited only to those who can procure a permission. Some things are exhibited which require more credulity than has fallen to our share to possess; such as the stone upon which John the Baptist was beheaded, and the rock from which the water gushed when touched by the rod of Moses. San Marco is a grand and dreamy structure, unreal, fantastic, solemn, inconceivable throughout.

We then entered the palace, and walked leisurely through the old galleries and council chambers, "where the ancient rulers of this mistress of the waters looked sternly out, in pictures, from the walls, and where her high-prowed galleys, still victorious on canvas, fought and conquered as of old." The halls are bare and empty now, yet retaining some evidences of the ancient importance in the richness and splendor of this structure. Crossing the Bridge of Sighs, which spans a narrow street high above the water, we entered by torchlight the dark and dismal dungeons of the old prison, the very sight of which caused me to shudder and wonder how the human heart could ever have invented such cruelties for the punishment of poor human nature. The cold, damp cells, the instruments of torture, the narrow bridge, and the lions' mouths—now toothless—where denunciations of innocent men were dropped, all remain as commentaries upon the doings of the wicked councils that sat in judgment upon the actions of men.

This is the city of palaces and churches, many of which contain relics and paintings of great value, a description of which would fill many letters.

An excursion to the island of Lido, where Byron used to bathe and ride, is generally made by persons who visit Venice. The beach is devoid of beauty, and the island barren and unattractive, except to those who consider beautiful every spot associated with the poet's name. On our return we stopped at the Armenian College, situated on a small island near the city. We were politely received by one of the priests, who kindly furnished us with an Armenian book published in the College, and introduced us to Lord Byron's tutor, now an old and infirm man, prepared, as he told us, to obey the summons of Almighty God.

While in Milan I gave you an account of the reception of the Emperor in that city, which was cold and formal, being the work of hirelings, and not the spontaneous outpouring of the heart of the great body of the people. In Venice it was pretty much the same, with the exception of the manner, being on the water instead of an open Piazza or broad street. It was midnight when he entered the city, his approach being announced by the thundering of cannon and the sound of a thousand bells. Not wishing to lose the sight, we threw our cloaks around us, hurried through the old Exchange, and stood on the Rialto, under which the procession of gondolas passed. The old bridge was magnificently illuminated with lamps of every color, the palaces on the Canal Grande were all lighted up, music of every kind filled the air, and dark gondolas glided swiftly along to join the procession. In a short time the youthful Emperor came along, and we expected to hear the greeting of the crowd on the Rialto, but all was silent as the grave; no voice was heard to say *Vive l'Empereur*, no face indicated approbation, but all seemed like a funeral, so silent and melancholy that I retired almost regretting that I had gone out.

LETTER THIRTY.

FLORENCE, Italy.

Trip from Venice to Florence, through Padua and Bologna—Appearance of Florence—Her Picture Galleries, Palaces, and Churches—English Church and People in Florence—American Residents and Artists—Flower Girls—Environs—The Grand Duke and Government of Tuscany.

IN two hours after leaving the city of the sea, the rail-cars brought us to the ancient town of Padua, celebrated as the seat of one of the oldest and most renowned universities in Europe, now fast going to decay, and interesting to the stranger only as retaining the armorial bearings of the members, which decorate the walls of the interior Cortite, and the statue of the celebrated Elena Lucrezia Cornaro Piscopice, known and admired for her beauty, purity of character, and universal accomplishments. The Duomo (Cathedral) and some of the palaces of Padua are very fine, but hardly worth mentioning after describing those in Venice. At Padua, we made a contract with a *vetturino* (hackman) to bring us to this city—a long but agreeable journey, occupying four days. This contract would amuse you exceedingly; being drawn up with as much precision as any legal instrument, specifying in plain terms what each party was expected to do, and containing certain restrictions and requirements, altogether necessary for travellers in Italy, who desire to have peace, and wish to avoid a thousand vexations. Our route between Padua and Florence presented many objects worthy of note, if I only had the time and space to bestow upon them. After crossing the Adige, and passing through a region of country which produces the finest vintage, we reached the Po, which is about the size of the Cumberland, and kept within its banks by levees, varying from ten to twenty feet in height. On the third day we entered Bologna, or the city of *sausages*, an ancient sombre-looking place, under a brilliant sky, with heavy arcades over the footways of the older streets, and lighter and more cheerful archways in the newer portions of the town. From the Observatory, situated near the centre of the city, we had an excellent view of the many fine churches—the tall leaning towers, built of brick, and inclining crosswise as if they were bowing stiffly to each other, and the broad plains in the environs, bounded by the lofty range of the distant Apennines. The colleges, and palaces too, and above all, the Academy of Fine Arts, where there are a number of interesting pictures, especially by Guido, Domenichino, and Ludovico Caracci, give Bologna a place of its own in the memory. Even though they were not, and there was nothing else to remember it by, the fact that it required six *visés* on our passports to get out of the gates, is sufficient to make a lasting impression upon us.

Leaving Bologna, we reached the foot of the Apennines, over which we were drawn by four dove-colored oxen, (nearly all the cattle in Italy are dove-colored,) and reached this city on the evening of the fourth day.

> "Of all the fairest cities of the earth,
> None is so fair as Florence."

Situated on the banks of the Arno, in a valley rich in all that is beautiful, and surrounded by lofty and well-shaped mountains, covered with bright villas and smiling groves, it offers a prospect well calculated to captivate the stranger, and entice the thousands who come here annually to spend the winter months. Aside from the beauty of its situation, and salubrity of its climate, Florence is distinguished above all other Italian cities, for the number, extent, and richness of her picture galleries and halls of statuary—palaces that furnish attractions for artists and all amateurs. Among these galleries, the most noted are those in the Uffige and Pitti Palaces, which contain some of the oldest and most valuable works of art now in Europe. "Here, open to all comers, in this beautiful and calm retreat, the ancient masters are immortal, side by side with Michael Angelo, Canova, Titian, Rembrandt, Raphael, Poets, Historians, Philosophers—those illustrious men of history, beside whom its crowned heads and harassed warriors show so poor and small, and are so soon forgotten. Here, the imperishable part of noble mind survives, placid and equal, when strongholds of assault and defence are overthrown; when the tyranny of the many, or the few, or both, is but a tale; when pride and power are so much cloistered dust." The central part of the Uffige palace is a circular room, called the *Tribune*, covered with a cupola, elegantly incrusted or inlaid with mother-of-pearl, paved with the richest marble, and ornamented with the rarest works of the pencil and the chisel. The first that attracted my attention, was the far-famed marble statue called the *Venus de Medici*, and considered by artists as an example of perfect art. It was much broken when found, and the restorations are so poor that the general effect of the statue is very much impaired. The Apollino offers an excellent example of the ideal form of the human figure as entertained by the old masters. The Lostutori, (group of wrestlers,) the L'Arrotino, (slave whetting his knife,) and the Dancing Faun, all exhibit very high qualities of the art, and are justly regarded as among the most valuable monuments of antiquity. The choicest paintings of the collection are also assembled in the Tribune. Here the great works of Michael Angelo and Raphael stand out in living colors, for the admiration of the world. The Virgin presenting the infant to St. Joseph by the first, and a *Venus* by the last named artist, are sufficient in themselves to give a reputation to any museum of art.

The Palazzo Pitti is a large and splendid structure built of rough stone, and now the residence of the sovereign. Its chief attractions are the paintings that adorn the large and well furnished rooms, and the Boboli gardens in the rear, occupying the most elevated site in the city, and filled with terraces, fountains, statuary, arbors, exotics, and every thing calculated to beautify and adorn the spot. Attached to the palace is a museum, superior in many respects to any that we have yet seen. The collection of wax figures exhibiting the human frame in all its parts are unequalled any where, while the collection of birds, minerals, and animals compare well with those in more celebrated museums. Connected with the museum is a room recently erected by the Grand Duke and dedicated to Galileo, who was a resident of Florence. In point of exquisite workmanship and elegant proportions it is well worthy to bear the name of the distinguished astronomer. The floor is of tesselated marble, and the ceiling frescoed, representing the life of Galileo. It contains a full-sized statue of the philosoper in one end, surrounded with his instruments and the busts of his pupils arranged in niches according to their different positions.

Besides the two palaces that I have just briefly described, Florence contains a number of private palaces which are always accessible to strangers, and have in them objects of curiosity no where else to be seen.

Like nearly all of the cities in Italy, Florence can boast of many fine public buildings, the churches taking the precedence. The Cathedral is a mammoth structure, built of tesselated marble, and surmounted by a double dome said to be the largest in the world. The interior is rather dark, owing to the smallness of the windows and the richness of the stained glass which excludes the light. Near the main building is a Campanile and Baptistery, also made of tesselated marble, and considered fine specimens of architectural taste. Next to the Cathedral the churches of San Lorenzo and S.

Croce are the most remarkable. The exterior of the first is nothing but a mass of rough and dingy brick-work, but internally it is extremely rich. The Medicean Chapel "is an illustration of the old story of the painter, who being unable to represent Venus beautiful, covered her with finery." The walls are entirely covered with the richest variegated marbles and *pietre duce;* agate, lapis lazuli, jasper, chalcedony, and other precious stones. Graceful and elaborate representations of flowers in mosaic exhibit on the walls the armorial bearings of the cities and states of Tuscany. This elegant chapel was really intended by its founder, Ferdinand I., for the reception of the Holy Sepulchre, but failing in his object, it was subsequently converted into the cemetery of the grand ducal family. Santa Croce is situated in the ancient part of Florence, and is the principal Church of the Black or Observatine Friars. The exterior is not finished, although it is one of the oldest edifices in the city, and the probability is that it will never be completed, as they would then have no excuse to tax the people. The interior is covered over with sepulchral slabs, most of which are in very low relief, but the monuments erected by the munificence of the city to the memory of Michael Angelo and Galileo exhibit the perfection of modern art. Several members of the Bonaparte family are interred in this church, besides many other persons of distinction. Speaking of churches reminds me to mention that I attended divine service in the English Chapel at the request of a friend, where I had not only to pay fifty cents admission to the woman at the door, but was compelled to listen to an old man's sermon written in his dotage and delivered by a beardless youth, who looked as if he had hardly finished his catechism. This church is supported by the English who leave their homes and come here to live economically, *hearing* that the Florentines live in *style* on less than nothing. There are a number of American residents now in the city, mostly artists, who come here to study the old masters, and obtain advantages that they have not in the United States. We visited the studio of our great sculptor, Hiram Powers, a few days since, and he was kind enough to show us a number of excellent pieces, viz., busts of Washington, Franklin, Clay, Webster, Calhoun, and others, besides a beautiful statue called the Fisher Boy, and the models of his two pieces called America and California. Mr. Powers has a reputation not only at home, but among the artists of Italy, that he may well be proud of. Florence is a charming place, and I cannot bring this letter to a close without alluding once more to its beauties. Every morning when we essay from our hotel, the bright faces of the flower girls greet us with a smile and happy good morning, place bouquets in the button holes of our coats, and dart off to the next passer-by with so much good-humor and playfulness that one cannot but feel kindly towards them and the busy world around. Wherever we go something pleasing presents itself for our contemplation. If we become tired of the streets and public places of the city, we can drive through shady groves and green meadows of the environs, where every thing is fresh, beautiful, and inviting. But there is no sweet without its bitter; the Grand Duke is old and imbecile, without the confidence of his people, and dependent on a foreign soldiery for his persoual safety.

LETTER THIRTY-ONE.

GENOA, Italy.

Trip from Florence to Genoa *viâ* Pisa, Leghorn, and the Sea—Appearance of Genoa from the Harbor—Fortifications—Palaces—Peculiarities of the City—Excursion to Villa Pallavicina—Return to Florence.

RAILROADS are so rare in Italy, and we are so heartily tired of diligences and vetturini, that we came to the conclusion to make a visit to the home of Columbus, as much for the sake of variety as a disposition to see the spot that gave birth to the discoverer of the new world. We started early in the morning, and in two hours found ourselves standing on the Leaning Tower of Pisa, so much admired and talked about abroad, and so insignificant when you draw near to it. When viewed through the highly telescopic medium of popular report, it appears something wonderful, while, in truth, it is hardly worth stopping to see. It has a cylindrical form, and measures fifty feet in diameter, and one hundred and seventy feet in height. It consists of eight stories of columns, in each of which they bear semi-circular arches, forming open galleries round the story. It is easy of ascent by a spiral staircase, and the summit is inclosed with an iron railing to prevent accidents. Seven large bells are suspended around the top, four of which are quite large and three small, and said to be remarkable for their sweetness of sound. The most extraordinary feature of the tower is its leaning tendency, being fourteen feet from the level of the base. It furnishes an extended and beautiful view of the Mediterranean, Leghorn, and the Apennines. Near the tower stands a group of buildings, comprising the Baptistery, the Cathedral, and the Church of the Campo Santo, which, taken together, form perhaps the most remarkable collection in the world. Removed from the ordinary transactions and details of the town, they have a singularly venerable and impressive character. It is the architectural essence of a rich old city, with all its common life and common habitations pressed out and filtered away. The Campo Santo (cemetery) is a curious old place, containing a great number of sepulchral slabs, monuments, and sarcophagi of antiquity. It was the first founded in Italy, and has given its name to every similar place of interment. Here grass-grown graves are dug in earth brought more than six hundred years ago from Mount Calvary, and ancient frescoes very much obliterated adorn the walls of this solemn burial place, subjects taken mostly from the Christian mythology, that is, the lives of the Saints.

Not far from Pisa is the city of Leghorn, (where Smollett was buried,) which is a thriving, business-like, matter-of-fact place, distinguished more for its commerce and manufacture of bonnets than any thing else, and particularly disagreeable to strangers, on account of the many annoyances they are subject to, in the way of passports, porters, beggars and rascals generally.

After going through the ordeal and paying an enormous price for our passage, we boarded the steamer, rested tolerably on a sofa, and woke up the following morning finding ourselves at anchor in the beautiful harbor of "*Genova la Superba.*" It was full of vessels; all seemed active and bustling, reminding me forcibly of her ancient importance and power among the cities of the world. The city is in the form of an amphitheatre, and rises gradually from the water's edge to the summit of the Apennines, which come into the sea just here. The two horns of the crescent, and several peaks in the mountain in the rear of the city, are surmounted with strong fortresses, which command the entire harbor, making it the most formidable place in the Sardinian dominions. Occupying a small compass, it is necessarily very compactly built, and viewing it from the sea, with its terraces rising one above another, garden above garden, palace above palace, and height above height, with its narrow streets and singular-shaped buildings, it presents a picture altogether different from any that I have yet seen. We went ashore in a small boat, had our baggage passed by slipping a small fee in the officer's hands, and in a few minutes found ourselves snugly ensconced in a hotel that was once the palace of some rich merchant in the times when Genoa was in her glory. The streets of the city are generally not more than six feet wide: no carriages are allowed, and every thing is conveyed on the backs of donkeys, mules, and men. As we wended our way through these dark and narrow thoroughfares at the heels of a cicerone, I could but wonder how the human race could exist in such places. I never in my life was so dismayed: the wonderful novelty of every thing, the unusual smells, the unaccountable filth, the disorderly jumbling of dirty houses, one upon the roof of another—the passages more squalid and more close than any in the Five Points of New-York, in and out of which, not beggars, but well-looking and well-dressed females, with white veils over their heads and great fans in their hands, were passing and repassing—the perfect absence of resemblance in any dwelling-house or shop to any thing we had ever seen, perfectly confounded us, and we were not at all disinclined when our guide intimated that it was time to return for dinner. The following day we were ushered into a more inviting part of the city, among the fine palaces. The Strada Nueva and Strada Balbi are somewhat wider than the streets we passed through yesterday, and are famous for the number and magnificence of the palaces that extend from one end of them to the other. We went into a number of them, and found that they were like those in Florence and Venice, which I have previously described. We will not soon forget the bright and happy day that we passed in rambling through these immense mansions, many of the walls of which are alive with masterpieces by Vandyck and other eminent artists.

Near Genoa there is a villa called Pallavicina, belonging to the Pegli family, and just completed, which surpasses in beauty any thing of the kind in Italy, and I may say all Europe. It is situated on a lofty hill on the road to Nice, and commands a beautiful view of the blue Mediterranean, the harbor of Genoa, and a vast region of country round about. There is nothing extraordinary about the palace, except the extensive marble terraces that surround it; but the out-grounds are laid out with great taste, and contain every thing calculated to beautify and adorn the spot. Observatories, rustic seats, grottoes, artificial caves, waterfalls, romantic bridges, boats, swings, fountains, flower beds, and every conceivable convenience are here congregated in a small space, and arranged in such a manner as to give it more the appearance of a paradise than a gentleman's country seat.

From Genoa we intend returning to Florence by way of Spezzia, Lucca, and the marble quarries of Carrara, the road running along the shore of the sea, and presenting a diversity of scenery no where else to be seen but in Italy. It was in the gulf of Spezzia that Shelley was drowned, and it was here that Napoleon intended to establish his stronghold, on account of the safety and commodiousness of the harbor, but was frustrated in his plans by the French Ministry.

LETTER THIRTY-TWO.

ROME, Italy.

Journey from Florence to Rome through Perugia and over the Via Flaminia—Etruscan Remains—Lake Thrasimene—Falls of Terni—Citadel and Aqueduct at Spoleto—First view of the Dome of St. Peter's Church—The Campagna Romana—Ponte Molle—Porta del Popolo—Piazza di Spagna.

"I am in Rome! Oft as the morning ray
Visits these eyes, waking at once I cry,
Whence this excess of joy? what has befallen me?
And from without a thrilling voice replies,
Thou art in Rome!"

IT is discretionary with travellers journeying from the Tuscan capital to the Eternal City to choose between one of three routes—to Leghorn, by railroad, and thence by sea to Civita Vecchia, the land route by Sienna, and another road passing through Perugia and Spoleto. For expedition the first is far preferable, but not so agreeable on account of the inferiority of the boats and the innumerable little annoyances that one is compelled to encounter in the way of passports, hotel keepers, porters, and beggars generally. The second route is shorter, but is less interesting than the third, and presents fewer objects of picturesque beauty. A diligence performs the journey in thirty-six hours, and a courier's carriage in much less time; while the vetturini require six and sometimes eight days. Wishing to see and learn something of the intermediate country, and not being pressed for time, six of us (all Americans) joined together and engaged a vetturino to convey us according to our pleasure within the gates of the Papal Capital. Our first day's journey brought us to Arezzo, a town containing ten thousand inhabitants, and noted as the birthplace of Petrarch, Vasari, Michael Angelo, and other men of distinction. Leaving early the following morning, we made an excursion a short distance from the roadside to Cortona, an ancient Etruscan city, situated on a lofty eminence, surrounded by a massive stone wall, and embracing evidences of Etruscan remains well worthy of the attention of the antiquary. It was founded by the Umbri, and claims to be one of the most ancient cities of the Etruscan league. We went into the Cathedral, which contains the great sarcophagus said to hold the body of the Consul Flaminius, and also into the Museum, where there is a small collection of antiquities, among which the coins and bronzes are the most remarkable. A bronze lamp, discovered in a ditch at La Fratta a few years ago, is the most interesting and valuable object in the collection. It is a round bowl, nearly two feet in diameter, with sixteen lamps around the rim, ornamented with heads of Bacchus, and a Gorgon's face on the bottom. The priest who conducted us through the Museum said that this lamp weighed one hundred and seventy Tuscan pounds.

Leaving Cortona, we soon found ourselves on the site of the battle of Thrasimene so celebrated in Roman history. It is just such a place as an accomplished general would select to take advantage of and destroy his enemy; with the hills of Gauladro on the one side and the lake on the other, encircling the plain upon which the sanguinary battle was fought so completely as to make it appear utterly impossible that any other result could have taken place. The lake which bears the name of the battle is a very pretty sheet of water, about thirty miles in circumference, and surrounded by gentle eminences covered with oak and pine, dotted here and there with a village and olive plantations. We spent the night on its shores at a place called Passignana, which I am sure not one of us will soon forget. The inn, like many others in Italy, was constructed for the accommodation of man and beast, and while we were sipping vile coffee and gnawing *goat cutlets*, our jaded horses were heard stamping below and biting their troughs, as a substitute for more wholesome provender. We made the best of it, however, and started before day the next morning for Perugia, where we made up in a good dinner for lost time, and passed several hours agreeably in examining the gateway, walls, bridges, and other Etruscan remains. On the roadside, near Perugia, is an old tomb, "Grotto di Volunni," discovered by a peasant in 1840, and remarkable for the perfect manner in which it represents the Etruscan mode of interment. It is approached by a long flight of steps descending to the entrance in the hillside, and consists of ten chambers, cut out of the living rock: the largest is twenty-four feet by twelve, and sixteen feet high; the nine others which open into it are of much smaller size, and contain old urns filled with broken bones, inscriptions giving a history of the deceased, lamps suspended from the ceiling, and figures representing the heads of Medusa, the Gorgon, and other characters. Not far from this we got upon the Via Flaminia, which passes through the valley of Clitumnus, and near the temple supposed to be the one described by Pliny as dedicated to the river-god Clitumnus, and celebrated in the writings of Dryden, Addison, and Byron. It is quite small, and now used as a chapel dedicated to St. Salvadore. At Spoleto we stopped a short time, and enjoyed the view from the citadel, which is one of the finest in Italy, and examined the celebrated aqueduct built by Theodelapius III., duke of Spoleto, 604. The citadel is now used as a prison, and contains at present more than five hundred convicts, many of whom were committed for political offences. The aqueduct, which supplies the citadel and town with water from a large spring in a hill opposite and separated by a deep ravine, serves both as a conduit and bridge for foot passengers. It is a work of considerable magnitude, and well deserves examination.

On the fifth day after leaving Florence we visited the Falls of Terni, which are situated in a quiet and romantic region five miles distant from the town of Terni. They have been so frequently described by writers of every grade that I deem it unnecessary to enter minutely upon its beauties, and will therefore give you only some idea of its general effect and peculiarities. The formation of the cascade was not, as one might conclude, the work of nature, but of art —for the purpose of draining the valley of the Velinus from the frequent inundations of the river, which was so charged with calcareous matter, that it filled its bed with deposits, and thus subjected the rich plains of Keeti to constant overflow from the lakes which it forms at that part of its course. The drainage of the stagnant waters produced by the overflow of the lakes was first attempted by the Romans more than two centuries before the Christian era—who caused a channel to be made for the Velinus, through which the waters of that river were carried into the Nera, over a precipice of several hundred feet. The bed of the river above the Falls is forty or fifty feet wide, and the rapidity of the stream is said to be seven miles an hour—flowing down three successive falls into a deep gulf from an altitude of nine hundred feet, sending the spray high into skies, which again

> "Returns in an unceasing shower, which sound,
> With its unemptied cloud of gentle rain,
> Is an eternal April to the ground."

Byron, in his beautiful description of the Falls, rather overshoots the mark, according to the ideas of Americans who have heard the mighty roar of Niagara. "The war of waters and the hell of waters" certainly express more than can be realized by an American viewing the cataracts of the old world. Terni, however, is a place well worth a visit, and in point of beautiful scenery and great height, I give it the preference to all the cascades and torrents that I have yet seen in Europe.

At Nurni we saw the remains of a ruined bridge which has for ages past been regarded as one of the noblest relics of imperial times. Two arches are still standing in a perfect state, exhibiting strongly the superior skill of the ancients in the art of masonry. It is built of large blocks of travertine, without cement, but so closely joined that it would be difficult to insert the smallest instrument between the layers. Anxious to reach the Eternal City, we hurried on, and at noon on the seventh day we descried in the distance the magnificent dome of St. Peter's Church. There it stood like a mighty giant amid innumerable towers, and steeples, and roofs of houses, rising up into the sky, and high above them all bearing the Holy Cross.

It is impossible to describe my emotions as we neared the city of so many historical recollections. I thought of its antiquity, its renown, its glory, and its present lowly state. Even my own brief history involuntarily passed before my mind's eye—the past fruitful in its recollections of pleasures and pains. Collegiate days glowing with Roman story, professional trials and juvenile troubles, all came up and suggested thoughts at once pleasing and painful. We soon entered on the Campagna Romana; an undulating flat where few people can live on account of the malaria, and where for miles and miles there is nothing to relieve the terrible monotony and gloom. We asked our *cocher* to point out the Coliseum and other ancient ruins, but he replied that they were all on the other side of the city. We gave up almost in despair, and were compelled to drive thirty miles over this Campagna without seeing any thing except a few old dirt hovels inhabited by villainous-looking shepherds, with long uncombed hair hanging over their faces, and closely wrapped in brown mantles, tending their sheep. As we approached the city, the appearance of the country became more pleasing, and the vegetation more abundant. Monte Maria, covered with pines and cypresses, bounds the prospect on one side—the hills of Albano and Frascati extend far away in the distance on the other—while the plain of the yellow Tiber was spread out before us. We crossed the *Ponte Molle*, and entered Rome in the afternoon by the Porta del Popolo—which opens upon a spacious and well-built square of the same name, ornamented with a fine fountain and obelisk brought from Heliopolis, the On of Scripture.

We expected to be examined pretty closely before they would permit us to pass through the gates, but to our utter astonishment the officer came to the carriage door and openly demanded a bribe of ten pauls—which we paid, (*of course*,) and drove on to our hotel in the Piazza di Spagna without any examination. We said not a word, but thought what a commentary upon the government of the Pope.

LETTER THIRTY-THREE.

ROME, Italy.

Visit to the Capitol—View of the City and Campagna—The Corso and public Squares of the Modern City—The Museum—Castle of St. Angelo—St. Peter's Church—The Vatican and other Palaces—The Pope, Cardinals, and Government of the Papal States.

"O Rome! my country! city of the soul!
The orphans of the heart must turn to thee,
Lone mother of dead empires, and control
In their shut breasts their petty misery."

OUR first care, after arriving here, was to look about, inquire, and select suitable apartments, conveniently situated for visiting the various sights of the city—an undertaking apparently trifling, but really of considerable moment to a man who has an eye to time and fatigue. Following the advice and complying with the wishes of friends, we made the proper arrangements at a hotel, situated near the Piazza di Spagna, at the foot of the Pincian Hill, the favorite promenade of the modern Romans. This work being finished, our next object was to mount some lofty height and survey the great theatre of so many historical recollections. Our *valet de place* informed us that the tower of the Capitol and the dome of St. Peter's Church afforded the best views, but that the former was the most desirable, being situated on the summit of the Capitoline Hill, which separates the ancient from the modern city, the work of the Popes from that of the Cæsars. Passing through the Corso, a long and narrow street, lined on either side with shops, palaces, and private houses, sometimes opening into a broad piazza, we came to a long flight of marble steps, blackened by time and ornamented with two colossal statues of Castor and Pollux, with their horses, besides the milestone on the old Appian Way, and other relics of antiquity. Walking through a piazza, ornamented with a fountain and bronze equestrian statue of Marcus Aurelius, we ascended a long and narrow flight of wooden steps, which led us to the summit of the tower. Here we realized, in one sweep of the eye, all the dreams of our boyish days and the hopes of later years. Like nectar, we drank in, to our heart's content, the beauties of a panorama rich in history, in memory, and in truth. The *Seven Hills*, the yellow Tiber, running out of its bank and spreading desolation in its course, the broad Campagna extending to the sea on the east, and the distant range of the snow-capped mountains on the west, formed the outlines of the picture—filled up on one side with the remains of the old Aqueduct, the Coliseum, the Forum, and innumerable temples, and on the other with the great dome of St. Peter's Church, spires without number, and the lofty palaces of the modern Romans. Descending, we went into the Museum, situated on the piazza alluded to above, and opposite the Conservatory. The building is small, and the collection much less extensive than that of the Vatican, and contains only a few first-rate works of sculpture. The most remarkable objects to be seen here are two ancient sarcophagi, elegantly worked, the bronze horse discovered in 1849 in the Vicolo delle Palme, the infant Hercules, also in bronze, statues of Agrippina, mother of Germanicus, Venus of the Capitol, the Faun, and the Amazon, all of which are executed in the most perfect manner. In the Conservatory, used for the sittings of the Senate, I observed some good paintings and exquisite statuary, particularly a collection in a room dedicated to Canova, embracing the busts of nearly all the modern artists of celebrity. Just back of the Conservatory is the Tarpeian Rock, which we approached through a small kitchen garden, and found it surrounded with dirty buildings and filled nearly up with rubbish from the streets. Enough remains, however, to point out

"The steep
Tarpeian: fittest goal of Treason's race—
The promontory whence the traitor's leap
Cured all ambition."

Leaving this fated place, we drove through the principal squares and streets of the modern city, and found them as reported, extremely filthy and disagreeable. The piazzas are generally ornamented either with fountains or Egyptian obelisks; while the narrow streets, paved with lava, are without sidewalks, and lighted at night with oil. The Corso is the only street in Rome on which a person may walk with impunity in inclement weather, and even here there is danger of being jolted into a mud-hole by a begging monk, or spattered from top to toe by some *Jehu* driving most furiously towards the goal of the ancient Capitol.

Rome, like Venice, is distinguished for the number and magnificence of her churches, a description of which would be not only uninteresting to you, but too great an undertaking to embrace in a single letter. Next to St. Peter's, which overshadows all the rest, the churches of St. Paul, St. John Lateran, Santa Maria Maggiore, and the church of the Jesuits, are particularly distinguished. St. Paul's is situated in the outskirts of the city, on the bank of the Tiber, and when completed will vie with any building in Italy. It is extremely rich in solid alabaster columns, mosaics, statuary, and paintings. To describe St. Peter's church seems almost a work of supererogation, after the thousand and one descriptions that have appeared from time to time in books and the letters of travellers. We will not attempt, therefore, to enter into any thing like a minute representation of this great building; but will merely write down our impressions after several visits. It is situated not far from the west bank of the Tiber, and opposite to the main part of the modern city. Crossing the Ponto St. Angelo, near the castle of the same name, we came in sight of the stupendous building. At first I was really disappointed in its dimensions and external appearance, and this disappointment continued until we entered the great door-way, walked through the various aisles and chapels, and ascended the mammoth dome, from which the greatness, the glory, the surpassing grandeur of St. Peter's was revealed to our bewildered senses. The exterior is not so beautiful or rich in architectural embellishments as the Cathedral at Milan, but take it all in all, it surpasses any edifice now in the world. The Piazza in which it stands, with its cluster of large and exquisite columns, and its gushing fountains, so fresh, so broad, and free, and sparkling, nothing can exaggerate, while the semicircular colonnades, sixty feet wide and about the same height, supported by four rows of columns, through which carriages pass, terminate in two galleries three hundred and sixty feet long and twenty-three broad, and communicate with the vestibule of St. Peter's. The entire structure is built of travertine, and decorated, the summit with colossal statues of saints, etc. To form some idea of the immensity of the Cathedral, I quote from another the following facts relative to the time of building and cost: "It required three centuries and a half to bring it to perfection, and its progress during that period extended over the reign of no less than forty-three Popes. The expenses of the works were so great that both Julius

II. and Leo X. resorted to the sale of indulgences for the purpose of meeting them. At the close of the seventeenth century the cost was estimated at £10,000,000, not including the sacristy and other parts since finished. The annual expenditure on repairs, superintendence, etc., is £6,300." Now that I have given you some idea of the extent, cost, and external appearance of St. Peter's, you must go with me through the vestibule and massive door-way into the interior, which comprises all that is beautiful and grand in architecture, mosaic work, statuary, and paintings. The nave is vaulted and ornamented with sunk coffers, elaborately decorated with gilding and stucco ornaments. Five massive piers, supporting four arches, separate the nave from each side aisle. Each pier is faced with two Corinthian pilasters, having two arches between them occupied by colossal statues of saints, etc. Numerous chapels, corresponding with the great arches of the nave, are arranged on either side of the church, and tend to break the general effect and reduce the appearance of the aisles. The pavement is entirely composed of marble, and the walls and piers are generally faced with plates of marble, varied with medallions and other sculptures. The vases for the holy water, sustained by cherubs, and the numerous statues and monuments of merit that fill up the niches and other vacant places, also add to the beauty of the interior.

The first object that fixes attention after entering, is the Baldacchino, or grand canopy covering the high altar. It is of solid bronze supported by four spiral columns of the composite order, and covered with the richest ornaments. The High Altar is immediately over the grave of St. Peter, and is surrounded by a circular balustrade of marble, from which are suspended more than a hundred lamps which are kept constantly burning night and day. In the centre of this holy place there is a statue of Pius VI., one of the finest works of Canova, representing the Pope in a kneeling posture, praying before the tomb of the Apostle. Above is the great dome covered with mosaics, and an inscription representing in letters of gold the following words: TV. ES. PETRVS. ET. SVPER. HANC. PETRAM. ÆDIFICABO. ECCLESIAM. MEAM. ET. TIBI. DABO. CLAVES. REGNI. CŒLORVM. Near the Baldacchino is the famous bronze statue of St. Peter, seated on a pedestal with the right foot extended, in order, I suppose, to give the multitude a fair opportunity to kiss its great toe. Go into St. Peter's when you may, you will find all true Catholics, irrespective of age, sex, or condition, paying homage to this cold and forbidding statue. Some who have an eye to cleanliness first wipe off the toe with their handkerchiefs, but the great majority just kneel, then touch the toe with their forehead and then their lips, apparently with great devotion and reverence.

Beneath the dome and under the canopy are the catacombs, or burial place of saints, heroes, and popes. With the aid of a wax candle in the hands of a priest, we were enabled to discover in the dark several fine monuments and an elegant sarcophagus of an ancient prefect of Rome, named Junius Bassus, in two stories of marble. These subterranean apartments are perfectly dry and pure, affording a suitable place for the reception of the good and the great. After going through the main body of the church and all of its various apartments, we ascended the dome by means of an inclined plane as high as the roof, and a winding staircase to the summit. Here, six Tennesseans and two other Americans entered the great ball, (capable of holding sixteen persons,) and looked down four hundred feet on the walking figures on the pavement below. Nothing can surpass the magnificence of this stupendous work, as viewed from the summit. It looks like a village of workshops, inhabited by those who are constantly employed in repairing the edifice. The view is also superb, embracing objects of great interest and beauty. Just below, under the shadow of the dome, are the gardens attached to the Vatican, in which the Pope sometimes passes his leisure moments. On the west, the white sails may be seen spreading to the breeze, bearing the barks of many nations, laden with the products of this balmy clime. On the south, the mighty monuments in the "city of the dead" rear their lofty heads so high that one cannot fail to be impressed. On the east, the distant mountains, half covered with snow, rear their dreary peaks high above the Campagna, reminding us that it is winter, while the Roman lady wears the garb of summer. With this feeble description we take leave of a structure where

"Majesty,
Power—glory—strength and beauty—all are aisled
In one eternal ark of worship undefiled."

At the head of the collections in the palaces of Rome, the Vatican or Palace of the Pope, with its treasures of art, its enormous galleries and staircases, and suite upon suite of immense chambers, ranks highest and is the richest. Many most noble statues, wonderful pictures, and curious antiquities are there, nor is it presumptuous in me to say there is a considerable amount of rubbish there, too. It is a stupendous structure, but being built at different periods it looks more like a collection of separate buildings than one regular palace, and hence its general appearance is any thing but prepossessing. It contains 4422 apartments, eight grand and two hundred smaller staircases. The space it occupies is immense, its length being 1151 English feet, and its breadth 767 feet. It happened to be a day of celebration when we visited the Vatican, and we saw for the first time a meeting of the Pope and his Cardinals, in the Capella Sistina, celebrated as containing the fresco painting of Michael Angelo, and Raphael's great masterpiece, called the Last Judgment. Being no great judge of the fine arts, I will not venture an opinion as to the merits of this much talked of work, and, indeed, it would be difficult for any one to give an opinion on account of the great damage it has sustained by retouches and the action of time. The celebration alluded to was exceedingly interesting. The Pope entered, clothed in his pontifical robes, made of white satin and spangled with gold, while the Cardinals, who are mostly old men, made their appearance in scarlet robes with long trains borne by pages. Not understanding the language, I of course could not enter into the particulars of the ceremony, and can only state there was a great deal of formality, and the most superb sacred music from the choir that I have ever listened to. The Pope is rather prepossessing in appearance, being tall, well formed, and graceful, with a countenance indicative of goodness and intelligence. Leaving him, however, for the present, let us return to our description of the Vatican, which is full of interest to the stranger. The Library is beautifully arranged, and contains 23,000 manuscripts, besides numerous volumes of great value. The manuscripts are rare and ancient, but accessible only by permission from the Pope, which is rarely granted on account of the great fear they have that they might be injured. The gallery of paintings is small but select, containing the masterpieces of the old painters. Here I observed the Gobelin tapestries, taken from the Cartoons of Raphael, which are considered very fine. The collection of Roman and Egyptian antiquities in this palace is unsurpassed. One might pass months and months in the examination of the numerous objects in the Vatican, and finally give up in despair.

Rome also abounds in many private palaces of great note, some of which contain rare paintings, statuary, etc. All are accessible, and their owners seem to take pride in exhibiting them to the world. Many of these elegant mansions, once the abode of luxury and wealth, are now vacant, and their occupants banished in foreign lands. Rome, like Florence, was too weak to govern herself, and consequently fell into the hands of a foreign power. The French are in possession of the city, which was once the mistress of the world. A regiment of Swiss guards are hired to protect the person of the Pope, whose political influence is on the decline. The people want a republic, and they are only waiting for an opportunity to renew hostilities.

LETTER THIRTY-FOUR.

ROME, Italy.

The Pope in state on the Corso—American Chapel in Rome—The Forum, Pantheon, Coliseum, and other ancient remains—Drive on the Appian Way—Excursions in the neighborhood of Rome.

"While stands the Coliseum, Rome shall stand;
When falls the Coliseum, Rome shall fall;
And when Rome falls, the world."

BEFORE entering into the precincts of the "city of the dead," about which so many learned disquisitions have been recorded, and so many orations delivered, I must describe to you briefly a procession on the Corso, and festival at the church of San Carlo, in which the Pope, his Cardinals, and the Senators of Rome participated. Such gala-days are not unfrequent in the Holy City, and consequently create very little excitement among the citizens; while the stranger from a far country, unused to such display and ceremony, is all alive to see and learn the *modus operandi.* Hearing that this festival was to take place at a certain hour, we walked from our hotel to the Corso, through which the procession was to pass. The street on either side was lined with the French soldiery, and the balconies, ornamented with yellow curtains, were occupied by well-dressed females, with flowers in their hands, as an offering to his Holiness. In a few minutes after our arrival, the Swiss Guards, dressed in a uniform introduced by Michael Angelo, and similar in appearance to the coat of many colors made by Israel in his old age for his son Joseph, made their appearance at one end of the long street, followed by a numerous train of carriages filled with the Pope, his Cardinals, the Senators and the High Priests of the city. The carriage containing his Holiness was exceedingly elegant, drawn by six spirited black horses, and mounted with six outriders. As it moved slowly along the Corso, the soldiery laid down their arms, every person fell upon his knees, and the Pope with the mystic sign of his finger, bowing first to the right and then to the left, created a scene at once solemn and impressive. Arrived at the church of San Carlo, he was taken out of his carriage, placed in a large arm-chair, and carried through the different aisles on the shoulders of his Cardinals, followed by a procession of priests, bearing torches, incense, etc. Two priests, holding in their hands enormous fans, made out of peacocks' feathers, walked on either side of the chair, and the females present were all dressed in black, and veiled so closely that it was impossible for the closest observer to obtain a furtive glance at their hidden faces. To go through the details of the ceremony would be uninteresting to you; suffice to say, that it occupied about three hours, and it is only one out of more than one hundred festivals that take place every year in the Eternal City.

After the conclusion of the various forms alluded to, the Pope repaired to the Vatican, and we to the American Legation, where we listened to an excellent sermon, delivered by a gentleman from the State of Michigan. Fifteen or twenty Americans were present, making one feel as if he were at home listening to the doctrines of divine wisdom from the lips of some familiar friend. The chapel is attached to the Legation, and is supported by voluntary contribution. It is the first and only Protestant church ever established in Rome —a privilege granted by the Pope to our present Chargé d'Affaires on account of the interest taken by him in the revolution of 1849, and the high regard entertained by the Pope for the people and government of the United States.

For the antiquarian, fond of searching out and deciphering ancient inscriptions; for the architect, who desires to see the highest achievements in his art; for the historian, who wishes to chronicle the mighty works of the past; for the artist, who wishes to catch inspiration from the living pictures of the old masters; and for the poet, who wishes to infuse into his verse the spirit of bygone ages, let him visit the Eternal City. Here they will find a field rich in all that is calculated to inspire the creative mind. Before going beyond the walls of the present city, there is much to see in the way of antiquities that I have not heretofore alluded to. The Pantheon still stands in a perfect state, and occupied as a church. It is situated in the herb-market, a small dirty piazza, rarely frequented at the present day, except by the lowest people. We have had no opportunity of examining the interior of the *rotunda*, on account of the water which was at times two or three feet deep on the pavement, from the overflow of the Tiber. The portico, which is composed of sixteen Corinthian columns of oriental granite, with capitals and bases of Greek marble, has been admitted by most writers to be beyond criticism, and indeed the entire structure fully merits the description given by Byron in his Childe Harold:

> "Simple, erect, severe, austere, sublime,
> Shrine of all saints and temple of all gods,
> From Jove to Jesus—spared and blessed by time,
> Looking tranquillity, while falls and nods
> Arch, empire, each thing round thee, and man plods
> His way through thorns—glorious dome!
> Shalt thou not last? Time's scythe and tyrants' rods
> Shiver upon thee—sanctuary and home
> Of art and piety—Pantheon! Pride of Rome."

Not far from this stately structure is the Dogana di Terra, or Roman custom-house, formerly the Temple of Antoninus Pius. Eleven columns of Greek marble in the Corinthian style still adorn the front of the edifice, but are much injured by time and the action of fire. Just beyond, at the foot of the Quirinal, are the remains of the celebrated Forum of Trajan, and the unrivalled column, which still stands the pride of Rome in the midst of its ruins. Most of the Forum was buried many feet under the surface, but the excavations of recent years have brought to light many beautiful specimens of architecture that would otherwise have been lost to the world. The fragments of many columns, made of Egyptian granite, still occupy their original position, and convey to the mind some idea of the extent and magnificence of the building that was once the pride of Rome. The space occupied by the ruins is now inclosed with a wooden fence, used by the washerwomen in the neighborhood for drying clothes upon. The square is built up badly, and quite as uninviting as the region round about the Pantheon. Ascending the Quirinal from the Forum, we went into the gardens of the Colonna Palace, which are remarkable for several pine trees of enormous size, and the massive fragments of a building, supposed to be the Temple of the Sun. Passing the Palace of the Pope and the celebrated fountain in the piazza on the summit of the Quirinal, we proceeded to the Viminal, upon which are the remains of the Bath of Diocletian, said to have covered many acres. The ruins of this structure are now apparent in a portion of a circuit of brick wall, in an immense hall converted into a church, called St. Maria of the Angles, and other large brick walls and arches used for different purposes. Some of the pillars of the hall still remain in their original position. We counted eight made of Egyptian granite which measured fifty feet in height, and five feet through. Every thing evinces what great amount of labor was bestowed by the ancients upon their baths. Many objects of interest are to be seen in this neighborhood, such as the barracks of Diocletian, the garden of Sallust, the Porta Salina, through which the Sabine women entered, and the Villa of Albano, celebrated for its gardens and great collection of rare statuary and paintings.

The most prominent objects of curiosity in the way of antiquities, occupy but a small space in and near the Capitoline and Aventine Hills. Just back of the Capitol is the celebrated Roman Forum, occupying the valley formed by the two hills. The floor of the ancient edifice is about twenty feet below the surface of the earth, but has been mostly excavated, and is now plainly seen. Fourteen columns are still standing, and the Arch of Septimus Severus is almost perfect. We descended into the prison near the Forum, in which St. Paul and St. Peter are said to have been confined; drank of the water out of the well in the centre of the dungeon; placed our hands in the print made on the wall by the head of St. Peter, when smitten by the soldier, and saw the hole through which he made his miraculous escape. The dungeon is about thirty feet under ground, and the entrance is occupied as a chapel, to which hundreds resort daily for the purpose of prayer. On the summit of the Aventine are the remains of the Palace of the Cæsars. The brick arches are used for stables, and the space occupied by the palace is now covered over with a garden of vegetables. Just beyond we passed through the arch of Titus, and the ruined temple of Venus, to the great Coliseum, which is without question the most stupendous ruin in the world. Most things, as seen through the writings of travellers, and the highly telescopic medium of popular report, usually fall short of one's expectations; but the Coliseum is, in truth, far ahead of any description that I have ever read; it cannot be exaggerated, but, on the contrary, richly merits all the high eulogiums bestowed upon it in ancient and modern times. It is not so perfect as the one at Verona, as much of the stone has been taken away and used for build ing the palaces of modern Rome. This unhallowed demolition, I am happy to say, has been prohibited, and Pope Pius IX. deserves much praise for his restorations here and elsewhere. Only two thirds of the original structure now remain, which is amply sufficient to verify the truth of the lines quoted in the commencement of this letter. It is built of large blocks of travertine, brick-work, and tufa; the Corinthian, Doric and Ionic orders prevail, and its shape, as usual, is elliptical. The arena, which was once the scene of gladiatorial spectacles, now contains the peaceful cross, promising for every kiss an indulgence of two hundred days, and fourteen statues of our Lord's Passion are arranged around it. A Franciscan monk preaches in the arena every Friday, and who that has ever listened to divine service in the Coliseum can fail to remember the solemn impressions created upon his mind on such an occasion?

Leaving this wonderful monument of ancient Rome, we procured a carriage and drove out on the Appian Way, which is not only interesting of itself, but passes through miles of ruined tombs and broken walls, that are full of historical recollections. The Baths of Caracalla first attracted our attention. They are situated on the eastern slopes of the Aventine, and are the most perfect of all the Roman thermæ, and with the exception of the Coliseum, are the most extensive ruins in Italy. They occupy an area not less than one mile in circuit, and give one a more correct idea of the extent and construction of ancient baths than either those of Diocletian or Titus. Passing through the Porta Latina, we stopped to see several Columbaria, (or tombs,) and among them the Columbarium of the slaves of Augustus. They consist of square vaults under ground, with rows of niches for urns, one above another. The bones of the deceased were placed in the urns, and inscriptions on the outside of the niche, showing the name, age, and death of each person. The tomb of the Scipios is the most ancient and interesting of all the tombs yet discovered; it is marked by a solitary cypress tree, and consists of a number of subterranean chambers, brought to light after having been undisturbed for more than twenty centuries. Several curious sarcophagi and numerous inscriptions of a very old date were excavated out of these chambers. Driving a little further, we passed the circus of Romulus, where the course of the chariots, the stations of the judges, competitors, and spectators, are yet as plainly to be seen as in old time; passed the tomb of Cecilia Metella, and entered the church of San Sebastiano, under which is the entrance to the catacombs, so celebrated as the place of burial, and also of the assemblage for the meetings of the early Christians. These passages have been explored for ninety miles, and form a chain of labyrinths sixty miles in circumference. We walked through various chambers, accompanied by a priest with wax candles, and found them to be nothing more than excavations out of the earth, and in appearance similar to our small caves. In one of the chapels of this church, the priest exhibited a stone in a glass case, upon which there is an impression of two foot-prints, said to be those of Christ when he visited St. Peter in Rome, who said to him, "*Domini quo vades.*"

Tired of looking at broken aqueducts, broken temples, and broken tombs, we returned to the city over an excellent road, called the Nova Appia, and entered the Porta San Giovanni, situated near the church of St. John Lateran and the Scala Santa, in which are the marble steps upon which Christ descended when he was sentenced by Pontius Pilate. This holy staircase is composed of twenty-eight steps, said to have belonged to Pontius Pilate's house, and to be the identical stairs on which our Saviour trod. Pilgrims ascend it only on their knees. It is quite steep, and at the summit is a small chapel, said to be full of relics, into which the people peep through iron bars, and then descend by one of two side staircases, which are not sacred, and may be walked on. Fifty to one hundred pilgrims, male and female, old and young, high and low, may be seen at any time ascending this staircase on their knees. I never, in my life, saw any thing else so ridiculous and absurd as this sight—ridiculous in the many incidents connected with it, and absurd in its senseless and unmeaning degradation. There are two steps to begin with, and then a wide landing. Those who are most zealous begin at the beginning and go up to the top very slowly, resting on each step to repeat a prayer and kiss a cross cut in the wooden planks that cover the marble. This covering has been renewed three or four times, having been worn out by the knees of the pilgrims. We saw two American gentlemen go up, merely for the sake of saying that they had performed the feat. They got on charmingly, as if they were doing a match against time, and were up and down before some of the ladies had accomplished their half dozen stairs. Most of the penitents came down looking as if they had been regenerated, and had accomplished some substantial deed, which it would require a great deal of sin to counterbalance.

The excursions in the vicinity of Rome are charming, and full of interest to the stranger, independent of the many changing views they afford of the broad Campagna. Hadrian's Villa, which was in early times so rich in every thing calculated to adorn a country-seat, still possesses an interest even in its ruined walls. Tivoli, where the river Arno is diverted from its natural course, and made to plunge headlong more than one hundred feet in the yawning caverns below, is also worthy of a visit. There, too, is the Villa d'Este, deserted and rapidly decaying, among groves of melancholy pines and cypress trees, where it seems to lie in state. Then, there is Frascati, and on the hill above, the remains of Tusculum, where Cato was born, and where Cicero lived and wrote and beautified his favorite home.

LETTER THIRTY-FIVE.

NAPLES, Italy.

Journey from Rome to Naples—The Pontine Marshes—The Town of Fondi—A Night at Capua—Arrival at Naples—The Hotels—Lazzaroni—The Bay and General Appearance of Naples.

"This region, surely, is not of the earth:
Was it not dropt from Heaven? Not a grove,
Citron, or pine or cedar, not a grot
Sea-worn and mantled with the gadding vine,
But breathes enchantment."

No people in the world are so much attached to each other, or evince in foreign lands so much clannishness, as the citizens of the several States of the American Union. The Englishman, the Frenchman, the German, and most travellers in this part of the world, go from one end of the continent to the other without forming a valuable acquaintance, and apparently caring very little for their own countrymen whom they meet *en route*. With the Americans, it is totally different; they generally travel in parties, always make inquiries at the hotels about their countrymen, and are pretty well posted relative to each other's movements. To illustrate this fact, I will merely mention that our party consisted of four while in northern Italy, and that we set out from Rome with our number increased to twelve, which I confess was rather too large for agreeability. We drove down the Corso after an early breakfast, gazed on the Capitol, Forum, and Coliseum, probably for the last time, and took leave of the "city of the soul" through the lofty Porta San Giovanni, from which begins the Via Appia Nova. All the forenoon was occupied in making our way to Albano, situated on a high hill, at the southern extremity of the broad Campagna. Here we stopped at a hotel that was a few years since occupied by some family, who abandoned it on account of the political troubles of the country. It is a magnificent building, commanding a view of Pompey's Villa, the sea, and the city of Rome. After dinner we proceeded as far as Cisterna, the place near which the "*tres tabernæ*" mentioned in the Acts of the Apostles were situated. Here the early Christians repaired to meet St. Paul on his way to Rome. I do not know what it was then, but this whole region is any thing but inviting at present. The habitations of the peasantry along the roadside are made in the rudest manner, being nothing more than a few poles placed on end and covered with straw, giving them the appearance of hay stacks. Having no floors, they build their fires in the centre, and the smoke escapes through the door, which is the only aperture. In one place, we saw an entire village laid out regularly and built up with these hay-stack habitations. The people living here are mostly shepherds, who spend their lives with their flocks and dogs, secluded from the world, and perfectly content if they make enough to keep soul and body together. Soon after leaving Cisterna, we entered the Pontine Marshes, which, in ancient times, contained the site of twenty-three of the most flourishing cities in Italy. An excellent road is made across them, shaded by a long, long avenue of elm trees. The marshes are twenty-four miles in length, and from six to fifty-two in breadth, covering some of the best lands in Italy, which might be easily reclaimed, if they were in the hands of an energetic people. At Terracina our *cocher* bribed the officers of the doganna, (which is a regular business,) and we passed into the Neapolitan dominion without the vexation of having our baggage overhauled—which, together with passports, is so annoying as to almost make one swear to leave the country. Passing the second night at Mola, situated on the sea in sight of Gaeta, where Pope Pius IX. found refuge during the troubles of 1848, we proceeded to the city of Capua, passing through the ancient town of Fondi, so celebrated in robber stories. I made a note of this place, because the people whom we saw in the streets presented many peculiarities of feature, dress and manner, differing entirely from any we have heretofore seen. One main street, or channel of mud and refuse, divides the town, in the centre of which is a square and churches, into which the beggars were pouring from all quarters. We stopped in the square to change horses, and in a few minutes our carriage was surrounded by a wretched set of hollow-cheeked and scowling beggars, who demanded charity in a tone of voice indicating utter despair and recklessness. The men were habited in frowsy brown cloaks, thrown over their shoulders after the manner of the Spaniards, with conical-shaped hats, and countenances fierce and haggard, remindng me strongly of the sieges and pillages enacted here in early times by Barbarossa and his companions. The women occupied the windows, encouraging by signs and words the group of miserable, naked children that surrounded us, to persist in their importunities for charity. Poor, ignorant, and degraded people! they know nothing of the comforts of life, the beauties of religion, or the duties of man.

Surrounded by this motley concourse, we moved on, expecting to reach Naples the same evening, but were disappointed; our horses gave out, and we were compelled to pass the night at Capua; and a miserable night it was. The town is occupied by the king's soldiers, and the hotels all appropriated, compelling us to seek lodging elsewhere. As a *dernier ressort*, we quartered ourselves in a large room, in a house belonging to a widow lady, which was also occupied by soldiers. A large brasier, filled with live coals, was placed in the centre of the room by the good lady's daughter, who retired in a most gracious manner, wishing us a comfortable rest; while we felt well assured that we would have no rest at all. I do wish you could have seen us, sitting cozily around that brasier, discussing the inclemency of the weather, our eternal horror of all *vetturini* and Italians generally, the great annoyance occasioned by the nocturnal visits of fleas and other vermin, the filthiness of Capua, and the rowdyism of the military. Having disposed of our spleen, we retired for the night—five of us in four beds, and our servants in the carriage. The following morning we sipped coffee in a miserable *caffee*, and left for Naples on the railroad, fully satisfied that Capua was not so seductive to a traveller now as the soldiers of Prætorian Rome were wont to find the ancient city of that name.

We reached Naples at an auspicious time; there was a storm at sea, and the whole bay was in commotion—dashing the waves over the quays, flooding the streets with water, and driving vessels furiously from their anchorage. It was a glorious sight; and hereafter, when I think of Naples, it will be in connection with that storm. The rain descended in torrents, and we reached our hotel, situated on the bay, some distance from the railroad station, perfectly drenched, and fully satisfied with the labors of the day.

The hotels in Naples are nearly all situated on the quays, and we were so fortunate as to secure rooms commanding a beautiful view of the bay, the islands of Capri and Ischia, Mount Vesuvius, the ancient cities of Pompeii and Herculaneum, besides a number of modern villages that skirt the shore. At certain hours of the day we enjoy this prospect exceedingly—early in the morning before the lazzaroni creep out of their hotels, and at noon when they are basking in the sun, or eating *maccaroni* by the yard at sunset. It is hard to associate agreeably the beauties of nature and the degradation of our poor species: to enjoy the one, we must be separated from the other. It is not well to find miserable depravity and wretchedness on the same canvas with the picturesque and enchanting: they do not harmonize; the effect of the one destroys our disposition to regard the other.

The bay, about which you have heard and read so much, is terminated by two capes—that of Misenum on the north, and of Minerva on the south—and is closed in by the island of Capri, once made notorious by the deified beast Tiberius. A part of the city extends to the west, in the form of an amphitheatre, on the hills of Posilippe, Saint Elmo, and Antignano; another part to the east in a plain, covered with villas from the Ponte della Maddalena to Portici and to Vesuvius. Towards the north, Naples is surrounded by a ridge of hills, which separate it from the Terra di Lavoro, or those fertile plains, the Campagna Felice, called by the ancient Romans their richest patrimony.

The shape of the bay, the position of Naples, the grandeur of Vesuvius, and the thousand distant beauties here assembled, combine to complete a picture that no pen can exaggerate.

LETTER THIRTY-SIX.

NAPLES, Italy.

The Piazzi Royal and its attractions—Strada di Toledo—The Museum—The Gardens of the Villa Reale—Grotto—Tomb of Virgil—Peculiarities of the City—Campo Santo—Excursions to Baiæ, Paestum, Vesuvius, Pompeii, and Herculaneum—The Neapolitan Government, etc.

IN the way of sights, as it is usually expressed, Naples does not compete with Rome, Florence, or Venice; there being only a few objects within the limits of the city deserving the stranger's attention.

Quality, however, will make up for quantity; and, although we have but few places to visit, they contain much to interest and instruct the inquiring mind. I do wish you could have been with us during our first day's ramblings, as it is utterly impossible for me to convey, on paper, all that came under our observation.

Setting out early in the morning from our hotel on the bay, we proceeded to the Piazza Royal, the great centre of attraction in Naples. Two bronze horses of exquisite proportions, presented to the King by the Emperor of Austria, occupy a space in front of the royal palace, which is, without exception, the most elegant structure of the kind that we have seen in Italy. A large body of soldiers are quartered here, to protect the person of the King, and visitors are not only required to present a permit from the proper authorities, but must undergo a rigid scrutiny, before they can enter the apartments. The armory is very extensive, and contains a large collection of ancient and modern weapons; many of the chambers are painted, in imitation of those of Pompeii, about which I will speak hereafter; the frescoes and oil paintings are very superior, and the Throne Room, which is covered with crimson velvet and gold, is particularly rich and elegant. Adjoining the palace is the great theatre of San Carlo, which turns out so many prima donnas for the operatic world. It is conceded by every one to be the largest and most magnificent play-house in Europe, and no one who has entered its walls can fail to be impressed with its capaciousness, richness, and convenience. Six tiers of great height encircle the body of the house, the fronts of which are exquisitely carved and gilded. The boxes are all lined with red velvet and damask curtains; the seats in the parquet are made entirely of iron, and so arranged that every one can see perfectly well; while the scenes and every thing connected with the stage are in perfect keeping.

We have attended several operas at San Carlo, but were disappointed every time. The boxes are rarely full, and the representation far inferior to many that I have seen in New-York and New-Orleans.

Before leaving the Piazza Royal, we must mention the church of St. Francis de Paola, which is the finest in Naples. It is a modern construction, in the form of a circular temple, with two rows of semi-circular porticoes, supported by marble columns. The interior abounds in rich chapels, and is decorated with paintings by Camuccini and other modern artists of celebrity. Proceeding up the Strada del Toledo, the great thoroughfare of Naples, we visited the museum, which is not so large as many others in Europe, but contains objects of curiosity no where else to be seen; particularly the relics excavated from the ruins of Pompeii and Herculaneum. Earthenware, glassware, and a great variety of fresco paintings, of a curious and somewhat obscene character, cut out of the walls in a perfect state, constitute the bulk of the collection from Pompeii—which can be seen and enjoyed, but as difficult to describe as the Egyptian hieroglyphics. In this collection I was particularly interested in a large mosaic, found at Pompeii, measuring twenty feet in length and ten in breadth, and representing a battle between Alexander and Darius. It is beautifully executed, and shows conclusively that they better understood such work in ancient times than at the present day. The Farnese Bull and the Hercules, two of the finest pieces of statuary of the kind in Europe, are exhibited in this museum. The first consists of a group of figures, representing Dirce, the wife of Lycus, in the act of being tied by the hair to a wild and furious bull. It is very massive—all in one piece of marble, and executed by two Greek sculptors, who were brothers, called Apollonius and Tarnisius. The Hercules, like Pompey's statue in the Spada Palace at Rome, is very large and fully developed, exhibiting all that is requisite in the combination of strength and symmetry. The attitude was well chosen, having the right hand resting on a marble block, over which is thrown the skin of the Nemean lion, with his club lying by his side; the left hand is placed behind, holding three Hesperian apples, and the following words are inscribed on the base: "*Glyconsthanaiis epoici.*" Among the numerous things marked Pompeii, we observed several loaves of bread, with the baker's mark upon them, as left in the shop when the lava rolled down into the city; also some paints of different colors, and cloth made out of *asbestos*. The library is quite extensive, containing many old and valuable works. The collection of bronzes are particularly fine, and the picture galleries filled with the productions of Penturicchei, Caracci, Schidone and Correggio, well deserve attention. All the things which I have enumerated are curious and valuable; but the collection of precious stones and cameos, belonging to the Farnese family, attract more attention and are more prized than any other branch of the Museum. The largest cameo in the world is here displayed to the gaze of the people, who would like to see its value appropriated to the relief of the poor, or some other laudable purpose, instead of being fastened up in a strong box, with a soldier to guard it, night and day. It was found, according to tradition, in the tomb of Hadrian by a soldier, who, ignorant of its value, disposed of it for a very trifling sum. By some means or other, it came into the possession of the King of Naples, and is now valued at one million of dollars. On one side I noticed the head of Medusa, and on the other that of Alexander, beautifully cut, and so ornamented as to increase the general effect of the stone.

After passing nearly the whole day in the examination of the curiosities in the various apartments of the Museum, we returned to our hotel through the gardens of the Villa Reale, situated on the bay, and forming the most agreeable and fashionable promenade in Naples. They extend along the shore of the bay for about half a mile, and are beautifully inclosed with an iron railing on one side, and a hedge of roses near the water's edge. Fountains, statues, evergreens, and flowers adorn the interior, and an excellent band of music plays every afternoon for the benefit of strangers, who congregate here at this season from all parts of Europe.

Not far from the gardens is the Grotto or tunnel, cut through the hill a third of a mile in length; the height is about one hundred and fifty feet, and the width sufficient for two carriages to pass. The road originally passed over the hill, and this grotto was made by the Cumacans and Neapolitans, to facilitate the communication between the two places. It is lighted, night and day, by means of lamps, and an old monk is stationed at the entrance nearest to Naples, in a little chapel cut in the rock, for the purpose of receiving alms for the poor from those who pass through the grotto. Just over this chapel, and about half-way up the hill, is the tomb of the great Mantuan Bard, said to have been placed here by order of Augustus, who desired the remains of the poet to be interred in Naples, his favorite residence. No traces exist either of the urn or columns. Its external form is that of a tower, rendered picturesque by the surrounding scenery.

In passing through the streets of Naples, the stranger is attracted by a number of little peculiaritiss, no where else to be seen, which I will merely mention, leaving your imagination to carry out the rest. The first and most prominent is that of the lazzaroni eating maccaroni by the yard, in the streets and public places, for the gratification of their appetites, and not unfrequently for the amusement of strangers, who pay for as much as they can eat, just to see the sight. Then come the female money changers, seated on stools behind tables filled with coppers, which they give in change, at a large profit, for silver and gold. Near these tables are another set, occupied by superannuated old men, with goose quills behind their ears and a small slip of paper before them, waiting patiently for some illiterate individual to come along and get them to write a love letter, or something that requires as much pains and particularity. In the morning, long droves of donkeys, with panniers on their backs, filled with vegetables and fruits, may be seen going from house to house, furnishing the people with such things as are procured at market-places in other cities. In the evening, two-wheeled wagons, drawn by three horses abreast, decked with smart trappings and a great abundance of brazen ornaments, may be seen going at a rapid rate, carrying laborers to their homes in the neighboring villages. It is astonishing how many poor creatures manage to get into one of these vehicles—the smallest of which contain sometimes six people inside, four in front, four or five more hanging on behind, and two or three more in a net or basket suspended below the axletree, where they lie, half suffocated with mud and dust. Exhibitors of Punch, buffo singers with guitars, reciters of poetry, reciters of stories, a number of low and cheap exhibitions, with clowns and showmen, drums and trumpets, painted cloths, representing the *elephant*, within, and eager crowds assembled without, assist to make up some of the peculiarities of Naples.

Leaving the city one morning, we followed a funeral procession to Campo Santo, the modern burial place, situated near the foot of Vesuvius. The deceased was some poor creature, unknown, and, I may say, uncared for in this world—as there was no one present to shed a tear or perform the last sad offices of affection. The body, on an open bier, borne on a kind of palanquin, was hurried along to the reception room of the cemetery, where it was divested of all clothing, and allowed to remain a short time, as a matter of form, in a coffin, used on all similar occasions, and then taken out and cast headlong, by the monks, into a pit nearly filled with bodies. At the request of the monk, we looked down this pit, and found it to be about forty feet deep and walled up with stone. It was an awful sight, I assure you, to see in one place so many bodies in various stages of putrefaction. I looked once, and that was sufficient: the sooner it is forgotten the better. These pits are used only for those who die in hospitals and prisons, and are unclaimed by their friends. There are three hundred and sixty-five, one of which is opened and closed each day in the year. Near this place for the reception of the poor and unfortunate, is a new and handsome cemetery, filled with costly chapels and vaults, for the reception of those who live in fine houses and are well-to-do in the world. The contrast is striking; but when one reflects that there is no distinction hereafter, all seems vanity and vexation of spirit.

No city in Italy affords so many pleasant excursions as Naples. Whether we turn towards the Miseno shore of the splendid watery amphitheatre, and go by the Grotto of Posilippo to the Grotto del Cane and away to Baiæ, or take the other way towards Vesuvius and Torrento, it is one succession of delights. Our first excursion was in the direction of Baiæ, celebrated for the beauty of its bay, and in ancient times for the number and magnificence of its villas. Horace preferred it to all other places. Cæsar, Pompey, Marius, and other distinguished men, had villas on the coast, which is regarded as more beautiful than that of Naples. Many places of interest are on the roadside, such as the lake called Agnano, surrounded by hills formed of the lava of extinct volcanoes. It is about three miles in circumference, very deep, and in constant ebullition from the vapors below. In its vicinity are remains of parts of the ancient Thermæ, called the Stuffe di San Germano, consisting of small rooms, in which the heat of the vapor rises to 39° and 40° of Reaumur. Near the lake is also the Grotto del Cane, mentioned by Pliny, l. 2, c. 90. It is about ten feet in depth, nine feet in height, and four feet in breadth. A light, inodorous vapor rises about six inches from the soil, and in the interior is without incrustations or any deposit of saline matter. This grotto, formerly called the Cavern of Charon, derives its present appellation from the experiments made on a dog, who would die at the end of two minutes if not restored to the open air. An old woman always stands at the door of the grotto with a little dog tied with a string, which has inhaled the noxious vapors so often that it goes through the forms of death as quietly as any other dog would gnaw a bone. Between lake Agnano and the town of Pozzuoli, is the Solfatara, called by the ancients Forum Vulcani, situated in a narrow plain, surrounded by the Monti Lucogei, or the Phlegrean Fields, which was considered, in the time of Pliny and Strabo, as a volcano not entirely extinct. Several apertures exhale a heated vapor, in which the smell of sulphur and ammonia predominate. Flames are visible during the night, when the fire is also more distinctly heard. The Solfatara appears to have been a mountain, the summit of which fell in by the violent action of a volcano. The noise produced by walking or the rolling of a stone on the surface would indicate that the interior is hollow. Numerous mineral waters exist near this spot, and the whole region round about shows conclusively that all is fire below. Leaving this place, we passed through Pozzuoli, stopping to see the ruined temple of Serapis and the Amphitheatre or Coliseum. Going a little farther, we passed along the shores of Lake Lucrin and Averno, near which are the ruins of the Temple of Diana, Mercury, Venus, and the Bay of Baiæ, so much lauded of old and so much admired at the present day for its safety and its beauty.

The following day, the same party took the opposite direction, and made an excursion to Paestum and the exhumed city of Pompeii, two of the most noted places in the vicinity of Naples. The former is remarkable for its ruins—the least aged of them built hundreds of years before the birth of Christ, and standing yet, erect in lonely majesty, upon the wild, malaria-blighted plain. The latter, situated sixteen miles from Naples, and near the ball of Vesuvius, presents a quiet and beautiful picture compared with the scene presented to the inmates of Diomede's house on the day of its destruction.

As I remarked in the beginning of my letter, nearly all of the movables have been carried to the Museum in Naples, but there is much remaining to prove the ancient importance of the place, and the curious structure of the buildings and streets; at every turn some little familiar token of habitation and every-day pursuits are presented to the eye for reflection,—the chafing of the bucket-rope in the stone rim of the exhausted well; the track of carriage-wheels in the pavement of the street; the marks of drinking vessels on the stone counter of the wine-shops, and the mills used for grinding the corn, all combine to render the solitude and deadly lonesomeness of the place ten thousand times more solemn.

The streets of Pompeii are both narrow and circuitous, with side-walks, and the name of each street cut on the curb-stone. The houses are built of small brick, and composed of one or two stories, generally inclosed in a square court surrounded with porticoes where the doors are placed. In the centre of the court is a well or reservoir of water for the use of the establishment. The rooms on the ground floor are without internal communication; they are small but lofty, the most of them without windows, being lighted alone from the door. The ceiling and walls are covered with painted figures of various descriptions, and the floors made of the finest mosaic. The most important buildings are those belonging, as is supposed, to Caius Sallustius, Vettius, Pressius, and Diomede, besides the Temples of Iris, the Temple of Music, Public Baths, Tragical Theatre, and Amphitheatre. They are all constructed pretty much on the same principle, and very little variety exists, except in the frescoes and mosaic. On the front steps of nearly every door I noticed in mosaic the word *Have* or *Salve*, (meaning welcome,) and in the cellar of Diomede's house, which is outside of the walls of the city, I noticed the impressions of two bodies in the ashes, hardened with the ashes, so impressed and fixed there, after they had shrunk inside to scanty bones. The skeleton found here is supposed to be that of Diomede, holding in one hand a key and in the other coin and gold ornaments, behind which was some inmate of his house holding bronze and silver vases, which they were attempting to save, but were destroyed in the act.

Between Pompeii and Naples are the ruins of the ancient city of Herculaneum, also buried by the eruption of old Vesuvius. The Theatre, which is all to be seen, was discovered in 1689 by some inhabitants of Rosina, who, having dug to the depth of sixty-five feet for a well, found remains of valuable marbles and inscriptions relative to Herculaneum. We descended a long flight of steps with lighted torches, passed through narrow passages, and actually stood upon the stage of the ancient theatre, in which the play was probably going on when the lava rolled down the burning mountain and buried them far, far beneath the surface.

Rosina, which occupies the ancient site of Herculaneum, is the great starting point for those who are ambitious to ascend Vesuvius. Here we procured ponies and a guide, and proceeded several miles over a narrow and rugged path to the foot of the cone, which we found to be only the commencement of our difficulties. Leaving the ponies at this point, we continued our course upward in various ways, according to the disposition and powers of endurance of each individual. The ladies were carried in a chair fastened on poles by four stout Italians, and some of the gentlemen in the same way. One of the party was an old gentleman from the States, remarkable for his rotundity and good-humor, and who was very uneasy all the while, fearing that something would give way and let him roll down in the ashes to the foot of the cone. To avoid all danger, he employed six stout men to assist him, who were disposed of in the following manner: two to each end of a rope fastened around his waist, two with straps over his shoulders, to which he held on with his hands, and two in the rear to scotch him when he got out of breath. It was a picture worthy of Punch, and worth all the labor and fatigue of mounting. After toiling, and panting, and laughing, for almost one hour, through ashes and snow, we reached the region of Fire. The day was clear, and the noonday sun was shedding its brightest rays over the broad sea down below, and tiny Naples in the distance, and every village in the country round, seemed more lovely and beautiful than ever. Unfortunately the volcano has been quiet for more than a year, and we were not permitted to see it in all its glory. The smoke, filled with sulphur, the noise and the heated vapors, were all that we saw, which was quite sufficient to convey an idea of its immensity and grandeur, without the lurid flames and red-hot lava. There are two craters on Vesuvius, one of which is almost extinct. We walked through the suffocating smoke around both of them, and when the wind blew from us we could see distinctly one hundred feet into the yawning gulf of fire. A young married lady from England, who constituted one of our party, accompanied me to the very brim of the crater, but it became so hot under our feet that we were compelled to retrace our steps hurriedly. After examining the crater to our satisfaction, roasting and eating a few eggs, and enjoying the extensive prospect around us, we commenced the work of descending the almost perpendicular cone, which is quite as amusing as ascending. The guides, anxious to give us all the assistance in their power, cautiously joined their hands, and made a chain of men; of whom the foremost beat, as well as they could, a solid foundation with their feet and sticks, down which we prepared to follow. The way being fearfully steep, and the ladies being unable to proceed alone, were taken out of the litter and placed, each between two careful persons, who being supported by the chain of guides, reached the foot in safety; while some of the gentlemen, in their hurry to get down first, lost their foot-hold and rolled over and over in the ashes, without any injury, and much to the amusement of those behind. Vesuvius is situated near the bay, and in sight of Naples, between two mountains called the Somma and Ottajano. Though separated, these mountains have a common base. It is supposed that formerly they were united, and that their separation is due to an eruption which rendered them craters. Vesuvius has the form of a cone; its perpendicular height is 3,375 feet, the circumference of the three mountains at the base is thirty miles. Three roads lead to the summit, that of St. Sebastian to the north, of Ottajano to the east, of Resenia, which is the most frequented, to the west. At this time the cone is covered with snow, while the vegetation flourishes in full vigor on the plains below.

The Neapolitan government, like that of all the Italian States, is in an unsettled condition. The King feels uneasy about his security, and relies more upon the valor of the ten thousand Swiss soldiers in his employ, than he does upon the fidelity of his own people.

LETTER THIRTY-SEVEN.

ALEXANDRIA, Egypt.

Departure from Europe—The Pass of Scylla and Charybdis—Mt. Ætna—Messina—The Island of Malta—Arrival off Alexandria—Strada Franca—Donkey Stand—Construction of the City—The Turkish Quarter—Pasha's Palace—Mud Villages—Private Slave Dépôt —Disorderly Funerals—Lake Mareotis—Pompey's Pillar—Cleopatra's Needle.

THE day we set sail from New-York, and bade adieu, perhaps for ever, to our native land, our feelings were altogether different, I assure you, from the day when we cleared the harbor of Naples, and gazed for the last time on the bright shores of Italy. On the ocean, we felt sad for the first day or so, because we had left friends at home to whom we are fondly attached, and a country from which neither time nor change can ever wean us; but on the deep-blue Mediterranean we had no regrets, no sadness; for we knew full well that we would soon reach the land of promise, where our pilgrimage would end, and our faces be turned once more to the shores of the United States.

After procuring a ticket from the police office, stating that we were in good health, we were allowed to go on board the French steamer from Marseilles and proceed on our voyage to the island of Malta. The frigate Independence was anchored in the bay—our flag was floating to the breeze, and the sweet notes of "Hail Columbia!" came softly to our ears as we glided over the placid waters. Twelve Americans stood on the deck, and returned the compliment from our frigate with three hearty cheers. The steamer turned the island of Capri, where old Tiberius once lived in debauchery, and the beauties of Naples soon faded in the distance. The following morning we came in sight of the snow-covered summit of Mt. Ætna, now reposing in its lofty majesty, glided swiftly along the base of the island of Stromboli, rising like a sugar-loaf from the sea, and passed safely between Scylla and Charybdis into the beautiful bay of Messina. Here we went ashore and rambled about the filthy streets and through the churches, where there is nothing to see, until we were admonished by one of the party that it was time for the steamer to start for Malta. From the sea the island of Sicily presents a broken aspect; but it is closely cultivated and rich in the abundance of all the tropical fruits. The next morning we entered the harbor of "La Valetta" before the sun was fairly up. We went ashore in a small boat, ascended the street of stairs, and were safely ensconced in a good English hotel, where we enjoyed, for the first time in many a day, a substantial breakfast. Valetta is clean and well built, and is the strongest fortified place in the Mediterranean—being built by the knights of old, who fled from Rhodes to this barren island for safety and solitude. Then the island was hardly known and but little cared for; while now it is the most important point for military purposes in the whole sea, and is regarded by the English as impregnable to the attacks of any foreign power. The entire fleet of the government in the Mediterranean is concentrated in this harbor, consisting of ten vessels, including one or two war steamers. We accepted the invitation of one of the officers of the navy, and went on board the Queen, one of the largest ships of the line, carrying 120 guns and 3,000 men. The officers were extremely polite in conducting us over the vessel and explaining to us the *modus operandi* in an action. Every thing seemed to be on a large scale; but I remarked at the time to one of my companions that they did not keep their decks in such order or manage their guns so dexterously as our American sailors. The palaces and cathedral, dedicated to St. John, the patron of the Order, are in a good state of preservation, and all occupied as residences and public institutions. The palace of the Grand Master is now the residence of the British Governor. It contains several fine halls, an armory, a few good pictures, and some curious tapestry. In the armory I observed many singular things, used by the old knights, and among them a cannon made of rope and lined outside with copper, spears, swords, and armor of various sizes and descriptions, brought from Rhodes. I tried on the armor of the Grand Master Vignacourt, which is inlaid with gold and curiously wrought. It was very heavy and cumbersome—so much so that I wonder how any man could do much fighting or moving about with it weighing on his person. The cathedral is not remarkable or attractive externally, but the interior affords a rich field for the study of the art and taste of the sixteenth and seventeenth centuries. The floor is a mosaic pavement, chiefly composed of the sepulchral monuments of the knights, whose effigies, in full costume, are represented in white marble. Some of the bells are said to have been brought from Rhodes, and in the chapel of the Madonna I noticed some six or eight keys, said to be those of the gates of Jerusalem, Acre, and Rhodes. The railing in front of the chapel is made of solid silver, which is so dim from age that one would never discover its value without being informed. Valetta is laid off at right angles, and built altogether of stone houses with projecting windows. The streets are kept perfectly clean, and the city is well supplied with water by an aqueduct, several miles in length, similar in construction to the old Roman aqueducts. The island of Malta is perfectly destitute of vegetation, and outside of the walls of Valetta and Citta Vecchia all is desolation and barrenness. The latter named place was at one time the chief town of Malta, but has been superseded by the modern city. It is now interesting to the traveller on account of the extensive catacombs, the bay in which St. Paul was shipwrecked, and the grotto where he lived as the guest of Publius.

After passing three days very pleasantly in that "little military hot-house," we departed on an excellent steamer, belonging to the French line, for the shores of Egypt. On the morning of the third day we descried in the distance the low coast of Barbary, and on the fourth we came in sight of Pompey's Pillar, which was the first object opened to our wistful eyes in the land of Pharaoh, Ptolemy, and Cleopatra. As we drew nearer to the ancient city we descried, through the mist and rain, the narrow Cape of Figs, upon which is the modern light-house and the Palace of the Pasha. The wind was blowing a perfect gale, and we stood out some time, waiting for a pilot to carry us into the dangerous harbor, but none came, and our captain, Frenchman-like, became impatient and resolved to go through the narrow inlet and run the chances of wrecking his vessel on the breakers. Fortunately we escaped all danger, passed along a line of merchantmen and vessels of war, filled with turbaned Arabs, and came to anchor beneath the lattice windows of the Pasha's seraglio. Here an amusing, and to some, frightful scene ensued. The anchor had scarcely reached the bottom when a number of small Arab boats crowded around the foot of the ladder to carry the passengers ashore; and all the shouting, screaming, pushing and shoving, that you could possibly imagine, we enjoyed on the occasion. The ladies on board were nearly frightened out of their wits, and no wonder, for the very sight of those terrible-looking fellows, with their dark flashing eyes, gleaming white teeth, "bearded like the pard," and armed with large scimetars, is enough to intimidate at first even the boldest. Waiting a short time for the grand farce to subside, we selected a boat and started, six in number, for the custom house. The rain came down in torrents, and our umbrellas were fastened on the trunks, and the fierce-looking Arabs refused to land us without receiving their pay in advance, with the view of extorting more if they liked. Having been warned by an old traveller of such tricks, we drew our empty pistols and gave them to understand, by signs, that we would do something terrible if they refused to land, which acted on them like a charm, and caused them to take up their oars and row in quick time. Finding no other conveyance, we all mounted donkeys and charged through the narrow and muddy bazaars at full speed to l'Hôtel d'Europe on the Strada Franca. It was really an amusing sight to see six long Americans mounted on donkeys about the size of a large goat, and followed by half-naked boys punching them up in the rear every few steps with a pointed stick. My friend from South Carolina was rather unfortunate in the donkey race, as he was not only rolled into a mud hole, but rolled over both by the donkey and the boy in such rapid succession that he failed to recover without being drenched from top to toe. Arrived at our hotel, which is quite large and conducted on the European principle, we commenced the work of sight-seeing, and preparing for our voyage up the Nile. The Strada Franca, or Frank quarter, upon which my window fronts, is decidedly the best built and most interesting part of Alexandria. It is a great square occupied almost entirely by Europeans, and used on all public occasions in preference to the Turkish quarter. The roofs of the houses are flat and surmounted by enormous flag staffs, indicating the residence of some consul or foreign minister. On Sundays and festivals a prodigious quantity of square yards of banner float from these, and give a very animated aspect to the scene. In front of each hotel there is a donkey stand, and woe to the stranger that ventures outside of the door without a big stick and the resolution to use it. The boys will crowd the donkeys around him, and each one cry out with a loud voice, "Master, master, very good donkey! bone, bone, Pasha's Palace, Pompey's Pillar, Catacombs, Slave Market, Turkish bazaar, yes,

yes," and the like, in such rapid succession that the stranger has no chance without knocking some of them down or retreating precipitately into the hotel. Alexandria is situated on a narrow and flat piece of ground, between Lake Mareotis and the Mediterranean; the streets are narrow, and the houses constructed mostly of crude brick. In the Turkish quarter the streets are covered over, so as to protect the inhabitants from the burning rays of the sun; the shops are about six or eight feet square, and the merchants' goods in proportion. Here the foreigner can be initiated somewhat in the manners and customs of Eastern life. The Turk sitting with his legs crossed and his person enveloped in the smoke of a large pipe; the females passing along with their faces covered, with the exception of their eyes, which are usually covered with *henna*, while their persons are entirely hidden by enormous black silk robes, giving them the appearance of inflated balloons; the caravan of camels loaded with fruits from the country, and the noise created by the shouts of the wild Arabs as they move along the streets, all combine to impress one strongly that he is among a peculiar people. After roving through the bazaars we visited the Pasha's Palace, situated on the Cape of Figs. The exterior is without attraction, but the interior is fitted up in a style both comfortable and elegant; the walls are covered with figured silk, and some of the floors are made of ebony, inlaid with ivory. The present Pasha is more civilized in his mode of life than his predecessors, having ordered a bed to sleep in, of European make, instead of lying on the floor like his subjects. My donkey-boy, who could speak a little English, was our only interpreter, and it was really amusing to see him walking over the fine floors of the palace with his bare and dirty feet, leaving a print at every step, while the servants of the establishment were stepping about lightly in silk stockings, fearing they would soil or scratch the polished surface. The harem adjoins the palace, but so closely watched, and constructed so as to prevent intrusion, that the most searching eye would fail to distinguish the beauties within. After gazing awhile at the walls and indulging our own thoughts, we were admonished by the donkey-boy that there was no admittance, and started off to see the reverse of life, in the mud villages that surround Alexandria. Here we had an opportunity of seeing the habitations and mode of life among the lower classes. The streets are from one to three yards in width, extremely tortuous and always dirty; the houses are constructed of corn-stalks, placed together and set upright, over which there is a coating of mud four or five inches in thickness; the roofs are flat, with pigeon boxes built over them, and they sleep on the bare ground with no covering, save a little straw. I noticed in several of these miserable hovels as many as twelve or fifteen human beings in a perfect state of nudity, living among yelping dogs and swarms of flies. Most of them were affected with ophthalmia, which is a disease of the country, and their only food seemed to be a few raw onions and garlic. No wonder that famine and the plague make such sad ravages among the benighted people; their mode of life, their filthiness and their indolent habits, all conspire to bring on disease in every shape, and render them miserable and degraded.

While in this quarter, we witnessed an Egyptian funeral, which was altogether different from any funeral ceremony we have ever seen. The corpse was placed in a square coffin, covered with gaudy trappings, and borne on the shoulders of four men, accompanied by a troop of boys in front, and women behind, who were making all sorts of motions indicating distress, and shouting at the very top of their voices. When they observed us looking at them, they increased their lamentations, and seemed to make light of the ceremony, by the performance of many antics too ridiculous to mention.

The slave markets of this city are not so extensive as those at Cairo, but are conducted on a scale sufficiently large to give one some idea of the institution in this country. They are purchased in Nubia and Abyssinia, by traders, for a mere song, and sold here and elsewhere for fifty or sixty dollars, according to the age and condition. We went into one of the dépôts and saw several hundred, mostly females, that had just arrived from these countries. They were perfectly black, and looked as if they had never seen a white face before. As soon as we entered, the master closed the door upon us, and would not let us out without giving them *backshish* (gift). The condition of the Egyptian slave is far worse than you have any conception. They are fed on onions, garlic, and stale bread—have hardly a rag to cover themselves, and are worked very hard. Our slaves are perfect lords compared to them; and notwithstanding all that the abolitionists may say, both at home and abroad, they are far better off than the slaves in Africa, or the laboring classes of any nation in Europe. I would not, under any circumstances, desire to agitate a question that has given rise to so much dissension of late in our happy land, but I feel it my duty to say that all Europe is against us, and more particularly the English. The subject is introduced on all occasions, and we are asked, even here, in this benighted land, if our slaves are not mal-treated and abused. Ignorant of our peculiar institution, and I may say of our country, they hold up this subject for our contemplation, and say to us that it is a system unworthy of the age. Having almost ruined and rendered bankrupt the citizens of her colonies by the abolition of slavery, they look with jealousy upon the cotton-growing region of our country, and will never rest until we dispose of the institution, or silence them in some other way.

Leaving the subject for the present, let us turn to the monuments of Alexandria, which are far, far more intresting than any thing modern. They speak of the past—the mighty past! when Egypt was in the zenith of her glory, and Europe in a state of barbarism.

Near the lake Mareotis, and on the road leading to the Mahmoudieh Canal, stands in majestic solitude Pompey's Pillar, the work of other times and other men! It rises a single shaft of ninety feet, and ten feet in diameter, surmounted by a Corinthian capital ten feet high, and is not only interesting on account of its monumental beauty, but designates the centre of the ancient city. It is far outside the present walls, and surrounded by Arab huts, in which poverty, misery and famine, and other destitution, stared me in the face. Cleopatra's Needle also stands to be admired and cherished for its antiquity. It was nearly buried at one time with sand, but recent excavations have exposed to view the centre obelisk, containing hieroglyphics yet to be interpreted, by those who pretend to have discovered the meaning of those rude signs. The obelisk is made of red granite, brought from Upper Egypt, is sixty feet in height, and entirely perfect, except the base and the top, which have been broken. On one side the characters are very distinct, and as clear as when it came from the hands of the sculptor; although on the other, the terrible sirocco, blowing upon it from the desert for so many years, has effaced some of the figures, and worn away the almost imperishable granite.

Finishing the sights of Alexandria, we called on Mr. McAuley, the American Consul General of Egypt, who is one of the most worthy representatives that I have met with from our government. He has not only furnished us with all the information and facilities for travelling in Egypt, but entertained us in the real old Virginia style.

LETTER THIRTY-EIGHT.

CAIRO, Egypt.

Departure from Alexandria—Our Boat—Canal of Mahmoudieh—The Rosetta Branch of the Nile—Cotton Farms—Villages—First View of the Pyramids—The Barrage—Desperate Affray with the Villagers of Embarbeh, and its Results.

BEING informed in Alexandria that all the good boats had been taken in Cairo, which is the usual place of commencing a voyage up the Nile, we procured from an English gentleman in that city a large and elegant *dahabieh*, called the *Zeynt al Nile* (Ornament of the Nile). The *dahabieh* and *cangia* are the boats generally used for the conveyance of passengers, and differ only in size, the former being more commodious and carrying more sail. Our boat has four cabins and three masts with lateen sails, like the generality of boats on the Nile, and managed by a *Reis* (captain) and fourteen Arab sailors. Several days were occupied in laying in stores for the voyage, and drawing up contracts with the owner of the boat and our dragoman, which requires as much precision and formality as a deed for a tract of land. All things being arranged to our entire satisfaction, we appointed a day for starting, and invited all our American friends down to the canal to see us off, when we drank in tolerable champagne to our country and each other, hoisted our banner and our private signal, and set sail from the famed city of Alexandria amid the cheers of our friends and the report of firearms. The Mahmoudieh canal, which connects the Rosetta branch of the Nile with the sea, is far from interesting, and the monotony of its banks is not relieved by the old-fashioned telegraphs, rising at intervals above the dreary plains, which extend on both sides of it to a seemingly endless distance. They communicate between Alexandria and this city, but convey intelligence so slowly that they are rarely used except for government purposes. The earth thrown up from the canal forms an elevated ridge, rising high above the adjacent lands, and the only objects that interrupt the uniform level are the mounds of old towns, whose solitary and ruined appearance adds not a little to the gloominess of the scene. This canal follows part of the ancient Canopia branch of the Nile, and the old canal of Fooah. It derives its name from the late sultan Mohammed Ali, who began and completed the great work in one year, at the cost of 7,500,000f. As many as 150,000 men are said to have been employed in digging it, among whom 20,000 perished by accident, hunger, and plague. Mohammed Ali, like Napoleon, never conceived a project without carrying it through in spite of all difficulties. He was a man with but little education, but great natural powers, and did much towards elevating the character and improving the condition of his country. At Atfeh this canal connects with the Rosetta branch of the Nile by a lock, through which the boats pass, after paying toll to the government. There is sometimes considerable detention on account of the great number of forms necessary to be gone through, but a few piastres will satisfy the Bey, and boats are allowed to proceed up the river without any further trouble. Atfeh, like nearly all the villages on the river as high up as this city, is built of crude brick made of mud and straw, with narrow streets, filled with dust, smoke, dogs, and sore-eyed Arabs. The mosques in the village are quite numerous, but uninteresting, being very inferior in an architectural point of view, and so much alike, that there is no necessity of visiting but one. All the Egyptians live in the cities and villages, except a few who lead a roving life in the deserts. Every morning and evening the cultivators of the soil may be seen with their implements going to or returning from their daily labor. The fields look fresh and green, promising an abundant harvest for the Pasha, who owns every thing, and furnishing a grateful prospect to those who visit the shores of Egypt to avoid the wintry blasts of the North. The Rosetta branch of the Nile is about twice the width of the Cumberland, the banks are low and caving, and the general appearance of the country very much like that of the lower Mississippi. This is the cotton region of the country, and if properly cultivated would produce the finest staple in the world. I went into some of the fields, and found stalks more than eight feet high, weighed down almost to the earth with cotton of a superior quality. Ten acres is about the largest quantity of land that I have seen in one field. The plough is the same as that used about three thousand years ago, and their manner of tilling the soil is so primitive, that its capabilities have never been developed. One of our southern planters might come here, and with proper attention, and our mode of cultivation, produce the finest staple in the world. The climate, the soil, and every thing conspire to make it one of the most desirable countries for the cultivation of the cotton plant on this side of the Atlantic.

On the evening of the fourth day, just above the village of Wardan, we descried for the first time the great Pyramids, which our dragoman informed us were thirty miles distant. The atmosphere was perfectly clear, the varied tints of the declining sun lingered on the horizon, and the great wonders of the world stood before our admiring gaze like huge mountains of stone in a desert where all was desolation and loneliness. We drew nearer and nearer, and on the following morning they seemed almost twice the size that they appeared when they first broke on our vision.

At the junction of the Rosetta and Damietta branches of the Nile, we passed through the *barrage* or dam of arches, commenced some years ago under the supervision of M. Linant, a French engineer, and still incomplete. The object of this gigantic undertaking is to retain the water of the river, in order that it may be used for irrigating the lands, when the inundation has retired, and supply the place of water wheels, which adds so much to the expense of cultivation. There are two dams, one across each branch, consisting of a number of well turned brick arches thirty feet in width. A large canal is to be carried directly through the centre of the Delta, and the quantity of water allowed to pass into this, and the two branches of the river, is to be regulated by means of sluices, according to circumstances. The principal arches of both dams are to be always kept open, but the lateral arches are to be closed when the river is low; by which means enough water will be furnished to fill the canals intended for irrigation of the interior. The entire structure is massive and graceful; but as the character of the river and soil is so much like the Mississippi, I fear that the foundations will give way, and that much

10

money and labor will be expended by the government without any beneficial result.

Just after daylight the following morning, the party were aroused by a terrible noise on shore, which turned out to be a fight between our crew and the villagers of Embarbeh about a log of wood. One of the party went out and endeavored to separate the belligerents, but his efforts were without avail: the wild Arabs seemed perfectly furious, and continued to beat each other with long sticks, which they always carry as a weapon of defence. Seeing that he could do nothing towards separating them, he started back to the boat, and was informed before reaching it, by one of the crew, that they had killed our *reis* (captain). This, however, turned out to be a mistake, as he was brought on board a few minutes after, severely wounded. At this stage of the difficulty the oldest member of the party went out with a double-barrel shot gun, and followed by a servant with a pistol in his hand. His object was not to renew the fight, but merely to maintain the right of navigation, and see that our men were permitted to track along the bank, which is the usual way of proceeding when they have no wind. The villagers planted themselves in front of our crew, and said they should not proceed; whereupon our friend raised his gun to intimidate them, when an athletic Arab rushed up behind and pinioned him, inflicting blows also on his person with their long sticks, which felled him to the earth. The servant who was aiding his master was also struck on the head and severely wounded in the neck by a pistol shot. At this stage of the action two other members of the party rushed out to their rescue with a revolver, holster pistol, and dirk-knife. As soon as they reached the top of the bank, between sixty and one hundred hostile Arabs rushed upon them with their sticks, but soon retreated under their fire, with the exception of two who seemed perfectly furious, and determined to murder them. Having fired off every barrel, the knife and bludgeons came into play, the sight of which induced the Arabs to retreat to a field of sugar-cane close at hand, and give our friends an opportunity of getting on the boat, which had left the shore and was floating down the current. All being on board, our crew poled on the opposite side to Boulak, while we re-loaded our guns in case of any further use. Several boats, crowded with Arabs, came over afterwards, but we were not molested, and succeeded in reaching the British Hotel in this city in safety.

The news of the affray preceded us, and all was excitement in the Frank quarter, where exaggerated accounts of the origin and results of the difficulty were circulating rapidly. Having a Vice Consul here, we immediately made known to him the whole affair, and drew up a statement of the matter for the benefit of the Pasha and Chief of Police. Some of the Arabs fled to the desert, but have since been caught and imprisoned, together with nearly every man in the village, and some of our crew. A few days afterwards we were all summoned by our Consul, who is a native, to appear before the Pasha and Chief of Police, to give in our evidence, and to point out those who were engaged in the fight. The wounded Arabs were brought in first, and made statements altogether false and ridiculous; no two of them concurred, and the Pasha seemed to regard their testimony as worthless. They all looked so much alike that we found it utterly impossible to point out one of them, or say, with any certainty, that they were engaged in the fight. During the investigation of the facts we appeared before the Pasha several times, and were always received with marked respect. Seated with our legs crossed, in the Turkish manner, on the cushions ranged around the room, we sipped coffee, smoked pipe, and conversed freely with him, while the poor Arabs were trembling in fear before us. Mr. McAuley, our Consul General at Alexandria, and our Vice Consul in this city, deserve much praise for the vigorous manner in which they have prosecuted our cause, and secured the rights of American citizens. The Arabs are not only to be bastinadoed publicly, but all damages paid, and the protection of the government guaranteed to us during our sojourn in Egypt.

Those of our party who were wounded in the affray are out of all danger, and we hope to continue our voyage up the Nile in peace and quietude.

LETTER THIRTY-NINE.

CAIRO, Egypt.

The Citadel—Joseph's Well—Palaces—Mosques—Bazaars—Frank Quarter—Old Cairo—Tombs—Nileometer and Isle of Roda—Festivals and sights—Excursions—The Pasha and his Government, etc.

CAIRO, the capital of Egypt and residence of Abbas Pasha, is much larger, and far more curious and interesting than Alexandria, the commercial metropolis of the country. In the latter city, Europeans have become so numerous and acquired such a strong hold, that it has lost much of its eastern character; but here the Arab and the Turk may be seen living in their own peculiar habitations, and enjoying their old customs and habits, in spite of the invasions of other races and the advancement of the age. One of my first rambles in Cairo was to the Citadel, situated on a lofty hill, forming the commencement of the great chain that extends along the east bank of the Nile, and commanding a superb view of the city and the surrounding country, taking in the arsenal immediately below the splendid mosque of Sultan Hassan, the numerous minarets of Cairo, and in the distance the Pyramids, with the valley of the Nile, to Sakkara on the south, and to the commencement of the Delta on the north. This strongly fortified place was constructed by Saladin to command and protect the city from the invasion of the Franks. While at work upon it they discovered a deep well near the centre, that had been cut by the ancients, and was then filled with sand, which they excavated, and brought another welcome supply of water to the Citadel by an aqueduct, which conveys a continuous stream from the Nile. It is called Joseph's well, and consists of two parts, the upper and lower well, and a flight of steps leads to the bottom, a depth of about two hundred and fifty feet. It is walled up with hewn stones. The water is drawn by means of donkeys attached to a wheel covered with buckets or earthen jars made for the purpose. Besides the well, the Citadel contains several objects worthy of notice, such as the Pasha's palace, a new work commenced by Mohammed Ali, the site of Joseph's Hall, and the arsenal. This palace, like all the rest built in modern times, is furnished almost entirely according to the French style, and contains only a few evidences of eastern customs, such as the baths and ottomans which were used in the early periods.

Returning from the Citadel, we entered the Mosque of Sultan Hassan, which is one among the finest of the four hundred mosques in Cairo, and regarded by the Cairenes as the best specimen of Saracenic architecture now extant. Its lofty and beautifully ornamented porch, the rich cornice of its walls, its minaret, and the arches of its spacious court, cannot fail to be admired by those fond of architecture, notwithstanding it is all coated with dust and dirt. The interior differs somewhat in form from the old style of mosques, consisting of an hypæthral court, with a square recess on each side, covered by a broad and beautiful arch. At the inner end of it are the niche of the *imam*, who prays before the congregation on Friday, and the *mumber* or pulpit around which the people may be seen at all times of the day kneeling and bowing their faces to the earth. Before saying their prayers they always wash their faces and feet in a pool of water in the centre of the court; and it matters not where they are, whether on the banks of the Nile or in the desert, they always perform these ablutions, turn their backs to the sun, and bow their faces to the earth twelve or fifteen times before finishing, repeating at the same time the prayers which they learn in childhood from the Koran. In the absence of water, they take sand and rub their faces and feet four or five times during the day. They evince great devotion and sincerity while on their knees, but as soon as they finish, they are ready to filch your purse, tell you a falsehood, or do any other rascality in their power. In the Mosque of Sultan Hassan I observed the tomb of Hagira, which bears the date of 764. It is surmounted by a large dome, like many others made of wood and plaster, on a basement and walls of stone, and ornamented with various figures out of the same material. On the tomb itself is a large copy of the Koran, written in beautiful and distinct characters, and over it are suspended three colored lamps, which are generally used in mosques. No one is allowed to enter a mosque without first taking off his shoes and depositing them at the door, and when he returns he is either compelled to fight his way through a crowd of beggars, who always hang about such places, or pay *backshish*, which is equally disagreeable, as you can never satisfy them, it matters not how much you give.

The narrowness of the streets of Cairo and their great irregularity may strike an American accustomed to broad thoroughfares as an imperfection in a large city, but their Oriental character fully compensates for this objection; and of all eastern towns none is so interesting in this respect as the Egyptian capital. In the bazaars, the mosques, and private residences, the same peculiarities may be observed, and no one can ramble through them without recalling his early impressions of "Arabian Nights." In the Frank quarter these peculiarities are not so striking, the hotels and houses generally being constructed more on the European plan, and the great square and gardens which adorn this quarter are filled in the afternoons by persons wearing the European dress. The gardens are beautifully shaded with the Acæin Lobbekh, and other ornamental trees, and the walks laid out with great taste, affording a delightful promenade for those who wish to enjoy the fragrance of flowers and inhale the pure air of this climate.

A visit to Old Cairo, which is situated on the river about three miles south of the city, fully compensates one for the donkey ride, and the quantity of dust he must necessarily inhale before reaching there. The streets are hardly wide enough for two persons to walk together. The houses are constructed of crude brick, one story in height; the inhabitants live like rats, all crowded together in rooms where there is but little light or ventilation. The Greek Convent, Mosque of Omar, and Ceptic Church are all very curious and interesting, on account of their antiquity. In the basement of the church we were shown a small apartment in which the Holy Family are said to have lived while in Cairo, and several pictures are hanging on the walls representing their flight into Egypt.

Opposite Old Cairo is the island of Roda, which Arab tradition fixes as the place where Moses was found by the daughter of Pharaoh. It is separated from the city by a canal, and contains on its southern extremity an elegant palace, recently built by Abbas Pasha for his mother, and the Mekkeeas, or Nileometer, of the ancient Egyptians. I had heard much of the Nileometer, and was disappointed to find nothing but a square well or chamber, with a graduated pillar in the centre for ascertaining the daily rise of the Nile, which is proclaimed every morning, during the inundation, by four criers, to each of whom a particular portion of the city is assigned.

The festivals and sights of Cairo are both numerous and curious. We witnessed the return of the Pilgrims from Mecca, which is one of their annual ceremonies. The procession contained many thousands, and the Holy Camel, elegantly caparisoned, was conducted through the streets with great pomp and parade. The Mooled e Nabbee, or "birth-day of the Prophet" Mohammed, is a *fête* that begins soon after their return and occupies a whole week. It is held in the *Uzbekieh* or great square in the Frank quarter, which is filled with booths, swings and other things erected on the occasion, giving it the appearance of a camp or fair. During this period the Saadieh derwishes, the modern Psylli, occupy their booths day and night, and perform all sorts of fanatical motions and juggling tricks with snakes, some of which are truly disgusting. On the evening of the last day the ceremony called the Doseh is gone through with, which no one can witness, except such people, without feelings of horror and disgust. On this occasion the sheikh of the Saadieh, mounted on horseback and accompanied by the derwishes of various orders, with their banners, goes in procession to the *Uzbekieh*, where these wild fanatics throw themselves on the ground, and being wedged close together permit the sheikh to ride over their bodies, and consider themselves as unfortunate if the horse fails to tread upon them. After this is over, a grand ceremony is performed at the house of their president, the Sheikh el Beker, the reputed descendant of *Abou Beker Saadieh.*

The bridal processions are also very curious, being composed entirely of females mounted on donkeys, after the manner of men, covered up with large silk robes, with the exception of their eyes, and each one uttering a shrill whistle as they pass along the streets. They go in single file from the lady's house to the house of her husband, and those who constitute the procession are paid as at funerals to increase the display and do the whistling.

To describe the various strange sights of this wonderful city would require a volume. Something new and interesting presents itself for contemplation every time we go out, and one may spend months here both profitably and pleasantly. The excursions in the neighborhood of Cairo are very numerous, and require a great deal of time to make them satisfactorily. Our first ride was out to Heliopolis, or the ancient city of On, mentioned in Genesis. It is situated five miles north of Cairo, and contains a large granite obelisk, remains of sphinxes, mounds of the old town, and the fountain of the Sun, all of which mark conclusively the site of that city. Returning, we passed by the old sycamore tree under which the Holy Family rested while in Egypt, and the tomb of El Ghoree, now in ruins. Like that of the Memlook Kings it is constructed of stuccoed brick-work, and covered with a dome ornamented inside with paintings and curious figures.

The gardens of Shoobra and the Petrified Forest are also objects of considerable interest. The former is attached to the Palace of Abbas Pasha, is laid out in the European style, and managed by Italian gardeners. The forest is in the desert, and consists of great quantities of petrified wood and fossils, embracing the crab, celiini, etc. Some of the wood measures as much as thirty feet in length, and abounds in great quantities. The most interesting excursion from this city is to the Pyramids of Ghizeh, situated off the west bank of the Nile, five miles from the village of the same name. Our party went over on donkeys, and occupied an entire day in examining the pyramids and the site of Memphis. The pyramids of Ghizeh, like those of Aboowash, Sakkam, and Dashoor, are situated in the desert, a short distance from the tillable land. They were originally cased with polished stone, which has disappeared with the exception of the upper part of the second pyramid. We ascended on the outside of the largest one to the summit in five minutes, with the assistance of two Bedouin guides whom we employed from the sheik, in order to avoid the trouble of being asked for *backshish.* There is a space about thirty-two feet square on the top covered over with the names of visitors, and the view is very extensive, embracing all the pyramids, the city of Cairo, the river for many miles, and the great desert on the west.

The exterior is built of a large block of sandstone which would have crumbled to pieces long since in any other climate. The interior is made with red granite, so well put together that it is as strong and as perfect in all its parts as it was when first completed. The passages leading to the great chambers are not more than five feet square, and the ventilation inside is so bad, that it is unpleasant to remain even a few minutes. So many persons have gone through these passages that they are worn perfectly smooth, and it was not without considerable danger that we groped our way with bad lights, and our eyes filled with dust, to the sarcophagus of the great king. A great number of tombs and mummy pits are scattered around the pyramids of Ghizeh, near to which is the great Sphinx, half covered with sand. Its head, neck, shoulders, and breast are still uncovered; its face, though worn and much broken, is mild, amiable and expressive, seeming, among the tombs around it, like a divinity guarding the dead. In view of the Sphinx, and close to the pyramids of Sakkara, is the site of ancient Memphis, of which little or nothing now exists, but a large colossus of Remeses II., a few fragments of granite, and some substructions. The colossus is broken at the feet, and part of the case is wanting, but its original size can readily be discovered, and may be estimated at forty-two feet eight inches in height, excluding the pedestal. The expression of the face is much better preserved than that of the Sphinx, and considered beautiful by the ladies who made the excursion with us.

The government of Egypt is nominally under the control of the Sultan of Turkey, to whom an annual tribute is paid; but in reality Abbas Pasha may be said to have things entirely in his own hands, and the connection is merely kept up for the sake of protection. England and Russia have their eyes at present upon this country, and fear of each other is the only thing that keeps them from taking possession of it. The motives for conquest on the part of the former country are increasing every year. The great overland route to India passes through this capital, and thousands of English subjects are settling in the country, creating interests that must eventually result in conquest. They have prevailed on the Pasha to allow them to connect Alexandria with Cairo by railway, against the wishes of the Emperor of Russia, and the British Consul General in Cairo has more influence with the Pasha than any other foreign ambassador and I may say even his own advisers.

10*

LETTER FORTY.

THEBES, Egypt.

Journey up the Nile—Grottoes of Beni Hassan—Osioot—Temple of Dendera—Thebes, Karnak, and Luxor—Temple and Dancing Girls at Esneh—Temple at Edfou—The First Cataract—Island of Philæ—The Nile above Philæ, and Incidents connected with the Journey.

HAVING ascended the Nile some distance above the first cataract, we are now at anchor opposite the ruins of the ancient city of Thebes, on our way back to Cairo; and I embrace the opportunity of writing a description of our journey, while the boat stands quietly along the shore, and all on board, except the faithful watchman, are wrapped in the arms of Morpheus.

We were detained ten days in Cairo, on account of the difficulty with the villagers of Embarbeh, which I alluded to in a previous letter; after which we set sail with the determination to avoid, if possible, any further trouble, and make our journey as agreeable and profitable as circumstances would admit. Our *reis*, in order to prevent any communication between the crew and those on shore, anchored the first night in the middle of the river, opposite Old Cairo, and started the following morning under a spanking breeze, long before we awoke. The next day brought us to Benisooef, the first large town, which is seventy-seven miles above Cairo. It is the capital of the province of Beylik, and residence of the Governor, whose palace can be seen from the river. Here the wind failed us, and we were compelled to *track* three days along the monotonous shore; but having guns and plenty of ammunition on board, we amused ourselves shooting at ducks, geese, and pigeons, which are abundant in Egypt. The novelty, also, of seeing the Arab sailors, in a perfect state of nudity, and their heads shaved close, with the exception of a small patch on top, by which they expect to be drawn into heaven, was sufficiently amusing to divert our attention from the slow progress we were making. Just before reaching Gebel Shekh Embarak, which is a lofty table mountain, approaching near the river, we were alarmed a second time by a large body of men and women, running to a point ahead of us, and armed with guns, pistols, and the *long stick* which they use so effectually in their difficulties. Thinking that some of those in the Embarbeh affray had pursued us, and aroused the villagers of Tokai to join them in an attack, we immediately loaded our guns and prepared the deck for an action, if they attempted to board us. It turned out, however, that we were not the object of their pursuit, but the Bedouins of the village of El Madal, who were attempting to take away their lands. Several guns were fired, and the Bedouins, retreated to the desert, leaving the villagers of Tokai in their rightful possession. A steamer came along about this time, and fearing the Pasha might be on board, they laid down their weapons in the grass and hid themselves very much after the manner of our western Indians.

Just before reaching Minieh, the second large town, there is a long, black-looking bluff, running close to the river, on the east bank, called Gebel e Tayr, (the mountain of the bird,) with a low stone convent, of the rudest nature, on its summit, named Sitteh (Sittina) Mariam el Adra, "Our Lady Mary the Virgin." It is inhabited by Copts, who live there like vultures, to spy out an apportunity of getting a few paras or piastres. Four or five of these creatures swam out to our boat, crying out at the top of their voices, "Ana Christian ya Hawagee!" One succeeded in getting on board; but our crew (who were all Mohammedans) pushed the others off, fearing that they would carry away all of our loose change. We gave the fortunate one a few piastres and an empty bottle, which he put into his mouth, darted into the water like a duck, and made for another passenger boat just behind us. We saw on the same day several Shereefs, on their return from a pilgrimage to Mecca. They claimed to be descendants of the Prophet, wore green veils, and carried a banner and drum with them. Like almost every Arab that we have met in Egypt, they cried out, "Backshish Hawagee!" and seemed to consider that their position entitled them to a gift from our hands.

At Osioot, the third large town, we stopped twenty-four hours, for our crew to make bread, which is required three times on a voyage up and down the Nile. They bake it in large ovens made for the purpose, out of meal from the *dhoura*, which is a species of maize, with a grain about the size of a pea. The bread is very dark, and becomes in a few days almost as hard as a stone, which they soften by boiling it, and mix in a few onions and garlic for seasoning.

This crude mixture constitutes their only food, except, occasionally, when they have a chance to steal a little sugar cane, or receive a sheep as a present from the Hawagee. Osioot is situated about one mile from the river, and is the largest, best built, and cleanest town in Upper Egypt. It is also the residence of a Governor, and contains some mosques and tombs of interest. Before leaving Osioot, Abbas Pasha came up from Cairo in a steamer, accompanied by two other steamers and the boat of the English Consul. We gave him thirty guns and lowered our flag, which is the usual mode of salutation on the Nile. Our salute was returned in a handsome manner, and acknowledged by the Pasha in person.

Speaking of steamers reminds me to state that there are now fourteen on the river, all belonging to the Government. One or two of them have been employed during the winter as passenger boats to the first cataract, and have succeeded well—carrying twenty or thirty persons, at £25 each, and performing the trip in eighteen days, including stoppages. In a few years the *dahabieh* and *cangia* will go out of use, and travellers up the Nile will perform the trip in one third of the time which it now occupies. At Geneh, which is about fifty miles below Thebes, we met a number of rafts, made of earthen water jars, several hundred feet in length. These jars are manufactured out of a porous clay, found in a valley near Geneh, which possesses the quality of filtering the water and keeping it as cold as ice in the warmest weather. They are made of all sizes, and are universally used by the Egyptians in preference to any other vessel. They are the very things we want in our country. I have taken such a fancy to them that I procured some of the clay, which can be analyzed and compared with the different qualities of clay in Tennessee. While in Geneh, we saw eight young giraffes, recently taken in Soudan by the wild Arabs, who intend presenting them to Abbas Pasha. They were beautiful animals, and looked entirely different in their wild state from the caged beast that we sometimes see in shows. Opposite Geneh, on the west bank, is the temple of Dendera, erected about eighteen hundred years ago, probably by Cleopatra, and dedicated to the goddess of Athor. Egyptian sculpture had long been on the decline before the erection of this temple. The plan is good, but the figures and hieroglyphics are not so well executed as those on the temples of Karnak and Philæ. It is, however, under roof, and more perfectly preserved than any ancient building in Egypt.

Thebes, Karnak, and Luxor contain objects of curiosity and wonder that would furnish the mind with food for six months' digestion. The great extent, magnitude, and beauty of the ruins cannot be exaggerated. "They stand in all the nakedness of desolation where they stood thousands of years ago, in the unwatered sands, in solitude and silence." At this day the temples of Thebes are familiar to every reader, by the descriptive pens of tourists. Artists have taken drawings of all their minute details, and I shall dismiss them very briefly. It was about noon when we entered the harbor of Thebes; the sun was shining upon it with meridian splendor; the inhabitants were seeking shelter in their miserable huts from its scorching rays; and the Europeans in the numerous pleasure boats scattered up and down the Luxor shore were enjoying repose beneath awnings stretched in front of their cabins. We had hardly made fast to the shore when a group of Arabs, smoking under the shade of some palm trees on a point above, discovered us, and came hurriedly down with books filled with recommendations, and proposing to act as guides in conducting us through the ruins. Securing one of these men who spoke a few words of French, and still fewer of the English language, we followed his footsteps first to the ruins of Luxor, which are situated on the Arabian side and very near the bank of the river. Although the temple is much hidden by the huts of the present inhabitants, there is much to see and learn of the ancient mode of building in the structure of the propylon, which is almost perfect and covered over with sculpture representing the battle scenes of an Egyptian warrior, designed and executed with extraordinary force and spirit. Near this magnificent gateway is the great obelisk, corresponding with the one in Paris, but more elegant in its execution, and better preserved than any now in Egypt. Between the obelisk and the great propylon are two colossal statues with mitred head-dresses, and made out of single blocks of granite, which are buried to the chest in sand, but still rising more than twenty feet from the ground. The temple is now occupied by a French physician, and a native who speaks a little English, and acts as consul for nearly all the nations of Europe. But great and magnificent as was the temple of Luxor, it falls into utter insignificance when compared with the wonderful ruins at Karnak, situated about one mile south of it. The road connecting the two places was originally lined with rows of solid granite sphinxes, most of which are now broken, and, for the most part, buried under the sand or hidden from sight by the *halfeh* grass. Four magnificent propylons terminate this avenue of sphinxes, through which the ancient Egyptians passed to offer up their devotions in the great temple. Here we beheld for the first time the wonders of this gigantic structure, which has been the object of admiration for ages past, and which defies all description. To stand in the large court and feast the eyes on the vast field of ruins which occupy more than a mile in diameter, is an easy and agreeable matter; but to convey to a distant friend any just idea of the magnitude and splendor of the temple is utterly impossible. To appreciate its beauties, you must see it with your own eyes and form your own conclusions. "No man can look upon these ruins without feeling humbled by the greatness of a people who have passed away for ever." Looking forward from the centre of the principal gateway, the vast scene of havoc and destruction presents itself in all the extent of this immense temple—with its columns, and walls, and immense propylons, all prostrate in one heap of ruins, looking as if the "thunders of heaven had smitten it at the command of an insulted God." The temple itself is estimated at 1200 feet in length and 240 in breadth; and the great hall measures 170 feet by 329, supported by twelve massive columns 66 feet high and 12 feet in diameter—besides 122 of smaller dimensions, about 42 feet in height, and 28 feet in circumference, divided in seven lines on either side of the central avenue. Passing out of the great hall, which is the most perfect part of the temple, we came to four beautiful obelisks, two of which stand on their original site, the others having been thrown down and broken by human violence. Next came the sanctuary, consisting of an apartment twenty feet square, the walls and ceilings of large blocks of smooth granite—the ceilings ornamented with stars on a blue ground, and the walls covered with sculpture and hieroglyphics representing offerings to Osiris, showing the strange uses of this sacred chamber, and portraying the low and degrading character of the Egyptian worship. Numerous chambers of similar dimensions surround the sanctuary, and beyond it is the columnar edifice of the third Thotmus, now in a dilapidated condition, but sufficiently perfect to convey an accurate idea of its dimensions and appearance. Those who have investigated the history of Karnak, represent its antiquity as surpassing that of any other building in Thebes, by at least one hundred years. But these are not half of the ruins of ancient Thebes. On the opposite or western side of the river we passed two whole days in rambling through tombs and temples, some of which are in an excellent state of preservation. The Arabs who rowed us over from Luxor landed the boat on a small island, and after much difficulty with the donkey boys who were eager to engage their animals, we were conducted to the ruins of the small temple palace, at Old Kooneh, dedicated to Ammon, the Theban Jupiter, by Osirei, and completed by Remeses II., the supposed Sesostris of the Greeks. This temple, as it now stands, presents a spacious hall supported by six columns, having on either side three chambers, one of which enters into a lateral hall, and the opposite one to a passage and open court. Upon the upper end of this hall open five other chambers, the centre one of which leads to a large room supported by four square columns, beyond which is the sanctuary itself; but this part of the temple is so much dilapidated that we could not form an accurate idea of its proportions. A short distance from the temple are two mutilated statues of Remeses II., of black granite—and a little beyond, a sandstone block of Remeses III. From this place our guide conducted us through a deep and barren valley called Biban el Mahook, the Tombs of the Kings, which are decidedly the most curious remains on this side of the river. We entered those numbered 17, 11, 9, 6, 1, and 14, all of which are exceedingly interesting, and of the same general character. No. 17, better known as Belzoni's tomb, is the best preserved and by far the most remarkable for its sculptures. We entered by a small door in the side of the mountain, without any inscription or ornament. The entrance hall, which is very beautiful, is about 27 or 28 feet in length and 25 in breadth, and leads through a square door into another chamber 28 feet long by 25, the walls covered with small figures drawn in outline, but perfect as if lately executed. Descending another staircase or passage, we passed through an elegant corridor into another apartment 24 feet by 13. This is called the Hall of Beauty—and fully merits the appellation. "The sides of all the chambers and corridors are covered with sculpture and paintings, the colors appearing fresher as the visitor advances towards the interior of the tomb; and the walls of this chamber are covered with the figures of the Egyptian gods and goddesses seeming to hover around and guard the remains of the honored dead."

Two French artists were copying the figures in this chamber by the light of lamps which illuminated the tomb so brilliantly that we could see the smallest figure with the utmost distinctness. These gentlemen have been in the tomb nearly two weeks without seeing the light of day, and seem to be perfectly enthusiastic on Egyptian sculpture and paintings. They received us with the greatest kindness, and made many inquiries about the condition of France and affairs in Europe. Taking a glass of champagne with them, we proceeded to the next apartment, called by Belzoni the Hall of Pillars. It is nearly square, being 28 feet long and 27 feet broad, supported by two rows of square pillars, and connected with a large saloon with a vaulted roof, 32 feet in length and 27 in breadth. Several other chambers of different sizes open into this room—one of which is unfinished, and the rest similar to the larger rooms. An alabaster sarcophagus formerly occupied the centre of the arched chamber, but like many other things, it has been removed to decorate some European museum. Every part of this tomb is in keeping. The corridors, chambers, and halls are ornamented with sculptures and paintings, representing gods, goddesses, and the hero of the tomb in the striking events of his life—priests, religious processions and sacrifices, boats and agricultural scenes, and the most familiar pictures of early Egyptian life, in colors as fresh as if they were painted but yesterday. That these magnificent subterranean chambers were used for the tombs of potentates there can be no doubt, as the sarcophagus in each one amply testifies; but that they were used for this purpose alone is clearly a mistake, and fully disproved in the book of Ezekiel, viii. 8–10: "Then said he to me, Son of man, dig now in the wall; and when I had digged in the wall, behold a door. And he said unto me, Go in and behold the wicked abominations that they do here. So I went in, and saw; and behold, every form of creeping things, and abominable beasts, and all the idols of the house of Israel portrayed upon the wall round about." The people of Israel regarded the Egyptians as models in every thing pertaining to architecture, and consequently the passage just quoted is quite as applicable to the one country as the other.

Leaving this interesting place, we crossed a high and barren range of hills to Medinet Abou, near which stand the two colossi of the plain and the palace of the great Remeses (the Remeseum, generally called the Memnonium). Medinet Abou is one of the four temples mentioned by Diodorus, and is far more extensive than any other on the western side of the river. The two colossi, one of which is called the Vocal Memnonium, stand in the centre of the plain, about forty feet apart, and face the river. They are made of a kind of spotted gritstone, and measure forty-seven feet in height, or fifty-three above the plain, and the pedestal, which is now buried about seven feet below the surface, completes to its base a total of sixty-eight feet. We walked around the mighty giants of the plain, once the wonder of the ancients, but we heard no sound either from above or below, and cannot therefore testify to the statement of Strabo, who heard distinctly the voice of the great Memnon. These wonderful statues have been frequently restored, evidences of which are quite visible; yet the desolating effects of time and the ruthless hand of the Arab have so mutilated their external appearance, that we could form only a faint idea of the features and expression of the face. The temple of Memnon or Remeseum is not so extensive as Medinet Abou, but far more interesting, and for symmetry of architecture and elegance of sculpture, I regard it as being equal to any other monument of Egyptian art. The greatest attraction about this temple is the remains of a stupendous syenite statue of the king, seated on the throne in the usual position of Egyptian figures—the hands resting on his knees, indicative of that tranquillity which he had returned to enjoy after the fatigues of victory. It is the largest statue in Egypt, and the greatest mass of hewn stone that I have ever seen—containing by estimation three times the solid contents of the largest obelisk, and weighing about eight hundred and eighty-seven tons. How the Egyptians could transport and erect a mass of such dimensions is a problem yet to be solved, and what means they employed to destroy it is equally wonderful. The throne and legs are completely destroyed and reduced to comparatively small fragments, while the upper part, broken at the waist, is merely thrown back upon the ground, and lies in that position in consequence of the fall. We examined several smaller temples of great beauty, and then proceeded to the Tombs of the Queens, situated three thousand feet behind the city. They possess few attractions after visiting the Tombs of the Kings, for those who are not interested in examining and deciphering the hieroglyphics. Near these tombs are innumerable mummy pits, in which I saw the ravenous Arabs digging for relics and hidden treasures. Indeed, the pleasure of one's visit to Thebes is almost destroyed by these grave-robbers, who hang around with their arms filled with skulls, hands, feet, and other portions of the human body, for you to purchase.

Fatigued by the labors of the day, we returned to our boat and set off for Esneh, the next large town on the river. As we passed by the ruins of the ancient Thebes, the sun was just declining behind the hills, revealing a picture surpassingly beautiful. The whole horizon was one sheet of brilliant and variegated colors—reflecting a thousand hues on the hill tops and temples, leaving an impression on our minds that can never be forgotten.

The following day we reached Esneh, situated on the west bank of the river. The only object of interest here is a temple that was excavated from the accumulated sand, by order of Mohammed Ali, in 1842. The portico is the only part that can yet be seen, which is sufficient to establish its ancient size and magnificence. I counted twenty-four columns, more than fifty feet in height, and five feet in diameter, covered over with figures and hieroglyphics. Excavations are now in progress by order of Abbas Pasha, which may bring to light something valuable. Esneh is the place where all travellers up the Nile stop to see the *Dancing Women* or *Almehs*, who are banished from Cairo on account of offences against the police, or the prejudices of the *Ulemas.* "The learning of these *learned women* has long ceased; their poetry has sunk into absurd songs; their dancing would degrade even the *motus Tonicus* of antiquity; and their title *Almeh* has been changed to the less respectable name of *Ghowagee*, or women of the Memlooks." The next place of interest is Edfou, where there is a temple built by the Ptolemies on a large scale. The walls are more than one hundred feet high, and beautifully adorned with figures, hieroglyphics, etc. It is built around a hollow square, and is nearly perfect in all its parts, giving one a very good idea of the extent and magnificence of such structures.

In the afternoon of the same day, we passed Hagar Silsili, or the chain mountain, near which are the great sandstone quarries, where the ancient Egyptians got most of their stone for building temples, etc. A number of grottoes and catacombs are cut in the solid rock, upon which are inscribed a variety of hieroglyphics and figures. This is the narrowest point of the river below the first cataract, and there is a tradition here that one of the ancient kings stretched a chain across the river to prevent the Ethiopians from passing. The temple of Ombos, now in a dilapidated condition, is situated on a high bluff, which overhangs the water between Hagar Silsili and Assouan, the ancient Syene. The river, as we approached the cataract, became much narrower, and quite shallow in places—so much so that we ran aground several times, and had the pleasure of hearing the wild cry of the sailors and the croaking of water wheels on the shore, which constitute the peculiar music of the Nile. Assouan is the stopping point for those who do not intend going beyond the first cataract, and at this season a large number of pleasure boats may be seen scattered along the shore. The town is like all Arab villages, and presents but few ruins of the ancient city, except some granite columns of a late date, and the sekos of a small temple, with the shattered remains of an outer chamber, and a portico in front. Opposite Assouan is the island of Elephantiné, now inhabited by Nubians, and covered over with the ruins of old houses and fragments of pottery. The only remaining ruins of Elephantiné are a granite gateway of the time of Alexander, the entrance to some edifice now entirely demolished, and portions of the old Nileometer.

Leaving our boat, which was too large to go over the cataracts at Assouan, we procured donkeys and rode up a distance of about five miles. Here we procured a small boat, managed by Nubians, and proceeded to examine the great cataracts of the Nile, about which you have heard so much. They are called by the natives E'Shellah, and are, in truth, nothing but rapids, whose falls do not exceed six feet, and passable at all seasons of the year. I expected to be disappointed with the cataracts, but I must say that I was more than disappointed. Compared to the rapids of St. Lawrence, or the numerous waterfalls in the United States, they diminish into utter insignificance. The boats are towed with ropes ; and now that the passage has been enlarged and the Nubians more skilful, there is litle fear of accidents. A number of amusing incidents occurred while we were loitering on the shore, which diverted our attention, for a time, from the scenery around. Forty or fifty naked Nubians were seen, all at once, to make their appearance from among the rocks, plunge into the river, and pass like an arrow over the cataracts, in the midst of the most furious rushing of the waters. I feared that some would lose their lives; but our venerable Reis, who sat smoking his chibouk, smiled at the idea, and remarked, in his own language, that they were Nubian ducks, and could not drown.

Just above the rapids, we saw two figures, with their clothes tied above their heads, sitting upon the surface of the water, apparently, and floating about like some inflated substance; which turned out to be a man and his wife, crossing from the island of Biggeh. Their bark was a log with a bundle of cornstalks on each side, too light to support their weight, yet strong enough to keep them from sinking.

About two miles above the cataracts is the island of Philæ, known in Nubia by the name of Anas el Wogood, and upon which stand the remains of the temple of Isis, commenced by Ptolemy Philadelphus and Arsinæ, and completed by succeeding monarchs. The island is small and shaped like an egg, presenting to the eye, from all points, a certain beauty and uniqueness no where else to be seen. The scenery around is wild and romantic, corresponding admirably with the position of the island, and so charming as to make one almost wish to pass the remainder of his days here. Next to the great temple of Karnak, I regard the temple of Isis as the most elegant structure in Egypt, containing many rich and perfect specimens of architecture, no where else to be found. The outside of the walls are ornamented with numerous figures and hieroglyphics, executed in a chaste and beautiful manner. No two of the capitals of the numerous columns are alike, all being different to display the beauties of the various orders. Very near to Philæ is the island of Biggeh, containing the remains of a small temple, dedicated to Athos, apparently commenced by Euergetes I. and completed by Ptolemy the elder. A red granite statue and a few broken fragments of stone, scattered over the surface of the ground, are all that remains to prove its existence and position. This island is inhabited by Nubians, who go entirely naked, except a piece of leather about six inches wide, cut in strings and tied about their loins. They are far more interesting to me in their appearance and character than the Egyptians. His figure is tall, thin, and graceful; his face is rather dark, but far removed from African blackness; his features are long and aquiline, somewhat resembling the Roman; the expression of his face is mild, amiable, and approaching to melancholy. The inhabitants of Nubia are extremely poor, but their wants are few, and they live accordingly.

Above Philæ, the barren hills become higher and run close to the river, leaving only a small strip of ground for agricultural purposes; but as we ascended only a short distance above this island, I will not attempt a description, but will state upon the authority of friends, that there is much to see between the first and second cataracts.

Satisfied with our voyage on the Nile, we returned to our boat, and are now floating sideways down the current, praying for a favorable wind, and hoping soon to return to Cairo.

LETTER FORTY-ONE.

JERUSALEM, Palestine.

Preparations at Cairo for crossing the Desert—Our Caravan—A Sheik of the Bedouins—Midnight alarm and loss of a Carpet Bag—Jerreed Tournament—Military Honors at El Arish—Five hours' separation from the Caravan in a Simoom—Five days in the Lazaretto at Gaza—Plain of Sharon—Ashdod—Two days in the Convent at Ramla—Journey to and first sight of Jerusalem.

HAVING made the grand tour in Egypt from the sea to the cataracts—or, in the language of the Bible, from "Migdol to Syene, even unto the borders of Ethiopia"—we were once more in the modern capital, making the necessary preparations for crossing the Great Arabian Desert. Three routes were presented for our contemplation, viz.: one by way of Petra, another by way of El Arish, and a third between the two. Parties were forming for each of the three routes, and we had our option which to join. Two of our friends, with whom we had journeyed for some months in Europe and on the Nile, desired to take the first, and we would have been pleased to continue with them, but two insurmountable obstacles stood in our way—time and uncertainty. This route requires forty days, which was somewhat longer than we wished to sit on the hump of a camel and gaze at nothing but burning sands and our own tracks; and then there was great uncertainty whether we would be permitted to enter Petra on account of the dissensions between the Akaba and Petra tribes, who had been at war with each other, and forbidden all foreigners to enter the city of Rock. Having disposed of this route, we were not long in making up our minds to accept the proposition of a friend from New-York, to enter into a contract with a Maltese dragoman, named Vincent Belluti, to carry us to Jerusalem by way of El Arish, and thence through the Holy Land to Damascus and Beirout. Vincent had the character of being an energetic man, good purveyor, and well acquainted with the way of managing the Bedouins. All was left to him, and I am happy to state that he realized my expectations in every particular. Independent of our own party, consisting of two young ladies and three gentlemen, we had the pleasure of being joined on the day of departure by an English gentleman from York, and his lady, who proved to be exceedingly clever, and contributed much towards making the journey agreeable, and the long days pass away almost imperceptibly. This couple will ever have my very best wishes, and hereafter when I think of the desert, their faces will come vividly before my mind's eye, and the many pleasant days passed in their company will be dwelt upon as among the brightest of my Eastern tour.

It was a gloomy day to me when we started for the Holy Land. Although the sun shed its genial rays on the blooming beauties of nature, and every thing seemed to invite us onward, yet I felt sad. It was the day fixed upon by the authorities for the punishment and exile of nine poor creatures who participated in the battle on the Nile. We were requested by our Vice-Consul to be present on the occasion, but I had not the heart to witness the severity of the Egyptian bastinado, with the knowledge that it was inflicted partly on my own account. But this was the slightest cause of our grief. We were about to part with tried friends, and leave a country replete with historical interest, and wander amid new and different scenes. Yes, we were to give up our quiet, easy-moving boat for a caravan of dromedaries and camels, to pitch our tents wherever the setting sun might find us, and instead of our faithful Arabs of the Nile, to have for our companions and protectors the wild rude Bedouins of the desert. All preparations, however, were made, the caravan waiting at the door of our hotel, loaded with tents, luggage, and provisions. The Bedouin Sheik and his swarthy tribe, armed with pistols, long sabres, and match-lock guns, were sitting cross-legged on a mat, smoking their pipes and waiting our commands. The dragoman, anxious to be off, was hurrying to and fro, seeing that all things were in their proper place. At last the signal was given. The Bedouins rose from their seats, adjusted their pipes on their backs, and moved off slowly towards the ancient city of the Sun (Heliopolis). It was at the time a grand sight to see thirty camels all tied together, and stepping steadily one after the other in the tracks of their long-bearded drivers; but the novelty soon passed away, and we now look at a camel with as much indifference as we would at an old cow grazing on a common. Some persons profess to admire this animal, but for my part I never wish to see another. They are any thing but prepossessing in appearance, slow and awkward in their movements, always complaining, and fit only for what nature intended them—beasts of burden.

The ladies did not fancy the idea of mounting at the hotel door, and to please them we rode on donkeys as far as the old sycamore tree, under which the Holy Family rested while in Egypt—a little to the south of Heliopolis, and of the *Bab el Hag*, over the plain where Toman Bey was defeated by Sultan Selim. Here we boarded for the first time in our lives the great "ship of the desert," and I assure you it was an amusing scene. The camels were arranged in a circle, and the Bedouins standing near by ready to assist us in mounting. The ladies were the first to make the trial, and I am certain that without the assistance of the dragoman and Bedouins, they never would have got farther than the second rising motion of the animal, without being pitched either behind or before. The gentlemen disdained the idea of being held on while the animal was rising, and insisted that they should be allowed to try it alone, upon which the drivers in their usual frank manner replied, *Tiebe* (very good). The consequence was, that two of the party were tumbled in the sand, and fully satisfied that they were unequal to the sudden and vigorous jerks of the rising camel.

Throughout all the East it is the custom to place the saddle on the back of the camel, as well as the horse, so soon as they are old enough for use, which is never removed until they die, or become unfit for work. The result is, that nine tenths of these poor brutes are constantly suffering from raw backs, much to the annoyance of the European or American traveller. I frequently endeavored to persuade the Arabs to pay some attention to this matter, but my efforts were always unavailing, as it is utterly impossible to get them to depart in the slightest degree from the usages of their ancestors.

To give you some idea of our *comforts* while riding, just picture to yourself a tall six-footer from Tennessee perched high out of his element on a blue mattress, underneath which was an enormous bag of beans, for the use of the animal *en route*, placed on a saddle similar in shape to a wood-horse, and according to my boyish recollection similar in point of ease. Thus elevated, imagine him with a broad-brimmed wool hat, covered with a green veil, holding in one hand a white cotton umbrella, in the other a coarse palm halter, moving at the rate of *three miles* per hour, and congeeing his body in the most ungraceful manner to the back of a beautiful young lady all the way from the Knickerbocker State. At four o'clock, the usual hour on the desert, we pitched our tents near the village of Bilbis, and in sight of the citadel and minarets of Cairo. While driving the pegs, an Italian quarantine officer came down from the village and endeavored to prevail on us to camp near his house, stating that the thieves were unusually bad, and that it was really dangerous to pass the night in the desert. The dragoman of our English friend, who is a sprightly Egyptian, and our own dragoman held a parley on the subject, and informed the *gentleman* that they knew full well how to manage the thieves, and for his own safety he had better keep clear of our tents during the night. Finding that he could make nothing out of the dragomans, the dirty rascal slipped round and claimed acquaintance with Antonio, one of our servants, and invited him to visit his house that night, and reminded him to put a bottle of brandy in his pocket. Now, although Antonio was sometimes fond of turning his little finger over his thumb, he politely declined this invitation, saying that he had no brandy of his own, and was too honest to take that belonging to his master. In a few minutes our tents were pitched near to each other, and the camels arranged in a circle round them, forming a kind of bulwark in case of an attack during the night. All being fixed according to the directions of the dragomans, the Bedouins gave their animals a few beans, examined their old firelocks, refreshed themselves with a few dried dates, and then prostrated their weary limbs on the desert sand, there to repose until the hour arrived for them to watch and guard the tents. At half-past five, the ringing of a bell announced that dinner was served, and all hastened to the large tent to partake of the first meal on the desert. Each one expressed their surprise to find every thing so neatly and so comfortably arranged: the iron-framed cots were all made up—a Turkish carpet covered the ground, and the table-cloth and napkins were as clean as I ever saw in any European hotel; and what was still more surprising, we were furnished with a bill of fare that would not disgrace the first-class hotels in London, and certainly much superior to any thing in Cairo or Alexandria. As you may be curious to know what constituted this bill, I will enumerate the several courses in their order, viz.: Soup, mutton, turkey, pigeons, rice, potatoes, pudding, fruits, sweets, and accompaniments. After the cloth was removed, coffee and pipes were served, according to the custom of the East, and we regaled ourselves in a manner truly oriental.

Whenever a party encamps near a village in Egypt, the sheik usually furnishes a guard who profess to be responsible for every thing, but are in reality not only thieves but a decided nuisance. As soon as their time for watching begins, they commence firing off their old matchlocks, in order to exaggerate the importance of their services, when in truth there is no real danger, the Bedouins of the desert being harmless as far as the taking of blood; and as for stealing, they do it on such a small scale, that no one is injured but the camel owners, who are generally able to bear the loss. This firing off of guns during the entire night is exceedingly disagreeable and annoying to the fatigued traveller, who desires repose after the labor of camel-riding during the day.

To give you some idea of the cunning and petty rascality of the Arab people, I will relate a little incident that occurred the second night near the village of Goshen. The sheik of this place furnished twelve men, who came to the encampment long before the usual time, and evinced a degree of vigilance in our behalf that aroused my suspicion as to their honesty. Sure enough, about the hour of midnight, we were alarmed in our sleep by the report of guns and sudden cry of *Bedouins! Bedouins!! Bedouins!!!* Thinking that the wild rovers of the desert were upon us, and that our time had come, we all simultaneously bounded from our cots, grasped the weapons beneath the pillows, and rushed out to meet our fate. All was confusion—the guard pretended to be much alarmed—the camel drivers were running to and fro expecting every minute that their all would be taken. The dragoman, however, was cool, and seemed to comprehend in an instant the whole affair. Search your tents, he cried, and see what they have taken. In an instant lights were produced and every one began to look for his property, when, lo and behold, a still small voice emanated from the *harem* (as the Arabs termed the ladies' tent) announcing the loss of a *carpet bag*. It seems that the guard pulled up the tent pegs, slipped out the carpet bag, and gave the alarm in order to impress us with the belief that it was the work of the poor *Bedouins*. After this, our own men kept a vigilant watch over the rascals, and the following morning we sent a deputation after the sheik of the village, who, like the patriarchs of old, exercises a paternal influence over the village and is expected to know every thing that transpires among his people. In a short time a venerable-looking man with long white beard and pipe-bearers in his train, made his appearance at our encampment, and declared by every thing that was solemn and holy that he knew nothing of the stolen property. Feeling confident that his men were the thieves, and that he knew all about it, we told him that if the bag was not produced immediately, we would put one of our men on the fleetest dromedary and send him back to Cairo to inform the Pasha of our loss. This threat seemed to give him great alarm, so much so that he ordered his men to prostrate themselves on the ground and receive the bastinado. We objected to this, and told him to carry them into the village if he desired to punish them, and not in the presence of the ladies—who were listening to the conversation, eager to get the many indispensables contained in the carpet bag. Finding that his proposition to inflict the bastinado failed to appease us, he proposed to hang two or three of them, or do any thing to prevent our making complaint to the Pasha. We told him that we were going to Salahieh that night, and if the carpet bag was sent on to us we would say nothing about it; but if not, we would inform Caraca Mustapha, who has command of seven hundred soldiers at that place. Paying no further attention to them, we ordered our camels to be packed and proceeded on our journey, passing through a number of ruined villages and cultivated land, where the old-fashioned water wheels and buckets are used as on the Nile.

Just before reaching Salahieh, we met Caraca Mustapha (who is Governor of that part of Egypt) taking a ride on horseback, accompanied by two mounted soldiers and a footman bearing his pipes. Our dragoman saluted his Highness, and informed him of the loss we sustained the night before at the village of Goshen, which seemed to make him very angry, particularly when he was told that they entered the *harem*, which is considered more sacred than their mosque. He replied that it was an unheard-of outrage, and if we would wait one day he would either restore the lost carpet bag or have the old sheik and all the guards severely bastinadoed. That night we enjoyed a comfortable rest, free from the alarm of thieves and the report of firearms; and long before we awoke the Governor had dispatched two officers, a flag-bearer, and eight soldiers to the village of Goshen. At ten o'clock the gentlemen of the party called to see the Governor in his tent, and were received with marked civility. He was seated on an elevated cushion in the Turkish fashion, and did not move when we entered—it being considered undignified to make the least physical exertion. We all took seats around him in the same manner on some matting placed on the sand, and conversed about half an hour, through our interpreter. We told him that we had been up the Nile, and were highly pleased with the country and its antiquities; spoke of our experience in riding camels, and told him that we kept them in shows at home, and paid so many piastres to look at them, which pleased him exceedingly. We flattered his troops, the beauty of his country, and the climate. Pipes and coffee were handed around in the usual manner by negro slaves, and he apologized for not being able to entertain us better. When we started to our tents we invited him to call and see the ladies, which he accepted in the most gracious manner, and returned the visit in less than fifteen minutes. The dragoman ushered him into the larger tent, and returned the same civilities that he had extended to us. As soon as the ladies made their appearance with their *faces uncovered*, the old Pasha seemed utterly overpowered, and was so much pleased, that I really think he would have done any thing in reason to amuse the party. After asking him about a thousand questions, which a woman alone could think of, we were invited out to witness a jerreed tournament, one of the favorite amusements in the East, and without exception the greatest display of horsemanship that ever came under my observation. The scene was truly Oriental. A grove of palms bounded the prospect on one side, the arid desert on the other, and the two encampments filled with camels, Arabian horses, and their gaily dressed riders, served to complete the picture. About fifty men participated in the tournament, and were equally divided and arrayed against each other. They were armed with the jerreed, made of palm branches, instead of the usual spear, which they throw with great precision at each other forty or fifty yards off. They are excellent horsemen, and to avoid the blows of the contending party they would frequently throw their bodies completely on the side of the horse while at full speed. They charge with great spirit, and the horses seem to enter into the combat with as much animation as the men themselves. They are cruel riders; I noticed the blood flowing in streams from the side and mouth of nearly every horse from the effects of their stirrups, which are made of iron in the shape of an old-fashioned shovel, and severe curb bits. During the exhibition, the Governor and his suite, consisting of several officers and pipe-bearers, were seated with us on Turkish rugs, and seemed highly gratified to see us enter so fully into their sports. The Governor's departure was as sudden as his visit. Rising without saying a word or even bowing to the ladies, he walked with great dignity to his tent, evidently satisfied that he had made a hit. Not wishing to disappoint him, we sent as a present three plated salvers and a silk scarf, which he accepted as a matter of course, and sent us in return a letter of introduction to the Pasha of El Arish.

The following morning we started off without the carpet bag, but we have been informed since that it was recovered, and the twelve men soundly bastinadoed. I had almost forgot to mention that we were joined at Salahieh by a large party of Pilgrims or Hadji from Mecca, who desired our protection from the Bedouins of the desert.

They had been absent from home nearly one year, and had nothing with them but two small donkeys to carry their water, and a little brown bread, which they mixed with herbs and boiled together in small kettles, shaped somewhat like the rind of a long melon. Every morning and evening they would scratch holes in the ground until they came to moistened sand, with which they rubbed their faces, hands, and feet, instead of the ordinary ablution practised where water is abundant. After this operation, they prostrated themselves and went through the ceremony of prayer. It is a solemn and affecting scene to see men out in the still and barren desert offering up to God and the Prophet the earnest devotion of their hearts. At noon of the seventh day we reached Teeneh, which occupies the site of Pelusium, once a place of great consequence. It was strongly fortified, being the bulwark of the Egyptian frontier on the eastern side, and considered the "key of Egypt." It was called in Scripture, "Sin." (Ezek. xxx. 15, 16.) Near this the unfortunate Pompey met his death, basely murdered by Ptolemy and his minister Photinus, whose protection he had claimed, B. C. 48. A long strip of date trees, a few wild Bedouins living in rude habitations formed of date branches, and an old fountain constructed either by the Romans or Napoleon, as a stopping point, is all that remains of this once important place.

While at the fountain "the daughters of the men of the city came out to draw water." They carried pitchers upon their shoulders, and like Rebekah of old, drew water both for us and our camels. Now Rebekah *was* a damsel very fair to look upon, a virgin without spot or blemish, well worthy of Isaac's love; but the damsels that greeted us were very different in their appearance, and treated us in a manner wholly unbecoming the gentle sex. After giving us drink, instead of offering us *meat*, and straw and provender for the camels, they called the men belonging to the village and endeavored to take away one of our camels, saying that our sheik owed them money and they intended taking their property. A great deal of loud talking and fierce looks were exchanged on both sides, and the matter was finally adjusted by the *dragoman*, who informed the men that the *Howadji* would not allow them to take the camel under any pretext. Soon after leaving the fountain we were overtaken by three friends from New-York, who left Cairo two days after us. They brought me letters from home, which came like manna to the children of Israel, at a time when I most needed them. It was the only package that I had received for many months, and you can easily conceive what pleasure they afforded me. Seated high on the hump of my camel, I unfolded the precious papers and read them over and over again, weighing each line and word particularly, in order to learn as much as possible from those that are nearest and dearest to me on earth.

The following day the same gentlemen and myself met with an adventure of somewhat rare occurrence. We started at eight o'clock in the morning with the caravan, but became impatient, and concluded we would try the speed of our dromedaries for a short distance, and then wait for them to overtake us. We moved on charmingly and at a rapid pace for about two hours, when all of a sudden the bright orb of day became obscured, the whole heavens darkened, and the wind commenced blowing most furiously. It was evidently a *simoom*, and our only hope of escape was in Him who rules the storm and directs the whirlwind. The sand drifted in such quantities that our track soon became obliterated, and our eyes perfectly blinded. Thirst also came upon us, and our only refuge from famishing was a small canteen filled with a mixture of brandy and water. Making our dromedaries kneel down close together, we ensconced ourselves behind them, and waited for the storm to subside. Five long hours, which appeared like so many days, passed away, and still we were alone in the broad desert waste, without guide, compass, or direction. At last the wind became more calm, the atmosphere clearer, and our hopes brighter. Mounting the camels once more, we pursued our course in the direction that we thought right; and while groping in darkness, we fortunately discovered in the dim distance the form of a man. That form I shall never forget. It was one of the Hadjis on the look-out for us, and without his exertions we would have had to pass the night alone in the broad desert. He informed us that the caravan was ahead, and with his guidance we overtook our friends just as they were pitching their tents. As soon as they discovered us, joy unspeakable burst from their lips; the ladies were particularly delighted, so much so, that they gave utterance to their emotions by a flood of joyful tears. They had given us up as lost, or murdered by the Bedouins, and you can easily imagine their feelings.

The day after this adventure we passed by a large lake nearly filled with sand. The water was salt, and the saline incrustation so thick that I lifted it from the surface in large flakes. The road that lies on its borders is replete with historic interest from the aggressive time of Nebuchadnezzar to that of Napoleon and Shacham Pasha. It was the debatable ground between Egypt and Syria, whether its possessors were Babylonians or Persians, Greeks or Romans, Saracens or Crusaders, and is called to this day *El Sikka Sultan*, Highway of Kings. Just before reaching El Arish, we were met by several mounted soldiers, and nearly all of the inhabitants, who went out to see their husbands and fathers. The women, robed in fine white, raised the shrill *whistle*, indicating joy; the men ran up to our drivers, grasped their hands, and touched their foreheads repeatedly, producing a scene at once novel and amusing. El Arish occupies the site of the ancient Rhinocalura of the Greeks, and the Botany Bay of the old Egyptians. It was to that place that condemned criminals were transported by the Pharaohs, having first their noses cut off, whence the name of the Land of Broken Noses. Here Baldwin the Second of Jerusalem died in the midst of his warriors, when on his way to conquer Egypt. The old Greek castle still contains a sarcophagus of a child belonging to one of the Ptolemies. Napoleon thought it, next to Alexandria, the most important military point in Egypt, and built a large stone fort there in 1789, which is now occupied by the Governor and a few soldiers. The place is now the quarantine for those going from Syria into Egypt, is surrounded by sand hills, and in sight of the sea. Upon the strength of the letter introducing us to Mustapha Bey, we had twenty-five mounted soldiers to escort us several miles, and one came with us as far as Gaza, an honor rarely conferred, and which we properly appreciated.

After leaving El Arish, we passed along the sea-shore to Refah, or Rhaphin, now marked by two solitary granite pillars, situated on an eminence. It is remarkable as the battlefield between Antiochus the Great and Ptolemy the younger of Egypt, when they contended for the empire of the East. On the plain before it the gigantic elephants were trained to war, and here Antiochus was defeated. Here, also, the bride of Solomon, even Pharaoh's daughter, was delivered into the hands of the elders of Israel, who were sent to receive her. It was undoubtedly one of the holy stations. While taking our luncheon under a tree near the columns. two old sheiks, accompanied by their men, came down out of the hills and demanded tribute money. Vincent paid them three piastres for each Frank in the party, the usual sum required from all Europeans. Our own sheik denied their right to receive the sum, and a quarrel ensued, which ended, as usual, in words.

That night we pitched at a place called Sheik Jude, a burying ground, where several tombs are standing. In the large tomb, the grave is covered with a green canopy, and contains a collection of old rags, pieces of wood, and other mementoes, hung about on strings by pilgrims who pass that way. While there, we witnessed a burial. The grave was dug about three feet deep, with a kind of mattock, and the dirt shovelled out with their hands, having no instrument to use for the purpose. The corpse was wrapped in a coarse blanket worn by the Arabs, and placed in the grave without any coffin. The following day we reached Kan Yoones, the Yenisus of Herodotus, which is situated on the borders of the desert and confines of Egypt. Here our five days' quarantine commenced, about which we could say much, and will always remember. The houses in Kan Yoones are constructed entirely of stone, daubed over with mud, are one story in height, and have flat roofs. Sultan Burkoot built a magnificent khan there, in which is a curious mosque. The fields about the town are inclosed with hedges of the prickly pear, and contain some orange, fig, and other fruit trees, that were very pleasing to look upon after journeying so many days in the desert.

Leaving Kan Yoones, we passed over a beautiful grass-covered plain, accompanied by the *Garde de Santa* to the quarantine establishment at Gaza. It is not my intention to inflict on you a description of quarantine regulations, or go into a dissertation upon the advantages or disadvantages attending such places, but simply to narrate a slight account of our stay at Gaza. The Lazaretto in which we were incarcerated is beautifully situated in the suburbs of Gaza, and consists of a large square inclosure made of stone, about fifteen feet in height, and stuccoed. A deep well of good water is in the centre, and the rooms for the accommodation of travellers might be rendered comfortable if they could in any way manage to rid them of the great quantities of vermin that infest that region, and almost devour a poor Frank alive, in spite of all his exertions to the contrary. They come out of the walls, the carpet, and every conceivable place in perfect regiments, too formidable to be resisted, which, added to the hootings of a thousand jackals in the neighborhood, you can readily conceive how we passed our nights. "And Samson went and caught three hundred foxes, (jackals,) and took firebrands, and turned tail to tail, and put a firebrand in the midst between two tails; and when he had set the brands on fire, he let them go into the standing corn of the Philistines, and burnt up both the shocks and the standing corn, with the vineyards and olives." (Judges xv. 4, 5.) The days were consumed in enjoying the beautiful scenery about Gaza, reading what few books we had in our trunks, conversing and smoking pipes, which we found decidedly more agreeable than fighting fleas and listening to the concerts of jackals over some dead carcass.

The evening before leaving the quarantine, a French medical officer, in the Turkish service, called to examine our tongues, and see that our baggage was properly fumigated. It was truly an amusing scene. The *Guardianos* drew us up in a line, and each one was required not only to exhibit their tongues, but to slap themselves violently under the armpits and other parts of the body, to convince the doctor (who stood about six feet off) that we had no symptoms of plague, or other diseases peculiar to the East. The ladies declared that it was an outrage, and that they would not submit to such an indignity; but the doctor was imperative, and informed them that they must either show their tongues or remain within the bounds. Gaza, as I before remarked, is beautifully situated, and surrounded by well cultivated gardens of tamarisks, figs, and olives; the mountains of Ghor, Moab, and Judah are fragrant with the perfume of the ranunculus, anemone, asphodel, and minorette. The population is about three thousand at present; the houses are built of stone daubed with mud, and covered on the top with growing grass.

The prison where Samson was confined was shown to us. It is constructed of hewn limestone, square in form, and now occupied by the Arabs for a dwelling place. Two black granite columns are lying in front of the prison, evidently of great antiquity, and two blind beggars were seated on the steps when we were there, reminding me strongly of Samson's blindness, and the sport made of him in his afflictions. About two hours' ride from the present town of Gaza is the hill upon which Samson is said to have carried the gates of the city. "And Samson lay till midnight, and arose at midnight, and took the doors of the gate of the city, and the two posts, and went away with them, bar and all, and put them upon his shoulders, and carried them up to the top of a hill that is before Hebron." (Judges xvi. 3.) The road for several miles after leaving Gaza passes through cultivated fields and olive orchards, which are really refreshing to the eye that had been accustomed to look for so many days on the burning sand of the desert.

Our next camping place was near a village that our drivers called Jabin, situated on an eminence in sight of the sea. A pond of water stands near the town, and a ruined mosque on its margin of great magnitude. Judging from the arches, niches, and a few black granite columns lying about, it must be of Roman construction. Asdood or Ashdod, mentioned in Scripture, was the next point of interest on our route. "And the Philistines took the ark of God, and brought it from Ebenezer unto Ashdod." (1 Sam. ii. 1.) It is now a miserable place, filled with dirty hovels and low people. An old ruin occupies the summit of the hill, from which we had a fine view of the beautiful plain of Sharon. "I am the rose of Sharon, and the lily of the valley." The Song of Solomon may be appropriately sung even now, for the eye of the traveller is delighted with a profusion of roses, tulips, the narcissus, the white orange lily, the carnation, and a highly flavored species of everlasting flower. This plain stretches along the coast from Gaza in the south to Mount Carmel in the north, being bounded towards the east by the hills of Judea and Samaria. The lands are broken up ready to receive the seed from the hand of the husbandman, and give full promise for a crop as abundant as those gathered by the old patriarchs.

On the evening of the nineteenth day we entered the *hospitium* of Ramla, the ancient Arimathea, and were received by the inmates with that cordiality for which they have always been distinguished. It is surrounded by a high square inclosure, has a garden inside, and every thing calculated to make the weary pilgrim comfortable. The neat little chapel in which we attended vespers occupies the site of Joseph's dwelling, who took down the body of Jesus from the cross and laid it in his own new tomb. Ramla is built also of stone houses, with round dome-shaped tops, and contains a population of five thousand. The only remarkable antiquity now remaining is a stone tower of great height and symmetry, built by the Crusaders in honor of the forty martyrs killed there. The view from the tower extends even to Jaffa, and it is supposed that St. George, the patron Saint of England, died there. Owing to the inclemency of the weather, we remained two days in the *hospitium*, and received a visit while there from one of the dignitaries of the town, who was formerly the Vice Consul for the United States, but was for some reason deprived of the flag by our Consul General at Beirout. In due time we returned his call, and were received in great state, for the simple reason that he desired us to intercede for him with the Consul General, and procure his reappointment. During our visit the subject of slavery was suggested by the appearance of a likely negro boy bearing coffee and pipes, which resulted in my gaining some information that I would have otherwise lost. When two slaves intermarry belonging to different masters, the owner of the man claims the male issue, and the owner of the woman the female issue; whereas with us the owner of the woman is entitled to both. Quite a strong attachment exists between the master and slave, and it is not unfrequently the case that they marry and live happily together.

At Ramla we took leave most cheerfully of our camels and camel drivers, to mount the fleet and spirited Arabian steed. I was fortunate in procuring an excellent animal, which I intend riding throughout all Syria. A ride of two hours through a cultivated plain brought us to the verge of the "hill country of Judea," where the road opens through a rugged ravine, and is formed in the dry channel of a narrow torrent. A scene of wild solitude and desolation surrounded our steps as we pursued our journey through the dark shadows of the mountain, reminding me forcibly of some of the beautiful scenery in Switzerland and our own country. Soon after entering the labyrinth of mountains we reached Latroun, or the "Thief Village," being the site of the place where the thief lived who was crucified on the cross with our Saviour. It is now nothing but a heap of ruined stone houses, occupied by reptiles and jackals. From the summit of the chain I looked back toward the southwest on the beautiful valley of Sharon, bounded by the Mediterranean, and before me opened the vale of Jeremiah and the ancient fortress called the Castle of Maccabees. Proceeding on our way through conical-shaped mountains, connected with each other at their base, and covered with dwarf oaks, box rose, laurels, and a few olive trees, we came to the Wady Beit Hanina, a long and slippery descent, over slabs of rock and deep gullies, worn by the winter rains. At the foot of this dangerous place we met the celebrated robber Abou Goosh, who used to lay all travellers under heavy contributions until subdued by the arms of Ibrahim Pasha. This man once formed the daring scheme of seizing on Jerusalem, and of establishing himself there, and had well nigh succeeded in the attempt. His various acts at length aroused the attention of the Porte, and a mandate was issued to Abdallah Pasha of Acre to imprison him. Since his release he has been perfectly harmless, and is now an officer of the government. He is one of the handsomest men that I have seen in the East, and apparently about fifty years of age. Passing through Turpentine Valley, we next came to the brook out of which the youthful David picked up the five smooth stones, with one of which he slew the gigantic Goliah. I drank water and gathered some pebbles from the brook as a memento of the spot. The brook now stands in pools, and is evidently a wet-weather stream. Crossing it, we saw the village of Heriet Lefta, and in the distance on the summit of a lofty hill El Bire. We then ascended gradually for about one hour, crossed another rugged flat covered with large loose stones, and descended once more to the *Holy City*. It has been remarked frequently by travellers in their descriptions that the approaches to the capital are extremely beautiful, but I must beg leave to differ with them. The circuit of hills that were once verdant with the olive, the fig tree, and the vine, are now blasted and deformed. The rocks that were sublime are now devoid of all beauty—the fields and gardens have no richness, and the valleys no fertility. "How doth the city sit solitary *that was* full of people, *how* has she become as a widow, she that was great among the nations, *and* princess among the provinces; *how* has she become tributary!"

LETTER FORTY-TWO.

JERUSALEM, Palestine.

First Impression of the Holy City—The Walks—Jaffa Gate—Tower of Hippicus—Our Hotel—Walk to Herod's Palace—The Church of Flagellation—The Via Dolorosa—Church of the Holy Sepulchre—Easter—The Sacred Fire—Folly of the Priests—Emotion upon entering the Holy Tomb.

"How hath the Lord covered the daughter of Zion with a cloud in his anger, and cast down from heaven unto the earth the beauty of Israel, and remembered not his footstool in the day of his anger."

No city assuredly presents a more signal proof of the vicissitude of all earthly affairs than the ancient capital of the Jews. When we behold its crumbling walls, its ditches filled up, and all its buildings encumbered with ruins, we can scarcely realize that our eyes rest upon that renowned city which once withstood the efforts of the most powerful empires, and for a time baffled even the armies of Rome, whose subjects now vie with other religious sects in paying homage and reverence to the mouldering edifices of the fallen city. When we consider its situation and the time of its greatest power, it is difficult to believe what history teaches us relative to its greatness and influence. It possessed none of those natural or artificial advantages that we now consider necessary to insure the growth and prosperity of a city. Situated on the rugged cliffs of Zion, Moriah, and Calvary, encircled by the lofty and barren mountains in its vicinity, remote from every great road, it seems not to have been calculated either for a considerable mart of commerce, or for the centre of a great consumption. But all of these obstacles were overcome, and Jerusalem flourished—proving what patriotism and religion can accomplish in the hands of a good government, or when favored by that Providence which rules and determines the destiny of all things.

The vicissitudes of this Holy City also present to the mind of the historian and politician a problem of the most interesting nature. At one time we see its citizens in bondage, the victims of a relentless tyranny, and menaced with complete extirpation. At a later epoch we behold them swept away as captives by the hands of idolaters; and at length they appear as the instruments of a dispensation which embraces the dearest interests of all the human race, and which, in happier circumstances than ever fell to their own lot, has already modified and greatly exalted the character, the institutions, and the prospects of the most improved portion of mankind in both hemispheres of the globe. Connected with Christianity, indeed, the history of the Hebrews rises before the reflecting mind in a manner far exceeding that of all other people. In opposition to their own wishes, they laid the foundations of a religion which has not only superseded their peculiar rites, but is rapidly advancing towards that universal acceptation which they were wont to anticipate in favor of their own ancient law. Abstracting his thoughts from considerations of this nature, a candid man must acknowledge that the course of events which constitutes the history of ancient Palestine, has no parallel in any part of the world. Eighteen hundred years ago, there dwelt in this country a singular and retired people, who differed from the rest of mankind in the very important circumstance of not being idolaters. At the same era all the other nations of the earth were the victims of superstitions of the most hateful and degrading tendency, darkening all the prospects of the human being, and corrupting his moral nature in its very source. Scorned and despised by those powerful empires, their teachings notwithstanding continued to gain ground on every hand, till at last the proud monuments of pagan superstition, consecrated by the worship of a thousand years, and supported by the authority of the most powerful monarchies of the world, fall one after another at the approach of our Saviour's disciples, and before the pervading efficacy of the new faith. The effects produced upon the "hill country of Judea" cannot be solved by reference to the ordinary principles whence mankind are induced to act or to suffer. They exceed all calculation, and it is in vain that we attempt to compare them to those more common revolutions which have changed temporarily the face of nations, or given a new destiny to ancient empires.

From my earliest recollections, when I learned the catechism from my mother's lips, the name of Jerusalem embodied more in my mind than all other names besides, and to the latest day of my life I shall retain a vivid recollection of my emotions when first I gazed upon those dark and mysterious walls that surround the sacred city. I paused and asked myself, Is this Jerusalem? Is this the cherished object of my pilgrimage? Is this the spot where our Saviour was crucified, buried, and resurrected? And at once all that I could remember of her history, from the patriarch Abraham to Godfrey of Bouillon, came quickly to my mind's eye.

The first object that met my vision in the suburbs were the remains of two enormous stone mills, erected by Ibrahim Pasha, and afterwards destroyed by the Turks. Then came the Turkish cemetery, and the Jaffa Gate, through which we entered. Passing under the shadow of the tall tower of Hippicus, we slided hurriedly down a steep and covered bazaar after the dragoman, knocking first against some slow-motioned Turk, smoking his long-stemmed pipe, and then against the awkward and listless female robed in pure white, and her face covered to avoid the gaze of the rougher sex. At last we reached in safety our hotel, which is very small, but comfortable, being situated in the vicinity of the site of King Solomon's Temple, and kept by a converted Jew named Simeon. Eager to see the sights of the ancient city, we procured the services of a guide, and proceeded first to Herod's second palace. It is constructed of marble—quite handsome and spacious, and the most perfect ruin in the city. Near by are the remains of the Castle of Antonio, and the Church of Flagellation, where our Saviour was scourged. This church is of recent construction, and is situated on the Via Dolorosa, opposite the site of Pilate's House. The walls of the chapel are adorned with paintings representing the sufferings of Christ, and figures in wax are also there to show how he was persecuted by his enemies. The Via Dolorosa is a long and narrow way, about ten feet in width, and certainly the filthiest place that I ever walked through. The different stations were pointed out by the guide representing our Lord's Passion. One was a hole in the side of the wall, said to have been produced when the Virgin stopped and wept; another, a broken column, upon which Christ fell with the cross; and another, the impression of his hand in the solid stone against which he rested himself. These stations are regarded as sacred, and to this day all Christians that pass along the Via Dolorosa stop and leave a kiss, soon to be wiped out by the Jews, who never fail to spit and scorn upon the holy places.

At the extremity of this renowned way stands the Church of the Holy Sepulchre, erected by the Empress Helena on Mount Calvary, where Constantine erected the original building. It is so completely surrounded with houses that it is impossible to obtain a good view of it. Its area is about three hundred feet in length, by a very irregular breadth, at such different levels that the "Chapel of the Cross" is fifty feet below the rock of Calvary. In front is a large court, its pavement worn with the feet of innumerable pilgrims, and vestiges of columns in the Byzantine style. At the entrance I noticed several Turkish doorkeepers seated cross-legged smoking their pipes. Within the vestibule, the first object of interest is a large slab of yellowish-looking marble, said to be the stone upon which the body of Jesus was anointed before its interment. Six huge candlesticks and candles to match are placed at each end, and constitute its only ornament. This is the first object of veneration to the pious pilgrims, who prostrate themselves and kiss it before visiting the interior. Passing on and turning to the right, we came to the chapel built over the sacred tomb, about forty paces from the foot of Calvary, and under the central dome of the church. This chapel is of an oblong shape, rounded at one end with small arcades, or closets for prayer. These are for the Copts, the Abyssinians, the Maronites, and other Christians who are not, like the Roman Catholics, Greeks, and Armenians, provided with chapels in the body of the church. At the other end it is squared off and furnished with a platform in front which is ascended by a flight of steps, having a small parapet on each hand, and floored with marble. This side is filled with gold and silver lamps, and a painting representing the ascension. It is divided into two apartments, the first containing the block of polished stone, about one foot and a half square, on which sat the angel who announced the blessed tidings of the resurrection to Mary Magdalene and Joanna, and Mary the mother of James. Here the worshipper divests himself of his shoes and head-covering before entering the mansion of victory, where Christ triumphed over the grave and disarmed death of its terrors. The tomb exhibited is a sarcophagus of white marble, slightly tinged with blue, being fully six feet long, three feet broad, and two feet two inches deep. It is broken across the top and one of the corners, and judging from appearances it must at one time have been exposed to the atmosphere, by which it has been considerably affected. It is made in the Greek fashion, without any ornament, and not like the more ancient tombs of the Jews, which are cut in the rock for the reception of the dead. A number of costly lamps are kept burning over it night and day—the gifts of different sovereigns in successive ages. It occupies about one half of the sepulchral chamber, and extends from one end of it to the other. A space about three feet wide in front of it is all that remains for the accommodation of visitors, so that not more than four can be admitted conveniently at a time. I paused a moment and contemplated upon the movements of those whose religious sentiments I thought better entitled them to precedence. It was a scene of deep solemnity, and will remain impressed on my mind until the latest day of my life. Although I could not agree with them in the belief that this was the tomb in which the body of Christ reposed for three days, yet it was a suitable emblem of his suffering and the scene of his resurrection. The religious devotees retired, and I went in alone, there to commune with my own heart, and dwell upon the many hallowed associations connected with the spot. My emotions are indescribable. I felt oppressed with intense feeling; the sanctity of the place took possession of my soul, and the presence of the great Jehovah seemed to rise before my vision like some bright spirit from the dreamy world. "Here the mind looks on Him who, though he knew no sin, entered the regions of mortality to redeem us from its power, and the prayers of a grateful heart ascend with a risen Saviour to the presence of God in heaven." Leaving the chapel of the tomb, I entered that belonging to the Greek Church, filled with tawdriness and bad paintings redolent of vulgar superstitions. A low pillar in it marks the centre of the earth, and the original clay of which our forefather Adam was moulded. From this chapel I entered a dark and narrow staircase to the summit of "Calvary, which is the centre, the grand magnet of the Christrian church. From this proceeds life and salvation; thither all hearts tend and all eyes are directed; here kings and queens cast down their crowns, and great men and women part with their ornaments; at the foot of the cross all are on a level, equally ready and equally welcome." On Calvary is shown the spot where the Redeemer was nailed to the cross, the hole into which the end of it was fixed, and the rent in the rock. While standing there gazing on a painting in a niche behind the altar, representing our Saviour on the cross, with the two

Marys on each side of him. I could almost imagine the dreadful scene of the crucifixion, when "the vail of the temple was rent in twain from the top to the bottom," and when Christ uttered that beautiful sentiment of forgiving meekness, "Father, forgive them; they know not what they do."

No man can visit Calvary without experiencing emotions that he never felt before, and never can feel again. It is a solemn, holy, and soul-absorbing spot—fit to be visited alone by those who can appreciate the sufferings, the goodness and loving-kindness of Him who gave up his life to save a sinful world. Descending from the mount, I entered by a long flight of steps the chapel of St. Helena, the mother of Constantine, in which is the vault where the true cross was found, an event that continues to be celebrated by an appropriate mass every year on the third of May. The place is large enough to contain fifty or sixty individuals; it is very dark and cave-like, but lamps are always burning that afford sufficient light for the pilgrim to see and kiss the painted image of the cross. The sword, spears, and tomb of Godfrey of Bouillon are exhibited in the church, and also the tomb of Joseph and his family of Arimathea, who asked the body of Christ from Pilate, and buried it in his own new tomb. It will soon be Easter, and the city is filling up rapidly with pilgrims from all parts of the Levant and Russia to witness the exhibition of the Holy Fire, and bathe their bodies in the Jordan. This exhibition, which is annually practised in the church of the Holy Sepulchre, is the work of the priesthood of the Greek Church, who teach the credulous multitude to believe that fire descends from heaven into the tomb to kindle their lamps and torches. The scenes exhibited on the occasion are far more ludicrous and disgraceful than any thing in the heathen world, and calculated to destroy all those devotional feelings that we would like to enjoy while standing near places hallowed by so many glorious associations.

LETTER FORTY-THREE.

JERUSALEM, Palestine.

Mosques of Omar and El Aksa—Remains of King Solomon's Temple—Birth-place of the Virgin—Pool of Bethesda—St. Stephen's Gate—Convents of Jerusalem—English Chapel —American Residents.

THE Mosque of Omar has not inaptly been styled the St. Peter's of Turkey. By all true Catholics the Cathedral at Rome is regarded as the great centre from and through which the Divine light is disseminated over the world; and so it is with the Mussulman race, whose religion acknowledges but two temples, one at Mecca, and the other at Jerusalem. Both were called El Haram, signifying a place consecrated by the peculiar presence of the Divinity, and are equally prohibited to Christians, Jews, and every other person who is not a believer in the Prophet. All other mosques are considered merely as places of meeting for certain acts of worship, and are not held so sacred as to require the total exclusion of those who do not profess the true faith; entrance into them is usually granted by application to the proper authorities; but the Sultan himself could not grant permission to an unbeliever either to pass into the territory of Mecca, or to enter the holy precincts of this mosque. Procuring the services of the English Consul's janissary, we ascended to the top of the Governor's house, situated in the vicinity of the mosque, where we had an excellent view of the inclosure and the exterior of the edifice. It occupies the centre of a large flat square in the eastern extremity of the city, and is circular in shape, and surmounted by a large dome which forms decidedly the most conspicuous object in Jerusalem. The Sakhara itself is a regular octagon of about sixty feet a side, and is entered by four spacious doors, each of which is adorned with a porch projecting from the line of the building and rising considerably on the wall. All the sides of it are panelled. The centre stone of one panel is square, of another it is octagonal, and thus they alternate all around; the sides of each running down the angles like a plain pilaster, and giving an appearance as if the whole were set in a frame. The marble is white, with a considerable tinge of blue—square pieces of the latter color being introduced in different places, so as to confer upon the exterior a very pleasing effect. The upper story is faced with small tiles painted of different colors, white, yellow, green, and blue; some of them are also covered with sentences from the Koran. At this height there are seven elegant windows on each side, except where the porches interfere, and then there are only six; the general appearance of the edifice being extremely light and beautiful, more especially from the mixture of the soft colors above and the delicate tints of the marble in the main body of the structure. The interior is said by those who have seen it to correspond in every way to the beauty and magnificence just described. The most conspicuous object of veneration in the mosque is a large irregular mass of calcareous rock, having an oblong shape, and containing, as the Moslems suppose, the impress of the angel Gabriel's fingers and the Prophet's foot—and like the Palladium of ancient Troy, is said to have fallen from heaven on the very spot where it now rests, at the time when the prophecy commenced in Jerusalem.

Within the same inclosure there is another mosque called El Aksa, which is a fine building, but far inferior to Omar. Between the two there is a beautiful fountain, which derives its name from a few orange trees overshadowing its water, and this space is supposed to be the site of King Solomon's Temple, about which so much has been said and written. While gazing from the house-top on this beautiful inclosure where the followers of the Prophet delight to saunter, or repose as in the Elysium of their devotions, my mind was occupied with thoughts too vast, too sacred, too absorbing to be reflected by the mere expression of language. Here it was that King Solomon, the "wise and the great, erected an house for the name of the Lord, and an house for his kingdom," on the summit of mount Moriah, where the Lord appeared unto David his father, in the place that David had prepared in the threshing-floor of Ornan the Jebusite. On the east side of the mosque our guide pointed out to us the remains of the outer wall of the ancient temple, which is made of hewn stone of great size, and of such antiquity that we broke large pieces off merely by striking them lightly. And here also is to be seen the abutment of a bridge recently discovered, which is supposed to have connected the temple with Zion Hill. This bridge is mentioned by the ancient historians, but until lately all travellers seem to have lost sight of it, owing probably to the fact that it was obscured by the *débris* of the city. Jewish tradition renders it almost certain in my mind that these remains constituted a part of the wonderful building; for on every Friday evening (the Jewish Sabbath) they assemble in a small paved court formed partly by the wall, and offer to God their prayers and lamentations in tones so piteous, so earnest, so beseeching, and so heart-rending, as to make even the followers of the Prophet pause and shed a tear of commiseration. On the opposite side of the mosque from the Jewish wailing ground is a small and unpretending house occupied by a Christian family, which is said to have been built on the very spot where Mary the mother of Christ was born. And near by is the Pool of Bethesda, which resembles an old reservoir, being nothing more than a large and deep basin walled up with stone, and perfectly dry, serving as a kind of receptacle for the filth of the city. St. Stephen's Gate is also in this part of the city, and opens on the valley of Jehoshaphat. In point of architectural beauty I consider it superior to the Jaffa Gate, or any other save the Golden Gate, which is now built up, to be opened at a time that no man can divine.

The convents of Jerusalem are very numerous, and some of them very beautiful, particularly those belonging to the Armenian and Greek churches. Nearly all of them are resorted to by the pilgrims, who are treated with the utmost kindness by the superiors and inmates. The chapel connected with the Armenian convent is the finest in Jerusalem, and contains many curious things of interest—such as the place where the head of John the Baptist was buried, and paintings of a strange and unnatural character. The English and Prussians have recently erected a beautiful chapel in the Gothic fashion near the Tower of David, and have a bishop stationed here who preaches twice every Sunday, in the English and Arabic languages. But like the American missionaries, they are doing but little towards reforming the Jews or Mohammedans. They are joined to their idols, and we had better let them alone. Since our arrival in Jerusalem we have formed the acquaintance of Dr. Barkley, an intelligent Baptist missionary from Virginia, who has given up the Old Dominion and brought an interesting family here, to bury them, as he says, by the grave of King David. Strange infatuation! It matters but little after life leaves the body where it is interred; but if there is a spot on this green earth where I would prefer to repose, it is my humble home in the far, far West, where those that I love may occasionally be reminded of our mutual joys and sorrows.

LETTER FORTY-FOUR.

JERUSALEM, Palestine.

Walk about Jerusalem—Potter's Field—Mount of Offence—Mount Zion—Pool of Siloam—Valley of Jehoshaphat—The Tombs of Zechariah, of Jehoshaphat, and of Absalom—Garden of Gethsemane—Tomb of Virgin Mary—Grottoes on Mount of Olives—View of the City—Sepulchres of the Kings—Grotto of Jeremiah, etc.

"And they took the thirty pieces of silver, the price of him that was valued, whom they of the children of Israel did value, and gave them for the potter's field, as the Lord appointed me."

HAVING visited over and over again the holy places within the walls of Jerusalem, we concluded to take advantage of a fair day to examine the interesting localities of the suburbs. Passing through the Jaffa Gate, we turned to the left, and soon came to a broken and time-worn cemetery called Potter's Field, which is undoubtedly the identical spot bought by the chief priests with the thirty pieces of silver to bury strangers in. The earth of this field has a peculiar reddish color, and quite different in appearance from the land in its vicinity. Strangers are buried there to this day; and the weary pilgrim, who knows not what a day may bring forth, looks on Potter's Field with a melancholy interest.

A little further on, and to the south of the Mount of Olives, are beheld the Mount of Offence, the scene of King Solomon's idolatry, and also Zion's sacred mount, distinguished both in the Old Testament and in the New. "Here the successor of Saul built a city and a royal dwelling; here he kept for three months the Ark of the Covenant;" here the Redeemer instituted the sacrament which commemorates his death; here he appeared to his disciples on the day of his resurrection; and here the Holy Ghost descended on the Apostles. Hallowed by so many glorious associations, the stranger, while standing on its summit, must experience emotions of a peculiar and agreeable character. Immediately in front of Zion Gate is the tomb of David, hidden from the view of the Christian observer by a mosque built over it.

Descending the mount by a path leading to the valley, we came to the Fountain and Pool of Siloam, so celebrated in the history of our Saviour's miracles. The brook itself is badly supplied with water, of an inferior quality, being warm and somewhat brackish. A short distance from the Pool, towards the north, we found the source of the scanty rivulet which is called here the Fountain of the Virgin, from the belief that she frequently went there to drink. It is inclosed with hewn stone, forming a recess about twenty feet lower than the surface, and under an arched vault of masonry, very well executed. On the hillside immediately opposite the Pool is a small Arab village, called Siloam, which presents a very dilapidated appearance, and wholly devoid of interest.

Proceeding up the deep and picturesque valley of Jehoshaphat, along the banks of the brook Kedron, we came to the Jewish cemetery, where the descendants of Jacob have been interred from time immemorial, and which is considered even to this day by that peculiar people to be the most sacred spot on earth. "Here they resort from the four quarters of the globe, to yield up their last breath; and a foreigner sells to them, for its weight in gold, a scanty spot of earth to cover their remains in the country of their ancestors." Each grave is marked by a flat stone laid over the top; and they are so numerous, that we thought at first it was nothing but a heap of rubbish at the foot of the declivity of Mount Olivet. Quite a number of Jews may always be seen walking about, or reposing under the olive trees in the cemetery. They are easily recognised by their peculiar dress, quick, piercing eyes, black eyebrows, and long heavy beards. They look pensive, silent, and alone in the world, ready, and even anxious, to die in the land of their fathers.

Proceeding slowly up this interesting valley, our attention was attracted to three conspicuous monuments—the tombs of Zechariah, of Absalom, and of King Jehoshaphat. The first mentioned of these is a square structure, hewn apparently out of the solid rock, and separated from the quarry out of which it is cut by a space of fifteen feet on three of its sides, the fourth side fronting towards the valley and the Mosque of Omar. This singular tomb reminded me very much of those in Egypt, although very insignificant in point of size, being only about twenty feet in length on the sides, and the same height in front, surmounted by a small pyramid of masonry. It has four half-columns, cut out of the same rock, on each of its faces, with a pilaster at each angle, badly executed, and resembling somewhat the Ionic order. We could discover no entrance to the tomb, which confirms our belief that the architecture was borrowed from the Egyptians. The tomb of Absalom resembles somewhat in size, form, etc., that of Zechariah, just described, except that it is sculptured with figures of the Doric order, and surmounted by a sharp conical dome, with large mouldings around its base, and on the top something like a torch. It is made up of such a strange mixture of styles, that we could not make up our minds to what age it belongs, believing, however, that it occupies the site of the one set up by Absalom himself. "Now Absalom, in his lifetime, had reared up for himself a pillar, which is in the King's Dale: for he said, I have no son to keep my name in remembrance; and he called the pillar after his own name; and it is called unto this day Absalom's Place." That of Jehoshaphat is in the same vicinity, but not so important as the two former.

A little beyond these tombs, on the hillside, is the famous garden of Gethsemane, where our Saviour was betrayed by Judas. "Then cometh Jesus with them unto a place called Gethsemane, and said unto the disciples, Sit ye here, while I go and pray yonder." This sacred place is now inclosed with a stone wall fifteen feet in height, and of modern construction. By applying at one of the convents in the city, we obtained permission to enter the garden, which is now laid out in flower-beds, and contains eight old olive trees, said to be the same that were standing at the time when Christ visited it with his disciples.

Immediately opposite the garden, towards the city, is a singularly picturesque cavern, in later ages called the Tomb of the Virgin. It is approached by a paved court, and has a very pretty front in the Grecian style. The descent into the cavern is formed by a handsome flight of steps, made of polished stone, being about fifty in number, and of great breadth. About half-way down are two arched recesses in the sides, which Thomas, our guide, told us contained the ashes of St. Anne, the mother of Mary, and of Joseph her husband.

Reaching the bottom of the cavern, we were shown by an old monk the tomb of the Holy Virgin herself, which is in the form of a simple bench covered with marble. Here the Armenians and Greeks say mass; and here the curious traveller stops to wonder and to doubt. In the immediate vicinity of this cavern our guide pointed out various places, meant to keep alive the remembrance of certain occurrences connected with the history of Christ and his people; such as the place where St. Peter and the two sons of Zebedee fell asleep when their Master retired to pray—the scene of the agony and the bloody sweat—and the spot whereon Judas betrayed the Son of man with a kiss; also the rock on which our Saviour stood when he predicted the sack of Jerusalem and the destruction of the Temple—the cavern where the Apostles were taught the Lord's Prayer—and another where the same individuals, at a later period, are said to have met together to form their creed.

The Mount of Olives has three separate summits, on the principal of which are a mosque, and the ruins of an old church, called the church of the Ascension, because it contains a stone in the floor with the impression of a man's foot upon it, supposed by the credulous pilgrims to be the identical spot from which Christ ascended into heaven. From the lofty minaret attached to the mosque, we enjoyed a magnificent view of Jerusalem and the country round about. Looking westward, the ancient city, rich in history and memory, is spread out like a map to the eye. Mounts Zion, Moriah, and Calvary are marked so distinctly, that there can be no doubt about their locality. The valley of Jehoshaphat, in all its extent, gives variety to the scene—while on the east the Moab mountains, Dead Sea, and Jordan complete the panorama.

Descending the mount, we went about one mile to the northward of the city to see the Sepulchres of the Kings, which are by far the most costly and singular remains of ancient architecture that we have seen about Jerusalem. Great doubt exists relative to their origin and intention; but from all appearances, they were evidently used as the last resting place of high persons. The whole work is hewn out of the solid rock, and so adorned with fruits and flowers, as to leave no doubt but that it was made at a great cost and labor. We approached it on the east side, through an entrance cut out of the rock, which admitted us into an open court about one hundred feet square. On the south side is a portico twenty-four feet long and ten broad, also cut out of the natural rock, and having an architrave running along its front ornamented in the most exquisite style. The entrance into the sepulchre is so much obstructed by large stones and rubbish, that we found it a little difficult to get in; but we succeeded at last in entering a large room about twenty-four feet square, excavated out of the rock in such a perfect manner, that any modern workman would be glad to imitate it. From this large room we passed into six others, all of the same construction, the two last being lower than the rest, and reached by a small flight of steps. All of these chambers, except the first, contain stone coffins, placed in niches found in the sides of the apartment. Some of these coffins are ornamented with the richest and most beautiful carving —equal in some respects to the old Roman sarcophagus. The most remarkable things connected with the Sepulchres of the Kings are their doors—of which only one remains, partly hidden by rubbish. It is one solid piece of stone, about six inches in thickness, and equal in other respects to an ordinary sized door. The carving resembles a piece of wainscot, and the entire mass turned upon two hinges in the nature of axles. These hinges constituted a part of the door, and were lodged in two holes of the solid rock—one at the top, and another at the bottom. On our return to the city, through the Damascus Gate, we stopped at the Grotto of Jeremiah, where that prophet is said to have resided, and where he wrote his book of Lamentations. "Jerusalem hath grievously sinned; therefore she is removed. All that honored her despise her, because they have seen her wickedness: yea, she sigheth and turneth backward."

LETTER FORTY-FIVE.

BETHLEHEM, Palestine.

Bethany—Road to Jericho—Fountain of Elisha—Plain of Jericho—River Jordan—Dead Sea—Convent of St. Saba—Tower of Simeon—Tomb of Rachel—Church of the Nativity, etc., etc.

BEFORE visiting the valley of Jordan, it is absolutely necessary for all Franks to procure the protection of the Jordan Sheik, and pay one pound sterling for tribute money. If you fail to attend to this matter, and start alone, you are almost certain to fall among thieves, who will deal with you as harshly as their ancestors did to travellers in the days of the good Samaritan. "A man went down from Jerusalem to Jericho, and fell among thieves, which stripped him of his raiment, and wounded him and departed, leaving him half dead." Our dragoman relieved us of all trouble; and on the day set apart for making this excursion, quite a large number of horsemen might have been seen wending their way through St. Stephen's Gate and the King's Dale towards the ancient town of Bethany. Our party was very large, consisting of the English Bishop of Jerusalem and his family and ten Americans, besides our guard and attendants. This is the greatest number of Americans that ever started together over that renowned road; and it is somewhat curious when we reflect that our countrymen know more about the geography of the Holy Land than any other people, and travel over roads that were considered old long, long before the discovery of the western continent.

Following the path that winds around the base of Mount Olivet, we soon came to the village of Bethany—now small and poor, the cultivation of the country around it being very much neglected by the indolent Arabs into whose hands it has fallen. Here we were shown the ruins of a house said to have belonged to Lazarus, whom Christ raised from the dead, and a grotto, which is represented as the veritable tomb wherein the miracle was performed. "Jesus, therefore, again groaning in himself, cometh to the grave. It was a cave, and a stone lay upon it." We descended by a long and winding flight of steps to the bottom, and found two chambers about ten feet square, walled up with stone on all sides. This was not all that we saw in Bethany. The dwellings of Simon the Leper, of Mary Magdalene, of Martha, and the spot where the barren fig-tree withered under the curse, were all pointed out to us. We are privileged, you know, to doubt as much as we please; yet it is pleasant to feel that we are in the vicinity of such places, if we do not hit exactly on the identical spot.

Leaving Bethany, we descended rapidly for about fifteen miles to the plains of Jericho, being several thousand feet below the Mediterranean. The road is exceedingly rugged, and passes through a barren and romantic region, covered over with volcanic substances. The only object of interest that came under our observation was the Khan Hudrur, supposed to have been built by the crusaders for the benefit of pilgrims going to the Jordan. Soon after entering the plain of Jericho, we came to Ain es Sultan, (Fount of Elisha,) the waters of which were sweetened by the prophet. Watering our horses there, we proceeded for about half an hour, and found our tents pitched near the ancient City of Palms, on the brink of the brook Cherith, that is before Jordan. Jericho, which is at present a miserable village, inhabited by wild and ruthless Arabs, derives all its importance from history. Of all its magnificent buildings, there remains only the part of one tower, said to be the dwelling of Zaccheus the publican, and a considerable quantity of rubbish, which is supposed to mark the boundary of the ancient city. All having beards, (except the ladies,) we concluded not to tarry long, particularly as we had no use for rams' horns, and started early the next morning over the plain to the Jordan. Before describing this interesting stream, I must not pass over the mountain of Quarantina, the supposed scene of the Temptation and fast of forty days endured by our Saviour, who,

> "Looking around on every side, beheld
> A pathless desert dusk with horrid shades:
> The way he came not having marked, return
> Was difficult, by human steps untrod;
> And he still on was led, but with such thoughts
> Accompanied of things past and to come
> Lodged in his breast, as well might recommend
> Such solitude before choicest society."

The words of the poet are true even now; for on all sides the mountain is dry, barren, and uninviting. It is, as described by St. Matthew, an exceeding high mountain, and its ascent both difficult and dangerous. A small chapel is to be seen on the top, and another half-way down on a projecting rock. Near the latter we saw a number of caves and holes, excavated by the over-pious, for the purpose of undergoing the austerities of Lent. From this renowned elevation we obtained the first view of the plain of Jericho and the valley of the Jordan. The descent from the mountains to the river is gradual, and the soil of the plain is of a white sandy nature, strongly impregnated with nitre, and covered with low and stunted shrubbery. We approached the sacred stream that winds through scenes rendered memorable by such great events, at the Pilgrim's Ford, where the Orientals say the waters stood and rose up in a heap, while the multitudes of Israel entered dry shod into their promised inheritance. "Here is the wilderness where John was baptizing, when our Saviour submitted to that solemn rite, and the manifestation of his divinity was fully witnessed to by the attestation of Heaven." Here thousands of pilgrims have repaired annually for ages from all parts of the world, to bathe in water which they suppose to be endowed with a cleansing moral efficacy. At Easter the assemblage is very great, and the scene curious in the extreme. Russians, Greeks, Armenians, Copts, Syrians, and a few Franks, all mingle together for a season, to perform the dearest act of life. Nearly all of them have on a white gown with a black cross upon it, which they put away after bathing for the purpose of being buried in. As soon as they reach the bank, they make a general rush—young and old, rich and poor, sick and sound, men, women, and children—into the stream. Many are drowned, but it matters not—the scene is sacred, and death is disregarded. The Jordan is exceedingly narrow and sinuous, and subject to great floods. We threw stones over it without any difficulty, and when we went into the stream, it was so rapid that it was almost impossible to maintain our foothold. Like many others before us, we filled our bottles with the holy water to carry home and baptize the dear little infants of our friends, and cut sticks from the *agnus castus*, or willow, to present to the old men of the church as memorials of the place.

Leaving the Pilgrim's Ford, we proceeded down the right bank about four miles to Lake Asphaltite, the most remarkable sheet of water in the known world. No person who takes any interest in the Bible, can fail to look with the deepest concern upon a scene which they may compare with the strange narrative presented in the book of Genesis, and to contrast it with the description there presented to them of its former beauty and fertility: "Abraham went up out of Egypt; his wife, Lot, his brother's son, and all that he had with him. Abraham was very rich in cattle, in silver, and in gold. And Lot also, who went with him, had flocks, and herds, and tents. And the land was not able to bear them, that they might dwell together; for their substance was great, and there was strife between the herdmen of Abraham's cattle and the herdmen of Lot's cattle." To avoid any contention, Abraham, in a compromising spirit, gave utterance to the following language: "Is not the whole land before thee? If thou wilt take the left hand, then I will go to the right; or if thou depart to the right hand, then I will go to the left. And Lot lifted up his eyes, and beheld all the plain of Jordan, that it was well watered every where, before the Lord destroyed Sodom and Gomorrah, even as the garden of the Lord." So Abraham went to the land of Canaan, and Lot occupied the virgin soil of the well-watered plain.

How different its aspect now! The fields once verdant with corn are now inundated, and the sinful cities of Sodom and Gomorrah buried beneath the poisonous bosom of the Dead Sea. Such was the will of Divine Providence, and all has been verified to the letter. A range of hills rise up abruptly on either side, destitute of trees and gloomy in their appearance. The water in the distance looks green, as if stagnant, though we saw nothing of this appearance when we came near to it. A slight ripple was upon its surface, and a great deal of froth was seen along the shore, which looked like a deposit of salt. Two of us went in bathing, and found the water as represented by travellers, exceedingly buoyant. The shore where we entered was shelving, and we waded out some distance before it was deep enough to swim. After coming out, our bodies were perfectly greasy, and where there was a scratch or pimple it became inflamed and annoying. Our hair and beard assumed a stiff and dead appearance, which lasted for many days. Pins and all other articles of metal about the person turned black immediately. Black sea-weed, gravel of different colors, and pieces of drift wood, were all that we saw near the water's edge. It is not true, as stated by some travellers, that no vegetation or living thing exists in the vicinity of the Dead Sea. We saw no tall and luxuriant forests, but an abundance of flowers and low stunted shrubbery. A flock of cranes flew over the sea while we were there, and birds of many kinds were chirping among the flowers.

Leaving the Dead Sea, we rode for three hours over a mountainous and desert country, to the Convent of Deir Mar Saba. This sacred retreat is singularly situated, half-way between the Dead Sea and the ancient city of Bethlehem. Nothing can be more dreary or lonely than Santa Saba. It is erected in a ravine, sunk to the depth of several hundred feet, where the brook Kedron has formed a channel which is dry the greater part of the year. The convent is on a slight eminence at the bottom of the dell; whence the buildings of the monastery rise by an almost perpendicular flight of steps and passages hewn out of the rock, ascending thus to the top of the hill, where they terminate in two square towers of great height. It is the largest and best conducted convent in the East, having as many as one hundred rooms, and every comfort that the weary pilgrim could desire. The chapel is large and well furnished. The skull room contains fourteen thousand skulls of persons who died or were killed in the convent; a curious sight, but unpleasant to look upon.

From Mar Saba we came to Bethlehem, (Beil Lahm,) the place of our Saviour's nativity. "Now when Jesus was born in Bethlehem of Judea, in the days of Herod the king, behold there came wise men from the east to Jerusalem." It is pleasantly situated on a high and terraced hill, surrounded by other hills covered with loose stones. The houses are mostly two stories high, built of stone, and have flat tops, upon which the citizens pass much of their time. The convent, which marks the place of the Redeemer's birth, was built by Helena, after removing the idolatrous structure said to have been erected by Adrian from a feeling of contempt or jealousy towards the Christians. At present it is divided among the monks of the Greek, Roman, and Armenian churches, to whom are assigned separate portions, as well for lodging as for places of worship, though, on certain days, they may all celebrate the rites of their common faith on altars which none of them have hitherto been allowed to appropriate exclusively. There are two churches, an upper and a lower, under the same roof. The former is nothing remarkable, if we except a star inlaid in the floor immediately under the spot in the heavens where the supernatural sign became visible to the wise men, and, like it, directly over the place of His nativity below. This last is an excavation in the rock, elegantly fitted up and floored with marble, and to which there is a descent of steps through a long and narrow passage. Here are shown a great number of tombs, and among them one in which are said to have been buried all the babes murdered by the barbarous Herod. From hence we were conducted into a handsome chapel, the floor and walls of which are composed of beautiful marble, having on each side five oratories, or recesses for prayer, corresponding to the ten stalls supposed to have been in the stable wherein the Saviour was born. This sacred place is irregular in form, because it occupies the site of the stable and the manger. It is thirty-seven feet six inches long, eleven feet three inches broad, and nine feet in height. As it receives no light from without, it is illumined by thirty-two lamps, sent as presents by different princes. At the further extremity of this small church, there is an altar placed in an arcade, and hollowed out below in the form of an arch, to embrace the sacred spot where Immanuel, having laid aside his glory, first appeared in the garb of human nature. A circle in the floor composed of marble and jasper, surrounded with silver, and having rays like those with which the sun is represented, is supposed to mark the very place wherein that stupendous event was realized. An inscription, denoting that "Here Jesus Christ was born of the Virgin Mary," was once to be seen in these words: "Hîc de Virgine Mariâ Jesus Christus natus est," but has recently been removed by the barbarous Greeks. Close to this altar is another denoting the manger in which the infant Messiah was laid. It is also made of marble, and bears a resemblance to the humble couch which alone the furniture of the stable could supply. Before it, is the altar of the Wise Men, a memorial of their adoration and praise at the moment when they saw the young child and Mary his mother. This convent is evidently of great antiquity, and, though frequently destroyed and as often renewed, it still retains its Grecian origin. Like most buildings dedicated to such purposes, it has the form of a cross, the nave being adorned with forty-eight columns of the Corinthian order in four rows, which are at least two feet six inches in diameter. Just back of the convent a tomb is pointed out as that of the Virgin Mary, but as there is also one in Jerusalem, there is no way of determining their claims.

Before leaving Bethlehem, we visited several interesting places in the vicinity, such as the ruined tower of Simeon, who upon beholding the infant Messiah expressed his readiness to leave this world—the Monastery of Elias, now in possession of the Greeks, and the Tomb of Rachel, rising in a rounded top like the whitened sepulchre of an Arab Sheik.

LETTER FORTY-SIX.

HEBRON, Palestine.

Pools of Solomon—Aqueduct—Convent of St. John—Hebron—Sepulchre of Patriarchs—Quarantine, etc.

THE Pools of Solomon are on the road between Bethlehem and Hebron, which, like all other roads in Syria, is exceedingly rugged and dangerous, being nothing more than a narrow path without any grades, filled with large loose stones. These large fountains originated, it is supposed, in a scheme for supplying Jerusalem with water. The reservoirs are three in number, and so arranged that the water of the highest may flow into the second, and the second into the third. Their shape is quadrangular; the breadth is the same in all, amounting to about ninety paces. In their length there is a slight difference: the first being one hundred and fifty paces long, the second two hundred, and the third two hundred and twenty. They are all built up with strong masonry, and plastered so as to render them tight. The springs whence the pools are supplied are very copious, and secured with great care, having no access to them but by a small hole leading into two large chambers neatly arched. The water is excellent, and conveyed as of old to Bethlehem and Jerusalem through an aqueduct formed of brick pipes, strengthened by the application of a peculiarly strong mortar.

Not far from these celebrated pools is the Convent of St. John's. It is situated in the desert, and built over the dwelling where the Baptist is supposed to have been born; and accordingly, under the altar, the spot on which he was brought forth is marked by a star of marble, with the inscription, "Hic precursor Domini Christi natus est."

From appearances this convent was at one time very elegant, having a beautiful cupola, and a pavement of mosaic; but at present it looks dilapidated and deserted.

About dusk on the same day that we left Bethlehem we pitched our tents in the suburbs of Hebron, (Habrown,) or according to the Arabic orthography by the moderns, El Hhalil. It is removed from the usual track of tourists, and possesses very few objects of interest. Like nearly all the towns in Syria, it is situated on a hill, with narrow and dirty bazaars. The country in the vicinity looks blasted and barren, and the people cursed with poverty. The cave of Machpelah, which Abraham purchased from Ephron the son of Zohar for a burying-place, is now appropriated to the worship of Mohammed. No Christian can gain admission, even with a firman from the Porte, and we had to content ourselves with a description given us by our guide, who said that it was elegantly and beautifully decorated. The Quarantine establishment here is similar in structure and arrangement to the one at Gaza. We visited it with the expectation of meeting some of our friends who crossed the Desert by way of Petra, but were disappointed. A party of English gentlemen were there, who informed us that the difficulties between the Akaba and Petra tribes precluded them from visiting the city of Rocks. After riding many days on the back of a camel, they had the mortification to find out that John Bull was no better than other people in the estimation of the Bedouins of the Desert.

LETTER FORTY-SEVEN.

NAZARETH, Palestine.

Return to Jerusalem—Beer—Village of Leban—Jacob's Well—Valley of Shechem—Nablous—Sebaste—Gennin—Mount Tor or Tabor—Sea of Galilee—Tiberias—Saphet—Nazareth, etc.

FROM Hebron we returned to the Holy City, where we remained two days in order to give the dragoman time to lay in a stock of provisions for our tour towards the north. The pious pilgrim might pass many months in Jerusalem agreeably and profitably; but the general traveller is more easily satisfied, and is willing to depart as soon as he has seen the different places of curiosity. Going out of the Damascus Gate, we passed by the Cave of Jeremiah, and Tombs of the Kings, to the summit of a lofty hill, where we turned our horses and gazed for the last time on the most remarkable city in the world. The dome of Omar's Mosque, the Tower of Hippicus, and the Church of the Holy Sepulchre were the last objects to fade from our vision. We looked at them long and steadily, believing that it was the last time we would be permitted to enjoy a panorama embracing so many hallowed beauties.

After riding two hours and a quarter, we came to the ruins of an ancient town upon a low bank on the left. Three fine arches of large hewn stones, apparently of the early Jewish time, stand like a crown upon its top; and on the right of the road, for the road must have formerly passed through the town, are spacious semicircular terraces in the rocks, with broad steps at regular intervals leading up to them, and from one to the other. These ruins are called *Atara.* Two towns are spoken of in the book of Joshua, under the name of Ataroth; one as being on the borders of Ephraim and Benjamin, the other as Ataroth-adar, "near the hill that lieth on the south side of the nether Beth-horon," which answers well in position to this place.

Moving onward over a narrow path covered with loose stones, we came into the region of country famous for one of the greatest prodigies recorded in the Old Testament—when "The Lord discomfited the five kings of the Amorites before Israel, and slew them with a great slaughter at Gibeon, and chased them along the way that goeth up to Beth-horon, and smote them to Azekah, and unto Makkedah. Then spake Joshua to the Lord, in the day when the Lord delivered up the Amorites before the children of Israel, and he said in the sight of Israel, Sun, stand thou still upon Gibeon; and thou, moon, in the valley of Ajalon. And the sun stood still, and the moon stayed, until the people had avenged themselves upon their enemies."

After a little more than four hours' ride from Jerusalem, we found our tents pitched at a copious fountain, near the village of Beer, which is the Michmash of Scripture, celebrated as the place where Jotham fled from the anger of his brother Abimelech, Judges ix. It presents the remains of an extensive *khan*, built in the time of the Crusaders; also the ruins of a beautiful church, erected, as tradition reports, by the pious Helena, on the spot where the Virgin sat down to bewail the absence of her son, who had tarried behind in Jerusalem to commune with the doctors in the temple.

The following morning we set out for Nablous, which is nine hours' ride from Beer, over a road quite as rugged as those described in a previous letter. The first object that attracted my attention was a low-browed cavern near the roadside, the bottom of which is covered with running water produced from springs in the mountain. We dismounted and made an examination. The walls are smooth, and two columns cut out of the natural rock in the Egyptian style stand in the centre of the apartment. We endeavored in vain to find out its name, and concluded that it must have been used for tombs. Near this place is the supposed neighborhood of that mystic Bethel where Jacob enjoyed his vision of heavenly things, and had his stony couch made easy by the beautiful picture of ministering angels ascending and descending from the presence of the Eternal. (Genesis xxxv.) Passing the village of Broot, situated on a lofty dome-shaped hill, we caught a glimpse of the blue waters of the Mediterranean, and then descended into the deep and beautiful vale in which Leban is situated, called Lebonah in the Bible. Here we lunched at an old fountain, over which there is an extensive stone ruin. While my friends were taking their *siesta*, I amused myself in an endeavor to use the Arab plough, but failed most signally. The *cows* ran away with me, and the rude plough bounded clear out of my hands, while the peasantry stood looking on convulsed with laughter. Late in the afternoon we entered the *diamond*-shaped valley of Machna, in which is situated Jacob's Well, *Aïn Yacoub* or Es Samascih, the scene of the memorable conference between our Saviour and the woman of Samaria. The Empress Helena built a church near the well, but it is entirely destroyed, nothing remaining but the foundation. The well is covered over with large stones, but there is a small aperture down which we looked, and cast some stones to try its depth. It must be nearly one hundred feet deep, and contains a great deal of water at present.

At this point we entered the narrow valley of Shechem, or Sychar, as it is termed in the New Testament—overhung on either side by two mountains, Gerizim and Ebal. These eminences are near the same height, and both replete with historic interest. 'Twas here that the sanction of the Divine law was pronounced—the blessings which attend obedience, and the curses which follow the violation of the heavenly statutes. "And it shall come to pass, when the Lord thy God hath brought thee in unto the land whither thou goest to possess it, that thou shalt put the blessing upon mount Gerizim, and the curse upon mount Ebal. Are they not on the other side of Jordan, by the way where the sun goeth down, in the land of the Canaanites, which dwell in the champaign country over against Gilgal, beside the plains of Moreh?" (Deut. xi. 29, 30.) The westernmost, Gerizim, is said by tradition to be the mountain on which Abraham offered up his son for the sacrifice, and here the children of Israel were commanded to build an altar to the Lord, and the blessings of the law were pronounced with a loud voice to the people from Gerizim, and its curses from Ebal.

A few minutes' ride from Jacob's Well brought us to the gate of Nablous, which has a population of eight or ten thousand, and is one of the most important places in the Holy Land. It is the Shechem of Scripture. "Then Jeroboam built Shechem in mount Ephraim, and dwelt therein; and went out from thence and built Peniel." (1 Kings xi. 25; John iv. 5.) Joseph was buried here, (Joshua xxiv. 32,) and the whole country round about is rich in Biblical associations. Its appearance, when viewed from the heights by which it is surrounded, is really beautiful, and I regard it as decidedly the most romantic-looking spot that we have yet seen in Syria. The inhabitants are the handsomest people in the East, having fine forms, light complexions, and dark piercing eyes. They are mostly Mohammedans, and look upon a Christian with a haughty bearing. Two long streets run parallel with the valley, entirely through the place, and are washed by a stream running in the centre.

We passed through the town amid shouts, jeers, and stones from the children, who are taught by their parents to revile even the name of Christian. We succeeded, however, in getting safely through, and pitched our tents on the north side of the town. There is a considerable trade, as well as several flourishing manufacturing establishments in Nablous. Within the town are six mosques, five baths, one Christian church, an excellent covered bazaar for fine goods, superior to any of the bazaars in Jerusalem, and an open one for provisions, besides numerous cotton cloth manufactures, and shops of every description.

The Samaritans at present in Nablous number only sixty-eight. They have a synagogue in the town, where they perform divine service every Saturday, and one school where their language is taught, and in which is preserved a manuscript of the Pentateuch, said to be three thousand two hundred years old. It is written on parchment and rolled in a brass box. We were required to take off our shoes before entering the synagogue, and as I stood gazing on the precious relics shown to us by an old Samaritan, whose beard was long and white, I was strongly reminded of the parable in the Bible.

Leaving Nablous, amid the piteous cries of the poor lepers that hung about our camp, we descended into the "Vale of many Waters," to the village of Beit Wadan, on our left, where turning more to the north, we mounted a ridge of low hills, where tillage and garden culture cease, and the soil is no longer deep enough for the growth of trees; but the stony ground is covered with the ranunculus, anemone, and lupine of great size, and dazzling brightness of blue and white. In one hour more, the valley of Sebaste is seen in the north, and in the extreme distance to the west, between the low peaks of rocky hills, the Mediterranean opens to the view. Sebaste is the Greek name given to the ancient Samaria by Herod the Great in honor of the Emperor Augustus. The view of Sebaste is quite picturesque, occupying the summit of a hill encompassed all round by a deep valley, and therefore capable of an easy and complete fortification. The Jewish historian describes at length the buildings erected by the Idumean prince, especially a citadel, and a noble temple which he intended to exhibit to future generations as a specimen of his taste and munificence. Evidences of this great structure are still existing. I counted as many as forty standing limestone columns, besides various fragments scattered about the hill-top. A very pretty ruin of a church, said to have been built by the Empress Helena, occupies the most prominent point on the hill over the place where St. John the Baptist was beheaded. In the body of this temple, we went down a staircase into the very dungeon where that holy blood was shed.

At this point, we left the territory of Ephraim and passed into that of the tribe of Manasseh. Pursuing our course northwards, we soon reached a little village where we were again stoned by the children. I was behind the party some distance, and passed through the village alone. The first intimation I had of the character of the people was given by a shower of stones from the house-tops, after which I was pursued and hooted at in the most insulting manner. The men and the women did not participate in this outrage, but stood by and gave countenance to the doings of their children. On the evening of the third day we encamped near the village of Gennin, situated in the plain of Esdraelon. From the evidence of its position and descriptions, as well as from that of its name, it is clearly the Ginea of Josephus, and most probably the En-Gannim mentioned as a city of the borders of Issachar, near Jezreel, and near the Kishon. (Josh. xix. 21 ; xxi. 28.) It has one mosque and about six or eight hundred inhabitants, and like the villages in the south, it is built entirely of stone.

Early the next morning we pursued our journey across the plain of Esdraelon, famous in many of the most memorable parts of the history of the Old Testament; famous during the conflicts of the third crusade, and famous in our own times for the stout resistance made by Gen. Kleber, with a small force of French infantry, to the overwhelming army led by the Turkish Vizier—a resistance which Napoleon, after a forced march to the support of his gallant colleague, with numbers still vastly inferior to those of the enemy, converted into a brilliant and decisive victory. It was called by the French the battle of Mount Tabor, though fought on the plain several miles from the mountain. Soon after leaving Gennin, Mount Gibeon became visible on the right. It is considerably higher than the surrounding mountains, and is somewhat in the shape of an irregular cone. Here it was, in the last fatal battle between Saul and the Philistines, that Israel fled, and her champion and his three sons were slain. Passing in sight of Mount Tabor and the Lesser Hermon, we reached in five hours the hills which separate the plain from Nazareth. Before leaving this plain, I must mention that it is by far the most extensive and fertile region that we have yet seen in

Syria. That part of it which lies near the villages is pretty well cultivated; while the vast body of the vale is open and useless. They plough here altogether with cows, whose movements are directed by the use of a long pole, with which they touch first one animal and then the other.

Six hours from Gennin brought us to the Latin convent in Nazareth, where we have excellent rooms and every attention from the holy fathers. Their hospitality is universally extended, for which they ask no remuneration. Gentlemen, however, always present the *Superior* with money to aid them in their charitable deeds. Our first duty, after washing up and treating our bodies to clean shirts, etc., was to visit the Church of the Annunciation, which forms part of the convent. From the nave a double flight of steps leads to the space containing the high altar. A narrow stairway between these descends to what is shown as the place where stood the house of the blessed Virgin: a single chamber or grotto, with a small recess beyond, in which an altar is raised, is said to be the spot where she received the annunciation that from her should be born the Saviour of the world. Back of this is a place said to be the abode of one of Joseph's neighbors, who took care of his house during his stay in Egypt. Another chapel is shown, said to occupy the site of Joseph's work-shop. Another contains a large stone on which Christ dined with his apostles. We visited the Greek and one other chapel while out, and also a school supported by the English Church. Nazareth, the modern Nazara, or Nassera, is situated on the side of a small valley surrounded by a great number of barren hills. From my window in the convent I have a view of the entire town. Mount Tabor, which is about four hours distant, and the Mount of Precipitation, where they intended to cast Christ headlong into the abyss below, (but failed to accomplish their wicked designs,) form prominent objects in the view. The population of Nazareth at present is about four thousand, of whom three thousand are Christians. The inhabitants are altogether different in their personal appearance to any that we have seen in the East. Most of them have long Roman noses, clear complexions, dark eyes, and intelligent countenances—showing evidently that they are a superior class of people.

Leaving the ladies and baggage at the convent, we made our excursion to Tiberias, which is one day's journey from Nazareth.

Two hours' ride brought us to Kefer Kenna, or Cana of Galilee, the village where our Saviour performed the first miracle. It is situated on a slope of a hill, from which there is a fine view of the extensive valley below. There is nothing to interest the stranger here, except two old stone pots or jars, made of the common rock of the country, and said to be the original vessels that contained the water afterwards converted into wine. These jars are shaped like a large mortar, and are exhibited in a small church belonging to the Greek communion. Five hours' ride from Nazareth brought us to the shores of Galilee. We did not go into the town immediately, but loitered along the water's edge, picking up shells and pebbles. The hot baths, so celebrated for their medicinal properties, are very near the lake, and fitted up in the Turkish manner. The water issues from the side of the hill in great quantities, and is so hot that I could not hold my hand in it one half minute. It is conveyed from the spring into a large circular basin made of white marble, and sufficiently deep for a man to swim. A large marble bath-tub was pointed out to us, by the Arab who had charge of the establishment, as being the same used by Ibrahim Pasha while at Tiberias. The water of the lake is clear but insipid, and judging from the washed stones high up on the shore, it must be subject to heavy storms. Some writers represent this sheet of water as being from fifteen to eighteen miles in length, and from five to six in breadth, which seems to be a mistake. Judging from the eye, I take it to be ten or twelve in length and three to four in breadth. It is surrounded by lofty but barren hills, which makes it look smaller than it really is. After passing some time in viewing the region round about this small sea, including the Mount of Beatitudes, where tradition says that Christ delivered his sermon, and a hundred other spots celebrated in history, we entered the walled town of Tiberias, now rapidly going to decay. Our dragoman conducted us to the house of a Jew, where we all slept in one room, and had an abundance of fleas and vermin of every description to keep us awake during the night. From Tiberias I could see distinctly the ancient sites of Bethsaida and Capernaum and the Mount of Beatitudes. Saffad is not far above the lake, celebrated for the beauty of its scenery, and being the place where the Jews suppose the Messiah will reign forty years before going to Jerusalem.

From Tiberias, we ascended a lofty hill, and crossed the plain of Galilee to the western base of Mount Tabor. The ascent of this sacred mountain is gradual, and requires one hour and a half to reach the summit. It is shaped something like a cone with the top knocked off, and a level area of an oval figure, extending about two furlongs in length and one in breadth, is seen on the top. It is inclosed with trees on all sides except the south, and is most fertile and delicious. Having been anciently surrounded with walls and trenches, there are remains of considerable fortifications at the present day. A thick wall of large stones may be traced quite around the summit close to the precipice, on several parts of which are relics of bastions. On the eastern side of the hill is a strong castle, and in the precincts of it is the grotto in which are three altars in memory of the tabernacles that St. Peter proposed to build, and where the Latins always perform mass on the anniversary of the Transfiguration. The mountain derives its celebrity from the opinion entertained among Christians since the days of Jerome, that it was the scene of a memorable event in the history of our Lord. It is situated apart from all the other mountains, and furnishes a view of the rarest beauty. On the northeast I saw in the distance the expanse of the Mediterranean, while all around the spacious and beautiful plains of Esdraelon and Galilee greeted the eye. Towards the south I had in view the high mountains of Gilboa, so fatal to Saul and his sons. A few points to the north appears the Mount of Beatitudes, and the high chain of Anti-Libanus covered with snow. To the southwest is Carmel, and in the south the hills of Samaria. Descending the mountain, we returned to the convent in Nazareth, where every thing is comfortable and inviting.

LETTER FORTY-EIGHT.

DAMASCUS, Syria.

Mount Carmel—Acre—Ladder of Tyre—Sidon—Residence of Lady Hester Stanhope—Beirout—The Druses—Balbec—Damascus.

FROM Nazareth we passed over a rough and mountainous country to Sephony, which occupies the site of the ancient Sephoni, described by Josephus as the largest city in Galilee. Here was held one of the five Sanhedrims of Palestine, the others being held in Jerusalem, Jericho, Gailasa, and Amathus. "It existed as a flourishing city till the year 339, when it was destroyed by the Romans in consequence of an insurrection of the citizens. The castle, once the acropolis of the city, stands on the top of the hill, nearly half a mile above the village." Soon after leaving Sephony, we entered the delightful plain of Zabulon—saw the well of Zabulon, and close to it the walled village of Kaffer Mender. The road now lies through the narrow vale of Abylene, bounded by low hills covered with oak trees, to the village of the same name. Two miles further is another well, at the foot of a hill on which is the village of Pere overlooking the plain of Acre, called sometimes the vale of Kishon or Megiddo. This vale is almost one continued swamp, crossed by tracks not always easy to find. Crossing the river Kishon, which traverses this plain, and in which the host of Sisera were swept away, we entered the dirty town of Caiaphus, situated on the bay at the foot of Mount Carmel. According to Pocock, this is the Porphyrion of the Romans, where Pliny says the Tyrian purple dye was made from the shell-fish of the coast. A grove of venerable olive trees adorn the road on either side to Mount Carmel, one of the most charming spots in the East. This sacred mountain is situated on the summit of a lofty promontory, commanding a magnificent view of the sea, and Acre, backed by the snowy ranges of Lebanon and Anti-Lebanon. The monastery is the largest and best fitted up establishment in the East. It is built of stone, three stories in height, surmounted by a large dome, under which there is an elegant and finely furnished chapel. We were received here by the monks with great cordiality. The Carmelites do not eat flesh, but live on fish, which they furnish to their guests in every variety; also pastry, and admirable wine, (the vino d'oro,) which they make from their own vineyards. Carmel is mentioned in the book of Kings, where Elijah ordered all Israel, and the prophets of Baal, and the prophets of the groves to assemble.

Descending the lofty steep, we pursued our way northward along the margin of the sea, crossing the Kishon and Belus, to the eastern gate of Acre, through which we rode and examined its bazaars and dismantled walls. The bazaars are well supplied, but Acre no longer presents the appearance of a well fortified city. Just back of it there is a handsome aqueduct and fountain of the olden time still in perfect preservation. The first object of interest beyond this is a lofty white promontory, corresponding with Mount Carmel, and from which the monastery can be distinctly seen. Not far from this we crossed the famous pass known by the name of the "Ladder of Tyre," and said to have been constructed by Alexander the Great. Being now in the land of ancient Phœnicia, of which Sidon was the capital, we soon came to the *Ras el Ain*, or the "Fountain Head." Here by the roadside are the remains of three large cisterns, in which the water stands at the depth of many feet, and whence it rushes through different channels and in strong currents to the sea. They are also called Solomon's cisterns, and are said to be those which supplied Tyre with water in the days of Hiram. A portion of the aqueduct still remains. Below the cisterns I noticed a grist mill with three sets of stones, moved by the volume of water flowing from above. Proceeding along the shore, we soon reached the ancient city of Tyre, now called *Soor*. It was one of the greatest cities in the East, and was destroyed by Nebuchadnezzar (573 B. C.) after a siege of thirteen years, (see Ezekiel xxvi. 4, 12, 21,) about one hundred and seventy years after its destruction by the Assyrians. The Tyrians built insular Tyre, which was taken by Alexander the Great, after a siege of seven months, by filling up the channel which separated it from the continent. After being successively under the power of the Greeks, the Romans, the Crusaders, and the Saracens, it finally fell into the hands of the Turks in 1289. Many relics still remain to prove the importance of the ancient city, such as portions of the old wall, and huge granite columns thirty or forty feet in length, lying about in different parts of the village, and on the sea-shore. The island is now completely connected with the main land. The present village of Soor contains a population of between three and four thousand, and has two mosques and three Christian churches. The site is now a flat and barren point projecting into the sea, with lofty mountains covered with snow in the background. We enjoyed the luxury of a bath in the waters where the shipping of this mighty city was once carried on, and I could not help thinking of the prophecies in the Bible, which are verified, I may say, almost to the letter.

We pitched our tents outside the walls of Soor on a hill of sand, and had the pleasure, about two o'clock in the night, of being aroused by a shower of rain falling on our beds, the tents having been carried away some time previous by a sudden gust of wind. Seeing that our chances of rest were completely broken into, we dressed and protected ourselves as best we could from the pitiless storm by wrapping the tent cloth over us. As you might imagine, we were in a terrible plight the next morning, but with our ardor for sight-seeing not the least abated. Leaving the ancient city of Tyre, where the fishermen spread their nets, we passed along the shore to a considerable stream called Nahr Kasmia, over which there is a beautiful bridge of one arch, constructed by the Romans, and in great preservation. Two hours more brought us to the promontory called Ras Sarfa, the Sarepta of the prophet Elijah. Here are several excavations in the rock, and scattered ruins lying between them and the sea. Not far from this is El Borek, where there is a fountain shaded with trees, and from which there is an aqueduct conveying the water to Sidon, now called Saida, situated on an elevated site commanding a view of Tyre, which is about twenty miles distant. Sidon is a much more beautiful and flourishing place than its sister city, but the prophecies of the Bible can be traced even here, by the most casual observer. A few hours' ride from the hill back of the city is still to be seen in a romantic situation Mar Elias, the residence of Lady Hester Stanhope, who gave up society, friends, and country, to live like a hermit in this desolate region, where her only associates were the untutored natives and an occasional traveller. The Arabs regarded her as a divine creature, and her influence over them was truly wonderful. Even to this day her memory is revered, and her secluded abode held sacred.

From Sidon we passed through gardens filled with orange and lemon trees to a very pretty stream called Nahr el Owely, over which there is an excellent stone bridge. After this the road to Beirout runs along the sea-coast—sometimes upon the sandy beach of the shore, and at others over rocky paths at a little distance from it. Just before reaching Beirout we entered a beautiful grove of pine trees, planted by the famous Fakr el Din, the prince of the Druses—then through a narrow way hedged in on both sides by sloping embankments of earth, crowned with the prickly pear, and so high that it appeared as if we were going through a dark tunnel. Our dragoman conducted us to a small hotel in the city, which looked so uninviting that we absolutely refused to take rooms, preferring to live in our tents, rather than suffer beyond human endurance. Finding that we were determined, he agreed that Demetrie's hotel a little way outside of the walls, on the sea-shore, was decidedly better. Now Demetrie is a Greek of remarkably fine appearance, and takes great pride in keeping the best house in Syria. He always dresses in the costume of his native country, and walks about the premises with the consciousness that he is the observed of all observers. Beirout, the ancient Berytus, is the principal seaport, and decidedly the most agreeable place in Syria. It is situated at the end of a long headland that projects into the Mediterranean, and is fortified on the land side by a high wall flanked with towers. The streets are irregular, and like those of most Eastern towns, are narrow and dark. The bazaars are large, and well supplied with silks and other costly articles. The population chiefly consists of Maronite Christians. A large number of American missionaries reside in this city, and have a chapel and flourishing school. One of the missionaries told us that they were doing a great deal of good in educating and training the natives to habits of virtue and probity, but for my part I could discover neither.

From Beirout we came to this city by way of the celebrated ruins of Balbec. Before starting, our *Moukris* played off on me one of the thousand and one tricks that a pilgrim is subject to. The horse which I rode through the Holy Land, called *Ahbeyen*, (best quality,) was missing, and an inferior horse brought in his stead. The party was ready to start, and it was too late to remedy the imposition.

One hour's ride from Beirout brought us to the base of the Lebanon range of mountains, over which our road passes. Notwithstanding a great trade is carried on between these two cities, and hundreds of pack-mules throng it every day laden with costly goods, I venture the assertion, that there is no highway in the world half so rough, or half so dangerous. We intended visiting Deir el Kammar and Damas, the chief towns of the Druses, but were prevented on account of the difficulties between the people and the Turkish soldiers. The government wishes to force the Druses to enlist as soldiers, but they refuse, and make forcible resistance. Several severe battles have been fought, and the Turkish troops forced to retreat to Sidon. The day after leaving the sea, we entered the broad and beautiful plain of Beka, or Cœlo-Syria, so called by the ancients as being the hollow country between the ranges of Lebanon and Anti-Lebanon.

Turning northward, we halted a short time at a Moslem village called Kerak, to see what the natives call Noah's Tomb. It measures over one hundred feet, and is about two feet in width. This tomb is supposed to be that of the great restorer of the human race, and is kept covered with green baize—the color of the Prophet. An Arab woman of uncommon personal beauty carried the keys of the door, and gave me a ring from her finger as a memento of the place.

Pursuing our way up the beautiful valley until the sun was low in the west, we came in view of the ruins of Balbec. About midway across the plain, and nearly two miles from the main ruins, are the remains of a small but massive octagonal temple, called by the natives *Kabet Douris.* It consists of eight smooth granite columns, covered with stone blocks of different material and workmanship. We pitched our tents in the court of the great temple, and enjoyed the first sight of its wonder and magnificence by moonlight. I have seen the Coliseum, the Roman Forum, the ruins at Thebes, and indeed all the ruins of Europe and Egypt, but I have never seen any thing to equal in grandeur and romantic loveliness this far-famed temple. One look at its majestic proportions fully compensated for all the fatigue, trials, troubles, and tribulations that we have experienced in this blighted country. I shall never forget the night we spent at Balbec; as long as memory holds her own, I will recur with pleasurable emotions to that dreary spot, where pilgrims for ages have stood and given themselves up to its all-powerful influence. One of the ladies of the party, who had an exquisite voice, ascended to the top of the great temple, and sang *Uncle Ned* and other familiar airs. I had heard them often before in the far west, but they were not half so beautiful as they fell from her lips. It reminded me of home and those old familiar faces that I may never see again.

But let this pass for the present, while I describe to you in a feeble manner the ruins of Balbec. The best preserved of the two temples is dedicated to the Sun, (Baal,) the larger to the "Gods of Heliopolis." The principal entrance to the large temple was by a Corinthian colonnade, with a handsome flight of stone steps. A wall of modern date has been built across it, flanked at each end by two square towers. Columns, cornices, pillars, and vast fragments of the building lay scattered about here in sad confusion. The columns in the large temple are about sixty feet in length, and seven feet in diameter, and I observed three stones in the outer wall measuring sixty-eight feet in length, fourteen in height, and sixteen and a half in breadth. These stones were conveyed by some unknown power from the quarry, half a mile distant, and elevated twenty-five feet above the ground. The six standing columns of the large temple present the most imposing appearance I ever beheld.

The Temple of the Sun stands nearly south of the great temple, and the best view of it is from the six columns. Four richly corniced pillars at the south-east corner are all that remain of the portico. A Saracenic tower has been built over them, and in front of the principal entrance is a high stone wall, apparently of the same age as the tower. Passing through a low gateway, we found ourselves in front of this magnificent portal. It is built in the richest and most florid style of Corinthian architecture. The centre, or keystone, has been forced partly out of its place, most probably the effect of some earthquake, to which the whole of Syria is more or less subjected. Over it is a carved eagle holding a caduceus in his talons, and garlands in his beak. The interior of the temple is richly ornamented, but the entire roof has fallen in. Not far from the east corner is a square Saracenic building, with an arched roof, so formed as to support another building, few traces of which remain; a staircase on one side leads to the top. Ibrahim Pasha converted this building into a magazine. A little to the north-east of this building, and across the river, is a small circular temple of the Corinthian order, embowered among trees. It is one of the most elegant edifices in all Syria. Unfortunately, it has suffered very seriously, in common with the other temples, from repeated shocks of earthquakes, which have left so little standing evidence of the vast and wonderful chambers of the ancient Balbec. Close to the temple is a large ruined mosque, which seems to have been built out of the fragments of the buildings, and contains a tomb supposed by Lord Nugent to be that of the *great Saladin.* The inscription is in Arabic, and is thus translated in Nugent's work on the East: "Under this tablet is laid, by God's power, his most mighty officer, to whom there was no rival; King of the Arabs—King of the Seas and Lands, King of all Nations—lover of peace and justice, the most intelligent servant of the *Most High God*, unto whom he built this sanctuary; the most noble, powerful, and wise; the honor of all the world; the greatest king—Saleh-alla-ed-Dhein, who by the wisdom of his mind won all these countries, as also the affections of all the people whom he subdued in the land of peace." This being the last object of interest in the ancient city of Balbec, we took one long and lingering look before starting to this city.

There is very little to interest the traveller on the road between the two places, except some bold scenery of the Anti-Libanus, and the celebrated cedars of Lebanon, mentioned in the books of Ezra and Ezekiel. Our first view of the plain of *Ghouta*, in which Damascus is situated, was sudden and grand. We came to it unexpectedly, and in an instant one unbroken view as far as the eye could reach, covered over with innumerable villages, mounds, and water-courses, was presented to the eye, forming a panorama of rare beauty. From the elevated position from which we first beheld Damascus, it looked to be in the shape of the figure six, but so much concealed by numerous groves and gardens that encompass it on every side, that our view was very imperfect. These gardens, which are chiefly private property, abound in fountains and summer-houses; and here under the shade of the walnut, the citron, the orange, and the pomegranate, the luxurious and idle Turk passes the greater part of his time during the summer months, lost to every thing around him but the smoke he is inhaling from his *chibook* or *arghile*. The principal gardens lie close to the town, between it and the mountain of Sulihizzeh, but they are scattered through the whole of the plantation around Damascus, which extends over a circumference of nearly twenty miles. Near the centre of this plantation stands the city, about six miles in circumference. Two of the branches of the river Barrada flow through the environs, and may probably be the cause of the luxurious vegetation; while the main branch of the river passes through the town, supplies the numerous plantations and baths, which contribute so much to the elegance, as well as general salubrity of this queen of Oriental cities

Descending from the mountain into the plain, we passed through a neat little village into a narrow lane, walled in on either side with large blocks of dried mud and gravel mingled together, and placed in the same manner that we build our stone walls. Entering the gate on the east side of the city, we passed through a number of well-filled bazaars to the Palmyra Hotel, kept by a Greek. It is the only hotel in Damascus, and excepting Demetrie's, in Beirout, it is the best in Syria. The external appearance of the house is not at all attractive, but the inner court and the apartments are really elegant. The walls are beautifully painted in the Oriental fashion, the ceiling inlaid with pearl, and fountains filled with pure water ornament the court, and the centre of each chamber. It is decidedly the most comfortable place that we have been into for many months—so much so, that I would like to remain here several weeks, but time is precious, and other engagements demand that we should see the city in a few days, and be off.

The morning after our arrival we enjoyed the luxury of a Turkish bath, in an excellent establishment adjoining the hotel. The operation is rather long, but so comfortable that we do not regret the time spent. As many of your readers are unacquainted with this Eastern luxury, I will briefly describe it in its appointments. We were first conducted into a large circular apartment with a fountain in the centre—towels and pipes hanging about in all directions, and elevated platforms on which are arranged couches for the customers. Here we undressed, had a cover placed about our loins and a white cotton turban on our heads, Placing our feet in high pattens, we were conducted slowly by two Turkish boys through three rooms of different temperatures. We remained about half an hour in the third room, and were then conducted into a fourth, of still warmer temperature, where we were soaped, kneaded, and hot water poured over us. We remained in the fourth room about one hour, and were then conducted into a fifth room, where we went down head and ears into a large basin of very hot water. In this we remained only a few minutes, when we were conducted to the couches in the first room, where we lay on our backs covered with sheets, and smoking *arghiles* until breakfast was announced. This last operation is decidedly the most agreeable, and constitutes the chief luxury of the bath.

After breakfast we went into the silk bazaars, and purchased a variety of scarfs and other articles peculiar to Damascus and Aleppo. They will be much prized by our lady friends at home—both on account of their beauty, and the fact that they were bought here for them.

The bazaars of Damascus are far more numerous and better supplied than those in Cairo. Each trade has a separate quarter for their goods, and they are better lighted and have a more elegant appearance than we have seen in any other Eastern city.

From the bazaars our guide conducted us to the private houses of several wealthy Jews, which constitute the greatest attraction of Damascus. We were received by the ladies with the utmost kindness. Refreshments were furnished, and every facility offered to see and learn their manner of living. The apartments are very numerous, and fitted up in a style peculiarly Oriental. The ladies are very fair, dress richly, but without taste, and exhibit their bosoms in a manner that would shock the females in our country. The coffee-houses are numerous and well furnished, generally speaking; they are open on all sides, except where partially covered with plants trained up the slender columns which support the roofs. Many of them project over some running stream, with orchards and gardens covering the opposite bank. Here, during the spring and summer months, the ear is greeted with the notes of singing birds, thousands of which shelter themselves amidst the luxuriant groves of apricot, mulberry, and Damascus plum trees, whose fruit is strangely mingled with the dense foliage of the elm, the ash, the willow, and the sycamore. I noticed one sycamore in the bazaar that was at least fifteen feet in diameter, also grape vines of enormous size. While we were sipping our coffee in one of these pleasant places, I observed five men standing around a large mortar pounding coffee. Four of them had pestles similar to those used with us for beating corn, but far heavier, each weighing forty pounds. The fifth man stood and stirred the coffee up with his hands amid the four pestles with a dexterity really wonderful. While pounding they sung a low and monotonous song, and exerted themselves in a manner that few ordinary men could undergo. They were all nearly naked, and the perspiration rolled down their bodies into the coffee in such streams that I disliked to drink the beverage. Although Damascus is a large and important city, there are but few objects in it to interest the Christian stranger.

Our guide conducted us to a small cellar, said to be the house of Judas, in which Ananias restored sight to Saul. A quarter of a mile from the eastern gate of the city, a spot is pointed out as the scene of his miraculous conversion, not far from which is also shown the part of the wall from which St. Paul was let down by night in a basket, to avoid the Jews, who were keeping watch at the gate to kill him. (Acts ix. 11–20.)

Mr. Burnet, of Cincinnati, who is a missionary residing in Damascus, pointed out to us the ruins of a temple near the great mosque, which has no name, nor is it mentioned in any of the books. Six huge columns, surmounted by a heavy cornice, are all that remains of the temple. It is admirably executed, and furnishes the best view of the city.

The population of Damascus is estimated at one hundred and fifty thousand, of whom twelve thousand are Christians, four thousand Jews, and the remainder Mohammedans. If the city was connected with Beirout by railroad it would flourish very rapidly; but the vast and magnificent plain in which it is situated is so isolated from the world, that they cannot expect to make much advancement.

This is my last letter from Syria. In a few days we sail for Smyrna and Constantinople, and if convenient I will furnish you with letters describing the remainder of our tour.

LETTER FORTY-NINE.

SMYRNA, Asia Minor.

Farewell to the Holy Land—Voyage to Smyrna—Our Steamer and Passengers—Island of Cyprus—Coast of Karamania—Islands of Rhodes, Samos, and Scio—Bay of Smyrna—The Quarantine.

LIKE the Jews, I always had, from the time I learnt my catechism at the Sunday school, a strong desire to see with my own eyes the scenes of Sacred History. To live and die, and be cheated out of this darling idea, was too great a privation, and I had no rest till the tour was accomplished. Now that I have visited all the Holy Places, and lingered sufficiently long to hear the wondrous story, and experience those ecstatic feelings that none can enjoy but the pilgrim, I feel content, and thank my God that my day-dreams have been realized. Something may transpire hereafter to induce me to revisit the Holy Land, but the privations, dangers, and annoyances that one must unavoidably encounter, will always incline me to live on the memory of the past.

From Beirout we embarked on the steamer Stamboul (belonging to the Austrian Lloyd line) for the city of Smyrna, having for our companions *en voyage* the Bishop of Jerusalem, (who is an intelligent Swiss,) a number of Turkish officers, nine Americans, and six hundred pilgrims. The deck was crowded to suffocation with a species of humanity no where else to be seen, except in the Orient. Most of them were Greeks and Armenians, besides many Turks and Persians, all mingled together in one great mass, looking more like pigs in a sty than human beings. They were returning from Jerusalem, where they went to pass the Easter holidays. Nearly all of them had long tin boxes filled with miserable paintings of the Virgin and our Saviour, which they procured in the Holy City to carry home as mementoes. I was a little surprised to observe magnificent diamonds on the fingers of some who dressed shabbily, and lived for economy's sake on nothing but vegetables. Indeed, there are many of these creatures who appear perfectly destitute, and yet count their thousands.

Early the following morning we cast anchor in the bay of Larnica, the principal town on the island of Cyprus, where we remained several hours for the purpose of putting off sixty or one hundred pilgrims. Cyprus is the most easterly island of the Mediterranean, off the coast of Syria. In ancient times it was believed peculiarly the favorite abode of Venus—a fable originating probably in the voluptuousness of its inhabitants. The island is seventy leagues in length from east to west, and thirty leagues in its greatest breadth; its circumference is one hundred and eighty leagues. It is traversed by two mountain ranges of considerable height, from which many streams descend, which once diffused verdure, and added to the beauty of the scenery. Under a good government and proper cultivation, Cyprus would be a valuable island. It produces grapes in abundance, from which an excellent wine, known in the Levant as the *Vino di Commanderia*, is produced. The leather, madder for dyeing cotton red, opium coloquintida, soda, and other valuables, are to be found there. Leaving Cyprus, we coasted the shores of Karamania, which are exceedingly barren and dreary; the hills rise abruptly from the sea, and are cultivated only here and there in small patches by a few straggling Greeks. This part of Asia Minor is very thinly populated, and considered unsafe to travel through, on account of the roving banditti that infest all that region.

Early on the morning of the fourth day we reached the city of Rhodes, situated on the north-eastern extremity of the island of Rhodes, and celebrated both in the annals of ancient and modern history. The inhabitants of the island obtained the sovereignty of the sea in early times by their superior knowledge of maritime affairs and navigation, and were conspicuous for their learning and the fine arts. It is better known at the present day as the residence of the Knights of St. John of Jerusalem, and the theatre of one of the most heroic defences on record. The island is about thirty miles long, eighteen broad, and one hundred and forty in circumference. The coast is indented with gulfs and winding bays, well protected by bold promontories. The soil was originally extremely fertile, but has been so much neglected of late years that it no longer bears that appearance. Rhodes, the chief town, is defended by massive fortifications and large square towers. It is no longer a place of importance; its ruined streets are gloomy and deserted; the houses are chiefly of stone, and many of them uninhabited. Several remains of the works of the knights are still to be seen in tolerable preservation. The street of the knights is straight and well paved, and some of the houses retain the armorial bearings of the knights, sculptured on the wall over the doors. The captain of the "Stamboul" pointed out to me the two rocks upon which stood the great *Colossus*, one of the seven wonders of the world, erected in honor of the sun, and dedicated to Apollo, to whom the whole island was consecrated. These two rocks, which are situated at the entrance of one of the harbors, are stated to be fifty feet asunder, and the statue tall enough for ships to pass between its legs. Judging from the eye, the distance appears to be greater. The Colossus was from one hundred and five to one hundred and fifty feet in length. Pliny states that this wonderful monument was the work of Chares, the disciple of Lysippus. Fifty-six years after its construction it was thrown down by an earthquake. It is said to have been the labor of twelve years and to have cost three hundred talents. It remained where it fell for nine hundred years, till A. D. 672, when Maowias, the sixth Caliph of the Saracens, sold the brass to a Jew, who carried it off, loading nine hundred camels with its remains. No scholar can reflect upon the past history of this little island, and view its present condition, without a feeling of sadness and regret. But such is the history of the world: the greatest works of man must pass away, and vanish for ever, while the immutable creations of God stand the shock of ages, reminding us of our own weakness.

Quite a number of small islands skirt the shores of Asia Minor in the vicinity of Rhodes; Stanchio, Lero, and others lie near the track of the steamers. All is desolation upon them; nothing presents itself but barren rocks, and an occasional hut of some poor Greek.

The island of Samos next attracted our attention. It is known as the birthplace of Pythagoras, Chœrilus the poet, Conon the painter, and several other distinguished characters. Herodotus here sought refuge from persecution, and composed the first books of his history. The modern Samonites were the first to join in the Greek insurrection, and they massacred or drove the Turks out of the island which they put in a state of defence.

The island of Scio was in ancient times called Chios, and considered the paradise of the Levant, on account of its natural fertility, beautiful scenery, extraordinary verdure, and the richness of the foliage covering the whole face of the country. The Sciotes also participated in the Greek revolution. In 1822 the whole island was desolated by conflagration, plunder, and death. The females were sold as slaves, the men and male children massacred, and many of the principal merchants hung. Thirty thousand were passed through the custom house as slaves, and of the 120,000 souls who composed the population but nine hundred remained, all of whom were swept away by the pestilence which followed. The island has improved much of late years, and recovered, to some extent, its former importance. "Ion the tragic poet, Theopompus the historian, who flourished in the time of Philip of Macedon, Theocritus the sophist, and Metrodorus the philosopher and physician, were natives of Chios, which is also one of the spots which contend for the honor of having given birth to Homer."

Passing through the strait of Scio, we soon entered the beautiful gulf of Smyrna, which is thirty-three miles long, and from five to fifteen broad. It is encompassed with high mountains clothed with verdure, and has numerous headlands and islands intervening between the entrance and the tower. It was exceedingly rough when we entered the gulf, and the mist obstructed the view very much, yet I could see enough to convince me that it merited all the praise bestowed upon it by ancient and modern writers. Passing the Castle of the Sea, situated on a low point near the water's edge, we saw for the first time the city of Smyrna, the queen of the cities of Anatolia, celebrated by the ancients under the title of the lovely, the crown of Ionia, the ornament of Asia. The ruined castle on the summit of Mount Pagus, the cypress forests of the cemeteries, the numerous mosques, minarets, and cupolas, all reminded me that I was approaching one of the cities of the *Seven Churches* mentioned in the 11th chapter of Revelations.

We weighed anchor near the city and discharged the mails before going to the *Lazaretto*, situated below the city, and in which we were compelled to remain three *long days*. Five days' quarantine is the time prescribed by law, but the day we entered was counted as one, and the day of our departure as another, leaving three days in the Lazaretto. These establishments are certainly the greatest nuisance that a traveller in the East is compelled to undergo. The one at Gaza was bad enough in all conscience, but it was very comfortable in comparison to this, which is badly managed, and was so much crowded during our confinement as to render it really dangerous in case of the appearance of one of the many maladies peculiar to the East.

Five Americans were crowded in a room about twenty feet square, four in another, and two ladies with the wife and children of the Bishop of Jerusalem in a third. Our beds and meals were furnished at the rate of two Spanish dollars per day by the proprietor of a hotel in Smyrna, and was in keeping with the quarantine. If you desire to know how we occupied our time, just pay a visit to one of our asylums or jails, and you can form a pretty correct idea of the pleasures that we experienced. After the fumigation of our trunks, and examination of our tongues, the French physician gave us *pratique*, and we "cut stick" as soon as possible for better quarters. It is a little astonishing that the nations of Europe and our own country do not take some steps to relieve their citizens of this abominable regulation, practised only to extort money from strangers.

LETTER FIFTY.

SMYRNA, Asia Minor.

Appearance of Smyrna—Mount Pagus—The Six Churches—Caravan Bridge—The Cemeteries—Donkey Ride—Encounter with Albanian Banditti—Beauty of the Women—American and French Vessels in the Harbor.

THE city of Smyrna has been the scene of desolation from its earliest history, having risen ten times from her ruins with new splendor. Its origin has been ascribed to Alexander the Great, who was admonished in a dream to build a city on this spot for the Smyrnians, who came from Ephesus. If he had dreamed with his eyes open, he could not have selected a point better suited, in every particular, for a large commercial emporium. Like San Francisco, it is far removed from the sea, with a harbor capacious enough to protect her vessels from the severest stress of weather.

"Over against the city once stood the famous temple of Cybele. But what the inhabitants most glory in, is the circumstance of its having given birth to Homer." The city at present is shaped something like an ellipse, and extends for nearly two miles along the coast. It is built on the acclivity of Mount Pagus, from which the material for building is mostly taken. The population of Smyrna is about 150,000; of whom 80,000 are Turks, 40,000 Greeks, 15,000 Jews, 10,000 Armenians, and 5,000 Franks. The followers of each faith have their distinct quarters allotted to them. Every trade has a bazaar set apart for it; and the streets present more the appearance of an Italian city than any I have seen since leaving Naples. The houses of the Armenians and Turks are mostly painted blue on the outside, and those in the Frank quarter are built of stone.

The most curious places about Smyrna are the cemeteries, filled with forests of tall and gloomy-looking pines. The tombs of the males, in the Turkish cemetery, are designated by a turban, cut in marble, on the top of the head-piece; and those of the gentler sex, by a rose—fit emblem of purity and love.

In going to the Caravan Bridge, the favorite resort for the Turks in summer, we had an opportunity of witnessing a caravan, extending about two miles, and loaded with fruits and silks. The silks were from Persia, and of the richest quality. I congratulated myself that I was not a woman, for they looked so tempting that I might have exhausted my *letter of credit.*

Smyrna is the great fig market of the world. Vessels from all nations can be seen loading with this delicious fruit. On the steamers and in the hotels they did not furnish us with the best quality, and gave as their reason, that the price was so great, that none but rich foreign people could afford to eat them.

Persons wishing to visit the six remaining churches of Ephesus, Laodicea, Philadelphia, Sardis, Thyatira, and Pergamos, usually make this their starting point. To see them all, requires some ten or fifteen days; and I have been informed by persons who have visited them, that the ruins in several are well deserving attention, and will fully repay one for the trouble, danger, and expense of the journey.

During our stay in Smyrna, we took a ride on that animal of animals called the *donkey.* Ah! I will not soon forget that ride. Without stirrups to diminish my longitude, or bridle to guide the stubborn beast, I was left to the mercy of a driver, who seemed to delight in the fun created by our ludicrous appearance as we passed through the bazaars. The people looked at me and then at my donkey, as if to say, What a long individual, and what a short donkey! strangers, can't you relieve the little fellow? Fortunately, we had been gazed at so often that our faces had become *hard,* and if such had not been the case the profusion of fancy beard on my face would have defied them to detect a blush. Passing almost through the entire length of the city, we revisited that detestable place known as the Lazaretto, where our old travelling companions, Messrs. E—g, P., and *F. P.*, were fighting against time. We were not allowed to enter the premises, but shook hands and conversed with them through the gratings. After giving in our experience, we bade them good-by, and hope to meet them somewhere in Europe. We then proceeded to the summit of Mount Pagus to enjoy the magnificent view of the city and bay, and to examine the ruins of the old castle, which is now deserted and fast falling to decay. A very large space is inclosed within the walls, and in the centre of it is the ruined mosque, supposed to have been the original church of Smyrna. Our guide pointed out portions of the old Hellenic walls, some of the relics of the Temple of Jupiter, the stadium, the place where Polycarp is said to have suffered martyrdom, besides the fragments of numerous busts, cornices, columns, and entablatures. Our examination was suddenly interrupted by the magic appearance of two men dressed in the Albanian costume, and armed *cap-à-pie*. They proposed to hold our donkeys, but we declined, and immediately started back to the city, having received intimation from our guide that they were brigands, and would in a few minutes summon their comrades and make us their captives. We had left our weapons at the hotel, and thinking that "discretion was the better part of valor," we made our little animals cut dirt faster, probably, than they ever did before. These brigands are the most desperate characters in all the East, and keep the Smyrnians in constant terror. Just before our arrival, they seized the Dutch Consul, while walking in his garden, and conveyed him to one of their dens in the country, hoping that some great reward would be offered for his return. No reward, however, was offered, and they sent in word to his wife that five thousand dollars ransom money would save her husband, and if it was not paid on a certain day, they would send in his head for her to make soup out of. This message induced the friends of the Consul to furnish the money, and he was permitted to return once more to the bosom of his family.

Smyrna from its earliest history has been renowned for the beauty and exquisite loveliness of its women. You can find isolated beauties in almost any country or clime, but it does seem that certain localities are peculiarly blessed, and set apart for the development of form and feature in its most perfect image.

> "Grace shaped her limbs, and beauty decked her face."

Well may the devotee of female beauty give utterance to the language of Prior as he strolls through the bazaars of this city. In symmetry of figure, regularity of feature, elasticity of movement, and general attractiveness, they fully merit all that has been said of them, and can vie in my estimation with the most attractive signoras of Italy or Spain. Next to a beautiful woman I admire a beautiful vessel, and here we have both. Napoleon III., feeling the necessity of strengthening the naval arm of his service, in order to cope with the old Beldam of the Sea, and the rising greatness of the Model Republic, has ordered a number of new screw frigates to be built on an improved plan, and every way superior to any war steamer now afloat. The vessel that I saw in the harbor at Smyrna is certainly the most beautiful and complete craft that my eye ever rested upon, and if she succeeds it will bring about an entire change in the present system, and steam will supersede the sailing vessels. "My voice is not for war," but it is sometimes inevitable, and the next great conflict of nations must be on the seas. The commerce of the United States is now spread over the world, our brave mariners can be seen in every latitude, and it is almost certain that we must be participants in such a struggle. Are we prepared? Are we able with our present navy to protect our ships in foreign seas, or even our seaboard cities from the devastations of war? No, no, no! England, France, and even Russia, outnumber us in their guns, and in point of steam power we are far, far behind. Most of our countrymen do not know or feel the necessity of giving strength to our navy, but those who have had the opportunity of investigating this matter will tell you that it is of more importance to us at this present moment than all else besides. We have a mighty destiny to work out, an increasing commerce to foster, and an extensive coast to protect. With a strong navy we have nothing to fear, but in our present condition we are liable to be crippled—nay, ruined. Do not understand me as the advocate of an unwieldy and expensive navy, for I believe it to be like a large standing army, a curse and drain upon the best interests of the country; but let us have a power on the sea equal to our requirements, and capable of sustaining and perpetuating the glory and greatness of a nation now moving rapidly to the perfection of human government, and the end of man's creation.

LETTER FIFTY-ONE.

CONSTANTINOPLE.

Departure from Smyrna—Island of Mitylene—Tenedos—Plains of Troy—The Hellespont—The Dardanelles—Gallipoli—The Golden Horn—Pera—View of Constantinople from the Tower of Pera.

AT Smyrna we took passage on the Austrian steamer for this renowned and beautiful city. We had for our companions a large number of pilgrims, and a full complement of cabin passengers, amongst whom I recognised Lord Henry, of England, whose acquaintance I formed during the past winter in Egypt. He is a young man, about eighteen years of age, well educated, and much more agreeable than the generality of English nobility. Coming out of the gulf of Smyrna, we had a fine opportunity of seeing the city to advantage. The sun was just sinking behind Mount Pagus, reflecting its rays on the domes and minarets of the mosques, presenting to the eye a panorama of extreme loveliness.

The first place of interest, after clearing the gulf, is the island Mytilene, the ancient Lesbos, one of the most important islands in the Archipelago, situated in front of the Gulf of Adramiti, and separated from the continent of Asia by a narrow channel varying in breadth from seven to twelve miles. The island now possesses but few remains of its ancient grandeur, and, like many other places, its glory is in the past. Many distinguished individuals were born here, among whom were "Theophrastus and Phanias, the two favored disciples of Aristotle;" Pittacus, the Greek sage; the poet Alcæus; the musician Phrynis, and Sappho the great poetess.

Our next stopping place was at the island of Tenedos, opposite to which we had a beautiful view of the plains of Troy, so celebrated in ancient history. Ida, capped with snow, and the amphitheatre of mountains which encircle the valley of Mendire, or ancient Scamander, are presented prominently in the panorama, giving beauty and romance to a spot more celebrated than any other in the classics. *Alexander Troas* contains many remains of broken columns, pedestals, etc.; and about one mile from the sea are some ruins on a very grand scale, called by our captain the palace of Priam. Passing Rabbit Island, we entered the Hellespont, the mouth of which is five and a half miles across. It is defended by two castles, built by Mohammed IV. in 1659, to secure his fleet from the insults of the Venetians, who used to come and attack it in sight of the old castles. Proceeding up the channel some distance, we found a Norwegian brig, loaded with coal, cast the night before on the shore in a storm. We attempted to draw her into deep water, but our efforts were fruitless. The captain seemed much distressed, and I truly sympathized with him; for being cast away on a foreign shore, among Turks, is no small matter. Soon after this we landed at the Dardanelles, where we had an opportunity of examining the two famous castles. The castles of Chanak-kalessi, or Sultanie-kalessi, on the Asiatic side, and Chelitbawris, or Kelidbahar, (the lock of the sea,) on the European shore, are called by the Turks *Bogaz-hissar-leiri*, and by the Franks the Old Castles of Anatolia and Roumelia. We did not have time to go on shore, but we could see the general structure of the castles, and the great mortars out of which immense balls are shot. The dimensions of one of these balls, as stated by Gibbon, are enormous. Napoleon carried one of them to France, and it is said that it required the strength of twenty-four men to put it in the vessel.

The town of Chanak-kalessi is the place properly called the Dardanelles, and derives its name from the extensive pottery carried on here. While the steamer was at anchor a number of *caïques* came out to us loaded with gilded pottery, for sale. The helmsman of one of the boats was the largest human being that I ever saw. He was as black as original sin, and so fat that his flesh hung about him in immense flakes; his weight must have been enormous, for the stern of the *caïque* was deep in the water, while the bow was high in the air, notwithstanding two other men and a large amount of pottery were placed in front to counter-balance his surplus rotundity. Just above the Castles is the narrow point in the channel where Xerxes' bridges are supposed to have been applied. This part of the Dardanelles is likewise celebrated as the place where the army of Alexander, under Parmenio, crossed from Europe. Here the Ottoman crescent was first planted in Europe by Suleiman, son of Orchan, A. D. 1360. Here Leander used to swim across to visit Hero. The same feat (which has been performed by many since) was accomplished by Lord Byron in one hour and ten minutes.

"If in the month of dark December,
Leander, who was nightly wont
(What maid will not the tale remember?)
To cross thy stream, broad Hellespont!

"But since he crossed the rapid tide,
According to the doubtful story,
To woo—and—Lord knows what beside,
And swam for Love, as I for Glory:

"'Twere hard to say who fared the best;
Sad mortals! thus the gods still plague you!
He lost his labor, I my jest;
For he was drowned, and I've the ague."

No traces of ancient Abydos are visible, except the foundation wall of a modern fort of considerable size, which occupies the summit of the lofty cliff overhanging the stream.

The next point of interest was the town of Gallipoli, the Calliopolis of ancient geography. It is situated at the mouth of the Propontis, in a strait about five miles in breadth, and is forty miles from the Isle of Marmora, famous for its quarries of fine marble. The town was once fortified, but is now without walls, its only defence being a square sorry castle, with an old tower, doubtless that of Bajazet. It is the see of a Greek Bishop, and was the first town that fell into the hands of the Ottomans, being taken by them nearly a century before the fall of Constantinople, A. D. 1357. On the south side of the city are some tumuli, said to be the sepulchres of the ancient Thracian kings, and north of the present town some ruins of the ancient city.

We entered the Golden Horn at night time, and with the rising sun of the following morn rose in all its grandeur this magnificent city, "the Roman Constantinople, the Thracian Byzantium, the Stamboul of the Turks." With eyes riveted on the expanding splendors, I watched, as they rose out of the bosom of the surrounding waters, the pointed minarets, the swelling cupolas, and the innumerable habitations, either stretching along the jagged shore, or reflecting their image in the mirror of the deep, or creeping up the crested mountain, and tracing their outline in the expanse of the sky. Entranced by the magnificent spectacle, I felt as if all the faculties of my soul were insufficient fully to embrace its glories. I hardly retained power to breathe, and almost apprehended that in doing , , I might dispel the glorious vision, and find its whole fabric only a delusive dream. After indulging for a time in a delightful reverie, we were reminded by the agent of the Hotel Europe, that life was not a dream, but a sad reality, requiring bread and meat to sustain it. This veritable agent was an Englishman, who had lived some time in Boston, and like many of his countrymen, who are initiated in the low tricks of Yankeedom, he proved a consummate deceiver. He agreed to take the party at eight francs each per day, but took care before we left the house to swindle us out of twelve francs per day in the way of extras. Well, let him pass; it is only once in a life-time, and if any of us should be sent as Minister to this Court hereafter, we will know better how to manage things. Our luggage was placed in a *caïque* and rowed to the custom-house, where it was opened, but passed without examination. *Stamboul*, or Estamboul, as it is called by the Turks, occupies the triangular promonotory which alone formed the imperial city of Constantine. Its suburbs are separated from the main city by the Horn and the Sea of Marmora, such as Galata, Tophane, and Pera. Our hotel is in the latter, which occupies the European shore, and inhabited pincipally by Franks. From the lofty Fire Tower of Pera, we had a commanding view of all Constantinople, the Golden Horn, and the Bosphorus, which I will describe in my feeble way hereafter.

LETTER FIFTY-TWO.

CONSTANTINOPLE.

The Baths—The Bazaars—Dogs—Fires—Slave Market—Palace of the Grand Vizier—Fire Tower of Stamboul—Burnt Column—Cisterns of Constantine—Caïques—Bridges—College of the Dancing Dervishes—Barracks—Sultan's Palace.

AFTER our confinement for so many days in the Lazaretto and on board the steamer, it was natural for us to think of the luxuries of a Turkish bath, and make arrangements to visit one of the numerous establishments of this city, about which we hear and read so much. Procuring a guide, we directed him to conduct us to the best baths in the city, whereupon he led us to a very large but indifferent establishment, which he informed us was the very best in Stamboul. It was certainly the most extensive, and the number of bathers much greater than we had seen at any other place; but in point of cleanliness and real comfort, I much prefer the baths of Damascus. The boys sent to attend us in the baths looked like lepers, and presented such a hideous appearance that we refused to let them touch us. A great number of Turks were in at the same time, and observing *Christians* undergoing ablution, they seemed somewhat disconcerted, and kept up such a whispering and ogling that we were glad to get out of the establishment. There are about a hundred and fifty baths dispersed through different parts of the city. Some of them are constructed of marble, but in general they are extremely common and uninviting. They are divided into a number of circular rooms lighted from the top by cupolas thickly perforated, and studded with small hemispherical glasses. The rooms are large enough to accommodate a number of bathers at the same time. The first or outer room is always the largest, and a number of Turks may be seen there lying on couches, reposing after their ablutions and enjoying their favorite luxuries, the pipe and coffee.

The bazaars of Stamboul are mostly covered, and have more the appearance of a row of booths in a fair than a street of shops. They are very dark, narrow, and intricate, so much so that it is absolutely necessary for the stranger to have a guide. Like all Oriental cities, they are severally allotted to particular trades and merchandise. One bazaar glitters on each side of you with yellow morocco; you turn into another adorned with rich Indian shawls, or cast your eye down a long vista lined with muslin draperies or robes of ermines and fur. The shops of jewellers and engravers of precious stones occupy one quarter; those of the goldsmiths another. This is the great diamond market, and one who has a perfect knowledge of the precious stones might make excellent bargains here; but all Franks usually come out of the bazaars most wofully cheated, and uttering maledictions upon the head of the Mussulman, who immediately repairs to the mosque to pray away his rascality. The Turks invariably ask a Frank more than double what they expect to get for their merchandise, and it is amusing to see them pursue a customer after leaving their shops and bring him back by the coat tail to sell an article for one third of the original price. Time was when the word of a Turk was sacred as a precept of the Koran; now he can no more be relied upon than a Jew or Christian. He has acquired a great facility of lying, cheating, and drinking; and if they continue to improve and adopt European customs, we may soon hear of them stealing and having but one wife.

The bazaars are usually so much crowded with women and dogs that one is compelled to move very slowly, especially as more ceremony is required than amongst the well-dressed crowd that throng Broadway. Really the dogs may be classed amongst the wonders of Constantinople, and are so numerous and noisy as to render them intolerable nuisances with any other people except the Turks. They are not owned by individuals as in other countries, but govern themselves—each having his own particular district, from which he dare not go without being assailed by the police of the invaded territory. Their litters are rarely removed, and they constitute the chief scavengers of the city. They are bountifully fed upon the offal from the butchers' shops, private houses, carcasses of animals, and trunkless bodies which they occasionally find on the shores. Mosques and their inclosures are strictly watched, lest they should be polluted by them, and some consider them susceptible of plague. At night their howlings are perfectly deafening, particularly when a fire breaks out, and their voices are mingled with the *passawend* crying, *Yangen var*, (there is fire,) from the top of one of the lofty fire towers. Constantinople is built principally of frame houses, and in the absence of reservoirs, engines, and organized companies, the devouring element frequently overwhelms in common ruin the property of the infidel as well as that of the true believer. If the fire be not quickly subdued, all the ministers of state are required to attend, and if it threaten extensive ravages the Sultan himself appears and gives encouragement to the efforts of the firemen by the power of a golden shower of sequins, which never fails to produce the immediate extinguishment of the desolating flames.

In the absence of fire, and the barking of dogs, Constantinople is the most quiet city at night that I ever visited. By ten o'clock every human voice is hushed; and not a creature is seen in the street, except a few watchmen and an occasional wanderer with his paper lantern. No stranger ever leaves this city without visiting the Slave Market, because slavery in any form attracts more or less the attention of the inquiring and reflecting mind, and more particularly in Constantinople, where the beauties of Circassia and the regions of the Caucasus are exposed to servitude far more degrading than we witness in other countries. But, horrible as this traffic is, under any circumstances, to my ideas and feelings, it loses in some degree its horrors when confined to the African race. By physical formation and power of endurance, by their mental inferiority, and their natural disposition to be governed, instead of to govern, we are forced to believe that they were intended by a higher power to be hewers of wood and drawers of water until the end of time. But the beautiful Circassian, the lovely Georgian, and the unfortunate daughters of poor down-trodden Greece, were created for higher and nobler purposes. It was with no ordinary degree of emotion that I entered the gateway of this celebrated place, where so many Christian hearts have trembled; and before reaching the hollow square where they were exposed, I brought to memory all the terrible realities that I could remember connected with its history; the tears of beauty, the pangs of brave men, and so down to the unsentimental exclamation of Johnson to his new friend Don Juan:

> "Yon black eunuch seems to eye us;
> I wish to God somebody would buy us."

The bazaar forms a hollow square, with small apartments around it, in which the slaves belonging to the different traders are kept. A large portico projects in front, under which, and in front of each chamber, is a low platform, similar to those in New-Orleans, where the merciless slave-dealer sits and dozes over his coffee and pipe. In time of war the markets are filled with captives, but even in this season of universal peace, the Nubians do not constitute the only beings of traffic. The Franks are not permitted at the present day to see the white slaves, except by particular favor; but I have been assured by those living here that the custom is still in vogue, and that the wealthy Turk repairs as of old to the market with his well-filled purse, and agrees with the commissioner, for a stated sum, to prostitute the daughters of the most illustrious families of Georgia, Circassia, or the provinces.

From the slave market we visited the Palace of the Grand Vizier, situated near the great Fire Tower of Stamboul. The building is quite extensive, on the European plan, but presents nothing extraordinary either in its external or internal appearance. Near the palace in Adrianople street still stands the celebrated *Burnt Column.* It is about fifty feet in height, but so much shattered and blackened by the frequent fires in the neighborhood, that it is impossible to make much out of it. Upon close inspection I discovered that it was made of porphyry stones, the jointures hid with copper rings. It is thought that Constantine's statue stood on it. By its inscription, it appears that it was erected by the Emperor Manuel Commenes. Not far from this column are the Cisterns of Constantine, now called *Binderick*, or the thousand and one columns, and *Yerebatan Serai*, the subterranean palace, in which a number of half-naked pallid wretches are employed in twisting silk by the light of torches. Returning to Pera, we stopped to examine the *caïques* on the Golden Horn. They are the wherries of Constantinople, and the number that ply on the waters is said to be about ninety thousand, and are hired like hackney coaches in other cities. They are formed of thin plank of beechwood, neatly finished and elaborately sculptured. The elegance of their construction, the extreme lightness of the material out of which they are made, and the dexterity of the oarsmen, cause them to skim over the smooth surface of the Horn with great swiftness. They have no seats; the passengers sit on rugs in the bottom, and are required to remain perfectly steady to prevent being turned over. They are always to be found waiting for hire during the day at the points of landing.

While crossing the Horn, I examined the bridges that connect Stamboul with Pera. They are made of boats placed certain distances apart, with locks for vessels to pass through, and are precisely the same in form and structure as those on the Rhine, which I described minutely in a previous letter. Just above the bridges are the ship-yards, and the strength of the Turkish navy, where a number of enormous vessels may be seen waiting for war. They are too large for service, badly equipped, and fit only to be looked at and ridiculed by foreigners. In an action with such powers as France, England, or the United States, the Turkish navy would be as nothing; but to the nations in the region of this city it appears to be something grand, magnificent, and terrible. Some of the Turkish vessels would reflect credit upon any country, if their people understood how to manage them. These vessels were constructed by American ship-builders, and it is to be regretted that they are so poorly manned. From the Horn we ascended the high hill upon which Pera is situated to the College of the Dancing Dervishes. The room in which they dance is circular, and the floor quite smooth. Before entering, we were required to take off our shoes. The chief man, or priest, was seated in the Turkish fashion, in a place apart from the rest, who were arranged in a circle around the room. The head-dress of the priest was of green, the color of the Prophet, and the dancers wore a tall brown hat, shaped like a cone, and without any brim. Their dress was something like those worn by the ladies in our country, having very full skirts, and made of a dark brown material. The dance is nothing more than a monotonous turning on their heels, with their arms extended, like children playing. They go at it with great earnestness, and continue turning until they fall on the floor perfectly exhausted and drunk.

Leaving the College, we walked through the principal street of Pera (which is entirely European) to the Barracks, near the Sultan's new palace. Here we saw several thousand soldiers reviewed by the principal officer, and I was somewhat surprised to see how well they handled the musket. The Sultan has a great many English and French officers in his service, who teach his soldiers the tactics of modern improvement nearly as well as can be seen among the nations of Europe. One thing you may be sure of, and that is the courage of the Turks. Fear is not in the Koran, and if they do not come out victorious, it must be attributed to some other cause.

The Sultan's new palace is not yet completed. It is constructed of white marble, and promises to be the most magnificent palace of modern construction. It is situated on the European shore of the Bosphorus, and I will describe it to you more minutely in my next letter.

LETTER FIFTY-THREE.

CONSTANTINOPLE.

Grand Muster of all Nations—The Seraglio—Column of Theodosius—The Armory—Mosques of St. Sophia, Achmedje, and Suleimange—The Hippodrome—Tomb of Sultan Mahmoud —The Seven Towers—Cemetery of the Janissaries—Visit to the Sweet Waters—Excursion on the Bosphorus.

No one but a follower of the Prophet is allowed to enter the sacred precincts of a mosque without a *firman* from the Sultan; and to render the visit less expensive, the Franks usually assemble in large numbers from the various hotels in the city, and proceed under the guidance of a *cicerone* to examine the consecrated retreats of the Mussulman, which but a few years since would have been attempted only at the peril of a man's life. Agreeably to arrangement, our party met at the Hotel Europe—among whom I observed representatives from all the nations that travel, and a majority from the United States. We crossed the Golden Horn in *caïques* to Seraglio Point, upon which stands the palace formerly occupied by the Sultans, but now vacant. The inclosures of this far-famed palace occupy the space of the ancient city of Byzantium on the extreme point of the east promontory, which stretches towards the continent of Asia, and forms the entrance to the Bosphorus. The Seraglio (the splendid work of Mohammed II.) is nearly three miles in circuit; it is in a triangular form, of which the longest side faces the city; that on the sea of Marmora the south; and the other, which forms the entrance of the port, the east. The apartments are on the top of the hill, and the gardens and conservatories below, extending to the sea. Although the compass of it is so great, the outside of the palace has nothing curious to boast of; having been built by different sultans, it presents the appearance of a heap of houses clustering together without any manner of order. The rooms are well furnished in the French style, the baths entirely of white marble, and the fountains exceedingly rich. In one room we saw a kind of armory in which are deposited specimens of the weapons formerly in use among the Turks, and of the strange and gorgeous costumes of the various dignitaries and officials of the empire, which are now displaced by the unpicturesque and incommodious imitations of

European costume, which the Sultan has condemned all his employees to wear. This collection is extremely rich, and realizes my idea of the magnificence of oriental armor. I noticed quite an extensive collection of French prints on the walls, representing the battles of Napoleon. The gardens and hot-houses are well filled with rare flowers, and the view from the Seraglio window is really superb. In one of the courts we saw the column of Theodosius, about fifty feet high, and of the Corinthian order. It is surmounted by a capital of verde-antique, and it bears the following inscription, "*Fortune reduci ob devictos Gothos.*" Just before leaving the Seraglio we were conducted into a small apartment containing the archives of the country, and the likenesses of all the sultans on a map. The bedstead of Constantine, ornamented with precious stones, was also exhibited in a room that contained a large mantel-piece covered all over with gems of the largest and rarest quality.

We next visited the Armory, situated near the Seraglio, in a building formerly occupied by the Greek Church. It contains a very large stand of arms, and many curious implements of warfare. Adjoining the Armory is a small collection of antiques, some of which are very interesting. From this building we repaired to the great mosque of Santa Sophia, which is without question the most magnificent building in the East. "It is the old Constantinople cathedral, dedicated to the Eternal Wisdom, *i. e.*, to the Second Divine Person, associated even by Solomon with Jehovah in the creation of the world." The fate of this illustrious monument of the new Greek architecture during the last fifteen hundred years, from its first construction down to the present time, is replete with interest to every one acquainted with the history of Constantinople.

"The building was completed by Justinian, who drove on Christmas-eve, in the year 538, with four horses, from the palace above the Augustion to the church, slaughtered 1,000 oxen, 1,000 sheep, 600 deer, 1,000 pigs, 10,000 cocks and hens, and during the three hours 30,000 measures of corn were distributed among the poor." Accompanied by the patriarch Eutychius, he entered the church, and then ran alone from the entrance of the halls to the pulpit, where with outstretched arms he cried: "*God be praised, who hath esteemed me worthy to complete such a work. Solomon, I have surpassed thee!*" After the distribution of the corn by the magister,

Stategius, three hundred weight of gold was divided among the people. St. Sophia is in the form of a Greek cross, of which the upper end, where stood the altar, is turned towards the east, the lower end towards the west, and the two sides towards the north and south. The east side is towards the square of the Seraglio (a part of the ancient Augustion). The south side is towards the walls of the Seraglio, extending opposite to them. Three of the sides are surrounded by vaulted colonnades, covered with cupolas. I was somewhat disappointed with the external appearance of this mosque, but the interior realized all my expectations.

From Santa Sophia we visited the mosque of Sultan Achmed, which also occupies a part of the Hippodrome, and is not only the chief of all the mosques, but it is the only one in the whole Ottoman empire which has six minarets, *i. e.*, two more than *Aja Sofia*, the Suleimange, and even the mosque of the sacred house at Mecca. The most remarkable feature in this mosque is the four enormous columns, whose thickness bears no proportion to their height, and each of which is divided into three parts. The circumference of each measures thirty-six yards. They support the dome, and rise outside at its four sides, like so many small towers. The cupola of the great dome is surrounded by four half cupolas, each of which is joined by two entirely round cupolas, which form, exactly behind the four pillars, the four corners of the mosque, which, therefore, appears on the outside to be composed of nine cupolas. The floor of the mosque is covered with a magnificent Turkish carpet, and Korans of every form, and in the most beautiful writing, lie on gilded altars inlaid with mother-of-pearl. None of the mosques is so rich in valuables of every kind, which are here partly preserved, partly suspended on the wreath of the lamps, and in the mosque itself. Its founder, Sultan Achmed the First, one of the most pious princes of the Ottoman empire, richly endowed this his favorite work, and his example was followed by the nobility.

The Hippodrome was at one time rich in monuments, but now only three remain in the Atmeidan, viz.: The obelisk of granite, or Thebaic stone, which was set up a second time by the Emperor Theodosius, is a four-cornered pyramid, of one single piece, about fifty feet high, terminating in a point, and covered with hieroglyphics, now unintelligible. Close to this is another monument with four faces, built with different pieces of marble; the top of it has fallen, and the rest cannot long continue. This obelisk was covered over with brazen plates, as is apparent from the holes made to receive the pegs that fastened them to the marble. The plates were certainly set off with bas-reliefs and other ornaments, for the inscription at the bottom speaks of it as a work altogether marvellous. Between the two columns is another brazen column, formed of three serpents, turned spirally like a roll of tobacco; its size diminishes gradually from the base as far as the necks of the serpents, and their heads, spreading on the sides like a tripod, compose a kind of capital. The heads have all been destroyed, and nothing remains of the brazen column but the lower parts. It is said to be of the very earliest date, supposed to have been brought from Delphi, where it served to bear up that famous golden tripod which the Greeks after the battle of Plateæ found in the camp of Mardonius.

From this interesting spot we went to the mosque of Suleiman the Magnificent, one of the most glorious monuments of Ottoman architecture, built under the greatest of the Ottoman Sultans, in a style of grandeur worthy of the splendor of his reign, by Sinam, in 1550, finished in 1555. The plan of this mosque is according to its divisions exactly the same as that of all the fourteen great mosques, and apparently built entirely after the pattern of St. Sophia, but with the view to surpass it. As regards the regularity of the plan, the perfection of the individual parts, and the harmony of the whole, I give preference to this mosque.

Tired of taking off our shoes, and hearing the Koran read to the people, we concluded we had seen enough of mosques, and went to the tomb of Sultan Mahmoud and his family, which is built of the purest marble, and fitted up in the most extravagant manner. The tombs in the interior are covered with black, inlaid with mother-of-pearl, on the top of which are a number of cashmere shawls of great value. Diamond and pearl work are to be seen in great profusion, and the stands containing the Koran are really elegant.

At the tomb we procured horses and rode to the Seven Towers, called *Jedi Kouli*, an isolated building at the west angle of the city, where the walls which cross the promontory connect the sea of Marmora. Few things in this city interested me more than my walk around the imperial castle, once a state prison, and the same which procured for Constantinople the proud name of the "well-defended city." Time has laid his ruining hand upon it, and the whole fabric is in a state of dilapidation. Three of the towers have nearly disappeared, and those remaining are two hundred feet high. Passing the Cannon Gate, through which Mohammed II. made his triumphant entrée into the Christian city, we were conducted to the cemetery in which the seventy thousand Janissaries were buried. The fatal mark of death by the bowstring is conspicuous on the tombs, as a warning to rebels that they cannot elude the vengeance of the Porte.

The following day we procured a *caïque* and rowed up to the Sweet Waters, situated at the extreme point of the Golden Horn. The place derives its name from a number of springs, whose waters are supposed to be sweeter probably than other springs. In fair weather this is one of the most beautiful excursions in the world. The Sultan and his harem resort here every Friday, and a great concourse of Turkish ladies and gentlemen to meet them. This was the only opportunity that we had of seeing the Sultan's *pets*, and the black eunuchs who attended them were so cautious that we only caught an occasional glimpse—enough however to convince us that we could select a much better harem in the Uuited States, if our laws were not so binding on the subject.

No one leaves Constantinople without making an excursion on the Bosphorus to the dark and stormy Euxine. English and Turkish steamers run in competition, and those living at the various villages along the European and Asiatic shores, have every accommodation, and transact their business in the city with as much facility as those living here. To describe the beauties of the Bosphorus to a distant reader would be beyond the power of the most gifted. Nothing can exceed the beauty of the scenery along its banks.

"The European with the Asian shore
Sprinkled with palaces; the ocean stream,
Here and there studded with a seventy-four,
Sophia's cupola with golden gleam;
The cypress groves; Olympus high and hoar;
The twelve isles, and more than I could dream,
Far less describe, present the very view
Which charm'd the charming Mary Montagu."

Either side is lined with the magnificent palaces of the various Sultans, numerous villages, and country seats of the foreign ambassadors. We remained one night at Buyukdere to enjoy the scenery by moon-light, and partake of an excellent fish supper prepared by our esteemed Consul, Mr. Brown. The next morning we visited our accomplished Minister, Mr. Marsh, who lives at the beautiful village of Terepiee. He is a ripe scholar, well acquainted with the Turkish language and history, and every way fitted to represent the interests of his country.

This is my last communication from the capital of the Orient. I never expect to see it again as I now see it. In a short time the power of the Sultan must give way, the character of his people change, and the glory of the Ottoman empire be submerged by the *Rushing* people.

LETTER FIFTY-FOUR.

ATHENS.

Departure from Constantinople—Island of Syra—The Peiræus—Modern Athens—Ancient Ruins and Localities—Excursions—King Otho and the Queen—The Greek Parliament—Visit to the Daughters of Marco Bozzaris—Maid of Athens—Mr. Hill and his School—Elizabeth of Crete—The Count's Daughter

HAVING remained sufficiently long in Constantinople to examine and enjoy all its wonders and peculiarities, we embarked on the same steamer that brought us, for the island of Syra, touching again at Smyrna and Scio. In addition to the party of Americans who accompanied us from Syria, we had Mr. Robert J. Morris and lady, of Philadelphia, and the widow Atkinson, of Dresden. Mr. Morris was our late Chargé d'Affaires at Naples, and acquired quite as much reputation for diplomacy as his wife for beauty and accomplishment. The widow is a woman of extraordinary intelligence, and speaks fluently several languages. She travelled alone, and was then *en route* to the Holy Land and Egypt. I gave her some notes on the East, which I hope proved of service to her in her lonely wanderings.

On the morning of the third day we cast anchor in the harbor of Syra, which is one of the most important points in Greece. The

Austrian Lloyd steamers stop there, and passengers from the East are required to perform quarantine on the boat for twenty-four hours, which is far preferable to being cooped up in a filthy lazaretto. With books to read, pleasant company and fine scenery, we passed our time delightfully. Syra (anciently called Syros) is a flourishing commercial town, and contains a population of fourteen thousand. Its prosperity began with the revolution, when refugees from all other parts found protection there, and built temporary hovels on the sea-shore. It next acquired importance as the stopping place of the Austrian and French steamers. Soon after our quarantine expired, we moved our luggage on a small steamer that runs to the Piræus, and went on shore to get breakfast at one of the hotels. Here we met C. L. M. Evangelides, our Consul. He is a Greek who received his education at Columbia College, New-York, and is now the head of a large and flourishing school. He is an energetic man, and seems to have the cause of Greece dearer to his heart than any of his fellow-countrymen that I have yet seen. We visited his school, were presented to his family, and received with the greatest hospitality. Among the pupils we saw a nephew of the celebrated Marco Bozzaris, who figured so conspicuously in the late war. The little boy is about fourteen years of age, and evidently possesses a great deal of character. He had just made his appearance in the school after an absence of three days on the island, having fled because his teacher punished him for some misconduct. He gave me his signature in the English and Greek languages, and wished me a safe return to my native land. Mr. Evangelides accompanied us through the town, and also to the old fountain at which the nymphs of the island assembled in the earliest ages. It exists in its original state, and is, as formerly, the rendezvous of love and gallantry, of gossip and tale-telling. It is near the town, and the most limpid water gushes from the rock. The inhabitants preserve a tradition, that the pilgrims of old, on their way to Delos, resorted hither for purification, and it is still regarded by them with a degree of religious veneration. The islands of Andros, Tinos, Delos, and Paros, are all situated in sight of Syra. The latter is celebrated for the extent and beauty of its marble quarries. The monument just completed in the Hôtel des Invalides in Paris over the remains of the immortal Napoleon, was carried from the island of Paros, and a block is now being prepared for the monument at Washington. While in the harbor we visited a war frigate belonging to Greece, and commanded by an old veteran of the Revolution. When he ascertained that we were Americans, his heart seemed to open towards us; the vessel was exhibited in all its parts, and the birth-day of the old man was honored with a heart-felt toast in good Samian wine.

We arrived at Piræus in the night, and the following morning we drove over an excellent turnpike road on the Plain of Attica to the Hotel d'Orient in Athens. It is unnecessary for me to describe the feeling that agitated my bosom when I entered the gateway of this renowned city. They were the same that I experienced when I stood upon the summit of the Capitol at ancient Rome, and when I knelt at the tomb of our Saviour in Jerusalem. I am in Athens! "*Athenæ! Athenæ!*" Oh! what a flood of memories rush upon the mind at the bare mention of her name!

"Son of the morning, rise, approach you here!
  Come—but molest not yon defenceless urn;
Look on this spot—a nation's sepulchre,
  Abode of gods, whose shrines no longer burn."

Modern Athens is a beautiful and flourishing little city, containing a population of about thirty thousand, and retaining, in many respects, the character of its ancient predecessor. The manners and customs of the Greeks have not undergone so great a change as in other countries. Their dress and mode of living, as far as they are able, correspond pretty much with those of their ancestors. We did not come here, however, to see modern improvements, but to gaze with our own eyes upon the remains of objects that have attracted the admiration of the world for ages.

Having procured comfortable quarters, we proceeded, with a Greek for our guide, down the main street of the modern city in the direction of the Acropolis, the great centre of ancient Athens. The first antique that attracted our attention was a small circular building of marble called the Tower of the Winds, or the water clock of Andronicus Cyrrhestes. It was erected to indicate the quarter from whence the wind blew, the hour of the day by the sun when the weather was clear, and by water when it was cloudy. The form of the tower is an octagon. Each of the eight sides faces the direction of one of the eight winds into which the Athenian compass was divided; and both the name and the ideal form of that wind is sculptured on the side which faces its direction. It thus served to the winds themselves as a marble mirror. The tower and bas-relief figures are nearly perfect. Near the tower on the right is the Gate of the Agorie, or new market place, which consists of four fluted Doric pillars, supporting a pediment, near which stands Adrian's market tariff, as legible, and nearly as perfect as on the day it was placed there. Proceeding a little up the hill, we came to a place where some men were excavating the dirt from the buried ruins supposed to be the place of the Assembly of the Three Hundred. Broken columns, large blocks of marble, pieces of statuary, and a number of other relics have been found, showing that it was once a place of considerable magnitude and importance. Having a permit to enter the Acropolis, and being anxious to see its wonders, we hurried up the steep ascent, and entered the gate leading to the celebrated fortress. The summit of the hill is inclosed by a rude wall, forming a circuit of 2,330 yards, and built on the edge of the perpendicular rock, which rises one hundred and fifty feet above the plain. The upper part of the walls are the works of the Venetians and Turks. Some parts are of extreme antiquity, others are generally attributed to Cymon and to Themistocles. The area inclosed is about fifteen hundred feet in length, while its greatest breadth is only five hundred feet.

The propylæon first attracted my attention after entering the walls. In its present state it offers a front of six marble columns, of the Doric order, and two wings with friezes, entablatures, etc. It is of considerable depth, with a similar portico on the other or inner side. Numerous fragments of statuary, inscriptions, etc., are collected here for exhibition. On the right of the flight of steps leading into the propylæon is the little temple of Victory, *apteros*, or without wings. "The history of this temple is curious. It was mentioned by Pausanias, and seen by Wheler and Spohn as late as 1581, since which period no traveller had been able to discover a trace of it. At length, in some works carried on by the present government, to clear the approaches of the Acropolis to their proper level, a Turkish battery, which stood in front of the propylæon, was removed, and in doing so, fragments of pillars and other ornamental architectures were discovered in great quantities; and, by and by, the floor of an ancient temple, which, of course, was immediately recognised as that mentioned by Pausanias." The fragments were collected and the temple re-constructed without deviation from the original foundations. Four pieces of the frieze are in the British Museum. The temple itself consists of the two porticoes, each of four fluted Ionic columns, connected by a cella of solid masonry. The dimensions are very small, being not above twenty feet long, and not so much in height; but the proportions are so pleasing, and its situation on the rock, from whence Ægeus is said to have thrown himself, is so striking, that it is upon the whole a very beautiful object, and an admirable introduction to the majesty of the Parthenon, one of the first ruins on the most renowned site in the known world—hallowed by the noblest recollections that can stimulate the human heart.

The site of the Parthenon is the highest point in the city. It is also the centre of the Acropolis, as the Acropolis was of Athens. It was built during the administration of Pericles, of white marble, from Mount Pentelicus. It is not my intention to enter minutely into a description of the localities and ruins of this city, because so many have preceded me, stored with all necessary knowledge, ripe in taste and sound in judgment, who have devoted to them all the time and research necessary to convey an accurate idea to distant readers, that I feel disposed to take only a cursory view, particularly of the ruined temple of Minerva, which is regarded as the noblest monument of architectural genius which the world ever saw. It consisted of a cell, surrounded by a peristyle, which had eight Doric columns in the fronts, and seventeen in the sides. The columns are two feet six inches in diameter, and thirty-four feet in height, standing on a pavement elevated several feet from the ground. The height of the structure was sixty-five feet. Within the peristyle, at both ends, was a range of six columns, five and a half feet in diameter, forming a vestibule to the door of the cell; there was an ascent of two steps from the peristyle into these vestibules. The cell was sixty-two and a half feet broad, and divided into two unequal chambers, the western of which was forty-three feet long. The ceiling of the former was supported by four columns, and that of the latter by fifteen columns. The whole dimensions of the temple were two hundred and twenty-eight feet long, and one hundred feet broad. "The frieze on the exterior of the cell and its two vestibules represented the procession to the Parthenon, on the grand quinquennial festival of the Panathenea." The only part of the work now attached to the temple, is that above the western vestibule. A great part of it is now in the British Museum. "In the frieze of the peristyle there were ninety-two metopes, fourteen in each front, and thirty-two on each flank of the temple. The whole edifice within and without was adorned with the most splendid works of art, by the first sculptors in Greece, and Phidias himself wrought the celebrated statue of the goddess of ivory and gold. The Emperor Hadrian beautified and repaired the Parthenon; but in 1687 the roof was destroyed by a bomb fired from the Venetian army under Morosini, which fell upon a part then used for a powder magazine."

Near the Parthenon, on the side of the hill facing the modern city, stand the ruins of the Erectheum, the temple of Minerva Polias, occupying the site of the sacred olive tree, produced by Minerva from the earth in her contest with Neptune for the soil of Attica. The cella is about ninety feet long, standing from east to west, intersected at its west end by an irregular transept; and at each of the three extremities thus formed a portico. The southern portico is supported by caryatides. The Archæological Society of Athens have restored several parts of the structure.

On the south-west side of the Acropolis our guide pointed out some remains of the theatre of Herodes Atticus, who called it the Odeum of Regilla, in honor of his wife. Close to this is the site of the theatre of Bacchus, or the Dionysiac theatre. It was built five hundred years before Christ, and but little remains to show the form or character of the building. The temple of Bacchus, a cavern at the summit of the theatre in the rock of the Acropolis, was converted by Thasyllus, the victorious choregus, into a small temple, on the entablature of which was the statue of Bacchus, which is now in the British Museum. It was placed just before two columns formed with triangular capitals to support tripods, which still exist.

The Stadium of Athens was on the south side of the Ilissus, not far from the Acropolis. A sloping bank runs parallel with the river, and in this slope a semicircular hollow, facing the north, has been scooped out of the soil, at right angles to the river. The shelving margins were once cased with seats of white marble—it is now a long and grass-grown hollow, retiring into the hillside.

Between this and the town we passed under the Arch of Hadrian, which stood between the two divisions of the ancient city. On the north-west side of the arch is the inscription, "This is Athens, the ancient city of Theseus," and on the south-east side, "This is (the Athens) of Hadrian, and not the city of Theseus." That is to say, that Hadrianopolis was on the south-east side of the gate, and the Thesean city on the north-west side. Between this arch, which is quite perfect, and the Ilissus stands the column of the Olympium, or Temple of Jupiter Olympus, the largest temple of Athens. It was commenced by Pisistratus, 530 years B. C., and completed by Hadrian, A. D. 145. All that now remains of this wonderful temple are sixteen Corinthian columns, six and a half feet in diameter, above sixty feet high, on an artificial platform supported by a wall—the remains of which show that the entire circuit must have been twenty-three hundred feet. The temple consists of a cell surrounded by a peristyle, which had two columns in front and twenty at the sides.

The Lantern of Demosthenes, now surrounded by the houses of the modern city, is the only remaining relic of a series of temples called the street of Tripods, from the circumstance of these temples being surmounted by tripods gained by the Choragi in the neighboring theatre of Bacchus. It is considered one of the most beautiful monuments of antiquity, and the capitals are most elegant specimens of the Corinthian order, refined by Attic taste.

The temple of Theseus is the last of the great monuments now remaining, but the first which attracted our attention when we first entered the city. "It was built thirty years before the Parthenon, 405 B. C., a few years after the battle of Salamis, by Cymon, son of Miltiades." It is a small but exquisite specimen of the Doric order, built of Pentelican marble, centuries of exposure to the air giving it a yellowish tint, which softens the brilliancy of the white. The roof of the cell of the Theseum is modern. It is now used for the Museum of Athens, and is filled with statues, fragments, and inscriptions. Three Englishmen were buried within the temple while the Turks had possession of the country.

Not far from the temple is the sloping stone, down which the Grecian dames used to slide on their backs as an antidote against sterility. The rock is perfectly sleek from constant use, and a number of little girls were following the example of their ancestors. Near this is the Pnyx, or hill where the meetings of the people were held, and where the most important questions of peace or war were decided. The remains are upon a platform, on a rocky height, to the west of the Museum Hill, and to the south-west of the Areopagus. It is fronted with blocks of stone of great size. The stone pulpit, called the *Bemă*, is an elevation like an altar, where the orators harangued the people. This, with the steps leading to it, and the seats beneath it, are hewn out of the solid rock, and are in perfect preservation. Its area is more than twelve thousand square yards. Between the Pnyx and the Museum Hill is a place hewn out of the solid rock, called the tomb of Socrates—now filled with filth. At the base of the Museum Hill are four small dungeons, called the prisons of Socrates. That in which Socrates is said to have been confined, and to have drank the poisonous cup, had its entrance from above. A few steps were cut in the rock, whence a ladder was let down.

The Hill of the Museum, where Musæus is said to have sung, and, dying of old age, to have been buried, is nearly as high as the Acropolis. It stands south-west of the city. On the summit are the ruins of the monument of Philopappus. It is of the Roman architecture, and much defaced.

From the Hill of the Museum we ascended the Areopagus, or Hill of Mars, so called from the fact that Mars was the first who sat in judgment upon it. "Here the Areopagites, distinguished alike for their character, rank, and official dignity, sat as judges on a rocky hill in the open air, and in the dark, that the judges might not be influenced by seeing and knowing the accuser and the accused. Here Orestes was tried for matricide, and Socrates for theism. Here, too, the Apostle Paul delivered his magnificent address to the Athenian people."

From the Areopagus we walked out to the olive grove of Academia, close below the hill of Colonos, and about half a mile from the city. It is still known by the same name as it was in Plato's time, and is now a garden of roses—a fit place even for the modern student to repair for repose. A small monument stands on the summit of Colonos to the memory of a German who died in Athens. From this classic retreat we returned to our hotel, and enjoyed the sweet strains of martial music in the public grounds. King Otho and the Queen were present, and we had the pleasure of seeing them on horseback, their favorite amusement.

The following day, Messrs. Delano, Sharp, Lynde, Johnstone, and myself started for the field of Marathon—an excursion of ten hours. We went in a carriage as far as the village of Kevisia, where we had horses to meet us. The road to Marathon passes through a hilly, barren, and uninteresting country. We approached the broad plain from Vrana, where we had an excellent view of Negropont, the sea, and the entire plain of Marathon. While gazing on this renowned spot, I was strongly reminded of my Greek Professor in the Nashville University, who endeavored to impress upon the class the dates of the two great battles of Marathon and Salamis. Every day the question was asked, and we invariably missed. At last we wrote them on the wall of the recitation room, where they can be seen, probably, to this day.

I little thought at that time that it would ever be my privilege to rove over a country hallowed by so many early associations. But here I am, and if Mr. C. should ever ask me again about the field of Marathon, I will take as much pleasure in describing it to him, as he did in impressing the dates. The mounds where the Persians, Athenians, and Miltiades were buried are still plainly visible. Sharp and myself had a race from Vrana to the tomb of the Athenians. His horse fell just before reaching the mound, and I won the champagne. The plain is very extensive, completely hemmed in on all sides by mountains, except the ocean side, and beautifully cultivated.

"The mountains look on Marathon—
And Marathon looks on the sea;
And musing there an hour alone,
I dreamed that Greece might still be free,
For standing on the Persians' grave,
I could not deem myself a slave."

The same party visited Mount Pentelicus the next day. It is situated ten miles from Athens, and is 3,500 feet above the level of the sea. The road as far as the base of the mountain is very fine, and even the ascent is good, and not at all difficult. The marble is beautifully white, and the principal quarry now worked half-way up the mountain. There are several others in different parts, all bearing marks of the work of the ancient Athenians. There is a grotto here, once used for a chapel; the altar and figures of our Saviour are still to be seen. The view from Pentelicus is very extensive, embracing the field of Marathon, Athens, the Acropolis of Corinth, Salamis, Negropont, and Parnassus. While we were on the mountain, a French war steamer was practising in the little harbor where the great battle of Salamis was fought. The smoke and fire of the guns could be seen distinctly, but we could not hear the report. As I stood gazing with my glass at the livid flames issuing from her guns, I was forcibly reminded of that celebrated engagement, the history of which I used to dwell upon with wonder and admiration in my school-boy days.

Returning to the city very rapidly, we ascended Mount Lycabettus, situated in the suburbs, and crowned with the small church of St. George. It is higher than the Acropolis, and furnishes decidedly the best view of the plain, and the peculiarities of the physical form which distinguish Athens so remarkably from all other places.

Having somewhat a taste for politics, I frequently attended the sitting of the Greek Parliament. The building is quite plain, but sufficiently large and good to answer all purposes. In the lower House the walls are filled with the names of those who distinguished themselves in the late Revolution. I noticed in the collection the names of Lord Byron, Marco Bozzaris, etc. A member occupied the tribune when we were there last, who spoke in a strain of eloquence that is rarely heard in modern times. He spoke in an ardent and enthusiastic manner, reminding me forcibly of the orations of Demosthenes and the orators who harangued the Senate when Greece was in the zenith of her glory. Most of the members were dressed in their national costume, which I admire exceedingly, and sat with their *fez* on in the same manner as in the English Parliament. The Senate is a very small body, compared with the House, and the members are mostly old men who have distinguished themselves in the cause of their country. The people of Greece have very little confidence in the honesty of their representatives, and seem to regard King Otho as a young man of very little capacity.

While in Athens we were invited to a party at the Piræus, given by the Rev. Dr. Buel, an American missionary, where we met the two daughters of the celebrated Marco Bozzaris, and the *Maid of Athens*, now Mrs. Black. The young ladies were dressed in the Greek fashion; conversed fluently in English; and are every way fit representatives of the great Suliote chief. The readers of Byron will be shocked to learn that the *Maid of Athens* united her fortunes with an English policeman named Black, and is now the mother of a whole host of little Blacks. This is what you might term a step from the sublime to the ridiculous; but when she informed me that Byron was in love with her mother and dedicated his poetry to her when but a child, it palliated, in some measure, my disappointment, and I excused her for propagating the Black race.

The next day we visited the American missionary school, established by the Rev. Messrs. Hill and Robinson, in 1830. They went as the agents of the Episcopal Missionary Society, and have succeeded in building up a school that would reflect credit upon any country. This is certainly an ever-changing world. Athens was once the great centre of learning and the fine arts. Here Socrates and Plato and Aristotle taught, and Cicero went to study; and young America is paying back the debt which the world owes to the mother of science. From the school-room we repaired to Mr. Hill's residence, where we had the pleasure of meeting a number of American and English families, several old Greek Senators and their daughters, besides a number of strangers from different countries. Among the guests was the daughter of a Swedish Count, who married an Athenian woman. This young lady was just sweet sixteen, and without exception the most beautiful and fascinating creature that my eyes ever rested upon. Her form and features were Grecian, with the fair complexion and vivacity of the Swede. She spoke six languages with great fluency, and was just making her *début* in society. I fell desperately in love *of course*—and what was a little strange, my friend Johnstone, of South Carolina, found himself in the same interesting situation. I had experienced the feeling before, and wondered to myself how I ever became so deeply enamored with a creature so different in every respect from the Count's daughter. Johnstone, however, seemed so earnest in his attentions that I yielded the field to him, and passed most of the evening with the adopted daughter of Mr. Hill, called Elizabeth, of Crete, who is not quite so beautiful in person, but in point of intellect and qualities of the heart, she has no superior. Hereafter, when I think of the classic city, the images of these two bright creatures will come vividly before me, and I will long to be once more in Greece.

LETTER FIFTY-FIVE.

CORINTH.

Adieu to Athens—Tomb of Themistocles—Islands of Egina, Hydra, and Spezzia—Gulf of Nauplia—Fortress of Palamede—Itch Kali—The Lion Monument—Ruins of Tirynthus—Ruins of Argos—Ruins of Mycenæ—Ruins of Nemea—Corinth—Gulf of Lepanto.

AGREEABLY to arrangement, a large party of English and American travellers assembled at the Piræus to embark for the Morea. The morning sun was shining most beautifully, shedding a halo of light over the marble ruins of the Acropolis, and presenting to the eye a picture of rare sublimity. As we moved over the plain of Attica, I stood up in the carriage and watched the dear old Athens, with the same feelings that agitate the lover's bosom when he bids good-by to the idol of his heart. Farewell, mother of Science, farewell! My eyes will never look upon your temples again, but the image of the mind will endure for ever.

Soon after leaving the Piræus we saw the moleheads to which the ancients attached a chain to prevent the entrance of hostile ships, and also the remains of the tomb of Themistocles, near the water's edge, and in sight of the scene of his glory. The foundations of the wall built by Themistocles are still visible.

About twenty miles from the Piræus is the beautiful island of Egina. We ran close to it, and had a fine view of the remains of the temple of Jupiter Panhellenius, situated six miles distant from the port.

The next island of importance was that of Hydra. One of the Boudouri family was on board, and gave me a very interesting account of the history of this island. It is extremely barren, but the inhabitants by industry and skill in navigation have built up a town at once beautiful and flourishing. View it on a summer's evening by moonlight, and it is one of the most magnificent scenes imaginable. The white houses hanging in the form of an amphitheatre upon a steep mountain, then appear like a mass of snow; and the lights sparkling in the distance from the open windows "show like stars of gold on a silver ground." The glorious share that this little island has taken in the regeneration of Greece has brought it conspicuously into notice, and to the latest posterity the brave Hydriotes will live the watchword of freedom.

Passing between the island of Spezzia and the Morea, we entered the deep and beautiful gulf of Nauplia to the town of the same name. Most of our party remained all night on the steamer; but Johnstone and myself went to a hotel in preference. As soon as our luggage was deposited, we took a walk up to the fortress of the Palamede, situated on a lofty and precipitous rock, seven hundred and fifty feet above the level of the sea. It is inaccessible on all sides, except at one point to the east, where it is connected with a range of barren, rocky hills, and was surnamed the Gibraltar of Greece. The view from the fortress is surpassingly beautiful—embracing the plains of Argos, Mycenæ, and the distant mountains of Sparta. The second fortress, that of Itch Kali, is built on a peninsular rock, rising above the town, at the foot of the Palamede. The summit is encompassed by walls, whose foundations are the only traces of antiquity in the immediate vicinity. Numerous batteries protect it on all sides. The Venetians attempted to make it an island, by cutting through the rock and letting the sea flow round it, in which they partially succeeded. Nauplia was for a time the capital of Greece, and improved rapidly during the stay of the Regency, but as soon as the Court was moved to Athens it fell back to its original importance.

Returning to the hotel, (which is without exception the filthiest I have ever seen,) I amused myself by smoking an old pipe belonging to the landlord, watching the soldiers in the square, and examining an engraving of Gen. Jackson, which was given to the father of the present proprietor by the captain of one of the vessels sent to Greece during Jackson's administration to furnish the revolutionists with arms. Oh that we could have passed that night at the Hermitage in the fair State of Tennessee, instead of fighting Greek fleas at the miserable locanda at Nauplia!

Early the next morning our friends who remained on the boat came ashore, and we all started together on horseback for the site of the city of Argos, now occupied by a village of the same name. Just outside the walls of Nauplia there is a large lion cut out of the solid rock in the hillside, some fifteen or twenty feet from the ground. I learned from Mr. Boudouri that it was cut by order of the government to perpetuate the memory of the Germans who fell in the late war. About half a mile further, on a slight hill in the plain, are the ruins of Tirynthus, or Tiryus, built for Proctus, by the Cydopians, architects from Lycia, about the year 1379 B. C. Some of the walls of the citadel are nearly perfect, exhibiting the best specimens of the military architecture of the heroic ages, being generally twenty-five feet thick. Proceeding rapidly over a fine turnpike road, we soon reached the village of Argos, seven miles from Nauplia. As this place possesses nothing of interest, I will allude only to the historical localities. The Acropolis, anciently called Larissa, occupies the summit of a rocky hill, and still preserves, amidst the ruined masonry, some remains of antiquity. At the foot of the hill are the remains of the theatre. It was very large, and the seats that now remain in a perfect state were cut out of the solid rock in the hillside. Above the theatre are the brick remains of a temple of Venus. Some parts of the ancient walls of Argos are still to be seen.

From Argos we turned our course towards the Gulf of Lepanto. Before entering the mountain pass, we left the road at the village of Krabata, to examine the ruins of Mycenæ, once the capital of Agamemnon, built by Perseus 1300 B. C., and destroyed by the Argives, after the Persian war, 466 B. C. Near the citadel our guide pointed out the Spelia, or Treasury of Athens, commonly called the tomb of Agamemnon. The building was constructed under the slope of the hill towards the Rema, or ravine of the torrent. It is an immense subterranean dome, nearly in a perfect state, and of curious workmanship. It consists of two chambers; the diameter of the dome of the first is forty-seven feet six inches, the height fifty feet. The inner chamber, which is rudely excavated in the rock with an arch-shaped roof, connects with the main apartment by a small door. Above the entrance of the door of the first chamber is a triangular window, and the entrance itself is roofed by a single slab of stone, nine yards long and nearly six wide. An old Greek was sitting down at the door, attending his sheep and goats which were in possession of the tomb. Crossing a deep ravine, we soon reached the walls of Mycenæ, and entered the capital of Agamemnon through the great gate at the north-west end of the town. This gate is the most perfect of all the remains. It is approached by a passage fifty feet long and thirty wide, formed by two immense walls. The gate is ten feet in height, and in the lintel are marks of bolts and hinges, and the pavement contains ruts caused by chariot wheels. The width of the top of the door is nine and a half feet. It was formed of two massive uprights, covered with a third block fifteen feet long, four feet wide, and six feet seven inches high in the middle, but diminishing at the two ends. Upon the soffit stands a triangular block of gray limestone, twelve feet long, ten feet wide, and two feet thick, upon the face of which are represented in low relief two lions, standing on their hind legs, on each side of a round pillar or altar, upon which they rest their fore paws; the column becomes broader towards the top, and is surmounted by a capital, formed of a row of circles, inclosed between two parallel fillets. This is the celebrated Gate of the Lions. The entire circuit of the citadel still exists, and in some places the walls are fifteen or twenty feet high.

From Mycenæ, we passed the ruins of the village of Phytæ, through a deep glen or pass, guarded by soldiers, to a solitary country house, where we stopped and partook of the old Greek's cheer. While here we were overtaken by Mr. Wise and family, the English Minister at Athens. They were also going to Corinth, and we volunteered our services to protect the young ladies from the dangers of the road.

Soon after leaving the little hamlet, we descended into a broad plain in the centre of which are the ruins of Nemea. The temple of Jupiter still retains some of its original appearance. Several standing columns and the broken fragments of the rest exhibit the plan and style of the temple. The form and decorations are Doric, with nearly Ionic proportions. The breadth of the temple was sixty-five feet, and the length more than double. At a short distance from the temple are other remains of the Doric order. Traces of the Nemean Theatre are to be found at the foot of a hill not far distant. There is also an old fountain on the side of the hill, and the caves supposed to be those of the Nemean Lion.

Two hours' ride from Nemea brought us in sight of the Acropolis of Corinth and the Gulf of Lepanto. One half hour more, and we were seated in a little locanda, about the size of a small log cabin in the West. There are but few remains of any thing in Corinth. The ruins of two buildings of the Roman town still exhibit, 1st. A large mass of brick work on the northern side, probably a part of one of the baths built by Hadrian; 2d. An ampitheatre excavated in the rock, on the eastern side of the modern town. Seven Doric columns, the remains of ancient Corinth, are still erect in the centre of the modern town. The Acre-Corinthus is eighteen hundred feet high, and considered the strongest fortification in Greece. The view from this point is very extensive and beautiful, embracing the Acropolis at Athens, Mount Parnassus, the entire gulf, besides numerous other places renowned in history.

The morning after our arrival at Corinth, we rode on horseback to a little village situated at the head of the gulf, where we joined a large party who crossed the isthmus, and embarked in a small Austrian steamer for Patras.

LETTER FIFTY-SIX.

TRIESTE.

Voyage from Corinth to Trieste—Patras—The Ionian Islands—Austrian Steamers—City of Trieste—Separation from Friends, etc.

WE performed the trip from Corinth to Patras in the night, and the first objects that arrested our attention in the morning were the tall peaks of Parnassus, St. Andrew's Church, and the town of Missolonghi, where Lord Byron breathed his last. Our captain informed us that he would remain in the harbor until the afternoon, which gave us an opportunity of going ashore and examining the place. Although Patras was the first town that suffered during the Revolution, it is now one of the most flourishing cities in the Morea. The new streets are wide and regular, running at right angles to each other, and several are built with arches. Its present prosperity is the result of the cultivation in the neighborhood of the dwarf vine, called *Uva passa di Corinto*, or Currants, which renders the greater part of the plain of Patras the most valuable soil in Europe. The church of St. Andrew is held in great veneration, as it is supposed to contain the bones of the Apostle, and also the stone which tradition connects with his martyrdom. The castle commands a very beautiful view of the vast bay, Mount Panachaicum, the distant summits of Zante and Cephalonia, Castle of Tornese, Mount Skopo, Mountain of Acarmania and Etolia, the Straits of Rhium, etc.

Soon after leaving Patras, some of our machinery gave way, and we were compelled to run to Zante with one wheel. Fortunately the sea was perfectly smooth, and we reached the island in safety in thirty-six hours. Zante, the ancient Zacynthus, is so celebrated for its beauty and fertility, as to be called the "*Fior di Levante.*" It is sixty miles in circumference, fifteen miles from Chiarenza, in the Morea, and ten miles from Cephalonia. The population amounts to forty thousand persons, of whom eighteen thousand reside in the city of the same name. The greater part of the island is formed by an extensive plain, which produces great quantities of currants. The town is the largest and most flourishing of all the Ionian seaports. Its extreme breadth does not exceed three hundred yards, but it extends along the coast for a great distance. Castle Hill, which rises precipitously immediately behind the city, is strongly fortified. The houses and streets of Zante are very much after the fashion of the Italian cities, and some of the churches are very fine. When we were there it was *Festa* day, and most of the citizens were in the streets enjoying themselves in various ways. Great quantities of mutton were roasted in the same manner as we do at our barbecues in America, and the people seemed to eat as though they were unaccustomed to meat every day.

At Zante we took the steamer Mahmoud, from Constantinople, and ran close to the islands of Cephalonia and Ithæa, and the coast of Albania, to the city of Corfu. Here the passengers all went ashore in small boats to see the celebrated fortifications. Quite an amusing occurrence took place as we were leaving the steamer. A German, who is attached to the Austrian Legation at Constantinople, stepped into our boat with a young girl who, the ladies thought, looked rather too *fast.* Of course they were very indignant, and one of the gentlemen of the party undertook to carry out, by loud words and threats, what the ladies considered an insult. I thought at one time that we would have a general *mêlée* in the little boat; but the difficulty was adjusted on the quay. Tne German apologized, and said he did not know it was a private boat. I enjoyed the fun exceedingly, and felt disposed to take sides with the German, because he was alone against six Americans. Corfu, the ancient Corcyra, is the most considerable of the Ionian islands. The Lord High Commissioner and the Parliament of the Ionian Islands have their head-quarters there; and the city, from the number of English residents, and the garrison, looks quite English. It was really a treat to meet so many that could speak our language after more than a year's absence from Great Britain.

Corfu is beautifully situated near the centre of the island, on the shore facing the continent. It is strongly fortified, and has withstood many sieges. Being at the mouth of the Adriatic, it gives England, in conjunction with Malta and Gibraltar, the entire command of the Mediterranean. The bay is completely land-locked, surrounded on three sides by the island, and on the other by the mainland, with only narrow exits to the north and south, not visible from the harbor itself. The high coast of Albania—the fortifications of the island of Vido—the citadel built on two lofty rocks extending into the sea —the palace of the Lord High Commissioner—the shady park filled with brave Highlanders, clad in their native uniform—and the distant mountains of the continent, form a panorama of great beauty.

Leaving Corfu, we proceeded on our way up the beautiful Adriatic, close to the barren and thinly populated coasts of Albania and Dalmatia. The sea was as smooth as a mirror, and the air so balmy that we passed our time principally on the deck. The day after leaving Corfu was Sabbath, and we had the Episcopal service read in the ladies' cabin by an English clergyman. The English, like the Catholics, always carry their prayer-books when they travel, something that we Americans, particularly the gentlemen, usually neglect.

We entered the small harbor of Trieste early the following morning. The captain, in compliment to Mr. Morris, our Chargé d'Affaires at Naples, hoisted the United States flag, and we cast anchor in the deep waters of the Austrian bay under the folds of the stars and stripes. And here let me bestow a compliment upon Austria which she richly deserves, and which all concede, save the English, viz.: That her steamers are the best in the Mediterranean, and her officers the most meritorious.

Trieste (Tergeste of the Romans) is the most flourishing city in the Austrian dominions. It owes its prosperity to the Emperor Charles VI., who, in 1719, made it a *free port*, and to Maria Theresa, who fostered it with her patronage. It has completely supplanted Venice, "the city of the sea," has a population of nearly one hundred thousand, and engrosses nearly the entire trade of the Adriatic.

The *Corso* is the principal business street, and will compare well in point of beauty and activity with any street on the continent; and some of the palaces of the rich merchants built in the Venetian style are really superb. The inhabitants of Trieste are a motley race, derived from all parts of the world. The Italian language is principally spoken.

This is the place of separation from friends with whom I have travelled for many months in Africa and Asia. Parting with those we regard is always painful. I never say *farewell* without a pang; but that sad word has been used so often, under circumstances far more affecting, that I can give it utterance now with comparative complacency. Some leave for Italy's sunny clime, some for the snow-clad mountains of Switzerland, some for the gay city of Paris, and some for the capital of Austria. We have passed many joyous days together, in countries replete with every thing calculated to awaken the highest attributes of the heart and the mind; and hereafter, when I bring to memory the past, my old companions will be with me again.

LETTER FIFTY-SEVEN.

VIENNA.

Departure from Trieste—Cave of Adelsberg—Gratz—Erzherzog Karl—Vienna Tailor—Austrian Money—Police Office—Volks-garten.

AFTER examining the quays, streets, and churches of Trieste, Johnstone and myself started in the diligence for Laybach, the terminus of the Vienna railroad. From the top of the lofty hill just behind

Trieste, we had an excellent view of the city and the Adriatic. It is a beautiful prospect, and as we moved slowly up the serpentine road, I looked mournfully upon the blue sea, and endeavored in vain to extend my vision to the dreamy city of Venice. I love Venice, not alone for its historical associations and unique beauty, but because some of the happiest moments of my life have been passed in her palaces and on her canals. My stay there appears more like a dream than a reality, and if the residue of my life could be as the time passed in Venice, I would not ask a better future. But away with such thoughts—we were in a lumbering diligence on a turnpike road, running through a broken and barren country, similar to that in the region of the Mammoth Cave in Kentucky.

About one mile from the village of Adelsberg is the cavern known by the name of the *Grotto of Adelsberg*, which is probably the largest subterranean passage in Europe. It is four miles in extent, and the formations upon the whole are more interesting than those of the Mammoth Cave. The chambers are not so extensive but better preserved, having been strictly guarded against the hand of the visitor, by the officers of the government. The entrance is in the face of a cliff below a ruined castle. Here the river Poik, after winding through the plain, sinks into the cave, and may be seen about one hundred and eighty yards from the entrance, by the light of the taper, struggling to make its way through the devious passages of the deep abyss. Like the Mammoth Cave, you enter a small hole closed by an iron gate, leading into a long, low gallery, to a vast hall one hundred feet high and more than three hundred feet long, called the *Dom*. This is the only part of the cavern known down to 1819, when a laborer working in the cave accidentally broke through a screen of stalactite, and discovered that this was "but the vestibule of one of the most magnificent of all the temples which Nature has built for herself in the region of the night." Rude steps cut in the rock lead down one side of this chamber to the river, which is crossed by a wooden bridge; and the opposite side is scaled in a like manner. You then pass through a range of chambers, varying in size, but by far the most interesting from the variety, beautiful purity, and quantity of their stalactites and stalagmites. The singular shapes of some of the formations have given rise to various names applied by the guides, according to the likeness which they discover in them to real objects, such as the throne, the pulpit, the butcher's shop, the two hearts, the bell, which resounds almost like metal, the curtain, a curious mass, about an inch thick, spread out in such a manner as to represent perfectly a piece of drapery, and beautifully transparent. The last and most remarkable chamber is called Mount Calvary, from a collection of fallen rocks in the centre, incrusted and partly cemented together by stalactitic matter. This chamber is very high, and the formations present a singular variety of beauty. On Whit Monday one of the chambers is converted into a ball-room, and the peasant lads and lasses assemble for miles around, and make the regions of darkness re-echo with sounds of mirth and music.

Returning to the village of Adelsberg, we proceeded in the diligence to Laybach, where we took the railroad for the Emperor's City, passing through Gratz and a section of country remarkably beautiful and fertile. At the Vienna gate our luggage was searched with more than ordinary care, but they failed to discover any contraband articles. We profited by a previous difficulty in Lombardy, and pocketed our weapons, which the Austrians seem to have a peculiar disposition to find in the possession of Americans.

We drove to the Erzherzog Karl, (Archduke Charles,) a fashionable hotel situated in the old city near the Cathedral and main street Grabbin. This hotel is conducted on a magnificent scale, and they charge a magnificent price. So much for being fashionable. The first question we asked of the landlord the next morning was suggested by the contrast between our dress and that of our neighbors at the breakfast table. We had been out of the reach of civilization so long that we had fallen far behind the fashions, and looked so rusty that we felt out of place, and hurried, after a hasty meal, to a *Grabbin* tailor, where we selected a wardrobe suitable, as we thought, for our purposes. In two days we were *comme il faut*, and felt prepared to meet the gaze of the most fastidious Brummell of the Erzherzog Karl. After changing our garb we hardly knew each other, and were frequently heard to exclaim, Johnstone, is that you? Yes! Mac, is that you? All this however was at the expense of our purse, which was well nigh empty when we took leave of the Grabbin tailor. Every thing is extremely dear in Vienna, much more so than any place we have visited. They attribute their high prices to the paper currency now circulating in Austria, valued at from 25 to 30 per cent. less than silver.

From our tailor's we proceeded to the police office for the purpose of procuring permission to reside a stated time in the city, for which we paid one florin each. A number of questions of an inquisitorial character were put to us, all of which we answered without hesitation, having no plots or conspiracies against the Emperor of Austria. The country has been in a state of siege ever since the troubles in 1848, and the authorities deem it necessary to preserve the most rigid scrutiny over the movements and actions of foreigners. Without permit under the seal of government we would be liable to incarceration at any moment, and the bare mention of jail in Austria makes a foreigner tremble in his shoes.

Being armed and equipped according to the law, we accompanied some friends to the Volksgarten, (people's garden,) which is one of the most frequented places of summer resort in Vienna. Two bands were playing when we entered, and both the best of their kind in all Germany. One was the Emperor's military band, and the other the band of young Strauss, son of the celebrated composer. I am not skilled in music, but somewhat of an *amateur*, and can safely say that these two bands are the best in the world. The Germans seem to have a natural fondness for the harmony of sweet sounds, and they have attained a perfection in music that no other people can arrive at. This place is resorted to principally by females, who dress in their best for the purpose of attracting the attention of the *fast* men and strangers. The garden is provided with two handsome coffee-houses, and a good restaurant, where you can sip the delightful beverage and enjoy the sweet strains of music at once. One portion is called *Paridiesgarten*, in which is a building copied with slight variations from the Temple of Theseus, at Athens, and contains Canova's group of Theseus killing a Centaur. Napoleon intended to decorate the arch of the Simplon at Milan with this fine piece of sculpture; but, falling into the hands of the Austrians after the wars, it was conveyed hither, and placed in the building constructed for its reception.

LETTER FIFTY-EIGHT.

VIENNA.

Vienna within the walls—The Glacis—Cathedral of St. Stephen—Capuchins—Imperial Vault—Augustines—Canova's Monument—Imperial Palace—Antiquities—Minerals—Museum of Natural History—Imperial Library—Jewel Office—Imperial Regalia—The Emperor's Stables—Opera, etc., etc.

UNLIKE any other city in Europe, the capital of Austria is divided into two distinct parts, called the old and new city. The old is strongly fortified with a wall and fosse that forms almost a complete circle, and separated from the new by a broad street, and the Glacis, which is beautifully ornamented with shade trees, and constitutes one of the most delightful promenades about the city. I propose in this communication to confine myself exclusively to Vienna within the walls, and leave the outside objects for another letter.

The first place of interest to the stranger is the Cathedral of St. Stephen, from the summit of which is furnished an excellent view of the suburbs, (which are far more extensive than the city itself,) the windings of the Danube, the Prater, and the four battle-fields of Napoleon, viz.: Lobau, Wagram, Aspern, and Essling. This cathedral is regarded by architects as the most perfect specimen of the Gothic order in Europe. The tower is particularly beautiful and exquisite in its proportions, diminishing gradually from its base to its summit in regularly retreating arches and buttresses. Half-way up the tower is the station of the *Fire Watch* for the city. "Each window-sill in this apartment has a provision for fastening a telescope, whose movements are marked by a stand on which it is placed, upon graduated circles placed horizontally and vertically. Registers have been constructed for each window, so that the telescope having been pointed to any object, and the corresponding horizontal and vertical numbers upon the graduated scale read off, the name of the object, whether building or street, is ascertained by reference to them. Thus the exact spot where a fire may break out is ascertained, and the intelligence is instantly conveyed to those below by inclosing a ticket inscribed with the particulars in a hollow brass ball, which is dropped down a pipe leading to the bottom of the tower. Thence it is transmitted to the fire-offices." The largest bell in the tower was made of one hundred and thirty pieces of cannon taken from the Turks after

15

their repulse from the walls. It weighs three hundred and eighty cwt. The roof is very steep, and covered with colored tiles, forming a colossal mosaic of the Austrian Eagle. The interior presents many beautiful specimens of Gothic architecture, but looks dusky and gloomy. At the time we made our visit, a great number of people from the country occupied the seats (most of them asleep) waiting to be confirmed. They entered the city in processions, with a man in front of each body bearing a large cross with a figure of our Saviour nailed upon it, and blood trickling from the wounds to represent his sufferings.

From the Cathedral, we went to the Capuchin Church, remarkable only for containing the burial vault of the Imperial family. It is shown by torchlight, under the guidance of a Capuchin brother. I counted about seventy metal coffins, some of which are very magnificent. Those of Maria Theresa, her husband Francis, and her son Joseph II., are the finest. Those placed there recently are perfectly plain.

The church of the Augustines was next in order. The chief ornament of this church is the beautiful monument of the Archduchess Christina of Saxe Teschen, by Canova, one of his most successful works. In the Todten-Kapelle, on one side of the aisle, are the tombs of the Emperor Leopold II.; of the great Austrian General Daun, erected by Maria Theresa; and of Van Swieten her physician, the person to whom Austria is indebted for the present system of universal education. In the Loretto Chapel we saw through a glass in the iron door the hearts of the Imperial family, preserved in silver urns.

From this gloomy vault we repaired to the abode of the living, where all the mirth, pomp and parade of poor frail humanity finds willing votaries. The Imperial Palace is an ancient building of various dates and irregular structure, and is not imposing from its architecture, but considerable extent. It consists of three courts, or quadrangles. The oldest part dates from the year 1210. In front of the palace is a large lawn, and extensive gardens. In the court called Josephplatz, formed by the new part of the palace, is a large and well executed equestrian statue of the Emperor Joseph II. It was erected to his memory by the late Emperor Francis, and is a creditable performance of the sculptor *Zauner*. In an adjoining court called Franzenplatz there is a colossal bronze statue of the Emperor Francis, erected by his son. The expression of the venerable sovereign in the act of blessing his people, with the motto "*Amorum meum populis meis*," is fine, but the drapery is clumsy and the limbs are awkward. It is the work of Marchesi of Milan. In the buildings connected with the palace are to be seen the most valuable cabinets of Vienna, a brief notice of which may not be uninteresting.

The Cabinet of Antiquities contains a very extensive collection of valuable curiosities, among which are several cameos of great size. One is "The Apotheosis of Augustus," an onyx eight and three-quarter inches in diameter. It is considered one of the finest in the world, and cost twelve thousand ducats. Others of Alexander the Great, Rozana, and the head of Tiberius are also remarkable. Here also is an agate dish twenty-eight and a half inches in diameter, which is so valuable as to have formed part of the dowry of Mary of Burgundy, wife of the Emperor Maximilian. Another very curious thing is the celebrated *salt cellar* made for Francis I. by Benvenuto Cellini. Twelve thousand Greek vases, and one hundred and thirty-four thousand ancient coins and medals, add to the value of this collection.

The Cabinet of Minerals surpasses in many departments every other cabinet in Europe, and is well arranged. Amongst the objects that attracted my attention particularly was a precious opal, the largest known, from Czerwenitza, near Kaschau, weight seventeen ounces. Choice specimens of chrysolite, from Greenland; wavellite, from Brazil; Styrian arragonite, and other rare minerals; also, a fine collection of diamond crystals, some splendid specimens of emerald, and the most extensive and complete assemblage existing of aërolites, or stones which have fallen from the sky in different parts of the world. One of the largest, a mass seventy-one pounds in weight, fell in 1751, near Agram. Near it I observed, much to my surprise, pieces from Davidson and Cocke counties, Tennessee, besides various specimens of coal and other valuable minerals from our State, contributed by my old Professor Gerard Troost, late of Nashville University. We have a larger showing in this cabinet than any of our sister States; and if our citizens would only turn their attention to the exhaustless wealth of our mountains, Tennessee in a few years would be more desirable than the gold regions of the new El Dorado on the shores of the Pacific. In this collection may be mentioned the large bouquet of precious stones, set in a manner to resemble various flowers, and made for Maria Theresa. It is extravagantly beautiful.

The Museum of Natural History, founded by Francis I. and at his private expense, is one of the most extensive and interesting collections of the kind in Europe. The ornithological department is very complete, containing in some instances six or eight specimens of the same bird, in order to show the change of plumage from youth to old age, and the difference between male and female feathers.

The Imperial Library contains one of the most valuable collections in the world. It owes its origin to the private collection of books formed by the Emperor Frederic III., and increased by successive contributions of later sovereigns. It contains nearly three hundred thousand volumes, and upwards of sixteen thousand MSS.; also three hundred thousand prints, embracing some of the finest specimens of the art. Amongst the curiosities may be mentioned a tablet of bronze, on which is engraved a Roman Act of Parliament, forbidding Bacchanalian ceremonies, dated in the year of Rome 507; the celebrated Tabula Peutingeriana, a map of the Roman empire in the fourth century; Charlemagne's psalm book, MS., in gold letters; a roll of Mexican hieroglyphics, painted on deer skin, and presented by Cortez to Charles V.; fragments of a MS. of Genesis; silver capitals on parchment, besides a great number of other things too numerous to mention.

The Imperial Jewel Office is inferior to several others in Europe, yet contains many precious stones and valuable antiques belonging to royalty. The regalia of Charlemagne, *said* to have been taken from his grave at Aix-la-Chapelle, and used at the coronation of the German emperors for many centuries, consists of a crown ornamented with uncut stones, a sceptre, orb, Dalmatic sword, gloves and shoes; the crown and sceptre of Rudolph II., the crown, sceptre, and robes worn by Napoleon at his coronation in Milan as King of Lombardy, constitute the chief attractions of this collection. Among the sacred relics I observed the holy spear and nails of the cross; a tooth of John the Baptist; a piece of the coat of St. John the Evangelist; several links of the chains of Saints Peter, Paul, and John; a piece of the true cross; a piece of the table-cloth used at the Last Supper, etc. Pre-eminent amongst the precious stones I noticed the Florentine diamond, worn and lost by Charles the Bold, at the battle of Granson, and found by a Swiss, who sold it for five florins. It weighs 133 carats, and an emerald brought from the Holy Land by the Duke of Austria, weighing 2,980 carats.

Connected with the Royal Palace, are the rooms containing the state carriages, royal stables, and riding school. We counted more than one hundred carriages, many of which are very ancient. The state carriages look very grand and costly, but heavy and uncomfortable. The sleigh in which Maria Theresa used to drive in also is exhibited, and a light buggy made in the United States for the London Exhibition. The horses kept at the palace are of the Spanish breed, and used exclusively in the riding school, which is a large room with galleries, and the floor covered with loose sand. The riding-master was present when we entered, dressed in full uniform, teaching four young princes how to sit in the saddle, and hold the reins. To a man from Tennessee it looked rather ridiculous, and I venture the assertion that many of our cotton-headed boys would mount the most fiery steed in the stable without saddle or bridle, and ride him to death. The grand stable opposite the palace contains more than six hundred of the best looking horses that I ever saw, not excepting the Sultan's at Constantinople, or the Royal Mews in England. The building is a perfect palace, finer even than the White House at Washington. The troughs are made of variegated marble, the racks of iron, and the floor covered with plaited straw. This stable is guarded day and night by soldiers, and if a horse is taken sick he is immediately attended.

The Opera House of this city is a very handsome building, and the company well sustained by government patronage. We frequently saw the young Emperor, his mother, father, and brother, occupying the box appropriated for the royal family. They seem devoted to amusements, and applaud the performances with as much earnestness as those who occupy the pit.

LETTER FIFTY-NINE.

VIENNA.

The Suburbs of Vienna—Belvidere Palace—Ambras Museum—Litchtenstein Picture Gallery —Picture Gallery of Prince Eszterhazy—Palace of Luxemburg—Village of Baden—Schönbrunn—Beer Halls—The Prater—A Russian Bear, etc.

In my last letter, I confined my observations to the objects of interest in the old part of the city, which is still the most fashionable and desirable quarter for the stranger to locate in, because it contains the best hotels, and all that pertains to royalty. The suburbs, however, are far more beautiful and extensive. The streets are wide and clean, the houses high and well built, and the stores arranged with great taste and beauty. Indeed, I admire the appearance of Vienna more than any city in western Europe—not excepting even Paris, which Americans generally consider the most beautiful and charming spot on the continent.

The first place we visited in the suburbs, was the Belvidere Palace, built by Prince Eugene of Savoy, who resided in it during the latter years of his life. There are two buildings, termed the Upper and Lower Belvidere. The lower is a very old building, now undergoing repairs. The Ambras collection of antiquities is in this palace, containing a number of antique sculptures, one of the best armories in Europe, besides many other curiosities too numerous to mention. One very remarkable curiosity in this collection, is an immense pair of antlers in the trunk of a large tree, which has grown completely around them, so that only the points project. The Upper Belvidere is a very extensive and handsome building, situated on a hill, and commands a fine view of Vienna and its environs. The interior is well furnished, and filled with a choice collection of paintings, embracing some by Raphael, Vandyck, Rubens, etc. Having occupied nearly a day in examining this palace, we concluded our programme by going through the Litchtenstein and Esterhazy Galleries. The former contains about fifteen hundred pictures, among which are valuable specimens of almost every school of art, and many of the very first excellence. The Esterhazy Gallery contains the rarest collection of the Spanish school to be found out of Spain —also some beautiful statuary and engravings.

The following day we visited the Palace of Luxemburg, situated about eight miles from Vienna. A beautiful avenue extends from the city to the palace, making it a pleasant drive in the heat of summer. This palace was the favorite summer retreat of Maria Theresa, and, although very plain and unattractive to one who has seen nearly all the palaces of Europe, it is yet interesting on account of its associations. The grounds are very extensive, and beautifully laid out, containing running streams, lakes, water-falls, Chinese, Grecian and Swiss cottages, etc. On an island, in the centre of one of the lakes, is an old castle, filled with all manner of curiosities. The first room is used for the armory—among which is that of the Emperor Charles V. I tried on his helmet, which is beautifully worked in bas-reliefs, representing the siege of Troy. The collection of weapons taken from the Turks is also very curious. The second room is in the rotunda style, containing the statues of the various Emperors of Austria. We were then conducted through a number of apartments containing representations of tournaments on stamped leather, and painted glass windows, representing the Golden Fleece. Connected with this old castle is a dungeon, and place where prisoners were tried. The judges sat in a circular tower, above the dungeon, and the poor victim was drawn up on a stick, tied to the end of a rope, and nothing but his head allowed to be seen, which was drawn through a small hole made for the purpose. Here the unfortunate offender was compelled to sit on a small stick, with an open dungeon many feet below him, until the cruel judges pronounced his fate. Thank God, the days when such barbarous practices were tolerated have passed away for ever even in Austria. As we crossed one of the rustic bridges, our guide gave a whistle, and in an instant a thousand fish, of all sizes, rushed towards us, to get the bread which they are accustomed to receive from visitors. A little farther we were shown the place where they formerly held their tournaments. The judge's stand, and lodges for the spectators, are also ornamented with frescoes. The interior is covered with loose sand, and is used, at the present day, for exhibitions, to gratify the taste of royalty.

From Luxemburg we drove to the pretty little village of Baden, celebrated for its warm baths, and a great place of holiday resort for the Viennese. After examining the baths, we drove to the beautiful valley of Helen, near by, where we saw the ruins of several old castles, and enjoyed some of the loveliest scenery in Austria. On our return, we had an excellent dinner at one of the hotels in Baden. The table was set in a beautiful arbor of flowers, and the place so inviting, that we remained until William, our guide, informed us that we would be late in getting into the city. We passed through the valley of Brühl, and the village of Modling, on our return, which is remarkable for its enchanting scenery; and just before entering the city, William pointed out the *spinning Cross*, about which there is a tradition of a lady who sat there until her lover returned from the wars.

The following day we drove to the Palace of Schönbrunn, the Emperor's summer residence. It is about two miles from Vienna, and was begun as a hunting seat for the Emperor Mathias, by Fischer, of Erlach, and finished by Maria Theresa. The interior is well furnished, and contains in the collection of paintings the portraits of Maria Theresa and Maria Antoinette. This palace was occupied by Napoleon in 1809, when the treaty of Schönbrunn was signed there, and his son the Duke of Reichstadt, who died there at the age of twenty-one, in the same apartment in the left wing overlooking the garden, and on the same bed, it is said, which his father had occupied. The place in the window where Strapps, the German student, shot at Napoleon, is shown, and also the grave of the rash youth. The gardens behind the palace are very extensive, and laid out in straight walks; long avenues trimmed and clipped like hedges, to a length of fifty or sixty feet, in the French style, and ornamented with statuary and fountains. The Gloriette, a temple with a colonnade of pillars, situated on an eminence back of the palace, furnishes an admirable view from its summit of Vienna and the surrounding country. There is also a Botanic Garden and Menagerie connected with the establishment. Just outside of the garden gate is the beautiful little village of Heitzing, where the Viennese congregate on Sundays and holidays for amusement. It is composed chiefly of villas and country houses, and in the churchyard I noticed the monument of Baroness Pillersdorf by Canova.

At the Casino of Dommeyer, we had an excellent dinner, in a room magnificently fitted up, and in which more than a thousand persons were dining, and listening to the strains of Strauss's band.

Returning to the city, we stopped at two or three large Beer Halls, where the laboring classes assemble to drink beer and smoke pipes. It is an amusing scene to watch how they enjoy their favorite beverage, and to listen to the good-humored remarks and honest jokes perpetrated on such occasions. Each establishment has a neat garden filled with small tables, at which it is not uncommon to see a German drink ten or a dozen mugs of beer at a sitting, and smoke twice as many pipes of tobacco. After tea we attended one of the balls for which Vienna is celebrated, and which certainly repays a stranger for going. The women generally are very unattractive, but dance and waltz a little faster than any people I ever saw. In length of stride I yield to no one, but in waltzing with a German woman I proved rather a *slow coacher*, for in an effort to keep time, I lost my balance and drew my partner with me to the floor, much to the amusement of the by-standers. Fortunately they took me to be a Russian, which palliated the matter somewhat, for I disliked the idea of risking the reputation acquired by our countrymen of being equal to any thing.

The next evening we procured an open carriage and drove out to the Prater, the Hyde Park of Vienna, only far superior to the pride of London. It consists of a series of low and partly wooded islands, formed by arms of the Danube, which separate from the main trunk to rejoin it lower down. The Prater is very extensive—contains a large number of deer—and is the favorite place for walking, riding, and driving. On our return we met the Queen driving in a beautiful light carriage drawn by four bays in the postillion style.

While in London we did not anticipate visiting Russia, and consequently did not procure the Russian *visé* on our passports, which rendered it necessary for us to call on the Czar's Ambassador. We made him four visits, but failed to accomplish our wishes at last. The first time we happened to be *three minutes* too late. The second time we had an interview with the *Bear*, and he informed us that *animals* of his nature would not recognise Americans unless endorsed by their Representative. It so happened that our Minister was on a tour in Italy, and we had to get a note from his Secretary, saying that we were good and peaceable citizens. Thinking that we had things right, we made our third visit, and were informed by the *Bear* that he did not recognise the act of a *cub*, and would not *visé* our passports without the seal and signature of the Minister himself. With our patience nearly exhausted, we hurried to the English Legation and procured the endorsement of Victoria's Ambassador, which proved acceptable to the *Bear;* after which we gave the old fellow a perfect tornado of abuse, and took particular pains to inform our Minister how we had been treated by his diplomatic friend.

LETTER SIXTY.

MUNICH.

Departure from Vienna—Scenery on the Danube—Linz—Peculiarities of Bavaria—Situation of Munich—Royal Palace—Hofgarten—Churches—Pinacothek—Glyptothek—Royal Library—Public Monuments—Bronze Foundry—Painted Glass Manufactory—Theatre—The King and his People.

FROM Vienna we took passage on a very good steamer of its kind, for the town of Linz, a distance of one hundred and twenty-six miles. The current of the Danube is probably the strongest in the world, and it requires very powerful machinery to propel a boat, and considerable skill to navigate it successfully. The steamers are constructed after the fashion of the old North River boats, and are quite comfortable in fair weather, but exceedingly unpleasant at night and in foul weather.

For the first fifty miles we found the scenery rather monotonous, the banks being low, and the river filled with small islands and sandbars. The appearance changed above this, and precipitious bluffs rise high out of the water, crowned by an old castle or convent, resembling in many respects that part of the Rhine between Cologne and Mayence. The most striking objects that came under our notice during the day, were the Benedictine Convent of Gottwick, an immense quadrangular building, situated on the summit of a hill seven hundred feet high, and presenting a peculiarly fine appearance from the river, founded 1072. The castle of Dunenstein, where in 1192–3 Richard Cœur-de-Lion was imprisoned for fifteen months by Leopold of Austria. The castle of Aggstein, an old feudal ruin perched on a lofty conical rock. The Convent of Molk, another Benedictine monastery, founded A.D. 1707. It is said that during

Napoleon's wars in 1808–9, the cellars of this convent supplied his army for several days in succession with fifteen thousand gallons of wine per day.

We reached Linz the morning after our departure from Vienna, took breakfast at the Archduke Charles, and engaged seats in the diligence (or Eilwagen, as the Germans call it) for this city. Having several hours of leisure before starting, we strolled to the summit of a lofty hill just above the city, which furnishes an excellent view of the romantic scenery of that neighborhood. Linz is well situated, and contains about twenty-six thousand inhabitants. The diligence road runs for some distance along the right bank of the Danube, and then passes through Loinbach, situated on the river Inn. Here we dined, changed diligences, and had our luggage examined at the Bavarian custom-house. The country from Linz to Loinbach is very pretty, moderately undulating, and highly cultivated. Riding all night in a diligence we found to be no joke, for the next morning we were completely worn out, dull and hungry; so much so, that we stopped at a beer-house and ordered a breakfast. Speaking of beer-houses, reminds me to mention that Bavaria is essentially the land of beer. It is as much the staff of life here, as bread in our country. Take their beer from them, and they are done. A Bavarian, it is said, will drink from ten to twelve measures per day, each holding more than a quart. There are in the kingdom upwards of six thousand establishments for brewing, and about one hundred millions of gallons made annually. The Bavarians are a peculiar people, not only in the quantity of beer they drink, but in their manner of living and dressing, particularly among the peasantry. The men and women wear high green hats shaped somewhat like a cone, with a feather stuck in one side. The men usually have high-topped boots, into which they dispose of a part of their corduroy pants, and wear a roundabout of the same material, ornamented with large flat metal buttons, placed in straight rows. The women wear short petticoats, finished off at the bottom with a broad red or yellow binding, which contrasts strikingly with their long black stockings and high shoes.

Munich is built on the banks of the Iser, in the midst of a plain neither fertile nor picturesque, and in a situation entirely destitute of natural advantages. Previous to the present century it was a place of little or no consequence, but by the fostering care of her rulers, its population has nearly doubled itself, and the number of fine buildings which have risen up on all sides within that period, have scarcely a parallel in any other European capital. But like many other towns created by political views, royal whim, or ill-judged speculation, it does not fill the wide area of its proposed site. The space over which the houses are scattered is so thinly peopled, that you can almost count every person in the streets. It owes its present prominent position, as the seat of the fine arts, mainly to the late monarch Louis, who spared neither pains nor expense in the accumulation of treasures to adorn his capital. The Royal Palace may be divided into two parts, called the old and new buildings. The old building, though vast in extent, and very fine in its day, has but little to interest you unless it is the *Rich Chapel*, dedicated by the Elector Maximilian to the Virgin, and so called from the expenditure of precious metals and stones upon it; its ceiling being of lapis-lazuli, its floor of marble and verde-antique, its walls of Florentine mosaic, and the altar, with all its appurtenances, as well as the pipes of the organ, of solid silver. There is also a *Treasury* in the old palace, containing the regalia and royal jewels; among them the Palatinate Pearl, half white, half black, and a great variety of expensive trinkets, a magnificent blue diamond set in the order of the Golden Fleece, several pink diamonds, many fine single stones, emeralds and sapphires of great size and value, the complete *toilette* of Amalia in enamel, and another of the Empress Josepha in lapis-lazuli; also, the crowns of the present King and Queen, of Henry II., and the Emperor Charles I.

The new palace is a massive structure, built in imitation of the Pitti Palace at Florence, and fitted up in a style now prevalent in Germany, which is a revival of the ornaments of the Loggie of the Vatican, and the still more ancient houses of Pompeii. The ball-room is very large, surrounded by a gallery, and ornamented with fine statuary. The floor is made of different colored wood, cut into small blocks. The Hall of Beauties and the Throne-room are also very superb. The palace contains many rare and beautiful pictures, and fronting it is the Hofgarten and English garden, where the citizens drive, promenade, and listen in the summer afternoons to the sweet strains of music.

Some of the churches of Munich are really superb, but I have described so many edifices of this description in my previous letters that I will merely mention those that are considered the first. Near the centre of the city, on one of the squares, stand the lofty towers of the cathedral, (*Frauenkirche*,) built entirely of brick, and very much like the first Presbyterian church in Nashville, in its general appearance. The style is heavy, and quite destitute of ornament. St. Michael's, or the Jesuits' Church, is built in the modern Italian order, and remarkable for its spacious interior, unsupported by pillars. The front is adorned with statues of our Saviour, and several distinguished characters of Germany. Thorwaldsen's monument of Eugene Beauharnois, Duke of Leuchtenberg, is in this church. It was erected by his wife, and consists of a full-length statue of the Duke, standing in front of the closed door of the tomb, divested of all earthly decoration; his crown and arms lie at his feet; his left hand is on his heart, his right holds a laurel crown, his action thus expressing the motto on the tomb: "Honor and Fidelity." The Muse of History on his right commemorates his deeds; on his left stand, in an attitude of grief, the Genii of Death and Immortality."

The church of St. Caijetan is also in the Italian style, and contains the burial vaults of the royal family.

The church of St. Lewis (Ludwig Kirche) is really a handsome edifice, of the mediæval Italian or Byzantine order. The walls and vaultings of the choir and transepts are adorned with frescoes, designed by Cornelius, and painted by his pupils, the fruit of the study and labor of ten years. These frescoes portray the leading points of the Catholic Christian faith, and reflect great credit upon the artist. The Basilica of St. Bonifacius exceeds in size and splendor any of the churches in Munich, and resembles closely the Church of St. Paul outside the walls of Rome. The interior, like St. Louis, is rich in frescoes by Hess, and contains some valuable paintings. The Parish Church of Maria Hilf, in the suburb Au, is a building of the Gothic style, and one of the most chaste and pleasing edifices I ever saw, and contains nineteen large windows of modern painted glass, representing subjects from the life of the Virgin, and equal in many respects to the glass in the ancient cathedrals. It was executed under the direction of Hess in the Munich manufactory.

From the churches of Munich one naturally tnrns to the galleries of art and science, for which this city is so distinguished; and first of all is the Pinacothek, or Museum of Painting. The building is the largest and richest of the kind in Germany, and contains a very extensive and rare collection of paintings by the old masters, the best of which have been copied on porcelain by the artists of this city. This institution also contains a very large number of rare engravings, and Greek vases of every variety. Not far from the Pinacothek is the Glyptothek, or gallery of sculpture—a chaste and classical edifice, of the Ionic order. The front is adorned with the statues of Vulcan, Phidias, Pericles, Hadrian, Prometheus, and Dædalus. In the pediment is Minerva surrounded by artists employed in the various branches of sculpture. The decorations of the different rooms are in keeping with their contents. "The walls are scaglioli of the richest colors, the floors are of marble, and the ceilings are decorated with fresco and stucco patterns, and with gilding." Each apartment is filled with the rarest collection of ancient and modern art. The Æginetan collection is the most curious, and entirely devoted to the marbles discovered in the island of Ægina in 1811. They adorned the two pediments of a temple, said to be that of Jupiter Panhellenius, in Ægina, and represent from the inscriptions certain noble actions of the Æacidæ. One group represents Hercules and Telamon fighting against Laomedon and the Trojans, and the other the contest of the Greeks and Trojans over the body of Patroclus, in which Ajax holds a prominent position.

Immediately in front of this building is another of similar dimensions of the Corinthian order, designed for the exhibition of works of art, but not yet complete. On the Ludwigsstrasse is a magnificent new building of great dimensions appropriated for the Royal Library, which is the largest in the world except the Library of Paris. The number of volumes is variously estimated from four to five hundred thousand, including MSS. Among the curiosities in this vast collection may be mentioned the Codex Alaricianus, or Laws given to the Visigoths by Alaric II. in 506; the Orations of Demosthenes, on paper made of cotton from Chios; the New Testament (Greek) in capital letters, of the 8th century; Albert Durer's Prayer Book; Luther's Bible, etc.

Munich abounds in public monuments, some of which compare favorably with the first works of art in Europe. In the market place of the old town stands a pillar (*Marianische-Sanle*) erected by Maximilian I., as a memorial of the victory acquired by him, in conjunction with Ferdinand II., over the Protestant forces of the Elector Palatine, near Prague, in 1638. It bears this inscription: "Rem, Regem, Regimen, Regionem, Religionem, Conserva Bavaris Virgo Maria tuis." The corners are adorned with figures of angels contending with four monsters—a viper, a basilisk, a lion, and a dragon, said to represent pestilence, famine, war, and heresy.

In the Karolinenplatz stands a bronze obelisk ninety-five feet high, erected by Louis I. to the thirty thousand Bavarians who fell in the Russian campaign under Napoleon, in 1812–13.

In the Max-Josephsplatz is a statue in bronze of King Maximilian Joseph, by Rauch, of Berlin. It was erected by the citizens of Munich, and is one of the finest specimens of the art in Germany. The most remarkable monument in bronze, now in Europe or the world, is that of Bavaria, in the suburbs of the city, designed by Schwanthaler, executed by Fr. Miller, and the admiration of all who behold it. This statue is almost equal in size to the celebrated statue of Rhodes, one of the seven wonders of the world. It is the figure of Victory holding a wreath in one hand, while the other rests on the head of a lion. The statue is sixty-one and a half feet high, on a pedestal twenty-eight and a half feet high, and the head is large enough to hold six or eight persons; a spiral stairway leads to the top, and an excellent view can be obtained from a small hole in the upper part of the forehead, of the broad plain in front, and the distant range of the snow-capped Alps. In the rear of this beautiful statue is a small temple of exquisite workmanship, designed as the receptacle of statuary.

On our return to the city, we stopped at the Bronze Foundry of Stiglmayer, which is very curious. The process of making such work was here explained to us. They had just completed a colossal statue of Patrick Henry, ordered by the State of Virginia to adorn the Capitol at Richmond. It was modelled by an American artist in Rome, and brought here to be cast. The Old Dominion has taken the initiative in a step which I hope will be followed by Tennessee and the other States of the Union. How appropriate and beautiful would it be to have an equestrian statue of Old Hickory to adorn the grounds in front of our Capitol, and to fill the niches of the rotunda with marble statues of such men as Grundy, Carroll, and Polk, who have served the State on the battle-field, and in our national councils. No city in Europe can boast of a more beautiful site or magnificent State edifice than the *Petra* of the west, and no State in the Union is better able to carry out the design of its eminent architect. Every Tennessean should be proud of that noble edifice, and our State Representatives in their appropriations ought to be directed by no mean spirit, but give with a liberal hand.

From the Bronze Foundry we visited the Painted Glass Manufactory, which contains some excellent specimens of this art. The process is tedious and expensive; the glass having to be heated seven times in the furnace, and the most equable temperature preserved, without which the work would be destroyed.

Our last evening in Munich was passed at the theatre, where we had an opportunity of seeing the King and many of the most eminent citizens. In his person the King is small and not very good-looking, but he is said to possess talent, and is a great patron of the fine arts. The Bavarians, like all other Germans, are devoted to music and amusements, and they spare no pains or expense to render such places attractive.

LETTER SIXTY-ONE

DRESDEN.

Railroads of Germany—Leipzig—Arrival at Dresden—Picture Gallery—The Green Vault—The Armory—Elbe Bridge—Promenades—Environs, etc.

AT Munich we procured tickets on the railroad as far as Hoff, on the Bavarian frontier, where we changed cars for Leipzig. When we reached the station at Augsburg the conductor came round to see if all the passengers had tickets, and upon examination I discovered that mine was either lost or taken from me. I could speak only a few words of the German language, and no one on the train could speak French or English. The bell sounded and the whistle blew, and yet no ticket could be produced. At last as a *dernier ressort* I exhibited my passport, showing that it was *en règle*, upon which I was permitted to proceed without my ticket. Now if this had happened in any other country but Germany, I would have been compelled to procure another ticket.

The following day at Nuremberg we were thrown into a car occupied by a venerable old gentleman and his daughter who spoke English fluently, and seemed eager to gain all the information she could relative to our country. Being unusually good-looking and intelligent, I became at once interested, and used all my endeavors to inform her correctly as to our institutions, people, and country. We travelled together for three days, and I am indebted to her for a fund of information that would have been otherwise lost.

The railroads of Germany are not so substantial, neither do they make as great speed as those of England or France, but they are much safer and more comfortable. The cars are divided into four classes, and the second class is quite as comfortable as the first in England. They make frequent stoppages, and never appear to be in a hurry—preferring to run slow and smoke their pipes leisurely, to making sixty miles an hour, with a chance of breaking somebody's neck. An accident is almost unheard of, and if a passenger gets his ankle sprained it creates as much noise as the death of a hundred persons in the United States.

The country between Munich and Leipzig is almost a perfect plain, and in many places deeply wooded with forests of low stunted pine, a growth peculiar to central Europe.

At nine o'clock on the second morning after leaving Munich we reached Leipzig, a city possessing but few attractions for the general tourist. It is the centre of the German book trade; has one hundred and twenty dépôts, fourteen steam presses, and above two hundred hand presses. Here it was that Napoleon fought one of the greatest battles recorded in history. He occupied the King's Hall (Konigshaus) while there, in which building died General Field Marshal Schwarzenberg. The University of Leipzig is one of the oldest and most flourishing in Germany, and is one of the few colleges on the continent which has retainrd its landed estates, most of the others having been deprived of their possessions, and now supported by annual grants.

We remained but a short time in Leipzig, being anxious to rejoin some friends in Dresden, which is only three hours distant on the railroad.

The capital of Saxony is very prettily situated on the Elbe, but the city itself is more pleasing at a distance than striking when examined in detail; for it has neither fine streets nor imposing public buildings. It is called the Florence of Germany on account of its beautiful situation, and the number of its excellent collections, and more particularly its Gallery of Paintings, which is without exception the finest north of Italy. Notwithstanding Dresden has been the frequent scene of war, devastation, and ruin, her galleries and vault of jewels have had the singular fortune to be treated with reverence by every hostile hand. Even Frederic the Great and Napoleon the Great refused to allow their soldiers to molest the works of genius and art. Here are collected with admirable taste some of the finest paintings in the world, by the old and modern artists. The porcelain collection is particularly fine, and the skill attained in painting on this material is truly wonderful. The artist first paints his picture on a plate of porcelain, which is then placed in a furnace and burnt in thoroughly so as to render it indelible. A coat of varnish is then added to it, and the effect is equal, if not superior, to a painting on canvas.

The gem of the gallery is Raphael's Madonna di San Sisto, executed a few years before his death, and equal to any of his works in Italy. It is a very large painting, and represents Pope Sixtus, from whom it is named, standing on one side gazing with pious awe upon the figure of the Virgin, "who is soaring up to heaven in all the majesty with which the Roman Catholic religion has surrounded her, bearing in her arms the divine child. The head of the Virgin is perhaps nearer the perfection of female beauty and elegance than any thing in painting." Opposite the Pope kneels St. Barbara, and below the group are two little angels with upturned eyes and countenances beaming with innocence and intelligence. This picture was purchased from a convent at Piacenza for eight thousand pounds.

Correggio's recumbent Magdalen next attracted our attention as a superior work of art. It is a very small painting, but one of the sweetest and most faultless pictures in the gallery. The head, neck, and arms are beautiful, and the face distinguished for its peculiar softness of outline.

The Vintage, by Rubens, is considered one of his happiest efforts.

My friend Johnstone and myself fell so much in love with the pictures just mentioned, that we searched out the most eminent artist in Dresden and had them copied on porcelain for the gratification of our friends at home.

From the Picture Gallery, we visited the celebrated *Green Vault*, connected with the Royal Palace. The accumulated treasures of ages here to be seen are truly wonderful, surpassing any thing of the kind in the world. Here are carvings in ivory and wood of every description, mosaics, beautifully cut crystals, precious stones, pearls, and jewelry of every description, beautifully arranged and classified in glass cases, heavily gilt. To describe things as they appeared to us would be impossible, and I will therefore only enumerate those that I most admired in the different apartments.

Room 1st.—Bacchus and his companions on a goat; a small piece of bronze work, excellently made. A ship made entirely of ivory. Cabinet covered with amber; box made of coral, pearl, and mosaic. Two silver tubs, four or five feet in circumference, heavily gilt. Hunting horn of pure gold, set with gems. The christening font of the royal family, very large and made of solid silver. A very large onyx cameo. Enamel of the Virgin, the largest existing, executed 1703. Pearls resembling the human form in their natural state. Golden egg inclosing a diamond ring. A round crystal, eight inches in diameter. Also, a beautiful collection of vases and pitchers made of crystal; carvings in wood of the fifteenth and sixteenth centuries; a cherry stone with one hundred faces cut on it; the largest enamel known, a Magdalen by Dinglinger.

The eighth, or last apartment, surpasses all the others in value and beauty. The most curious works here were executed by Dinglinger, an artist who is termed the Saxon Benvenuto Cellini. The Court of the Great Mogul is a wonderful display of art. It represents the Emperor Aurengzebe upon his throne, surrounded by his guards and courtiers in the most appropriate costumes, according to the description of Tavernier, to the number of one hundred and thirty-eight figures, all of pure gold enamelled. The variety of character and the true expression of each of the figures, deserve the minutest inspection. This elaborate trinket, begun in 1701, employed the artist eight years, and cost $58,400. In this room I also noticed a very large specimen of uncut Peruvian emeralds, given by

Rudolph II. to the Elector of Saxony, and a portion of a mass of solid silver from Hirnmedsfurst mine at Freiburg. The Saxon regalia include the Electoral sword borne by the Saxon princes at the imperial coronations; the decorations belonging to a miner's uniform, made for the Elector John George, 1676; a large collection of chains, collars, and orders, among which are the garter, golden fleece, and Polish Eagle, worn by Saxon princes. Last of all comes the glass case filled with the most precious suits of the most costly jewels. The first division contains sapphires—the largest of them, an ancient specimen, was a gift of Peter the Great; the second, emeralds; the third, rubies; the fourth, pearls—one set of native Saxon pearls, from the Elster in Voigtland, which are of course inferior to the Oriental. Among sixty-three rings, there are two which belonged to Martin Luther, one a cornelian bearing a rose, and in its centre a cross; the other his enamel seal ring, bearing a death's head, and the motto, "Mori sæpe cogita." The fifth division is devoted to diamonds. The diamond decorations of the gala dress of the Elector consist of buttons, collar, sword-hilt and scabbard, all of diamonds; the three brilliants in the epaulette weigh nearly fifty carats. But the most remarkable stone of all, which is considered unique, is a *green brilliant*, weighing one hundred and sixty grains, forty carats each. The sixth division is also filled with diamonds, including the Saxon order of the Rue Garland, and seven orders of the Golden Fleece, etc. This wonderful collection of costly articles surpasses any thing of the kind in the world. The valuables in the Tower of London, about which the English boast so much, are nothing in comparison. Satisfied with our day's work, we returned to the British Hotel, and occupied the evening in discussing the wonders of the *Green Vault.*

The following day we visited the Armory, which contains one of the finest collections in Europe, and is more extensive than the Ambras collection at Vienna, or that in the Tower of London. "It contains all the weapons, offensive and defensive, of chivalrous warfare; all the trappings and accoutrements of the tournament and other wild sports of feudal ages. Wealth and skill appear to have been exhausted in the materials and decorations of the armor. The elaborate workmanship of gold and silver and ivory expended on the smaller arms, as the hilts of swords, stocks of guns, bits and stirrups; the rich damasking of the plate armor and gun barrels, and the carving and inlaid work so profusely bestowed, are sufficient to excite wonder and admiration." The first room contains specimens of painted glass of the fifteenth and sixteenth centuries, many articles of old furniture, cabinets, etc., among which I noticed two beautifully carved tables, made of a cypress tree of immense diameter. The work table of the Electress Anne, (1585;) a cabinet given to Martin Luther, by his friend the Elector John Frederic, containing relics of the great reformer; a great number of ancient drinking horns, vessels, goblets, cups for all varieties of potations. Some of these articles are upwards of seven hundred years old. The hunting horn of Henry IV., King of France, is in this collection; also, the travelling table of Augustus I., inlaid with silver, and containing a complete medicine chest, and other conveniences for travelling.

The second room contains the tilting armor of the fifteenth and sixteenth centuries, used by the Electors of Saxony. Two suits of armor are made of solid silver, and some intended for small boys are very interesting. In the times when these things were used, they commenced wearing them very early in life until they became grown-up men. The armor of Christian II. is said to have cost fourteen thousand dollars.

The third room is occupied almost entirely with parade arms, and armor employed in the tilts and tournaments in the times of chivalry.

The fourth room is filled with arms for use in the field, and not for show, being less ponderous and unwieldy than those in the preceding apartment. A large part of them have been worn in battle by the Saxon princes and other historical characters, and are chronologically arranged.

The fifth room contains firearms, from their earliest invention down to the present time, showing the gradual improvements that have been made. One of the oldest weapons in this collection is a rude sort of pistol, supposed to date from the end of the fifteenth century, a mere iron barrel eleven and a quarter inches long, with a touch-hole in the side. It was fired, not by the flint falling on the steel, but by the friction of a file upon a piece of fire stone. The file was inserted in a groove by the side of the touch-hole, and was then covered with powder, and the fire-stone screwed down tight in contact with it. When the file was slightly drawn out, the friction served to ignite the powder. The first step after this was the pistol fired by means of a piece of lighted tow; then came the wheel-lock, with flint and steel. Specimens of the different varieties are here preserved in perfect order.

The sixth room is filled with costly stuffs used at the coronations and other festivities of Augustus II. and III., Kings of Poland; trappings and harness for horses, of the richest materials; splendidly worked bits and stirrups and housings for sledge-horses, on which the most elaborate ornaments have been expended. One set of harness is of gold, splendidly enamelled and set with rubies, another of silver set with pearls.

The seventh room is fitted up with a Turkish tent, taken at the siege of Vienna; and its contents are chiefly Turkish and Eastern arms.

The eighth room contains an ethnographical collection, the garments and weapons of various barbarous tribes.

The ninth and last room contains riding equipments and parade trappings. In this apartment we were shown a saddle of red velvet, and the boots used by Napoleon at the battle of Dresden, also a wax cast of Napoleon's face taken after death.

From this interesting collection we visited the Elbe bridge, one of the finest structures of the kind in Germany. It is built entirely of stone, and commands a beautiful view of Dresden and the valley of the Elbe. "It was built with funds raised by the sale of dispensations from the Pope for eating butter and eggs during Lent."

Like most of the cities of Germany, Dresden abounds in pleasant promenades, and its environs are really superb. The Saxon Switzerland embraces the most romantic scenery in Germany, and is considered inferior to none in Europe, save the bold and magnificent scenery of the little Republic.

LETTER SIXTY-TWO.

BERLIN.

Appearance of Berlin—Unter den Linden—Monuments—Royal Palace—Palace of the Prince of Prussia—Museum—Picture Gallery—Egyptian Museum—Theatre—Brandenburg Gate—Count Raczynski Gallery—Thiergarten—Bellevue—Consultation with an eminent Surgeon—Pecuniary Difficulties, etc.

SIX hours' ride on the railroad from Dresden, through a level and barren country, brought us to the capital of Prussia, which is situated in the midst of a dreary plain of sand, destitute of either beauty or fertility. It is surprising that Frederic the Great selected such a site, but still more surprising that it should have grown up, notwithstanding, into the flourishing metropolis of a great empire. Its walls measure twelve miles in circumference, and its population exceeds four hundred thousand. Most of the objects calculated to interest the stranger are situated in the street named *Unter den Linden,* from a double avenue of lime trees, which form a delightful promenade in the centre, while on each side of it runs a carriage road. It is the Broadway of the city, and the view along it is terminated by the magnificent Brandenburg gate. Just in front of our hotel (Hôtel du Nord) is one of the finest bronze equestrian statues in Europe, recently erected by the present King in honor of Frederic the Great. It stands on a bronze pedestal, ornamented with bas-reliefs, and presents a pleasing effect to the eye. Just beyond this statue, in the Lustgarten, is a large and beautiful fountain, and in front of the Picture Gallery is an enormous basin twenty-two and a half feet in diameter, and cut out of a bowlder found near the city. At this point one may stand, and simply by turning on the heel view all that is interesting within the walls of Berlin. The Royal Palace first claims our attention, not on account of any architectural beauty, (for it is nothing but a mass of brick rendered dingy and gloomy by the action of time,) but the many historical associations connected with it. In the second story of this building, Napoleon pronounced his *Berlin decrees* from the middle window. The best furnished and most interesting rooms are those occupied by Frederic the Great. The *White Hall,* recently fitted up at great cost, £120,000, and decorated with the statues of the twelve Brandenburg Electors, and the eight Prussian provinces, is very beautiful, but inferior to the ball-room in the Royal Palace of Munich. In the third story of this palace is the Kunstkammer, (chamber of art,) soon to be removed to the New Museum. It contains some curious things, but upon the whole, it is a poor affair. The Palace of the Prince of Prussia is the finest in Berlin, yet inferior to several others in Germany.

The Royal Library is also in the same vicinity; a large and tasteless building containing five hundred thousand volumes and five thousand MSS. Among its curiosities are Luther's Hebrew Bible, the copy from which he made his translation, with marginal notes in his own hand; the MS. of his translation of the Psalms, with his corrections in red ink; the Bible and prayer-book which Charles the First carried to the scaffold, and gave before his death to Bishop Juxon, etc.

The Museum facing the Lustgarten is quite a handsome edifice, built on piles, as the spot on which it stands was previously a branch of the Spree which has been filled up. At the right side of the entrance is a group in bronze, representing the combat of an Amazon with a tiger. The walls of the front are adorned with frescoes by Cornelius. The main entrance leads into a beautiful rotunda ornamented with statuary and Gobelin tapestry. The lower story is filled with statuary, vases, and bronzes, and the upper story is occupied as the picture gallery. It contains a vast number of paintings, of but little value, and to one who is acquainted with the works of art in the galleries of Italy, Paris, Munich, or Dresden, it is but a poor treat. The new Museum, which is connected with the old building, is one of the most beautiful structures in the city. The walls and columns are covered over with frescoes in imitation of the designs on the great temples of Egypt; and the rooms are well filled with valuable Egyptian antiquities. Near the Museum are the Barracks and the University building. The number of students in the University is said to be fifteen hundred, among whom are several young men from the United States. The society of Berlin, like that of Boston, is distinguished for the number of its literary characters. The most talented men of Germany are here employed either in an official capacity, or as professors of the University.

Before leaving the Lustgarten, I must allude to the Theatre, which is the finest in Germany, and in many respects equal to San Carlo at Naples, or the Scala in Milan. The scenes are admirably arranged, the boxes richly cushioned and gilded, and the room adorned with fine statuary. The King sometimes gives magnificent entertainments here in a ball-room connected with the theatre.

Passing through the avenue of the Linden to its extremity, we came to the Brandenburg Gate, built in imitation of the Propylæon at Athens. The summit is adorned with a car of Victory, which was carried to Paris as a trophy by Napoleon, but recovered after the battle of Waterloo. After its return they bestowed upon the goddess the eagle and iron cross which she now bears.

A short distance outside the gate is the palace containing Count Raczynski's gallery of pictures, embracing some excellent specimens of modern German art; and at the extremity of the Thiergarten is the royal palace of Bellevue, which is exceedingly plain, but contains a beautiful collection of modern paintings belonging to the King, among which may be mentioned: Huss Preaching to the Peasants, a large and beautiful picture by Lessing; Destruction of Jerusalem, by Bendermann; Samson breaking the Pillars of the Temple; the Dying Father bestowing his benediction on his children; the Rape of Hylas, an excellent piece—the female figures are faultless; Adam and Eve discovering the body of Abel, by Begas, very fine. An old soldier with his coat covered with *decorations* acted as our guide. He is said to be very familiar with the King, and always offers him snuff, and converses in perfect freedom with his Majesty.

Returning to the city from Bellevue, I called with a young gentleman from Charleston, who is connected with the Medical College, to consult an eminent surgeon about one of my fingers that was injured in the difficulty on the Nile. After examining it very closely and asking me many questions, he looked very wise, and advised me to pass the summer at some watering place—saying that it was the only remedy he could suggest. At first I thought the man was joking, but when I discovered that he was really in earnest, I paid his bill, and told him that Americans never went to watering placas for a weak finger.

When we arrived in Berlin we were completely out of money, and were much surprised to learn from the bankers on our letters of indication, that no letters had been received for us from London. We had no acquaintance in the city, and as a *dernier ressort* we called on our Minister, who kindly vouched for our respectability, and relieved us of the anxiety that necessarily attends a man in a foreign country with an empty purse.

LETTER SIXTY-THREE.

BERLIN.

Excursion to Potsdam—Tomb of Frederic the Great—Palace of the Prince of Prussia—Bellevue—Russian Colony—Sans Souci—New Palace—Statue of the late Queen of Prussia, etc.

POTSDAM may be appropriately termed the Versailles of Prussia, being a town of palaces, and the residence of the Prussian princes during the rising fortunes of the royal family. It is about one hour's ride from Berlin on the railroad, and owes all its beauty and splendor to Frederic the Great, whose remains now repose beneath the pulpit in the Garnison Kirche. His sword, originally laid upon the metal sarcophagus, was carried off by Napoleon and lost; but over the tomb and on each side of the pulpit are placed the eagles and standards taken from the French by the Prussians.

A short distance from Potsdam is the palace of the Prince of Prussia, lately erected in the Gothic style, and by far the most convenient and beautifully situated palace in Prussia; and just beyond, on a high eminence called Bellevue, the present King is building a kind of summer look-out, which will furnish an admirable view of Berlin and the surrounding country. In the same vicinity is the Marble Palace, so called from the extensive use of marble in its decorations; and the Russian Colony, or village, consisting of eleven log houses, built entirely after the Russian fashion, and a neat little chapel surmounted by three bulk-shaped domes. This village and a piece of land was given by the late King to the colony sent here by the Emperor.

A few hundred yards from the Brandenburg Gate are the palace and gardens of Sans Souci, the favorite summer retreat of Frederic the Great. The palace, recently restored and fitted up as a residence for the present King, but without altering its original plan, stands on the highest terrace, and is a low and unpretending building. At the extremities of the terrace are the graves of Frederic's favorite dogs, and of his horse that carried him through many of his battles. Like Byron, he desired to be buried with his dogs, but neither of their wishes were complied with. "This spot was the favorite resort of the old warrior; here he was brought out in his arm-chair, surrounded by his dogs, a short time before his decease, to bask in the sun." "*Je serai bientôt plus près de lui,*" were nearly his last words. Within the building we saw his bed-room where he breathed his last; a clock, which he always wound up himself, and which stopped at the moment of his death, and still points to the hour of his decease, 20 minutes past 2. Our guide also pointed out Voltaire's room, the walls of which are covered with figures, said to be epigrams on his character and habits, viz.: a monkey, meant as a portrait; parrots, from his volubility; stork, from his migrations, coming in summer, quitting in winter.

Just in the rear of the palace is the famous Wind Mill of Sans Souci, which still belongs to the descendants of the miller who refused to sell it to Frederic, who desired to appropriate its site for his garden. Some years ago adverse circumstances compelled the owner of the mill to part with it, but the King generously paid off his debts and allowed him to retain his property, saying that it belonged to the history of Prussia.

The gardens of Sans Souci are very extensive, and laid out in the French style. A broad avenue runs through them, at the extremity of which is the New Palace, a vast brick building, erected at an enormous expense by Frederic, by way of bravado, at the end of the seven years' war, to convince his enemies that his finances were in good condition. This mammoth structure contains upwards of seventy apartments; it was completed in six years, and built on a spot previously a morass. The interior is fitted up in the most elaborate and extravagant manner, and the ceiling and walls of the large room in the centre of the building are lined completely with shells and minerals in very bad taste.

In the garden of this palace is a small building called the Antique Temple, containing a beautiful recumbent statue of Queen Louisa, by

Rauch. It is no larger than life, and represents her asleep. The features are regular, the figure excellent, and the entire piece superbly executed.

LETTER SIXTY-FOUR.

St. Petersburg.

Voyage from Stettin to St. Petersburg—Our Vessel and Passengers—The Gulf of Finland—Cronstadt—First View of St. Petersburg—The Neva—New Bridge—English Quay—Police Regulations—Our Hotel—Dinner at the U. S. Ambassador's.

It is just four hours and a half from the capital of Prussia to Stettin on the Oder by the railroad. Stettin is a place of some commercial importance, and is the point from which the Russian steamers embark for this city. The banks of the Oder below Stettin are exceedingly low, and the country reminded me very much of the region below Londonderry, in Ireland. After getting out of the river, we passed between some low and barren islands and the main shore, for a great distance before entering the sea. Our vessel was a war-steamer, built in Liverpool, and very good, I should think, for such purposes, but wholly unsuited to convey passengers between such important points, as most of them have to sleep on the floor and on the seats in the cabin. There is one improvement in the structure of this vessel which I think might be adopted even on our river steamers, where accidents are more numerous than on the sea; and this is in the wheel-houses, the tops of which are made in the shape of boats, capable of holding eighty persons each, and can be unshipped at any moment in case of accident.

The following morning we descried in the distance the coast of Sweden, and met an English steamer bound for London. As nothing of particular interest occurred during the day, I will give a brief of our passenger list. The captain and second officer were Germans, the crew slaves, or *souls*, as they are called in Russia. Next comes Prince Trubitskoie, of Moscow, a sour-looking individual, who had been on a tour of pleasure with his wife and child. The Princess is a tall, dark-looking lady, with a very long, but pleasant face. The child is perfectly beautiful, but completely spoiled, having an English, French, and other attendants. Then comes a jolly old

Commodore of the London Yacht Club, on his way to St. Petersburg, to enter his craft in the Regatta for the prize awarded by the Emperor. I recognised him as a brother Mason, and gained considerable information from him relative to the structure of yachts in different countries. Next comes a very nice young Englishman, who is one of Victoria's messengers. The Russian Consul at Marseilles, a large fat personage, with a Greek wife and pretty daughter. Two Austrian and two Prussian Generals going to Russia to witness the grand annual review of the military, having been invited by the Emperor. One of the Austrian Generals was very particular in his attentions to a German opera singer, who seemed well inclined. Then comes a young Russian nobleman with a French mistress, another with a greyhound, and another very fond of champagne. But the richest character of all was an old French woman from Cologne, who was quite smutty in her conversation, and kept the passengers continually in a roar of laughter. One morning she made her appearance on deck in her petticoat, and assigned as the reason, that the ladies' cabin *stunk* so badly that she could not go into it, and that she would not allow any of the servants to finger her things. Most of the passengers spoke English, and all spoke French —consequently our voyage was very agreeable.

On the morning of the third day we entered the Gulf of Finland, which is two hundred miles long and very wide. During the day we saw one or two towns on the Finland shore, and a number of small barren islands; also numerous sails, mostly of small craft.

Early the next morning, being the fourth day from Stettin, we landed at Cronstadt, where we were boarded by a whole phalanx of policemen and searchers of luggage, passports, etc.

Cronstadt is a strongly fortified place, containing twelve or fifteen thousand inhabitants, including the garrison. It is the water-gate of St. Petersburg, for here most ships coming from seaward anchor; the smaller vessels run up to the mouth of the Neva, carrying the freight and passengers over the shallow bars between the places. Here is also the chief station of the Russian fleet, the chief custom-house, and the harbor for vessels of war, which will contain about thirty ships, and is protected by a mole four hundred and fifty fathoms in length from the violence of the waves. After being detained here two or three hours, we got on a small steamer which landed us safely at the examination office on the English quay. On the right shore of the gulf from Cronstadt we saw the town of Oranienbaum, and a little further on, the gilded towers and park of Peterhoff, which are situated on a slight acclivity; but after they are passed the banks again become low, and present from a distance the only feature of the Finnish shores, interminable flats. At length a golden spot, sparkling in the sunshine, and of dazzling splendor, together with a tall and taper spire, shooting like a needle to the sky, and rising apparently from the water, are seen, and these are the first indications that prove that the great city founded by Peter the Great is near at hand. This golden spot is the gilded dome of the Isak Church, which may, in fair weather, be seen from Cronstadt, a distance of sixteen miles. The spire is that of the Admiralty. Aside from these two objects, the approach to St. Petersburg is anything but prepossessing, being situated on a number of low islands, formed by the winding of the Neva, and built up on the side next to the sea with indifferent-looking houses. But when we reached the English quay the appearance of things began to improve, and the wonders of the European city opened upon our eyes. We landed near the new bridge, one of the greatest monuments of the city, and one of the finest structures in Europe. It was built by Americans; has seven stone arches, with an iron-railing of great beauty. The contractors lost $80,000 by the contract, but like honest men they completed the work in good faith. We were required to pass through a line of policemen into the examination office, where we were detained more than two hours. The examination was more searching than we ever underwent before in other countries. They turned my little trunk upside down, and took all my books, even my Bible, away from me; then we were required to sign our names in several books before we were allowed to depart. Leaving this vexatious place, we endeavored to procure lodgings at Miss Benson's, an English boarding-house, but she was full, and we had to go to the Hotel Russe, or Klaie, where we succeeded in getting tolerable rooms.

The day after we arrived in this city we dined with Gov. Brown, our Ambassador, from Tennessee, and his Secretary, Mr. Wright, of New-Jersey. They live together in a well-furnished suite of rooms in the vicinity of the Winter Palace, and not far from the Newski

Perspective, the Broadway of St. Petersburg. We were received at the Legation, not by a Frenchman in kids or a Russian in furs, but by one of Afric's sons, who exhibited his ivory so invitingly and shook our hands so cordially that we almost forgot that we were in Petersburg, and imagined that we were entering the mansion of a Southern planter. In a few minutes after we arrived dinner was announced, and we had hardly taken our seats when the sweet strains of music greeted our ears from the court. The dinner could not have been better, and I must say that we passed the most agreeable evening here that we have spent in Europe. The Minister is a man full of the milk of human kindness; agreeable in conversation, and fully alive to the interests of his country. His Secretary is an accomplished gentleman, possessing all those high traits of character calculated to captivate in society or shine in official station. These gentlemen will ever have our best wishes; and if they should devote their lives to foreign missions, may they in future get into a more comfortable berth.

LETTER SIXTY-FIVE.

St. Petersburg.

Passport System—The Newski Perspective—Churches—Peter's Log Cabin—Corps des Mines—Admiralty—Palaces—Monuments—Excursion to Peterhoff—The Neva—Pickpockets.

In my last letter I made allusion to the difficulties we encountered with the police when we landed in this city; but that was hardly a beginning to what we were afterwards subjected to. To save time we engaged the services of a well-known *commissionaire*, named Craft, to assist us in getting our passports properly arranged. After waiting impatiently at the police office for about two hours, we were ushered into the presence of a number of very dignified-looking men, dressed in full uniform, who eyed us from top to toe, asked various questions of an inquisitorial character, and required our signatures on several different sheets of paper. We were then marched off to another police office about four *versts* in the opposite direction, where we were again questioned and required to sign papers. After this operation was gone through with, they returned our old passport and furnished us with a Russian passport to go to Moscow, for which we paid two *rubles* and fifty *kopeks*. During our absence at Moscow, Craft had our names published three successive days in the Police Paper, announcing our intention to leave Russia at a certain time. When we arrive at Moscow another passport will be required to allow us to return to St. Petersburg, for which we pay three rubles more, and when we leave Russia we are required to have still another passport for Sweden. Oh, what a country to an American accustomed to live, move, and act freely! It is utter martyrdom. I would not be compelled to live under such a government for the mineral wealth of Siberia.

From the police office we drove in a drosky down the Newski Perspective, one of the most magnificent thoroughfares in the world. Here all is life and movement, and no ten yards of ground are passed that do not present a scene or subject that will arrest the attention of the stranger. It is four versts (three miles) in extent, very wide, with a gutter in the centre, and paved with blocks of pine wood in some places, and stones variously placed in others. The buildings on this street are lofty and fine, the shops well furnished, and the signs of enormous size, covered with paintings representing the articles sold within. Many splendid equipages are to be seen here, besides innumerable droskies (peculiar to Russia) driven with Jehu speed, and the driver crying out "*Padi, padi*,"—make way, make way. The drosky is the most curious vehicle I have yet seen, and as we rode in them very often, a sort of description will not be out of place. It is on four low wheels, with a long cushioned seat running lengthwise, on which the rider sits astride, as on horseback, and the passengers likewise if they choose, but they usually sit sideways and have no support for the back. It is drawn generally by two horses, one in shafts with a high arched bow over the neck, called the *douga*, and the other called *le furiens*, in traces alongside —this last being trained to curve his neck and canter while the shaft horse trots. The horses are small, but well formed, and move along with great spirit and rapidity. The drosky is the Emperor's favorite vehicle, and when the weather is pleasant he may be seen almost any day driving unattended through the streets.

St. Petersburg abounds in churches, nearly all of which are used by the followers of the Greek faith, multitudes of whom may be seen at all hours of the day, kneeling at the shrines of the different saints. The most conspicuous edifice for public worship is the Isak Church, the finest structure in Russia, and inferior only to St. Peter's at Rome, and the Cathedral at Milan. The immense dome that surmounts the building is covered with pure gold, and the interior is elegantly adorned with malachite columns and other precious stones from Finland and Siberia.

Crossing the Neva over the Isak bridge, we visited the church of St. Peter and St. Paul, which is situated in the citadel, and conspicuous for its beautiful and slender gilt spire, similar and hardly inferior in height to that of the Admiralty. Aside from the spire, there is nothing attractive about the church, except its being the resting place of Peter the Great and his imperial successors. The preceding sovereigns of Russia were buried in the Arkhangelskoi Sabor in Moscow. Whoever has seen the monuments of the French, Austrian, and Italian sovereigns, will wonder at the simplicity and absence of ornament in this final abode of the Russian Emperors. The simple coffins are placed in the vaults, and over them in the church is nothing further in the shape of a monument than a stone coffin-shaped sarcophagus, covered with a simple pall. The names of the deceased are embroidered in letters of gold. On the tomb of the Grand Duke Constantine lie the keys of some Polish fortresses. Peter III., to whose remains Catherine refused interment in this place of sepulture, rests there now. Paul placed both Catherine's and his father's there. A hundred cannon, impregnable bastions, and a garrison of three thousand men defend the place, which can be desecrated by hostile hands only when St. Petersburg lies in ruins. The Russian princes are the only ones in Europe buried in a fortress.

From this church we drove to the humble little cabin of Peter the Great, situated on the upper end of the same island. It was built of round logs, pretty much in the western style, one story high, and divided into three apartments. The inner room was his bedchamber, the adjoining one his chapel, where the pictures he worshipped are still preserved, and the third apartment was used for his reception room. Here are preserved numerous relics belonging to that remarkable man. The boat which he is said to have constructed, and the sails he used, are also shown. The Emperor Alexander, to preserve the cabin, had it covered with a casing which gives it the appearance of a neat frame cottage. It was here that the present great city was first commenced. A number of lights were burning in the chapel when we entered, and devotees to the shrine were constantly kneeling.

We next visited the *Corps des Mines*, one of the most remarkable establishments in the capital. The building is grand and imposing from the river, but when you approach it the effect of a severe climate is plainly marked upon its walls. Like many other institutions, it was founded by Peter the Great, for the purpose of training and forming a corps of mining engineers, who would be able to explore and work the mines of Siberia and other mineral countries belonging to the vast possessions of Russia. It is not in order at present, having been taken to pieces for the purpose of making some improvement. The Museum attached to this establishment is one of the best arranged and most valuable in Europe. Among the many curious and precious things I will merely mention a few, viz.: Seventy-three crystals of emeralds, each crystal measuring from an inch to an inch and a half in length; a block of malachite weighing four thousand pounds, and valued at £318,478; a piece of native platina, weighing ten and a half pounds, and valued at £1,434; also, seven hundred and fifty pieces of native gold, one piece weighing eighty pounds, another piece eight inches in length and five broad, and valued at £26,236; a single crystal of beryl, weighing about six pounds, is considered the finest known specimen, and valued at £6,521. Besides numerous other mineral specimens, I noticed a great number of plans for mining machines, and among them one for sifting, and one for crushing gold. The collection of swords and other articles of steel manufactured in Siberia are very beautiful, and far superior to any thing I thought them capable of making.

Recrossing the Neva, we went to the Admiralty, situated on the great square of the city, from which diverge all the principal streets. From the spire of this building we had an admirable view of the city, and the windings of the river. St. Petersburg, as I before remarked, is badly situated, and covers an immense space. The city is too large for its population, and the fine wide streets present a desolate appearance from this lofty eminence.

After satisfying ourselves with viewing the vast expanse covered with palaces and stately buildings, we descended into the great square and examined the monuments so celebrated for their beauty. In front of the Senate House, and facing the Neva, is the equestrian statue of Peter the Great, the finest work of its kind in the world. It stands on a huge block of uncut granite from Finland; the Emperor's face is turned towards the Neva, his hand outstretched as if he would grasp land and water, and under the feet of the horse an enormous serpent is uncoiled with its head attached to the horse's tail to sustain the equilibrium.

In an open space between the Etat Major and the Winter Palace stands the greatest monolith of modern times—the column erected to the memory of the late Emperor Alexander, a single shaft of red granite, which, exclusive of pedestal and capital, is upwards of eighty feet in height. This beautiful monument is the work of Monsieur Montferrand, the architect of the Isak church. The base and pedestal are also composed of an enormous block of the same material, of the height of about twenty-five feet, and nearly the same in breadth; the capital measures ten feet, the statue of the angel on the summit fourteen feet, and the cross seven feet—in all about one hundred and fifty feet. As the whole of St. Petersburg is built on a morass, it was thought necessary to drive no less than six successive rows of piles, in order to sustain so immense a weight as this standing upon a confined base. On the pedestal is the following inscription: "To Alexander the First, Grateful Russia." Unfortunately, a sort of worm is at work on this beautiful structure, which has caused the column to crack in several places.

The following day we drove to the Hermitage, but were refused admittance on the plea that we had on frock coats. Hurrying back to the hotel, we put on dress coats, and then made a second effort, when another difficulty presented itself. "The Emperor was in the palace, and strangers were not admitted until he left." Feeling confident that the fellow lied, I offered him a silver ruble, which soon cleared the way. Indeed the Russian, like the Italian, may be bribed to do almost any thing.

The Hermitage is the largest and most magnificent palace in Petersburg, and second only to the new imperial palace at Moscow. It is situated on the Neva, and is connected with the Winter Palace by means of passages on the first floor. (What we call the second floor is always called the first in Europe.) It was built by the Em press Catherine, in order that she might have a place to retire in her leisure moments, there to enjoy the conversation of French philosophers and men of learning; and here, after the duties of the sovereign had been transacted in the Winter Palace, she was wont to pass the evening surrounded by all that could gratify the eye or the senses; musicians displayed their talents, artists their work, scientific men their speculations, and political men their opinions; for in accordance with the ukase suspended in all the apartments, perfect freedom and equality reigned, and the pictures which we see elsewhere only as allegorical representations of art and science-loving princes, were here every day realized. On the roof was a garden of flowers, shrubs, and trees, heated in winter by subterranean stoves, and illuminated in summer by variegated lamps, under the prismatic colors of which the brilliant assemblage wandered. We ascended a beautiful flight of marble steps into a large hall of great beauty, containing fifteen or twenty large malachite vases. We were then conducted through a number of rooms filled with paintings by the best artists, and cabinets of rare workmanship, containing many precious stones. Among the paintings I was particularly attracted by the "Destruction of Pompeii," by Brulloff, on a canvas more than twenty feet square. Abraham offering up Isaac—a very large and well executed work. Among other things, I was interested in some articles of furniture made after patterns by Peter the Great. A large variegated vase or basin from Siberia. Two mosaic tables of extraordinary workmanship and beauty, representing on the top the principal buildings of the different cities in Italy. A machine representing a gilt peacock, standing on a gilt tree, and inclosed in a glass case, is very remarkable. A dressing box made entirely of large diamonds, and a sculpture gallery filled with handsome statuary of modern Roman artists.

From the Hermitage we crossed over to the Winter Palace, which is also very splendid, and the residence of the Emperor. The throne room is handsome, but did not come up to my expectations, being inferior to several in Europe.

Next in point of splendor is the Marble Palace, built by Catherine for Prince Gregory Orloff. The Taurida Palace, so called in compliment to Potemkin, the conqueror of the Khan of the Crimea, and presented to him by Catherine. Michaeloff Palace, by the Emperor

Paul, and dedicated to St. Michael. The Annitchkoff Palace on the Great Prospect, built by the Empress Elizabeth, and bestowed on Count Razumoffsky, then twice purchased by Catherine and twice given to Prince Potemkin. The Palace of the Grand Duke Michael, the residence of the Emperor's brother, is decidedly one of the handsomest palaces in Petersburg.

About twenty-five *versts* from the city is the summer residence of the royal family, prettily situated, but not at all remarkable. The town of Peterhoff is exceedingly neat, and the palaces look comfortable. The grounds are extensive, and the fountains very large, but inferior to many in France and Italy. After roving all the morning through the gardens and parks at the heels of a stupid German *valet-de-place*, we dined at a very good restaurant, and returned in the afternoon to the city. The next day we accepted the invitation of Mr. Wright, our Secretary of Legation, to visit the islands above the city. At his instance we took a small steamboat at the quay, and sent the carriage to meet us, affording a fine opportunity of seeing the Neva and the summer villas of the citizens of Petersburg. We stopped at a place of amusement, where we heard the band led by Gungl, who played at the Inauguration ball of Gen. Taylor. After the music ceased we entered a room where model artists were being exhibited, and while we were admiring the different postures of the artists, some *light-fingered* scoundrel relieved my pocket of a purse containing one hundred rubles, and some other valuables. I tried to philosophize, but it was of no use. I could not divest myself of the fact that my pocket was empty. Philosophy is a very good horse in the stable, but out on a journey in a foreign land, far away from home, he does not work so well. Fortunately, my friend Johnstone was flush with circular notes, and there was no danger of starving. Our Minister and his Secretary both offered to let me have any amount, for which I shall ever feel grateful—particularly when I see a pickpocket's victim.

LETTER SIXTY-SIX.

MOSCOW.

Journey from St. Petersburg to Moscow—The Railroad—Russian Serfs—English Hotel—Sunday in Moscow—The Kremlin—Monasteries—The Riding School—Bazaars—Tea Houses—Amusing Incident, etc.

FROM the capital we turned our faces in the direction of the burned and rebuilt city of the Czars—Moscow, with gilded cupolas, the holy Moscow, the sanctified city, the Jerusalem of Russia, beloved of God and dear to men. A few years ago the diligence was the only conveyance for the traveller between the two cities, over the best Macadamized road in Europe, shaded with trees, and with handsome post houses under the direction of the government; but this is no longer the mode of communication, for even Russia has imbibed the spirit of progress and improvement, and American engineers have constructed for them a railroad similar to those in their own country. The contractors have realized great fortunes, and secured the good opinion of the Emperor, by constructing a road that we would term second class in the United States. The bridges over the Volga, and several smaller streams, are built entirely of iron, and far more creditable than the road. When we arrived at the station we found it densely crowded with spectators, anxious to witness the starting of the train. The doors of the station-room were closed until a stated time to all except the military, who were permitted to take their seats leisurely in the cars, while those who had no *buttons* were compelled to "*wait for the wagon.*" In no country have I seen the military so arrogant and overbearing. About eighty versts from Petersburg is the ancient city of Novogorod, now rapidly going to ruin. Some parts of it are still in good condition, but the city which covered, three centuries ago, an area of sixty-three versts in circumference, with a population of 400,000 inhabitants, is doomed and her greatness departed.

The country through which the railroad passes is perfectly level and barren, thickly wooded with forests of stunted pine as in Germany, and thinly populated. The villages are numerous, but look forlorn, being generally the property and occupied by the serfs of the seigneurs, and consisting of one long street, with houses on both sides, built of logs, the better sort squared, with the gable-end to the street, the roofs projecting several feet from the houses, and sometimes ornamented with rude carving and small holes for windows. The Russian serfs differ from slaves in other countries, in the important particular that they belong to the soil, and cannot be sold except with the estate; they may change masters, but cannot be torn from their families or birthplace. One eighth of the whole peasantry of Russia, amounting to about seven millions, belong to the government, and occupy the imperial demesne, and pay an annual tax. The rest belong to the nobles, and are the absolute property and subject to the absolute control of their masters, as much as the cattle on their estates. Some of the serfs have been enfranchised, and become burghers and merchants of great wealth; but they cannot rise above a certain point. It is from this class that Russia recruits her immense standing army, or, in case of invasion, raises in a moment a vast body of soldiers. It is frequently asked: "What have such men to fight for? They have no country, and must be devoid of all those impulses that animate the bosom of a man fighting for his fireside and his home." The only solution that I can give is the singular fact, that with the Russian serf there is always an unbounded love for the Emperor. Next to their God is their ruler on earth, for whom they will fight to the death.

When we arrived at the Moscow station a host of drosky drivers surrounded us, each one eager to convey us to the hotel. We could not speak a single word of their language, but were perfectly *au fait* in the language of signs. Selecting the man with the best physiognomy, I slapped him on the shoulder, gave him a knowing look, pointed to our baggage, and ejaculated "Howard's," the name of a well-known English boarding-house. In a few minutes we were quietly seated in his drosky, and conveyed rapidly to the right place.

It was Sunday morning when we reached Moscow, and the sound of the church-going bell reminded me of home; the gathering for church, and the greeting of friends at the church door. But he who has never heard the ringing of bells at Moscow, does not know its music. Imagine a city containing nearly seven hundred churches and innumerable convents, all with bells, and these all sounding together, from the sharp, quick note, to the loudest, deepest peals that ever broke on the ear, struck at long intervals, and swelling on the air as if unwilling to die away. Sunday is also the day for ob serving national manners and customs. We dined at an early hour, and under the escort of our obliging landlord we drove in a drosky to a great promenade of the people, called *L'Allée des Peuples.* It is the great rendezvous of the merchants and shop-keepers of Moscow. The grounds are ornamented with extensive avenues, and provided with every thing necessary for the enjoyment of the various national amusements. Soldiers are stationed at every point to preserve order, and every one seemed to be happy; but the principal attraction for us, as well as the people, were the Bohemian or gipsy girls. Wherever they moved, a crowd gathered round them. They were the first that I had seen of this remarkable people, coming from no one knows where, and living no one knows how; wanderers from their birth, and with a history enveloped in mystery. The men were now here to be seen, nor were there any old women about; and these young girls, well dressed, and some of them very pretty, moved along in parties of six or eight, singing, playing, and dancing to admiring crowds.

From this place we drove to Pedroski, the promenade for the nobility, where all the rank and fashion of Moscow were vieing with each other in style and magnificence. The grounds around the old château of the great Peter are handsomely disposed and ornamented with trees, and the carriage promenade equal to any in Europe. It is a straight road, more than a mile in length, through a dense forest of beautiful trees. For two hours before dark, all the equipages of the nobility parade up and down this promenade. On either side of the road is a walk for foot passengers; and behind this, almost concealed from view by the thick foliage, are little cottages, arbors, and tents, furnished with all kinds of refreshments suitable to the season.

Fortunately for us, our landlord had an arrangement with the managers of the different apartments in the Kremlin to allow his guests to enter without the trouble of procuring tickets from the authorities. So at eleven o'clock on Monday morning we repaired to this renowned place—the centre of the great city, and a spot around which linger a thousand hallowed associations. The first thing that attracted our attention was the "*Spass Vouta,*" (gate of the Redeemer,) through which we entered the walls that surround the triangular inclosure of the Kremlin.

It is the *porta sacra* and *porta triumphalis* of Moscow; through it entered the triumphant warriors of Ivan Vassilievitch, after the conquest of Kasan and Astracan, and those of Michaelis and Alexis after the victories obtained in the Ukraine. Over this gate is a picture of the Saviour, under a glass, and before it hangs a large lamp, in a massive metal frame; this is suspended by a heavy chain, and under it, to wind it up, stands a complicated machine, that jarred and rattled here in the time of the Czar Michael. A man whose sole business is to wind it up, has a table beside him with wax tapers, which he sells to be lighted before the picture. This shrine is an object of the greatest reverence with the Russians, although few know what it represents, it hangs so high and the colors are so faded. This forms a passage through the lofty tower of about twenty paces long; and every one, be he who he may, Mohammedan, Heathen, or Christian, must take off his hat, and keep it off until he has passed through to the other side. Even the Emperor and the haughty officer take off their hats; and if the stranger should so far forget the custom, he will hear the gently murmured warning, "*Shlapa, shlapa, batrushka*," (the hat, the hat, father.) Passing through the gate, we find a noble esplanade, commanding one of the most interesting views of Moscow, and having in front the range of palaces of the Czars. These palaces present a combination of every variety of taste, and every order of architecture, Grecian, Italian, Tartar, and Hindoo, rude, fanciful, grotesque, gorgeous, magnificent, and beautiful. The next object was the Czar Kolokol, (King of Bells,) which is elevated on a massive pedestal of granite close to the tower of Ivan Veliki. It is the largest bell in the world, being twenty-one feet three inches high, twenty feet five inches in diameter, and is in no part less than three inches in thickness. It was cast by the command of the Empress Anne in 1730, and bears her figure in flowing robes on its surface, beneath which is a deep border of flowers. The tower on which it was suspended was burnt in 1737, and the fall buried the enormous mass deep in the earth, and broke a huge fragment from it about six feet long and three feet wide. It now stands the object of religious veneration by the Muscovite, and the wonder of all travellers. Here too is the largest cannon in the world, its dimensions being about fifteen feet in length, and six or seven feet in diameter. It is placed on a carriage, but is too heavy (forty-five tons) ever to be serviceable. After looking at this large piece, we walked through the Arsenal and examined the cannon taken by the Russians from the French, Poles, and other nations. They are numerous, and show conclusively that her armies have fought many battles, and gained not a few victories. Ascending the lofty tower of Ivan Veliki, which is the highest and most remarkable in Moscow, we obtained the best view of the city and its environs. Unlike St. Petersburg, the city is situated on high and rolling ground, the streets are very crooked, the houses low and their roofs painted green, which imparts to the city a singular and unique appearance. From this point the eye takes in at once the windings of the Moskwa, clusters of domes amounting in all to nearly two thousand, the Sparrow Hills from which Napoleon first viewed the sacred city, and innumerable objects interesting in their nature and pleasing to dwell upon. But to return to the tower, which rises without ornament to the height of more than two hundred feet, surmounted by a gilded dome upon which, as on all other gilded domes within the Kremlin, (about sixty in number,) the cross is displayed above the crescent. We gained the summit by a small staircase, and the view from each story, which serves as a belfry, stimulated us to renew our exertions to reach the top. In the first of these stories hangs, in solitary grandeur, a bell, which, but for the mightier one below, would appear stupendous. To ring it is of course impossible; even to toll it requires the united strength of three men, who, pulling with separate ropes, swing the vast clapper round, making it strike the bell in three different places. In the belfry above are a number of other bells of great size and weight. Descending from the tower of Ivan, we entered the New Imperial Palace, recently completed by the present Emperor at an immense cost. It is connected with the Terema, and presents a striking contrast with the ancient structure, showing the improvement in architecture. The exterior of the New Palace is very imposing, but its great and unequalled beauty is displayed in its internal arrangement. We entered by a lofty flight of white marble steps adorned with chaste malachite vases, and were then conducted slowly through the various apartments.

The state rooms are fitted up with a degree of taste and splendor no where else to be seen. The floors are made of ebony and rosewood cut into small blocks and inlaid with mother-of-pearl—the walls covered with different colored silks—the pillars and ceiling covered with fine gold—the panels of the doors set with diamonds and other precious stones—the paintings by the best masters, and the furniture in keeping with the whole. In a word, it is the finest palace in the world. The Treasury has recently been removed to a fine marble building connected with the New Palace, and its precious contents arranged with great taste. The first room that we examined contains a number of elegant vessels used by the old Emperors. The second room is filled with flags and white eagles taken from the Poles. The third room contains a great many curious antiques—such as a saddle made of red velvet and set with precious stones, presented to Constantine by one of the Sultans; the crowns of Peter the Great and his brother, besides several others, including a Polish crown; the magnificent robes in which the present Emperor was crowned; a throne covered with turquoises of large size; also, a throne of John III., made of ivory, beautifully ornamented with bas-reliefs, and sent as a present from Greece; crown of the Empress Anne, covered with massive diamonds, and surmounted with an immense natural ruby and diamond cross. The last room on this floor contains a large collection of Turkish and other armor of interest, and in the rooms below I noticed a small iron bedstead taken from Napoleon, with his portrait hanging near it. A large number of old state carriages and sleds are to be seen here, showing that the moderns have made many improvements. These carriages are very long and heavy, whereas those made at the present day are light and comfortable.

From the Treasury we went to the *Uspenski Sabor*, or Cathedral of the Assumption, founded in 1325, and rebuilt in 1472. According to the national taste, a church must be crowded with pictures and shrines, and thus in this cathedral eye and spirit are bewildered with the glitter of gold and the glare of color. The whole church is gilt within; even the heavy pillars that support the five cupolas are covered with this material from top to bottom, and the walls the same; and on this golden ground large fresco paintings have been executed, the subjects taken from the Bible. In this cathedral the Emperors are crowned, and the Patriarch formerly officiated here. I do not admire the architecture or general appearance of this building, which is peculiar to Russia, and far behind the age. Among the objects of curiosity in this cathedral is a representation of Mount Sinai of pure ducat gold, a present from Prince Potemkin. On the summit stands a golden Moses, with a golden table of the laws; and within the mountain is a golden coffin to contain the host; it is said to weigh 126,000 ducats. A Bible, the gift of Natalia Narishkin, the mother of Peter the Great, is so large and the cover so laden with gold and jewels, that it requires two strong men to carry it into the church. The emeralds on the cover are an inch long, and the whole binding cost 1,200,000 rubles. The great chestnut wood throne seat of Vladimir the Great, within a house of brass-work, which they say is in imitation of the tomb of Christ—and also a miraculous picture of the Saviour. Here, too, is to be seen a nail, said to be of the true cross; a robe of the Saviour, and a part of one worn by the Virgin. There is also a picture of her, said to have been painted by St. Luke, and brought from Constantinople by one of the early Czars. Here are the tombs of the Patriarchs of the Greek church, one of whom, St. Philip, and honored by a silver monument, dared to say to Ivan the Terrible, "We respect you as an image of the Divinity, but as a man you partake of the dust of the earth." The greatest curiosity, however, is the golden shrine of the Patriarch Necosi in the sacristy, whose mouldering skeleton is here presented, together with his wooden spoon.

Behind the Cathedral of the Assumption stands the house which formerly belonged to the Patriarchs of Moscow, now called the *Synodalni Dom*, because a section of the Holy Synod has its office here. It contains the library of the Patriarchs, their treasury, and their wardrobe; and in the church attached to it is preserved the holy oil that is used in baptizing all the children of Russia. The Arkhangelski Sabor (cathedral of Archangel Michael) is also in the Kremlin. In this church are the tombs of the early Emperors, and the celebrated boy Dmitri, so much worshipped by the Russians. The most remarkable looking church in Moscow is in the Red Square, just outside of the sacred gate, the architect of which had his eyes put out after its completion, so as to prevent his building another.

From the Kremlin, we visited some of the monasteries in the suburbs, which constitute the largest, and next to the churches, the most numerous class of buildings. The monks of Moscow wield a great influence in the community.

Returning to the city, we stopped to see the Riding School, which has the largest unsupported roof in the world. I stepped it off, and found that it measured 192 paces in length, and 51 paces in breadth. Some years ago the Emperor reviewed 9,000 soldiers in the building. The roof is constructed similar to the bridges made of arches and braces.

The bazaars of Moscow are quite Eastern in appearance, differing entirely from those in Petersburg; and the shop-keepers are so eager to sell to those passing, that they go so far as to take hold of your coat-tail, and almost drag you into a bargain.

The Russians are great tea-drinkers, and their tea houses are as numerous as the restaurants of New-York. These houses are divided off into small rooms furnished with tea-tables. The waiters all wear long white shirts over their trousers, and look exceedingly neat. The Russian manner of making and drinking tea is altogether different from any other people. The waiter brings in two pots, one filled with boiling water, and the other half full of tea. He first pours a little tea into the cup, and then a little water. After this he empties more water into the tea-pot, and fills the cup therefrom. The Russian usually calls for a *pair of sugar*, meaning two lumps, which he holds in his fingers, and bites it off as he sips. He always empties his tea in a saucer, which he holds under the bottom on the ends of his fingers. He will drink ten or a dozen cups sometimes without rising from the table; and the merchants always conclude a bargain by taking a cup of tea.

Just before leaving Moscow we made the acquaintance of Mr. Williams, of New-York, who is one of the railroad contractors, and has been a resident of Russia nine years. He seemed very glad to see us, and gave me the most cordial shake of the hand that I had felt for many a day. Quite an amusing incident occurred while we were in his company. He proposed that we should take our seats in the car before the station door was opened, saying that he would carry us through. When we reached the door the guard said that we should not pass, whereupon Mr. Williams caught him by the collar and held him out at arm's length, until we walked through. It was an amusing scene, and created great commotion among the passengers, who could not understand how a plain-looking individual without buttons dared to act in such a manner. They soon learned, however, that he was an American, which explained the whole affair.

LETTER SIXTY-SEVEN.

STOCKHOLM.

Voyage from St. Petersburg to Stockholm—Revel—Helsingfors—Abo—Arrival in Stockholm—The Park—King's Palace—Churches—Haga—Drottningholm—Jenny Lind's Parents—The Swedes, etc.

HAVING returned from Moscow to the capital, we engaged passage on a Russian steamer for Helsingfors in Finland, where we changed to a steamer for this city. We were too late to secure berths, and were compelled either to take a bench in the cabin or be detained another week in Petersburg, the very idea of which would have induced me to take the deck without mattress or covering. Although Russia is an extraordinary country, and her cities present innumerable attractions, yet the many annoyances that fetter the stranger at every step render it intolerable for an American who is permitted to move about at full liberty in his own happy country.

When we reached Cronstadt, the port of Petersburg, we encountered a violent storm, which lasted only a few minutes; but this was long enough to do considerable damage to our little steamer. The day was very inclement, and running along the low flat coast of the gulf, without any particular object to interest us, was any thing but agreeable. At noon the next day we reached Revel, the capital of Livonia, where most of our passengers left us. This city in early times possessed considerable importance, but since the annexation of the country to Russia, St. Petersburg has taken all her trade. An old Russian, who was *en route* for Finland, went up into the town with us to see the corpse of a Livonian prince in one of the churches. As the story goes, he was denied the honor of burial because he could not pay his debts, and his body was cast into a cellar. Several hundred years afterwards it was discovered in a perfect state, and is now exhibited in a case deposited in the church. Unfortunately the funeral obsequies of some countess was going on in the church, and we were denied the privilege of seeing this natural mummy. We arrived at Helsingfors about midnight, and being very sleepy, I hurried on board the Swedish steamer and disposed of myself in the best berth. In a few minutes a broad-faced German entered, and walked directly to my berth. I knew in an instant from his expression that he intended to lay claim to it, but having the right of occupation, I determined to lie low and keep dark. After considerable difficulty, he succeeded in arousing me from a *deep slumber*, and speaking in his vernacular, said that I was in his berth. I looked at him a moment, and by a shake of the head gave him to understand that I did not speak his language. He then spoke to me in French, and received the same shake of the head. Taking me to be a Russian, he went off and enlisted in his service one of the Czar's subjects, who also received the ignorant shake. Failing to make me understand in his language, he tried the Swedish, but without effect. By this time the German became impatient and somewhat enraged, and as a *dernier ressort* brought up the engineer, who was a John Bull, and no mistake. With an air peculiar to all Englishmen, he spoke out in a loud voice, saying, "Do you speak English, sir?" to which I replied by the same shake of the head. Having exhausted all the languages that they could bring to bear, they naturally came to the conclusion that I was either deaf and dumb or a fool. John Bull, however, to make the matter certain, asked me in the name of God what language I did speak, to which I replied, American—a response that almost convulsed him with laughter. As soon as he recovered, he informed the German that I was a Yankee, and he had better let me alone, for all h—ll could not move me. Taking John Bull's advice, the German sought out another berth, and left me to finish my nap.

Our course the next day lay between the coast of Finland and the numerous little islands scattered along the shore, forming a distinct channel from the main sea. The whole country is barren, and covered with everlasting pine, which appears to be the chief growth of Eastern Europe. In the afternoon we reached Abo, where we remained one day. Soon after landing, an Englishman who was acquainted with the town accompanied us through the principal streets, which are wide and clean; and wound up the proceedings of the day in a snug little *café* situated in a grove, and attended by a pretty and graceful Swedish girl. Abo is inhabited mostly by Swedes, who are easily distinguished from the Russians, being much better looking and far more polite. At one time Abo was a flourishing town, and the seat of a university, which has been removed to Helsingfors. At present there is a goood deal of ship-building going on in the place, and the Emperor has contributed largely to aid a company in fitting out sixty vessels for the whale service. Several of them are completed, and judging from their appearance, they are well built, and will answer the purpose for which they are intended.

As we were leaving Abo, many persons, mostly ladies, assembled on the quay to take leave of their friends, and I was particularly attracted by their grace and ease of manner. Voltaire very aptly terms the Swedes the French of the North. I was considerably interested in a parting scene between a young man and his wife. She was going to Stockholm, to be absent two weeks, and was as much affected as if it was for two years. They kissed, and kissed, and kissed, until I thought their lips would be seriously damaged, or become glued together. At dinner I observed another Swedish custom, that differs entirely from any thing I ever saw. Before taking their seats at the table, they usually assemble around a small side table, and take what they call soup, or snaps, which consists of a kind of liquor extracted from potatoes, bread and butter, cheese and radishes. After walking around the soup table about ten minutes, they take their seats at the dinner table. We crossed the Gulf of Bothnia in the night, and early on the morning of the fifth day from Petersburg, the *Kelner* aroused us to see the scenery on the narrow inlet leading to Stockholm, and the approach to the city, which is very beautiful. We landed at the quay near the King's Palace, and proceeded without any examination of baggage to the Hotel du Commerce, situated in the centre of the city. The hotels of Stockholm furnish only apartments, and the stranger, to get a respectable meal, must be regularly introduced to the Merchants' Club, where he pays one dollar and a half banco entrance fee, and dines *à la carte*.

After dinner we crossed the water in a small boat managed by athletic women, to the Park, which is very extensive and handsomely adorned. In the centre there is a small palace belonging to the

King. The citizens of Stockholm have their amusements in the Park. In one part of it is a very good theatre, where we witnessed an exhibition of monkeys, dogs, and goats. The man who has charge of these animals is a perfect Alex. Selkirk of a fellow, and their performances are truly wonderful.

The next day we visited the King's Palace, which is the largest house in the city, covering a great space, but quite plain both externally and internally. It is built on a hollow square. The rooms are mostly small, and the ceiling low. There are some paintings and statuary here, but nothing of particular note. The library is quite extensive, and contains, among other books of interest, the Bible of Luther, with extensive notes on the margin in his own hand-writing; also, a remarkable looking book, of enormous size, called the *Devil's Bible*, written on parchment prepared of three hundred asses' skins. This Codex is a war-prize taken in Prague during the Thirty Years' War. In a square on the south side of the palace is a tall and slender obelisk, commenced by Gustavus III., and completed by Gustavus X. On the north side is a splendid bridge of granite, which spans the water that divides the city. The central part rests on a small island, and underneath the arch is a very good restaurant. In the square, on the opposite side of the bridge from the palace, stands a very handsome equestrian statue of Gustavus Adolphus.

The churches of Stockholm are quite handsome, but possess few attractions to one who has visited nearly all the churches of Europe. Cathrina church is the most prominent object in the city, and was founded in 1656, on the height where Christiern the Tyrant had the bodies burnt after the massacre, and where afterwards a wooden chapel was built by John III. Its name was given to it by Carl Gustaf, after his mother, and that monarch also presented to it two large bells, which he had taken in Poland. After having been ruined by fire in 1723, it was rebuilt from drawings by Buyhomaster Adelcrantz. A dome was then constructed over the centre of the church, and its beautiful canopy is supported without the aid of a single pillar. It is said that the architect, fearing the dome would give way, killed himself; but his work still stands in its original beauty.

Ridderholm's church, situated near the centre of the city, is also very handsome, particularly the spire, which is made of cast iron, and exceedingly symmetrical. The reason for putting up an iron spire was to save the church from lightning—it having been struck three times. The church is filled with mausoleums, the finest of which are the Caroline and Gustavian graves, on each side of the church. It was in this church that Senator Carl Nilsson Farla took refuge when the rich Bo Jonsson Grip pursued him, excited by his raging jealousy. Carl Nilsson laid hold so fast of the corner of the altar that it broke, but Bo Jonsson hewed him in twelve pieces. This happened in 1383. In memory thereof, a stone divided into twelve parts has been laid in the floor just on the spot where the murder was accomplished. There are also some valuable ornaments in the way of trophies taken in the old wars, to be seen in the church.

A few miles from the city is the royal summer residence, called Haga. In 1786 Gustaf III. laid the foundation of a great palace, but of which only the ground walls ever were finished. Among the minor buildings then constructed, that called Lilla Slottel (the little palace) was often inhabited by Gustaf III. The park is extensive and very handsome, and is adorned with a kiosk, a temple, urns, and constructions of many kinds. I was particularly attracted by a small foot bridge in imitation of a seine drawn by two huge figures representing negroes,—also, two gondolas, richly gilded, and adorned with the heads of the wild boar and rhinoceros. In different parts of the grounds I noticed large balls, made of green glass, and placed on a pedestal in the sun, in which could be seen the entire view round about in a small compass.

About one hour's run on the steamer from Stockholm is the summer palace of Drottingholm, on Lofon. It has been the royal seat as far back as the days of heathenism, and was then named Thorsund. Queen Cathrina Jagellonica had a stone house built there, and King John III. visited it frequently, especially for the sake of the game forest he kept up there. But the year after the death of Carl Gustaf, the little palace was burnt, and the present new edifice was constructed by the Queen Dowager Hedvig Eleonora, at her own expense. The whole region was originally low and marshy, but stone vaults were constructed where the present gardens are, rocks were blasted, and the sunk lands were cleared by canals. The palace is quite extensive and well furnished, but the park is the chief attraction about the place.

Returning to the city, we made a visit to Jenny Lind's parents, who are now quite old and infirm. They are exceedingly plain, but seem very proud of their distinguished daughter, who has kindly given them all the comforts of life out of her earnings in the United States. The Swedes generally are proud of their Nightingale, but heap maledictions upon her for uniting her fortunes with a Jew.

The Swedish ladies are without exception the most polite, graceful, and beautiful women of the north. Some of them are truly charming; and owing to the scarcity of the other sex, every stranger becomes at once a lion.

LETTER SIXTY-EIGHT.

COPENHAGEN.

Trollhattan Canal—Polhem and Gullo Falls—Gottenburg—Voyage to Copenhagen—The Round Tower—Magdalene or Lady Church—King's Palace—Monuments—Thorwaldsen's Museum—Private Museum—Frederic Park—The Danes.

AT Stockholm we took passage on a small steamer called the Polhem for Gottenburg. It is the most indifferent boat on the canal, but we were compelled to take it, or remain in Stockholm for a month. I determined to pass the first night on deck, but found it so cold towards morning that I gladly retired to my berth. In a few minutes I fell asleep, but it was short and disturbed; the atmosphere was so heated that I almost suffocated. Most of our passengers were ladies, on their way to the bathing places near Gottenburg, and amongst them was a young lady of considerable musical talent, and a great friend of Jenny Lind's—also a Swedish Baroness with two interesting daughters.

After running all day through lakes and between the islands of the Baltic, we entered the great Trollhattan canal, which is without exception the most wonderful work in Sweden, and superior probably to any canal in the world. It is fed by the lakes, and always has an abundance of water, sufficient for the largest vessels. Early on the morning of the second day we crossed Lake Roxen and Lake Boren, and reached Borenhault about noon. Here we passed through a succession of locks to Motala on lake Wetter. The canal between Lake Boren and Lake Wetter is cut out of the solid rock, and runs up a very steep ascent, the latter lake being much higher. These locks are wonderful works of art, that will ever redound to the honor of the engineer. The following day we crossed Lake Wenner, and visited the Polhem and Gullo Falls, situated a few hundred yards from the canal. These falls are but little known by European travellers, but are exceedingly beautiful, and far more interesting than the falls of the Rhine or Nile. At this point the canal descends through a great number of locks into the Hissengen. It is cut through solid rock, and very deep, giving it more the appearance of a tunnel than a canal.

We reached Gottenburg early the fourth day, and stopped at Blom's Hotel, which is the best in the city, but very poor. Soon after breakfast I received a visit from the two little daughters of the Baroness, and took a long walk with them through the public gardens. When I bade them adieu, they seemed much affected and cried bitterly. One is about ten and the other eight years of age, both beautiful and unusually intelligent. About two hours after the separation the servant returned with a present from one of them, with the message that I must not forget her when I returned to my far-off home. No, little Swede, I can never forget you! Often hereafter will I recur with pleasure to the time when I dandled you on my knee, and listened to the sweet tones of your voice. You are a child now, young in years, and with a mind and heart plastic to all surrounding influences. Time and other scenes will soon obliterate my memory, but in this heart I will ever cherish the few brief days of love that you bestowed on me, and which older heads and hearts have denied.

Gottenburg is more devoid of sights than any place of its size in Europe. It is situated in a plain surrounded by hills. On the outskirts there is a very pretty avenue of trees, and a public garden, which are all that is worth looking at. The city looks old and dilapidated, the streets dull and inanimate, and the shops poorly furnished.

We were compelled to remain four days in that city, from which we came on a splendid iron steamer to Copenhagen. Pretty soon after our arrival we, as usual, inquired for the best point to view the city, and were conducted by a *valet-de-place* to the summit of the Round Tower, a lofty brick structure near the centre of the city, which is attached to a church, and furnishes an admirable view. The Queen sometimes ascends this tower in a carriage drawn by four horses, but always walks down. I noticed in a little room on the summit a number of astronomical instruments, and infer therefrom that the tower is also used for an observatory. Close to the tower is the finest church in the city, called the Magdalene or Lady Church. The chief attractions in it are the colossal statues of Christ, the Virgin, and the twelve Apostles, by Thorwaldsen, the great Danish artist. The figure of Christ is represented with outstretched arms, and occupies a place above the altar. The Virgin has wings, and is kneeling on a carpet in front of the altar, holding in her hands a basin shaped like a shell, and the twelve Apostles are arranged on either side of the church in their order. These fourteen pieces are made out of the best Italian marble, and executed in the most beautiful manner.

From the church we visited the King's Palace, a massive and unprepossessing structure, resembling a barn more than a palace. In the third story there is a large collection of paintings of a negative character, and in the public square I noticed a bronze equestrian statue of Christian I., treading on the prostrate body of the King of Sweden, with four allegorical figures seated on each corner of the pedestal. Outside of the gate on the road leading to Fredericsburg is a tall obelisk erected by the peasants to Frederic VII. after he released them from bondage.

The most remarkable object in Copenhagen is Thorwaldsen's Museum. The building is square, with a court inside, and the exterior is ornamented with frescoes, representing boats bringing the artist's marble from Italy, and the people carrying the blocks to the museum, and the multitude gazing on the scene with expressions of astonishment. This museum contains all of the artist's models, but very few pieces in marble. The interior walls are ornamented with bas-reliefs in marble, some of which are very fine, especially a procession of figures representing the different vocations of life. His Eve I consider good, but inferior to some that I have seen in Italy. Near this museum is another of a different kind, belonging to a private gentleman. It is very extensive, and embraces curiosities from Greenland, Iceland, Kamtschatka, South America, and China. I was particularly interested in the collection from Greenland, showing the costumes and customs of that far-off and remarkable race. Their clothes are well cut, and made of skins; their summer houses are also made of skins, in the shape of tents, and have the cellular tissue of animals for windows. Their cooking utensils are made of a soft kind of stone, and their beds are elevated about one foot from the ground. The collection of sleds, etc., from Greenland, is exceedingly interesting. In the collection from China we saw the likeness of the present Emperor and his wife, recently taken from life; also a great variety of curiosities no where else to be seen. Close to the museum is the Exchange, a very large building, surmounted with a sharp spiral steeple, and occupied principally with small shops; also a church with a staircase on the outside of the spire, leading to the summit.

About two miles from the city is the Frederic Park, one of the country seats of the King. The park is very handsome, but the palace is plain and much out of repair. On the road near the park are a number of neat cafés and gardens, where the people congregate in summer. Returning to the city, we stopped at a place called Tivoli, where there are all sorts of amusements, and where all classes meet. After walking about the gardens, gazing at the people, monkeys, parrots, etc., we sat down and listened to a very good concert, then tried our hand at shooting with an air gun, and took a ride on a railway so constructed as to run both up and down an inclined plane. I noticed at this place many peculiarities of dress amongst the peasantry. The women usually wear a green gown with a large red-figured border round the skirt, and sleeves made very large above the elbow. They wear on the head a handkerchief half folded, tied under the chin, and the other half hanging behind, or nave a cap of gold or silver work, fitted on the back of the head. The men dress pretty much as they do in Germany, with roundabouts, large buttons, and large hats. From all I can see there exists no great difference between the Danes and Swedes, in appearance, manners, and customs.

LETTER SIXTY-NINE.

HANOVER.

Voyage from Copenhagen to Kiel—Hamburg—The Alster Basin—The Bourse—Trip to Hanover—The Theatre—Royal Palace—Waterloo Column, etc.

AT Copenhagen we took passage on a splendid iron steamer belonging to a company in Lubec for Kiel in the Holstein. As we were coming out of the harbor I noticed four new yachts belonging to the English Royal Club. They were very handsomely fitted out, and were returning to London, one of them having won the cup in the regatta at St. Petersburg. During the day we ran close to the low coast of Denmark, and the following morning we were landed safely at Kiel, where we took the railroad for Hamburg. The country between the two places is rather flat, but in a high state of cultivation, and produces well. There is a great deal of bog land on the line, and seeing the peasantry cutting and piling up the peat, reminded me forcibly of my tour through the South of Ireland. Reached Hamburg, or Altona, its suburb, in three hours, and took apartments at one of the hotels on the Alster, in the new and most beautiful part of the city. The Alster is a large and splendid basin, covered with pleasure boats, fowls of nearly every description, and other objects pleasing to the eye. An avenue of trees extends entirely around it, forming a delightful shade over the promenade, on which pavilions and other places of public resort are erected. The hotels on the Alster are numerous, and far superior to any in Europe.

The most prominent object in the old part of the city is St. Michael's Church, from which can be obtained the best view of Hamburg and the surrounding country. It has one of the loftiest steeples in Europe, being four hundred and fifty feet in height, and used as the station of the fire watch. Every hour the watchman blows a trumpet from the windows to let the people know that he is vigilant.

Hamburg is situated about eighty miles from the mouth of the Elbe. It is one of the four remaining Free Towns, and is chiefly remarkable as the first trading seaport of Germany, being to the north what Trieste is to the south. It is intersected by canals, called *Fleethen*, (Fleet ditches,) and in this respect, in the antiquated appearance of its houses in the old city, and in the trees growing in its streets, bears a resemblance to the towns in Holland. Four thousand vessels enter the port yearly, and more emigrants sail for the United States than from any other port, except Liverpool. It was once a fortified town, and was twice occupied by the French under Davoust in 1813. The ramparts no longer exist, being levelled and converted into delightful boulevards or gardens, neatly laid out, which extend nearly round the town and between the two Alster basins.

The Bourse of Hamburg is situated in the new part of the city on the Adolphs Platz, and is one of the largest and most convenient establishments of its kind on the Continent. One o'clock is the hour when the merchants assemble, at which time from five to six thousand may be seen on any day dealing in stocks. Near the Exchange is the Merchants' Bank, a very superb structure, with the vault under ground and covered with water. I noticed also in this neighborhood a building with an engraved front. The figures are engraved in the stone, and the effect is very fine.

At Hamburg we took a steamer for a small town above, where the railroad terminates, and reached Hanover in eight hours, passing through an undulating and highly cultivated country. The capital of this kingdom is situated in a plain on the Leine, a small stream, and has about forty-five thousand inhabitants. It does not present an imposing appearance at a distance, and there are but few objects within to attract the stranger. The new theatre, not yet finished, is a very large building, and externally the finest in Europe. The finest buildings are collected around a square called Waterloo Platz, which serves also as a parade ground. In the centre of this square is the Waterloo Column, one hundred and sixty-two feet high, surmounted by a figure of Victory, and inscribed with the names of the Hanoverians, privates as well as officers, who fell in that battle. On either side of it are extensive barracks. The Royal Palace is also on this platz, a very extensive building and well furnished. In the plate-room I noticed a collection of mediæval antiquities, relics, etc., some of them brought from Palestine by Henry the Lion, under the care of the Ober Hof-Commissar. In a small circular temple near the palace we saw Leibnitz's bust, much injured by persons throwing stones at it.

In the old town several antique Gothic houses still exist, and are curiously ornamented. Leibnitz's house, with stone ornaments and scriptural bas-reliefs on its front, is considered one of the most interesting objects in the city. Like most of the towns in Germany, Hanover boasts of her avenues and gardens of public resort. A grand double avenue of limes, more than two miles long, extends from the town to the Royal Palace of Herrenhausen, the favorite residence of George I. and II. The building is now deserted and out of order, but the gardens are still kept in beautiful style, and contain statues, hot-houses, and jets d'eau. In the *Mausoleum* we saw a monumental effigy of the late Queen Frederica, by Rauch, and our guide pointed out the spot where the Electress Sophia, mother of George I., and granddaughter of James I., fell dead while taking her evening walk.

LETTER SEVENTY.

AIX-LA-CHAPELLE.

Trip from Hanover to Aix-la-Chapelle—The Baths—The Redoute—The Dom Kirche—Hôtel de Ville—Summary of my Tour—Conclusion.

AT Hanover a young German from St. Louis, who had emigrated some years ago from Baden, got into the same car with us, on his way to his mother home to visit the friends of his youth. From his appearance and conversation we soon learned that he was a mechanic, of small means, but strict honesty. At Minden our passports were examined, and his found without the *visé* of the proper authorities in Hamburg. The officers would not allow him to proceed, and his funds were so near exhausted that any detention would leave him without a dollar. Our sympathies were aroused in his behalf, and we expostulated with the officers, but without effect. Seeing that he had no other alternative but to return to Hanover, we made up a purse for him, and explained what the law required. I shall never forget the remark he made when he bade us good bye. With a firm grasp of the hand, and a countenance beaming with gratitude, he exclaimed, "Gentlemen, you have my heartfelt thanks for your kindness. There is no country like America; and if God spares me to return, I will never make another track on this continent!"

A ride of ten hours from Hanover brought us to the banks of the beautiful Rhine, and the ancient city of Cologne. We stopped at the Bellevue, the same hotel that we occupied more than a year ago, while on our way to Switzerland. This is the first time we have crossed our track, and as I described Cologne before, I will pass on to the curiosities of this renowned watering place. Aix-la-Chapelle was called *Aquis Granum* by the Romans, and remains of their baths are still to be found near the warm springs. Charlemagne raised it to the rank of second city in his empire, and made it the capital of his northern dominions, appointing it the place of coronation for the German emperors. In the middle ages it was honored with the privileges of a Free Imperial City, and acquired considerable importance as a manufacturing town, especially in the manufacture of cloth, for which it is celebrated even to the present day. It was the scene of many Diets of the Empire, and of several councils of the Church; and in later times it has been distinguished by the congresses held there. After the Peace of Paris it was taken from France, to which it had been united by Napoleon, and made a part of the dominions of the King of Prussia.

Agreeably to recommendation, we stopped at Mullen's Hotel, opposite the great fountain. The situation is good, because we can see all the *élite* and fashion of this renowned place assembled every morning and evening to drink the mineral waters. Most of the springs are hot, and the magnificent baths throughout the city are supplied directly from the main fountain. A walk of nearly a mile through a beautiful avenue brought us to a little town called Borcette, that boasts of two of the largest and best springs in the vicinity of Aix. The water of one is so hot that I could not hold the glass in my fingers, and that of the other pleasantly cool. This place is patronized by the poor, who are unable to stand the high prices in the city. On the way a noble viaduct is passed, which carries the Cologne railway over the valley of Burtscheid. It is very lofty, constructed of brick, and contains a great number of arches.

About half a mile north of Aix, on the opposite side of Borcette, beyond the Sandkard Thor, is the hill called Louisberg, two hundred feet high, surmounted by a pyramid or obelisk raised for trigonometrical purposes. The view from the summit is extensive, and the country exceedingly beautiful. On the lower slope stands a handsome restaurant and café, the Belvidere, with a saloon commanding a noble prospect. Returning to Aix, we visited the *Redoute*, or gaming-house, which corresponds with what they call the Kursaal at other watering places. The building is quite inferior compared with those at Baden and Wiesbaden. Games of hazard, rouge-et-noir, roulette, etc., are carried on very extensively night and day. The tables are let out to a company by the government, who are compelled to apply a large portion of their profits to the improvement of the town.

The most interesting object in Aix-la-Chapelle is the *Munster* or *Dom Kirche*, (Cathedral,) which occupies the spot where Charlemagne had erected "the chapel" after which the city was named. "He designed it to be a burial place for himself, causing it to be constructed in the form of the Church of the Holy Sepulchre of Jerusalem. It was consecrated by Pope Leo III., with a ceremony worthy of its spendor. The original church was destroyed by the Normans, and rebuilt as it now stands by the Emperor Otho III. in 983, in conformity with the old plan. The tomb, in which once reposed the remains of Charlemagne, is marked under the centre of the dome by a large slab of marble, with the words 'Carolo Magno' inscribed upon it. A massive brazen chandelier hangs above it, the gift of the Emperor Frederic Barbarossa. In the vault below, the body of Charlemagne was seated on his throne, as one alive, clothed in the imperial robes, bearing the sceptre in his hand, and on his knee a copy of the Gospels. On his fleshless brow was the crown, the imperial mantle covered his shoulders, the sword Joyeuse was by his side, and the pilgrim's pouch, which he had borne always while living, was still fastened to his girdle." These precious relics were taken from the vault by Barbarossa and used in the coronation of succeeding Emperors of Germany. They are now preserved at Vienna.

The *throne* in which the body of Charlemagne was seated alone remains here. It is an arm-chair, made of slabs of white marble, which during the coronation were covered with gold. The choir of the church contains a pulpit, covered with plates of silver gilt, richly ornamented with carvings in ivory and precious stones. The sacristy is very rich in relics, such as the skull of Charlemagne inclosed in a silver gilt case something like a barber's block, and his arm-bone, and part of one of his legs, the hunting horn of Charlemagne formed of an elephant tusk, a locket of the Virgin's hair, and a piece of the true cross—two relics of which he wore around his neck, in his grave as well as when alive. The leather girdle of Christ, on which may still be seen the impression of Constantine's seal—the cord which bound the rod that smote him—the sponge which was filled with vinegar—that arm of Simeon on which he bore the infant Jesus—some of the blood and bones of St. Stephen—some manna from the wilderness—and some pieces of Aaron's rod, are still preserved.

The *Grandes Reliques* are shown only once in seven years, from the 15th to the 27th of July. The last exhibition took place in 1853. So sacred is this ceremony held, and so high is the privilege esteemed of obtaining a glimpse of them, that pilgrims resort to the spot from all parts of the country in vast crowds. "These relics were presented to Charlemagne by the Patriarch of Jerusalem, and by Haroun al Raschid. They are deposited in a rich shrine of silver gilt, the work of artists of the ninth century, and consist of—1st. The robe worn by the Virgin at the Nativity; it is of cotton, five feet long. 2nd. The swaddling-clothes in which Jesus was wrapped; they are of cloth, as coarse as sacking, of a yellow color. 3rd. The cloth on which the head of John the Baptist was laid. 4th. The scarf worn by our Saviour at the Crucifixion, bearing stains of blood. Intermixed with these religious relics are many curious antique gems, some Babylonian cylinders, and the like, which serve as jewels to ornament the saintly treasure. The church-plate, and articles of goldsmith's work, shrines, ampuls, reliquaries, crosses, chalices, etc., render this sacristy a perfect museum of art."

From the cathedral, we went to the Hôtel de Ville (Rathaus) in the market place, a large and antique stone building erected in 1353, on the site of the Palace of the Frankish Kings, in which Charlemagne was born. It is remarkable as the place of meeting of the two congresses of 1748 and 1818. The King of Prussia has appropriated a large sum of money for the repair of this building, which is now in progress.

CONCLUSION.

In the series of letters published in your valuable paper I have, in a feeble manner, endeavored to acquaint your readers with all the incidents of note that came under my observation, during a tour of two years; and as I do not intend going over the same ground, this will be my last. In reviewing the contents of these letters, which were written for the benefit of friends at home, we naturally recur to the commencement of our tour. Those who have perused them followed us across old ocean's wave to our mother country, thence to la belle France, up the beautiful Rhine, over the snow-capped Alps into classic Italy. Leaving the shores of Europe, they followed us across the deep-blue Mediterranean to the land of the Pharaohs, up the Nile into Nubia, over the sands of the great Arabian Desert to Jerusalem, the mother of cities. They have knelt with us at the Holy Sepulchre, and all the shrines of Palestine; they have roved with us through the cities of the Orient, and through Greece, the land of Poets, Philosophers, and Orators. Once more in Europe, they have accompanied us through all the German States, and the dominions of the Czar as far as the *Sacred City* (Moscow). Retracing our steps as far as St. Petersburg, they have gone with us through all the countries of the North, even to the point where the sun is visible for three days above the horizon.

During the period of our wanderings we have had ample opportunities of seeing and learning the peculiarities of the various countries on the three continents, and comparing them with our own happy land. What has been the result? Do we return dissatisfied with the land of our nativity? or are we willing to live and die there?

Nature has given us a country of virgin soil, capable of producing every variety of products, and our mountains are filled with untold wealth. The rivers of the United States are more numerous and better fitted for navigation than those of any other country in the world. Our government is the perfection of human wisdom, and onr people are not only familiar with its principles, but able and always willing to defend them. Some of our colleges will compare favorably with the oldest and most renowned in Europe, and in point of general intelligence, no country can claim superiority over us.

In the sciences and the fine arts we, of course, cannot set up our claim for eminence, but in a short period we may even boast of these things.

With such a country, and so much to make one happy, how can any sensible American ever wish to abandon it? Let those who speak of disunion, who have sectional prejudices, or who are blindly led by party rule, make the tour of the Old World, and if I am not greatly mistaken they will return home with national ideas, national love, and national fidelity.

FINIS.

SIMMS' REVOLUTIONARY TALES.

UNIFORM SERIES.

New and entirely Revised Edition of WILLIAM GILMORE SIMMS' Romances of the Revolution, with Illustrations by DARLEY. Each complete in one vol., 12mo, cloth; price $1.25.

I. THE PARTISAN. **III. KATHARINE WALTON.** (In press.)
II. MELLICHAMPE. **IV. THE SCOUT.** (In press.)
V. WOODCRAFT. (In press.)

"The field of Revolutionary Romance was a rich one, and Mr. Simms has worked it admirably."—*Louisville Journal.*

"But few novelists of the age evince more power in the conception of a story, more artistic skill in its management, or more naturalness in the final *denouement* than Mr Simms."—*Mobile Daily Advertiser.*

"Not only *par excellence the* literary man of the South, but next to no romance writer in America."—*Albany Knickerbocker.*

"Simms is a popular writer, and his romances are highly creditable to American literature."—*Boston Olive Branch.*

"These books are replete with daring and thrilling adventures, principally drawn from history."—*Boston Christian Freeman.*

"We take pleasure in noticing another of the series which Redfield is presenting to the country of the brilliant productions of one of the very ablest of our American authors—of one indeed who, in his peculiar sphere, is inimitable. This volume is a continuation of 'The Partisan.'"—*Philadelphia American Courier.*

ALSO UNIFORM WITH THE ABOVE

THE YEMASSEE,

A Romance of South Carolina. By WM. GILMORE SIMMS. New and entirely Revised Edition, with Illustrations by DARLEY. 12mo, cloth; price $1.25.

"In interest, it is second to but few romances in the language; in power, it holds a high rank; in healthfulness of style, it furnishes an example worthy of emulation."—*Greene County Whig.*

SIMMS' POETICAL WORKS.

Poems: Descriptive, Dramatic, Legendary, and Contemplative. By WM. GILMORE SIMMS. With a portrait on steel. 2 vols., 12mo, cloth; price $2.50.

CONTENTS: Norman Maurice; a Tragedy.—Atalantis; a Tale of the Sea.—Tales and Traditions of the South.—The City of the Silent—Southern Passages and Pictures.—Historical and Dramatic Sketches.—Scripture Legends.—Francesca da Rimini, etc.

"We are glad to see the poems of our best Southern author collected in two handsome volumes. Here we have embalmed in graphic and melodious verse the scenic wonders and charms of the South; and this feature of the work alone gives it a permanent and special value. None can read 'Southern Passages and Pictures' without feeling that therein the poetic aspects, association, and sentiment of Southern life and scenery are vitally enshrined. 'Norman Maurice' is a dramatic poem of peculiar scope and unusual interest; and 'Atalantis,' a poem upon which some of the author's finest powers of thought and expression are richly lavished. None of our poets offer so great a variety of style or a more original choice of subjects."—*Boston Traveller.*

"His versification is fluent and mellifluous, yet not lacking in point of vigor when an energetic style is requisite to the subject."—*N. Y. Commercial Advertiser.*

"Mr. Simms ranks among the first poets of our country, and these well-printed volumes contain poetical productions of rare merit."—*Washington (D. C.) Star.*

RUSSO-TURKISH CAMPAIGNS OF 1828 *AND* 1829.

With a View of the Present State of Affairs in the East. By COLONEL CHESNEY, R. A., D. C. L., F. R. S., Author of the Expedition for the Survey of the Rivers Euphrates and Tigris. With an Appendix, containing the Diplomatic Correspondence of the Four Powers and the Secret Correspondence between the Russian and English Governments. One vol., 12mo, cloth; Maps; price $1.00.

"A condensed detail of facts, and the result of personal observation, it is replete with instructive matter: a record of one of the most striking events in modern history; a guide to the formation of correct judgment on the future. Good maps, and minute descriptions of the principal seats of the past and present war; a statistical account of the military resources of Turkey; its present state and prospects; its political and commercial value—occupy an interesting portion of the work, which we heartily recommend to the attention of our readers."—*London Critic.*

"It fills up a vacant niche in the history of the times which seems to be required to give a proper understanding of the difficulties which have resulted in the present European war."—*Springfield Post.*

"This work, which, under any circumstances, would have excited great interest, is worthy of special attention now, from its relation to the eastern contest."—*Albany Argus.*

"Though abounding in information, it is clear, straightforward, and as free from overstatement and irrevelant speculations as the 'Commentaries of Cæsar'"—*New York Evening Post.*

THE RUSSIAN SHORES OF THE BLACK SEA,

With a Voyage down the Volga and a Tour through the Country of the Cossacks. By LAURENCE OLIPHANT, Author of "A Journey to Nepaul." From the Third London Revised and Enlarged Edition. 12mo, cloth; Two Maps and 18 Cuts; price 75 cents.

"The latest and best account of the actual state of Russia."—*London Standard.*

"The book of a quick and honest observer. Full of delightful entertainment."—*London Examiner.*

"Mr. Oliphant is an acute observer, and intelligent man, a clear and vigorous and succinct writer, and his book embodies the best account of Southern Russia that has ever appeared. His account of Sevastopol will find many interested readers."—*Boston Atlas.*

"This book reminds us more of Stephen's delightful 'Incidents of Travel' than any other book with which we are acquainted. It is an interesting and valuable book. He was as sharp at seeing as a live Yankee, and he has given us the fruits of his observations in a very graphic and interesting style."—*Boston Traveller.*

A YEAR WITH THE TURKS;

Or, Sketches of Travel in the European and Asiatic Dominions of the Sultan. By WARRINGTON W. SMITH, M.A. With a Colored Ethnological Map of Turkey. 12mo, cloth; price 75 cts.

"Mr. Smith has had rare opportunities. Few men have crossed and recrossed the empire in so many directions—and many are the errors, the false reports, the misconceptions as to fact or motive which are here corrected by an able and impartial witness."—*London Athenæum.*

"One of the freshest and best books of travel on the Sultan's dominions."—*New York Commercial Advertiser.*

"The reader obtains an excellent and reliable idea of the actual condition of the people, of the mongrel races, and the present state of the Sultan's dominions. There is a vivid interest in the narrative, and abundance of real information."—*Boston Transcript.*

THE BLACKWATER CHRONICLE;

A Narrative of an Expedition into the Land of Canaan, in Randolph County, Virginia, a Country flowing with Wild Animals, such as Panthers, Bears, Wolves, Elk, Deer, Otter, Badger, &c., &c., with innumerable Trout, by Five Adventurous Gentlemen, without any Aid of Government, and solely by their Own Resources, in the Summer of 1851. By "THE CLERKE OF OXENFORDE." With Illustrations from Life, by Strother.

"This is a handsomely-printed and beautifully-illustrated volume. Those who have a taste for field sports will be delighted with this cleverly-written narrative of the achievements and experiences of a hunting party in the hunting-grounds of the Old Dominion."—*Savannah Daily News.*

"A queer, quaint, amusingly-written book, brimful of drollery and dare-devil humor. The work overflows with amusement, and has a vignette-title and other beautiful illustrations, by Strother."—*Yankee Blade.*

"A pleasant book of American character and adventure, of interest geographically, sportively, and poetically. The authorship is of a good intellectual race; the "Clerke of Oxenforde," who figures in the title-page, being own brother to the author of "Swallow Barn," which, as everybody knows, is the "Sketch-Book" of that land of gentlemen and humorists."—*Literary World.*

MINNESOTA AND ITS RESOURCES;

To which are Appended Camp-Fire Sketches, or Notes of a Trip from St. Paul to Pembina and Selkirk Settlements on the Red River of the North. By J. WESLEY BOND. With a New Map of the Territory, a View of St. Paul, and One of the Falls of St. Anthony. In One Volume, 12mo. Cloth. $1 00.

"To the immigrant to the northwest, and to the tourist in search of pleasure it is worthy of being commended for the valuable and interesting knowledge it contains."—*Chicago Daily Tribune.*

"The work will surprise many, as it opens to us a new land, shows its vast resources, and treats its history with all the accuracy that could be acquired by diligent research and careful observation, during a three years' residence."—*Boston Gazette.*

"It contains notices of the early history of the country, of its geographical features, its agricultural advantages, its manufactures, commerce, facilities for travelling, the character of its inhabitants—everything, indeed, to illustrate its resources and its prospects." *Puritan Recorder.*

"We have seen no work respecting the northwest of equal value to this."—*Christian Intelligencer.*

THE YEMASSEE.

A Romance of South Carolina. By WILLIAM GILMORE SIMMS Author of "The Partisan," "Guy Rivers," &c., &c. New and Revised Edition. With Illustrations by Darley. 12mo Cloth. $1 25.

"A picture of the early border life of the Huguenot settlers in South Carolina. Like Scott's novels, it is a mixture of history and romance."—*Hartford Christian Secretary.*

"It is written in an uncommonly glowing style, and hits off the Indian character with uncommon grace and power."—*Albany Argus.*

"The whole work is truly American, much of the material being of that character which can be furnished by no other country."—*Daily Times.*

"The delineations of the red men of the south are admirably sketched while the historical events upon which the work is founded are vouched for by the author as strictly true."—*New Bedford Mercury*

SKETCHES OF THE IRISH BAR.

By the Right Hon. RICHARD LALOR SHEIL, M. P. Edited with a Memoir and Notes, by Dr. SHELTON MACKENZIE. Fourth Edition. In 2 vols. Price $2 00.

"They attracted universal attention by their brilliant and pointed style, and their liberality of sentiment. The Notes embody a great amount of biographical information, literary gossip, legal and political anecdote, and amusing reminiscences, and, in fact, omit nothing that is essential to the perfect elucidation of the text."—*New York Tribune.*

"They are the best edited books we have met for many a year. They form, with Mackenzie's notes, a complete biographical dictionary, containing succinct and clever sketches of all the famous people of England, and particularly of Ireland, to whom the slightest allusions are made in the text."—*The Citizen (John Mitchel).*

"Dr. Mackenzie deserves the thanks of men of letters, particularly of Irishmen, for his research and care. Altogether, the work is one we can recommend in the highest terms."—*Philadelphia City Item.*

"Such a repertory of wit, humor, anecdote, and out-gushing fun, mingled with the deepest pathos, when we reflect upon the sad fate of Ireland, as this book affords, it were hard to find written in any other pair of covers."—*Buffalo Daily Courier.*

"As a whole, a more sparkling lively series of portraits was hardly ever set in a single gallery It is Irish all over; the wit, the folly, the extravagance, and the fire are al alike characteristic of writer and subjects."—*New York Evangelist.*

"These volumes afford a rich treat to the lovers of literature."—*Hartford Christian Sec.*

CLASSIC AND HISTORIC PORTRAITS.

By JAMES BRUCE. 12mo, cloth, $1 00.

"A series of personal sketches of distinguished individuals of all ages, embracing pen and ink portraits of near sixty persons from Sappho down to Madame de Stael. They show much research, and possess that interest which attaches to the private life of those whose names are known to fame."—*New Haven Journal and Courier.*

"They are comprehensive, well-written, and judicious, both in the selection of subjects and the manner of treating them."—*Boston Atlas.*

"The author has painted in minute touches the characteristics of each with various personal details, all interesting, and all calculated to furnish to the mind's eye a complete portraiture of the individual described."—*Albany Knickerbocker.*

"The sketches are full and graphic, many authorities having evidently been consulted by the author in their preparation."—*Boston Journal.*

THE WORKINGMAN'S WAY IN THE WORLD.

Being the Autobiography of a Journeyman Printer. By CHARLES MANBY SMITH, author of "Curiosities of London Life." 12mo, cloth, $1 00.

"Written by a man of genius and of most extraordinary powers of description."—*Boston Traveller.*

"It will be read with no small degree of interest by the professional brethren of the author, as well as by all who find attractions in a well-told tale of a workingman."—*Boston Atlas.*

"An amusing as well as instructive book, telling how humble obscurity cuts its way through the world with energy, perseverance, and integrity."—*Albany Knickerbocker.*

"The book is the most entertaining we have met with for months."—*Philadelphia Evening Bulletin.*

"He has evidently moved through the world with his eyes open and having a vein of humor in his nature, has written one of the most readable books of the season."—*Zion's Herald.*

ISA, A PILGRIMAGE.

By Caroline Chesebro'. One vol., 12mo, cloth, price $1.00.

"The Pilgrimage is fraught throughout with scenes of thrilling interest—romantic, yet possessing a naturalness that seems to stamp them as real; the style is flowing and easy, chaste and beautiful."—*Troy Daily Times.*

"Miss Chesebro' is evidently a *thinker*—she skims not the mere surface of life, but plunges boldly into the hidden mysteries of the spirit by which she is warranted in making her startling revelations of human passion."—*Christian Freeman.*

"There comes out in this book the evidence of an inventive mind, a cultivated taste, an exquisite sensibility, and deep knowledge of human nature."—*Albany Argus.*

"It is a charming book, pervaded by a vein of pure ennobling thought."—*Troy Whig.*

"There is no one who will doubt that this is a courageous and able work, displaying genius and depth of feeling, and striking at a high and noble aim."—*N. Y. Evangelist.*

"There is a fine vein of tenderness running through the story, which is peculiarly one of passion and sentiment."—*Arthur's Home Gazette.*

LECTURES AND MISCELLANIES.

By Henry James. One vol., 12mo, cloth, price $1.25.

"A series of essays by one of the most generous thinkers and sincere lovers of truth in the country. He looks at society from an independent point of view, and with the noblest and most intelligent sympathy."—*Home Journal.*

"This is the production of a mind richly endowed of a very peculiar mould. All will concede to him the merit of a vigorous and brilliant intellect."—*Albany Argus.*

"A perusal of the essays leads us to *think*, not merely because of the ideas which they contain, but more because the ideas are earnestly put forth, and the subjects discussed are interesting and important to every one."—*Worcester National Ægis.*

"They have attracted much attention both here and in Europe, where the author is considered as holding a distinctive and prominent position in the school of modern philosophy."—*Albany Atlas.*

"The writer wields a masterly and accurate pen, and his style is good."—*Boston Olive Branch.*

"It will have many readers, and almost as many admirers."—*N. Y. Times.*

NAPIER'S PENINSULAR WAR.

History of the War in the Peninsula, and in the South of France, from the Year 1807 to 1814. By W. F. P. Napier, C.B., Col. 43d Reg., &c. Complete in one vol., 8vo, price $3.00.

"We believe the Literature of War has not received a more valuable augmentation this century than Colonel Napier's justly celebrated work. Though a gallant combatant in the field, he is an impartial historian."—*Tribune.*

"Napier's History, in addition to its superior literary merits and truthful fidelity, presents strong claims upon the attention of all American citizens; because the author is a large-souled philanthropist, and an inflexible enemy to ecclesiastical tyranny and secular despots."—*Post.*

"The excellence of Napier's History results from the writer's happy talent for impetuous, straight-forward, soul-stirring narrative, and picturing forth of characters. The military manœuvre, march, and fiery onset, the whole whirlwind vicissitudes of the desperate fight, he describes with dramatic force."—*Merchants' Magazine.*

POETICAL WORKS OF FITZ-GREENE HALLECK

New and only Complete Edition, containing several New Poems, together with many now first collected. One vol., 12mo., price one dollar.

"Halleck is one of the brightest stars in our American literature, and his name is like a household word wherever the English language is spoken."—*Albany Express.*

"There are few poems to be found, in any language, that surpass, in beauty of thought and structure, some of these."—*Boston Commonwealth.*

"To the numerous admirers of Mr. Halleck, this will be a welcome book; for it is a characteristic desire in human nature to have the productions of our favorite authors in an elegant and substantial form."—*Christian Freeman.*

"Mr. Halleck never appeared in a better dress, and few poets ever deserved a better one."—*Christian Intelligencer.*

THE STUDY OF WORDS.

By Archdeacon R. C. Trench. One vol., 12mo., price **75 cts.**

"He discourses in a truly learned and lively manner upon the original unity of language, and the origin, derivation, and history of words, with their morality and separate spheres of meaning.'—*Evening Post*

"This is a noble tribute to the divine faculty of speech. Popularly written, for use as lectures, exact in its learning, and poetic in its vision, it is a book at once for the scholar and the general reader."—*New York Evangelist.*

"It is one of the most striking and original publications of the day, with nothing of hardness, dullness, or dryness about it, but altogether fresh, lively, and entertaining." —*Boston Evening Traveller.*

BRONCHITIS, AND KINDRED DISEASES.

In language adapted to common readers. By W. W. Hall, M. D One vol., 12 mo, price $1.00.

"It is written in a plain, direct, common-sense style, and is free from the quackery which marks many of the popular medical books of the day. It will prove useful to those who need it"—*Central Ch. Herald.*

"Those who are clergymen, or who are preparing for the sacred calling, and public speakers generally, should not fail of securing this work."—*Ch. Ambassador.*

"It is full of hints on the nature of the vital organs, and does away with much superstitious dread in regard to consumption."—*Greene County Whig.*

"This work gives some valuable instruction in regard to food and hygienic influences."—*Nashua Oasis.*

KNIGHTS OF ENGLAND, FRANCE, AND SCOTLAND.

By Henry William Herbert. One vol., 12mo., price $1.25.

"They are partly the romance of history and partly fiction, forming, when blended, portraitures, valuable from the correct drawing of the times they illustrate, and interesting from their romance."—*Albany Knickerbocker.*

"They are spirit-stirring productions, which will be read and admired by all who are pleased with historical tales written in a vigorous, bold, and dashing style."—*Boston Journal.*

"These legends of love and chivalry contain some of the finest tales which the graphic and powerful pen of Herbert has yet given to the lighter literature of the day." —*Detroit Free Press*

MOORE'S LIFE OF SHERIDAN.

Memoirs of the Life of the Rt. Hon. Richard Brinsley Sheridan, by THOMAS MOORE, with Portrait after Sir Joshua Reynolds. Two vols., 12mo, cloth, $2.00.

"One of the most brilliant biographies in English literature. It is the life of a wit written by a wit, and few of Tom Moore's most sparkling poems are more brilliant and fascinating than this biography."—*Boston Transcript.*

"This is at once a most valuable biography of the most celebrated wit of the times, and one of the most entertaining works of its gifted author."—*Springfield Republican.*

"The Life of Sheridan, the wit, contains as much food for serious thought as the best sermon that was ever penned."—*Arthur's Home Gazette.*

"The sketch of such a character and career as Sheridan's by such hand as Moore's, can never cease to be attractive."—*N. Y. Courier and Enquirer.*

"The work is instructive and full of interest."—*Christian Intelligencer.*

"It is a gem of biography; full of incident, elegantly written, warmly appreciative, and on the whole candid and just. Sheridan was a rare and wonderful genius, and has in this work justice done to his surpassing merits."—*N. Y. Evangelist.*

BARRINGTON'S SKETCHES.

Personal Sketches of his own Time, by SIR JONAH BARRINGTON, Judge of the High Court of Admiralty in Ireland, with Illustrations by Darley. Third Edition, 12mo, cloth, $1 25.

"A more entertaining book than this is not often thrown in our way. His sketches of character are inimitable; and many of the prominent men of his time are hit off in the most striking and graceful outline."—*Albany Argus.*

"He was a very shrewd observer and eccentric writer, and his narrative of his own life, and sketches of society in Ireland during his times, are exceedingly humorous and interesting."—*N. Y. Commercial Advertiser.*

"It is one of those works which are conceived and written in so hearty a view, and brings before the reader so many palpable and amusing characters, that the entertainment and information are equally balanced."—*Boston Transcript.*

"This is one of the most entertaining books of the season."—*N. Y. Recorder.*

"It portrays in life-like colors the characters and daily habits of nearly all the English and Irish celebrities of that period."—*N. Y. Courier and Enquirer.*

JOMINI'S CAMPAIGN OF WATERLOO.

The Political and Military History of the Campaign of Waterloo from the French of Gen. Baron Jomini, by Lieut. S V. BENET U. S. Ordnance, with a Map, 12mo, cloth, 75 cents.

"Of great value, both for its historical merit and its acknowledged impartiality."—*Christian Freeman, Boston.*

"It has long been regarded in Europe as a work of more than ordinary merit, while to military men his review of the tactics and manœuvres of the French Emperor during the few days which preceded his final and most disastrous defeat, is considered as instructive, as it is interesting."—*Arthur's Home Gazette.*

"It is a standard authority and illustrates a subject of permanent interest. With military students, and historical inquirers, it will be a favorite reference, and for the general reader it possesses great value and interest."—*Boston Transcript.*

"It throws much light on often mooted points respecting Napoleon's military and political genius. The translation is one of much vigor."—*Boston Commonwealth.*

"It supplies an important chapter in the most interesting and eventful period of Napoleon's military career."—*Savannah Daily News.*

"It is ably written and skilfully translated."—*Yankee Blade.*

LEE'S TALES OF LABOR.

SUMMERFIELD;

Or, Life on a Farm. By DAY KELLOGG LEE. One vol., 12mo; price $1.00.

"We have read it with lively and satisfied interest. The scenes are natural, the characters homely and life-like. and the narrative replete with passages of the profoundest pathos, and incidents of almost painful interest. Above all, 'Summerfield' is in the deepest sense religious. and calculated to exert a strong and wholesome moral influence on its readers, who we trust will be many."—*Horace Greeley.*

"It aims to teach the lesson of contentment, and the rural picture which it draws, and the scenes of home happiness with which it makes us acquainted, are well calculated to enforce it."—*Atlas.*

"There is a great deal of life and nature in the story, and in some of the scenes there is a rich display of wit."—*Albany Argus.*

"It has a flavor of originality, and the descriptions are generally excellent; and, what is something of a peculiarity at present in writing of this kind, not overburdened with words."—*Literary World.*

THE MASTER BUILDER;

Or, Life at a Trade. By DAY KELLOGG LEE. One vol., 12mo; price $1.00.

"He is a powerful and graphic writer, and from what we have seen in the pages of the 'Master Builder,' it is a romance of excellent aim and success."—*State Register.*

"The 'Master Builder' is the master production. It is romance into which is instilled the realities of life; and incentives are put forth to noble exertion and virtue. The story is pleasing—almost fascinating; the moral is pure and undefiled."—*Daily Times.*

"Its descriptions are, many of them, strikingly beautiful; commingling in good proportions, the witty, the grotesque, the pathetic, and the heroic. It may be read with profit as well as pleasure."—*Argus.*

"The work before us will commend itself to the masses, depicting as it does most graphically the struggles and privations which await the unknown and uncared-for Mechanic in his journey through life. It is what might be called a romance, but not of love, jealousy, and revenge order."—*Lockport Courier.*

"The whole scheme of the story is well worked up and very instructive."—*Albany Express.*

MERRIMAC;

Or, Life at the Loom. By DAY KELLOGG LEE. One vol., 12mo; price $1.00.

"A new volume of the series of popular stories which have already gained a well-deserved reputation for the author. As a picture of an important and unique phase of New England life, the work is very interesting, and can scarcely fail of popularity among the million."—*Harper's Magazine.*

"The work is extremely well written. It is as interesting as a novel, while it is natural as every-day life."—*Boston Traveller.*

"Merrimac is a story which, by its simple pathos, and truthfulness to nature, will touch the heart of every reader. It is free from the least tinge of that odious stilted style of thought and diction characteristic of the majority of the novels with which the reading public are deluged."—*N. Y. Commercial Advertiser.*

"Another plain, straightforward, absorbing work from a pen which before has added riches to our literature, and honor to him who wielded it."—*Buffalo Express.*

"It is written in a genial spirit and abounds in humor."—*N. Y. Courier and Enquirer.*

www.ingramcontent.com/pod-product-compliance
Lightning Source LLC
LaVergne TN
LVHW020108110826
845151LV00001B/94